IDEAS

and

BELIEFS

of the

VICTORIANS

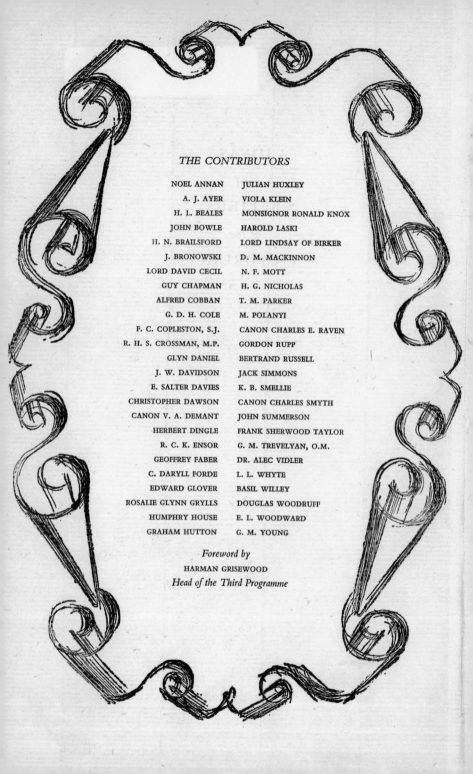

THE CONTRIBUTORS

NOEL ANNAN	JULIAN HUXLEY
A. J. AYER	VIOLA KLEIN
H. L. BEALES	MONSIGNOR RONALD KNOX
JOHN BOWLE	HAROLD LASKI
H. N. BRAILSFORD	LORD LINDSAY OF BIRKER
J. BRONOWSKI	D. M. MACKINNON
LORD DAVID CECIL	N. F. MOTT
GUY CHAPMAN	H. G. NICHOLAS
ALFRED COBBAN	T. M. PARKER
G. D. H. COLE	M. POLANYI
F. C. COPLESTON, S.J.	CANON CHARLES E. RAVEN
R. H. S. CROSSMAN, M.P.	GORDON RUPP
GLYN DANIEL	BERTRAND RUSSELL
J. W. DAVIDSON	JACK SIMMONS
E. SALTER DAVIES	K. B. SMELLIE
CHRISTOPHER DAWSON	CANON CHARLES SMYTH
CANON V. A. DEMANT	JOHN SUMMERSON
HERBERT DINGLE	FRANK SHERWOOD TAYLOR
R. C. K. ENSOR	G. M. TREVELYAN, O.M.
GEOFFREY FABER	DR. ALEC VIDLER
C. DARYLL FORDE	L. L. WHYTE
EDWARD GLOVER	BASIL WILLEY
ROSALIE GLYNN GRYLLS	DOUGLAS WOODRUFF
HUMPHRY HOUSE	E. L. WOODWARD
GRAHAM HUTTON	G. M. YOUNG

Foreword by
HARMAN GRISEWOOD
Head of the Third Programme

IDEAS

and

BELIEFS

of the

VICTORIANS

*an historic revaluation
of the Victorian
Age*

Sylvan
Press

This series of

talks broadcast on

the B.B.C. Third Programme

was first published in 1949 by

Sylvan Press Limited

24 Museum Street,

London WC1

Printed by Page & Thomas Ltd., Chesham,
and bound by Novello & Co. Ltd., London

CONTENTS

MAN AND NATURE

Foreword

HARMAN GRISEWOOD

THOSE WHO undertook the preparation of these talks hoped that they might prove to be of some enduring value as a contribution to the study of the Victorian Age. The fulfilment of these hopes is greatly helped by the appearance of the series in book form. Very few, if any, can have heard all the talks. The series went on for four months and the programmes, for sound reasons, were placed at times that varied a good deal between six o'clock and eleven. There is, besides, a wide area over which the Third Programme cannot be heard at all. This volume, therefore, must afford to many the first practical opportunity of enjoying the series as a whole. But it is important to realise that the original conception was not at all that of a book. Readers will notice, for instance, a looser organisation than would be natural in a work that was planned to be read continuously.

For the listener, broadcasting is essentially discontinuous. In a sense it should be so. Each item heard should be a completed experience. Even in a talk planned as one of a series there should be the minimum of carry over. But the reader on the other hand should be aware of the unity of what he reads even when circumstance compels interruption.

The planning of this series needed to keep in mind a double and seemingly contradictory aim. It had to be built upon a ground plan ; the result had to manifest a unifying principle. And yet each of the items had to possess a measure of independence. The listener should not feel that he was being invited to attend a course of studies. Each talk should be made enjoyable as a separate item and yet there should be a communicable coherence stamped upon the whole series.

Considered professionally as broadcasting this effect is generally agreed to have been achieved. But with the appearance of the talks in print and with the opportunities for cross reference and re-reading which print affords, it may be helpful to call attention to the ground plan rather more insistently than would be appropriate for the radio listener. The plan itself grew organically under various influences and according to the needs of the material itself as it emerged. I have thought it best briefly to tell the story of how the project came about and developed.

It was some time in February 1947 that Mr. Barnes, then Head of the Third Programme, at an informal meeting of Talks Division somewhat startled his hearers by the unexpected announcement that he would like all the talks in the next few months to be about the Victorians. With a view to bringing this intention closer to a practical result he engaged the services of a research assistant, Miss Jean Rowntree. She started work in May of that year. Her written instructions began thus :

"We plan a number of broadcasts to take place this autumn in which we intend to examine the assumptions of the Victorian Age, those suppositions which were unquestionably accepted and therefore determined action, and to appraise its ideals and re-assess its controversies with a view to shedding some light on matters which puzzle us today."

Most serious readers reckon themselves to be pretty well read in one or two aspects of the Victorian period. But few will have read comprehensively enough to illustrate, at all important points, a critical survey of the period as a whole. An orderly grasp of so much documentation requires great energy of mind. Miss Rowntree was to complete her work in three months. She was to interrogate a number of consultants. She was to draw together the threads of her already wide reading and concentrate her attention under five headings :

1. Man's Relation to God.
2. Man's Relation to Nature.
3. Man's Relation to his Fellow Men.
4. Man's Relation to Woman.
5. Man's Relation to the State.

" We do not aim at completeness ", the instructions continued, " nor yet at narrative. People are easily interested by personalities and we envisage making some use of the biographical method in the broadcast result. It would be useful, therefore, obviously to use certain persons and their lives, letters and conversation to exemplify certain trends and aspects of the period."

On August 4th Miss Rowntree completed her report—a fascinating review of about one hundred pages. At the end she wrote, " It looks as if you will need at least thirty programmes—which I suppose will be out of the question ". In the result there were fifty-seven talks, including one discussion of an hour's length, and twenty-six readings—eighty-three programmes.

Following the report there remained the huge task of organising the series. This was the work of Talks Department (Director, Norman Luker) and in particular of four producers, Miss A. Kallin, Mr. R. Lewin, Mr. J. B. Taylor and Mr. P. Laslett, who worked as a group under the chairmanship of Mr. W. M. Newton (Assistant Director of the Department). It was clear that there was no chance of its starting in the autumn. The problems of meeting such a requirement as this are, of course, even more formidable than the problems of stating it. There was a vast work of selection involved. The ground plan itself in its detail depended upon the availability of speakers. Genuine specialists in the period are surprisingly few. Twenty weeks was not long in which to accomplish what had to be done and at the same time to keep running the normal supply of current broadcasting requirements. At the end of the year enough detail had been decided upon in the earlier sections of the plan for a starting date to be fixed. The opening was arranged for February 1st—about one year after Mr. Barnes had first sketched out what was in his mind.

The *Radio Times* carried a synopsis of the whole series. The last part of the synopsis at this stage was necessarily somewhat provisional, but it traced pretty well the course that was actually followed. The headings of its five sections are as follows :—

Section 1. A group of talks on The Theory of Progress.

Section 2. A group of talks on Victorian Religious Belief and Controversy, the moral climate that nourished the sense of personal responsibility, the beliefs that gave it stamina, the misgivings that weakened it, and the influences that undermined it.

Section 3. A group of talks on Man and Nature : the secularisation of thought through the application of scientific method to all fields : the retreat of metaphysical and spiritual ideas before the terrestrial and the secular.

Section 4. The Liberal Idea.

Section 5. The " Working-out " of Victorian Ideas.
Provisionally, the two main approaches are seen as (*a*) The weakening of the ties on the individual in his relations with others (e.g. family, neighbours and employers) and the growing realisation of the inadequacy of Victorian ideas to cope with major problems (Negative aspect), and (*b*) the growing positive appeal of collectivist ideas, especially of the State.
These two tendencies, which are presumably aspects of a single process, to be shown at work in a comprehensive rather than a serial analysis of Victorian social institutions.

" The Series ", it was said in a short preamble, " will examine the assumptions of the Victorian Age, appraise its ideas, and re-assess its controversies in the belief that such an examination will shed light on the urgent issues of today. Each talk will stand on its own as a piece of broadcasting, but as the series unfolds it will be seen that the talks fall into certain groups as indicated in the outline ".

Reflection upon the arrangement of this synopsis and the points chosen for it will, I believe, give a coherence to what follows that might otherwise be lost. The reader will be able to discern more of the unifying principle that was at work in its design than would be possible for all but the most attentive listener. It will be seen that limits were deliberately set. Many would have chosen those limits differently. But however the material was chosen there were bound to be omissions. Bundles of letters indeed were received telling us what we had left out. Not many, however, were able to point to anything we had left untouched that would have been truly to our purpose.

Lastly, the reader will do well to remember throughout that what he is reading are broadcast scripts and not a collection of articles or essays. It is part of the professional work of the BBC staff to persuade a writer who is practised in the arrangement of words for print to employ what is for him often a new literary skill—the technique of writing for speech. And it is not merely " speech " that is the aim but speech of a particular sort. Oratory will not do. The lecture style is not as a rule quite natural enough. The style required is not yet established in our literature but there are signs that it will be. This book may be an important step in that direction. It is significant that three among the very few living masters of style should have applied themselves seriously to the broadcast talk and should have brought it to a highly skilful condition : Mr. Desmond MacCarthy, Sir Max Beerbohm and Mr. Harold Nicolson have made the broadcast talk something more than journalism. It may turn out that they will have established a new departure in our literary tradition, a new technique of the spoken word. There are many examples of enduring literature that were not made under the impulse of print. There is the whole of our dramatic literature—the most public of all literary styles. There is the Diary of Pepys—one of the most private. Neither is directly concerned with print. So the broadcast talk has an illustrious cousinship which should encourage those who feel that print is not the only form of publication that makes a reputation worth striving for.

This book, therefore, may have an importance even beyond that of its subject ; an importance as illustrating a technique ; an importance for the traditions of our literature. Its right appraisal, therefore, is a delicate matter not lightly to be undertaken. These few words of preface are meant to help this task forward, and the reader in his enjoyment of the book.

Introducing the
Ideas and Beliefs of the Victorians

G. M. TREVELYAN

I HAVE been asked to join in this introductory programme in my double capacity as an historian and as a relic of the Victorian Age, for I was already twenty-five when the Queen and the century came to an end together.

I have no intention tonight of trying to epitomise the ideas and beliefs of the Victorian era, for they were various and mutually contradictory, and cannot be brought together under one or two glib generalisations. But as all the thought of the age arose out of the circumstances of the age, I think this introductory talk can be best devoted to a rough outline of some of the governing conditions of life in nineteenth-century Britain. Later talks will be more abstract, on the thoughts and feelings of men. This first talk will be factual, on some of the circumstances that conditioned their thinking and feeling.

The BBC has chosen the time for this series well. The period of reaction against the nineteenth century is over ; the era of dispassionate historical valuation of it has begun. We can by this time examine without prejudice what we have inherited from the Victorians, what we have improved away, and what we have lost ; how like we are to them and how unlike. The period to be covered cannot be strictly confined to the reign of Victoria (1837–1901). To see the origin of Victorian ideas and conditions in which the early Victorians were brought up, we must look back to 1815, the end of the Napoleonic wars, the age of Cobbett and Lord Eldon, of Shelley, Byron and Scott. The close of the century, the age of Gladstone, Salisbury and the Fabian Society, of Hardy and Meredith, of the Savoy Opera, and the grand old Victorian Bernard Shaw, presents a very different scene. For the main characteristic of the Victorian era was constant change, variety and self criticism.

Between these two points in time lies an age of many achievements and many famous men. Economic historians call it the Railway Age. The name marks it off from the eighteenth century and the Regency, the world of stage coaches and canals ; and distinguishes it no less from the twentieth century, the Age of the Internal Combustion Engine—motor traction, submarines and aeroplanes.

Yes, it was the Railway Age, though the steam-engine did not put the horse out of action as motors have done. It was George Stephenson of Tyneside who began the Railway Age. The mine-owners wanted him to shift their coal, but his locomotive steam-engine shifted everything else as well. The Railway was as native to Britain, as Parliamentary Government, Franchise Reform, Free Trade, Freedom of the Press, Slavery-Abolition, Factory Inspection, Grants in Aid, Trade Unions, "Public Schools", and Income Tax. All these British policies, though many of them had their roots in earlier English history, came to their strength in the nineteenth century.

The Railway Age in Britain was also an age of Peace and Security. We enjoyed internal peace, though it was seriously threatened by the economic and social maladjustments that came in the train of the Industrial Revolution. But we managed, by a gradual process, to mitigate these evils enough to preserve civil peace, and by a series of Reform Bills we democratised the system of Parliamentary government which we had inherited in an aristocratic form from the eighteenth century. Britain alone of the great European countries saw no barricades in 1848, and was proud of it. And the Chartists in the end got their way without fighting. The British Labour movement remained law-abiding and Parliamentary.

External peace and security were also ours. For a hundred years after Waterloo, Britain and her trade and her colonies were peacefully protected by the sheathed sword of naval power, and by the existence of a navy which held the surface of the sea, and in those days feared no attack either from below its surface or from the sky overhead. So long as the navy was there, Britain could not be invaded—or bombed. " Our right little, tight little island " we boasted with truth was our " inviolate, isle ". After the fall of Napoleon, no great power dominated Europe or threatened our security. Our only wars were small affairs in the Crimea, in Africa, in India.

The other governing condition of the period, closely related to that peace and security, was ever-increasing wealth. Until, after 1870, American and German competition began to be acute, we had enjoyed a start over all the world in methods of machine production—in textiles and above all in iron and steel. Our capital and our engineering skill developed foreign lands and drew the tribute of dividends in return. We became the great creditor country. We were called "the workshop of the world". And London was the world's financial centre. In exchange for our money and our machine-made goods we garnered in our small island the food and luxuries of all lands, brought to our ports by our unrivalled merchant navy.

At the end of the century Britain's wealth, that is her command over goods, was enormous. Its distribution among the classes of the community was shamefully uneven ; but that was already less bad than in the days of Peterloo, the Corn Laws and the Chartists. At the time of Queen Victoria's two Jubilees (1887 and 1897) goods were cheap, taxes both direct and indirect were very light, and real wages were much higher than half a century before. So all classes joined heartily in celebrating the Queen's long reign, because it had been a period of progress in well-being, since the "hungry 'forties" which old men still remembered. There were still appalling slums and slum life, but it had been worse before.

It was in the nineteenth century that Australia, New Zealand, South Africa, and in part Canada, received their English-speaking populations. Taught by the results of George III's folly, the statesmen and Parliaments of Victorian England had the wisdom to grant to the white Colonies responsible self-government, though our wisdom in that matter stopped short of Ireland. By the loosening of the bonds of empire, the Empire was saved.

And it was the England and Scotland of the nineteenth century that supplied the population of those new lands. The birthrate in all classes was so high that our industrial expansion at home was rendered possible. The population of Great Britain rose from under twelve millions in 1811 to thirty-seven millions in 1901. And during those same years the tide of

2

emigration founded these new Britains overseas. As we should not now be capable of peopling vast empty territories, it is as well that we did it just in time, while we were still a very prolific race.

A century of peace, security and wealth was in many respects favourable to the higher aspects of civilisation. In the nineteenth century our fortunate ancestors were not precluded by national poverty from obtaining the books they wanted to study, from making or buying beautiful things or from travelling to see them. The shores and mountains of their own island were opened to them by the new railways, and they had free access to the Alps, to Italy and all the ancient lands of Europe, made significant to them by their study of history and the Classics, by the writings of Shelley and Byron, Ruskin and Browning. It was an age of cheap and rapid book production, patronised by a very large leisured and semi-leisured class, and by prosperous professional and artisan classes. There was a very large public for the many good writers whom England then produced out of these same leisured and professional classes—poets, novelists, historians, scholars, essayists, humorists ; many of their names are still household words today, even if too few now read their books. It was a time of active political, philosophical and religious speculations, carried on in an atmosphere of freedom, with the impact of Darwin and Huxley to stimulate it with new conceptions of the universe. It was good, serious stuff that was read. The competition of cheap journalism and literature, aimed at the lowest level of intelligence, only became dangerous at the latter end of the century.

Throughout the whole period, science, thought and literature were ahead of the arts. Owing to the destruction of craftsmanship in the machine age, the fashion in architecture, furniture and many of the arts of life was deplorable at the time of the Great Exhibition of 1851. Mass production had destroyed quality and taste. But under the leadership of William Morris and others even these things took a turn for the better. But the fact remained that for the bulk of the population the influences of village and rural life had given place to the sprawling ugliness of the industrial city.

The nineteenth century saw a very great advance in the sentiment and practice of humanity—to the old and weak, to the poor and unfortunate, to women and children. If we were put back in the year of Waterloo, we should think our ancestors fine fellows but rather brutes. In the next generation Dickens was the great popular exponent of the new humanitarian sentiment. Our English love of liberty, of justice and humanity, for which we have just fought two world wars, came to us direct from the Victorian Age, though the roots lie in centuries further back.

BERTRAND RUSSELL

THE DAILY life of our own time is so filled with uncertainties and haunted by dread of disasters, that the period when Victoria was on the Throne has already acquired all the character of a golden age. But to those who lived in it, it had not quite this comfortable character. It opened with a dread of revolution ; its central position was darkened by doubt ; and its end was overshadowed by the loss of industrial supremacy and fear of the growing German menace. It is true that in 1837 there were some solid grounds for self-satisfaction. We had beaten the French and were securely supreme on the seven seas. We were the workshop of the world, and had, as yet, no reason to fear industrial competitors. Our Empire was the greatest there had ever been, and was still growing. We believed ourselves to be spreading freedom, enlightenment, and true religion in every place to which our influence extended. The nations of the Continent, it was thought, would limp after us, though there was no chance that they would catch us up, for were they not all lazy and immoral ? Mr. Podsnap expressed the general opinion on foreign nations in the immortal words : " They do—I am sorry to be obliged to say—as they do ". Nor was this view confined to what might be called the intellectual lower orders. James Mill, having been told by someone that there were German philosophers of whom some people thought well, devoted a whole week to studying them, at the end of which he remarked : " I see well enough what poor Kant would be at ". This mood was the natural outcome of industrial monopoly, naval supremacy, and a vast Empire.

But even at that time there was quite another side to the

picture. The great bulk of the wage-earners lived in appalling poverty and worked intolerably long hours. The new Poor Law saw to it that those who could not get employment, even on these harsh terms, should have an existence even more painful than that of the most unfortunate of those who had obtained work. Ancient beauty was being obliterated by a plague of industrial hideousness. Even the well-to-do could not be quite comfortable, since there were rumblings of revolution. The French Revolution had happened not so long ago, and in England there were agitators who, it was thought, might at any moment rouse the maddened wage-earners to bloody insurrection. It is not always easy to realise in reading history that the actors in any period, unlike ourselves, did not know the future. We knew that Victorian England developed peaceably, but the contemporaries of the Chartists did not know this.

At the time of Peterloo many large country houses kept artillery in readiness, lest they should be attacked by the mob. My maternal grandfather, who died in 1869, while wandering in his mind during his last illness, heard a loud noise in the street and thought it was the revolution breaking out, showing that, at least sub-consciously, the thought of revolution had remained with him throughout long prosperous years.

Then there was another fear, more intense than it is easy for us to understand; I mean the fear of free thought. Free thought— so the men of that time believed—not only led to eternal damnation, but had other even more regrettable consequences. Had it not in eighteenth-century France led straight to the guillotine? How could the propertied classes hope to retain their wealth unless the poor remained pious? On this ground education, except for the well-to-do, was thought undesirable, and it was feared that if the poor could read they would read Tom Paine.

A President of the Royal Society said : "However specious in theory the project might be, of giving education to the labouring classes of the poor, it would in effect be found to be prejudicial to their morals and happiness ; it would teach them to despise their lot in life, instead of making them good servants in agriculture, and other laborious employments to which their rank in society had destined them ; instead of teaching them subordination, it would render them fractious and refractory, as was evident in the manufacturing counties ; it would enable them to read seditious pamphlets, vicious books, and publications against Christianity."

There was passionate rebellion against the evils of the time. Carlyle, in thundering and eloquent denunciations, maintained that his own age was less happy than the twelfth and thirteenth centuries. Robert Owen invented Socialism. The Chartists were thought to have a chance of success by violent revolution. And somewhat later Christian Socialism, led by Ruskin and Charles Kingsley, devoted itself to destroying complacency.

In spite of these things, however, for those who were not poor the age was on the whole a happy one. The evils which were perceived were remediable, and, to a considerable extent, remedied. Mr. Bumble and Dotheboys Hall, realities at the beginning of the period, were only a memory at the end. When education was made universal and compulsory, it was found that the wage-earning classes read not Tom Paine but the picture papers. Wages rose and hours of labour grew less and child labour was nearly abolished ; public health was improved enormously ; in spite of the lessening intensity of dogmatic belief crime rapidly diminished. And all this gain to the poor was achieved without loss to the rich.

In such a world the perception of present evil was bearable, since men felt that they knew what to do about it, and that it would soon be lessened. Such an environment was a stimulus to energy. Whereas we, when we become conscious of what is wrong with our time, are puzzled to find a remedy that has any chance of being adopted, and the baffled feeling that results in us is apt to lead to listlessness and cynicism, faults from which the Victorians were singularly free.

In intellectual matters there was a gradual softening of dogma analogous to the softening of social relations. *Essays and Reviews* showed that a clergyman might be unorthodox without ceasing to be a clergyman, and it was judicially decided that he need not even believe in hell.

Darwin threw down a challenge to the old rigidities, and his doctrine of evolution made everything a matter of degree, obliterating the absoluteness of white-and-black, right-and-wrong. It seemed that there had once been animals of which it could not be said with any certainty whether they were men or apes. This was most unfortunate.

It seemed that everything, instead of being so or not so, as in the logic books, was only more so or less so. And in this mush of compromise all the old splendid certainties dissolved.

After Darwin, the Victorians were obliged to suffer other shocks. Germany and America outstripped Great Britain in the production of iron and steel, and whether for this reason or some other a new respect for German philosophy arose. Kant was no longer " poor Kant " and the War Minister could avow himself an orthodox disciple of Hegel.

The Victorian Age, especially in its central portion, had many great merits surpassing, I think, any to which we can lay claim. It did great things in science ; Faraday and Maxwell, for example, though less famous than Darwin, were scarcely less important.

After the fear of revolution had died down, the Victorians became liberal and tolerant to a very remarkable degree. When Gilbert and Sullivan made fun of the Army and Navy nobody objected except Queen Victoria, and she only to the extent of refusing to bestow a knighthood on Gilbert. Nowadays such levity would be thought most reprehensible, and probably inspired by Moscow.

The theological discussions between Huxley and Gladstone in *The Nineteenth Century* are models of mutual tolerance. Marx and Kropotkin, who would nowadays be of interest to Scotland Yard, were unmolested. Although many men thought Darwin wicked, no one thought of making a law against evolution such as was enacted in Tennessee. The Metaphysical Society, which consisted of a small collection of eminent men, debated in correct Parliamentary style the question of the existence of God. A member who had not been present enquired anxiously of one who had : " Well, is there a God ? " To which the answer was : " Yes, we had a very good majority ". Toleration existed even in directions where people of our time are most apt to suppose that it was absent ; George Eliot was not ostracised.

The Victorian Age tackled its own problems with vigour and success. They were, it is true, easier than our problems because they were internal and did not require international co-operation. Few foresaw our problems, but I do not think they could be blamed for that. They found a country deeply divided against itself—" the two nations " as Disraeli called it—a country full of brutality, misery, and ignorance. At the end the country was closely integrated ; all the worst horrors of early industrialism had been mitigated ; universal compulsory education had been in operation for thirty years ; and democracy had been achieved except for the exclusion of women. All this without any violent upheaval. It is a good record ; I wish it could be hoped that the present age could have one as good.

LORD DAVID CECIL

I DON'T know how much people nowadays do read the great Victorian authors, but certainly if they don't they ought to. They have much more in common with us, both in what they write about, and the angle from which they treat it, than the writers of any other period. In fact, to the literary historian two hundred years hence, the literature of the last one hundred and thirty odd years is likely to appear of a piece. That of today will be the later phase of a period that began with the romantic movement. The tone is altered, but the problems and pre-occupations which form the subject-matter of serious literature are the same.

They are the problems and preoccupations of a period of change and uncertainty. Up till the nineteenth century, English life and thought had rested on a set of unquestioned values, derived partly from the Christian religion and partly from the Classics. From then on, a succession of forces got to work to undermine those values.

Religious faith was shaken first by the Rationalist movement, and later on by the scientific discoveries of Darwin and Huxley. And not only religious faith. The ideal longings which glow in the hearts of men seemed to have no counterpart or justification in the physical universe of which he is the inhabitant. Could he be sure that anything was good or bad, man began to ask himself ; and if so, why ? This uncertainty showed itself to every sphere of human activity, politics, sexual morals, the relation of parent and child. And the general feeling of insecurity was increased by the fact that the enormously enlarged power of man over matter brought about by scientific discovery was altering the average person's mode of living from year to year.

Darkly and irresistibly the huge force of material progress rushed onwards towards no set end.

The minds of the writers rushed on with it, but seldom with any great feeling of confidence. Some of them were vaguely exhilarated by the motion of rushing, others were giddy and frightened, and looked wistfully back to the safety and stability of the old beliefs. But since nobody knew quite where they were going, nobody was so serenely sure of what they thought right and wrong, as Jane Austen, for instance, had been. For no common standard had arisen to take the place of the old structure of values which the revolutionary movements were destroying.

The Victorians were always vigorous and sometimes hopeful. But they were worried : worried about God, worried about the poor, worried about the position of women, worried about sex, worried about democracy—worried, in fact, about much the same things as we are. For though most of them proposed a solution to one or other of these problems, none of these solutions had been able to satisfy the majority of people sufficiently to be taken for granted.

The interest of Victorian literature lies largely in the fact that the authors are asking just the same questions as we are. They differed widely in their interests and their points of view. Some writers took the view that progress was a good thing. What with science and democracy and rational agnosticism, they thought we were on the way to a happier and better society. But they were not so certain of it as not to be nervously irritable with people who did not share this opinion.

Their opponents were equally irritable. Tempestuous Carlyle, for instance, thought that the whole age was careering down the road to ruin. He condemned the democratic idea as pernicious nonsense; and propounded as the only remedy a sort of mystical belief in authority, which led logically to the totalitarian philosophies of today. Matthew Arnold was another man who believed in authority, though in a primmer, more refined form. He believed in saving mankind by higher education. If we were compelled to be cultured enough, he said, we might be able to choose and to blend what was good in the new and good in the old in such a way as to find some stable standard.

Yet another recipe for salvation was proposed by Ruskin and Morris, the fathers of Socialism : socialism of the ardent, dreamy humane English kind. They preached the advantages of an ordered and equalitarian society in which men worked for the good of all and the love of their craft. If this were established, they thought, the other questions would settle themselves.

Ruskin was also concerned with another problem of his time and ours : the place of the artist in society and the relation of art to life. He solved it on moral lines : the artist, he said, must work not for himself but for God and the community. A very different view of the subject was taken by Pater, first and greatest prophet of aestheticism. Art, he said, needed no justification, and the contemplation of beauty was simply and in itself the highest fulfilment of man's nature, and should be his chief activity. A great many important modern writers—notably Virginia Woolf and the Sitwell family—represent development of this Paterian point of view.

Some of the Victorian poets too talked about the relation of art to life. They were also deeply occupied with the religious question. Many like Tennyson came to no very cheerful conclusion on the matter. They, as he put it, " faintly trusted the larger hope ". Others like Browning, or Emily Brontë worked out a private faith founded on personal religious experience ; and there were those who, horrified by the tragic and insoluble riddle of the universe as revealed in the light of rationalist science, frankly professed themselves pessimists. Thomas Hardy sang beautifully the vanity of all things human.

He said the same things in fiction. But for the most part the novelists, intent on observing the comedy and pathos of work-a-day human life, were less concerned with ultimate questions. However, they were exercised about political and social issues. They attacked prisons and the poor laws and snobbishness. They did not think things ought to be left as they were. And with Charlotte Brontë and George Eliot, woman's position appeared as a question. As a matter of fact, George Eliot has all the Victorian worries, religious, political, sexual. Her sad profound intelligent novels raise most of the important questions of her day and ours.

Certainly then, to read the Victorians is not to escape from our present discontents. But it is to view them with a new eye. For the Victorians were not like us temperamentally ; they had not been knocked about so much by wars and revolutions. With the result that they approached their themes with a tumultuous energy, a splendid determination to discover some positive belief or other out of the confusion with which they were faced. This is very heartening, even when their conclusions are melancholy ; and all the more so because their vision of the world is all aglow with a full-blooded emotional force, that now melts in pathos, now sparkles out in robust humour, now soars upward in a flight of rhetorical eloquence. For—and it is here that they are so superior to us—they were not self-conscious. They were not ashamed to show their emotions. They are called sentimental because they are honest, because they do not mind admitting that the spectacle of heroic actions and mother love and innocent childhood fill their eyes with tears. We could do with some of this full-blooded temperament. For we suffer from emotional squeamishness, from the snobbish nervousness of being thought sentimental. And our books seldom satisfy the demands of the heart as those of the great Victorian authors do.

It is more doubtful if you will find the solution they offered to their problems completely satisfying. Progressive scientific optimism certainly has not the prestige it used to have as a creed. Nor has the belief in higher education or authoritarian government. Aestheticism has retained its attraction better. But alas, it is not very practical. It is hardly possible to live the life of a pure aesthete in 1948 England. Speaking for myself, I think the mystics turn out to have the best of the argument ; or, failing them, the pessimists. Surely Hardy and Emily Brontë have penetrated deeper into the true nature of human experience than have their contemporaries. However, many people I know will not agree about this. There are still people, I am told, who believe that mankind can be saved by science or education or political action. Anyway, whatever side you take you will find eloquent support for your views among the great Victorians.

CHRISTOPHER DAWSON

ALTHOUGH SO much has been written about the Victorian Age, I believe that it is only just becoming possible for us to see it in its proper perspective, for the real significance of an age is always hidden from its immediate successors. It is only after the passing of a century that historical understanding becomes possible.

This means that we are still too close to the later Victorians —the generation of Arthur Balfour and Walter Pater—to understand them. But the early Victorians like John Stuart Mill and John Henry Newman and Charles Darwin are now candidates for immortality and we can know and judge them in the same way as we know Adam Smith and David Hume and their world, or worlds. And as the early Victorians are in many respects the most remarkable of all the Victorians and have left the deepest mark on Victorian culture, we are already in a position to begin understanding the Victorian Age as a whole.

Now the paradox of Victorianism is that for half a century it has been a by-word for all that is stuffy and conventional and reactionary ; whereas in actual fact it was a great revolutionary age—an age in which Britain did more to change the world than she has ever done before or since. The famous passage in the Communist Manifesto, in which Karl Marx speaks of the world-transforming revolutionary activity of bourgeois culture, was inspired by the achievements of the new industrial civilisation that had been developed in England during the first half of the nineteenth century. No doubt, Marx was not thinking of England alone, since he realised that what was taking place was destined to change the world. And in fact all the great currents of ideas and political change that we associate with Victorian England, like the rise of modern science and triumph of Liberalism and the ideal of progress and social reform, were never peculiar to England, but were also characteristic of nineteenth-century culture in general on the Continent and in the United States.

All the same, the middle-class revolution, which Marx wrote about, was a specifically British achievement. In the 'forties it had only begun to affect France and Belgium while Germany and the rest of the Continent still remained an agrarian society in which conditions were much the same as they had been a hundred years before. The English were the pioneers who built the new railways and financed the new enterprises which transformed European life. And it was England that found its own solution to the problem of the new age and went a long way towards imposing this solution on the nineteenth-century world as a whole.

Now the key to this Victorian solution and the dominant feature of the Victorian Age was its achievement of social peace. The great conflicts which had disturbed the earlier part of the nineteenth century and which still persisted in most of Europe died down in England rapidly, almost miraculously, in the middle years of the century. While war and revolution continued to rage on the Continent and while the great new democracy of the West was torn asunder by a tremendous civil war, England continued to become more and more tranquil, more and more prosperous and more and more convinced of the merits of constitutional liberty and peaceful progress and reform.

On the Continent the party of Order and the party of Progress stood armed on opposite sides of the barricades, and they could only advance over the bodies of their opponents. In England both parties alike claimed to represent the cause of progress and the cause of order and they went forward side by side ; so that Victorian government was really the government of a common front under alternative party leadership.

It is easy to criticise this Victorian achievement as an illogical and philistine compromise, which sacrificed political ideals to material interest and allowed social evils to go unredressed so long as they did not interfere with the interests of the dominant class. But that is a very superficial judgment. For the Victorian compromise was the work of idealists, and the more intense and sincere was their idealism, the stronger was their devotion to compromise. This is true not only of politicians like Peel and Gladstone, but also of the philosophers and political theorists like John Stuart Mill and Walter Bagehot, and poets like Tennyson and Browning. And this is the characteristic which distinguishes Victorian England most thoroughly from the rest of the nineteenth-century world. For in France and Germany and Italy and Russia the idealists tended to be the extremists, who despised compromise and regarded the moderates as men without the courage of their convictions. It was only in England that we find a strictly constitutional movement for a limited practical reform, like the repeal of the Corn Laws, transformed into a kind of crusade led by men like John Bright who were able to appeal at once to men's economic interests and to a perfectly sincere sense of moral idealism.

That this was possible was due to the religious background

which formed such men as Bright and Shaftesbury and Glad-stone, and which underlies the general acceptance of common moral ideals which is the basis of the Victorian solution.

The strength of this religious element in Victorian culture has been realised perhaps more clearly by foreign observers than by the English themselves. It was already recognised by the con-temporaries who knew England best, such as Guizot in the 'forties, while in our own time the late Elie Halévy made it the central thesis of his classical *History of the English People of the Nineteenth Century*. It is only from this angle that it is possible to compre-hend that combination of moral idealism, social conformity and intellectual nonconformity that makes the Victorian Age so puzzling to the modern mind. In the Victorian Age the spiritual energy which had been accumulated by a century of intensive religious activity came to the surface and produced a social and intellectual harvest extraordinary in variety and profusion. This is to be seen not only in the men who retained their religious convictions, like Newman and Martineau, or Gladstone and Bright, or Shaftesbury and Maurice ; but equally in the leaders of philosophic thought, like J. S. Mill and Herbert Spencer and in the founders of the Secularist sects, like Robert Owen, the Socialist, and Holyoake, the Co-operator, and Con-greve, the Positivist, who inherited so many of the characteristics of their nonconformist predecessors. In this respect Victorian England has a good deal in common with the England of the seventeenth century. The Radicals and the Chartists were the spiritual descendants of the Puritans and the Levellers, and in both cases the intensity of religious life generated a profusion of new ideas and new political and social forces. But there remains the great difference that religion in the seventeenth century was a principle of strife and social disunion, while in Victorian England it was a great guarantee of social peace and social co-operation.

If this is so, how are we to explain the revolutionary achieve-ment of the Victorian Age of which I spoke at the beginning ? The fact is that the most revolutionary changes in life and culture have very little to do with political revolution in the ordinary sense. To prove this we have only to compare Victorian England with nineteenth-century Spain. In Spain more than anywhere else in Europe, the nineteenth century was an age of civil war and revolution, but at the close of the century Spanish society and culture were probably less changed in essentials than those of any of the great European peoples. In England, the rejection of political revolution was the condition which made the immense social changes of the Victorian Age possible. And here again it was religion that was the vital issue. England and Spain were both highly religious countries. But in England religion acted as oil on the bearings of the social mechanism, whereas in Spain, it was oil poured on the flames of civil war. The difference was not in the quality of the oil, but in the use to which it was put.

All the same, in England, no less than in Spain, and indeed everywhere in the world, the second half of the nineteenth century witnessed the gradually increasing secularisation of culture. The Victorian Age was great because, unlike the contemporary culture of continental Europe, it was able to apply the accumulated reserves of its religious tradition to the contemporary social situation. But it failed to preserve those resources, and as they were gradually exhausted the Victorian culture itself lost its strength and its spiritual vitality. One has only to compare the faces of the early and late Victorians—the portraits of the generation of Gladstone and Tennyson and Darwin and Manning with those of the generation of Swinburne and Pater and Campbell Bannerman and Balfour—to see what a great change had taken place. But it was not the breed of men, but the world of ideas that had changed. The beliefs of early Victorian England may seem to us a strange compound of mutually inconsistent orthodoxies—the bleak rationalism of the Utilitarians and the narrow pietism of the Evangelicals, but they were like flint and steel to one another, and from their contact there sprang the spirit of moral idealism and the passion for reform which burn like fire beneath the hard surface of the age of iron and steam.

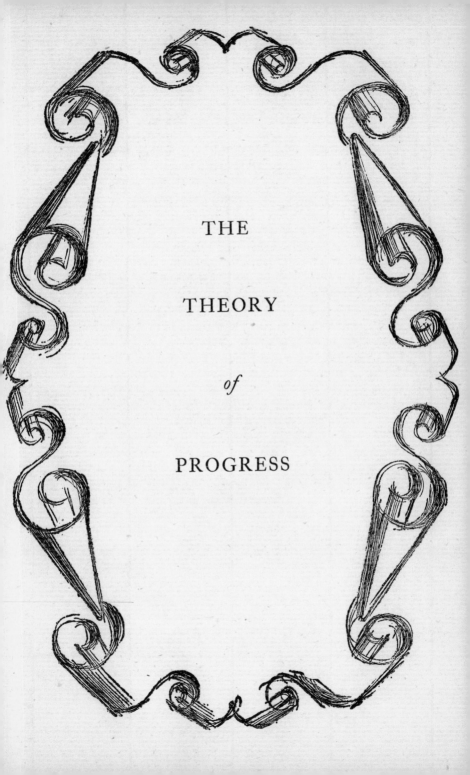

THE

THEORY

of

PROGRESS

Origins and Development of the
Idea of Progress

JOHN BOWLE

SOME OF you may remember two caricatures by Sir Max Beerbohm which contrast the Victorian vision of progress with our own : one depicts a substantial and bewhiskered bourgeois pointing with complacent relish to a larger replica of himself ; the other portrays a lean and disillusioned figure, a band of black crepe about his left arm, contemplating without enthusiasm a large question-mark against a murky sky.

Today, in the gaunt opening of the Atomic Era, the Victorian idea of progress has worn thin. Yet as we look back upon the colour and enterprise, the rich variety, the drive, of the Victorian Age, the disparagements of a Lytton Strachey seem to have worn not better. And the central, the most characteristic, belief of the Victorians, was the idea of progress. Must that idea be written off ? Is it one more delusion, the reflection of fortunate circumstances, of the complacency of a newly emancipated middle class ? I do not believe it.

On the contrary, I believe that our own age, so tormented and disillusioned, may well come to be regarded as the opening of a new era of widening experience and achievement ; and those who hold this belief will find, as one of last Sunday's speakers well remarked, some magnificently eloquent support for their views in Victorian literature.

What, then, did the idea of progress mean to the Victorians ? I should venture to define it as a belief in the steady, cumulative and inevitable expansion of human awareness and power— material, intellectual, spiritual. In the words of Tennyson, contemplating the threat of class war :

" Science moves, but slowly, slowly creeping on from point to
point,
Slowly comes a hungry people, as a lion creeping nigher
Glares at one that nods and winks before a dying fire,
Yet I doubt not through the ages an increasing purpose runs
And the thoughts of men are widened with the process of
the suns."

We are today apt to be sceptical about ideas which demand
faith. A modern idea of progress—and I think there are grounds
for one—must be modified into an hypothesis, based on well-
attested and far-ranging sociological and historical research. But
for many of the Victorians the belief seemed self-evident. And
no wonder ! " The rapid increase in natural knowledge," said
Huxley, " is the chief characteristic of our age ". Their idea of
progress was first, then, anthropocentric—the Diapason closing
full on Man.

The great achievement of the Victorian Age was to put
organised professional science on the map ; the use of knowledge
as power over environment " for the betterment of man's estate ".
Their outlook was therefore predominantly confident (though
there were many misgivings). This outlook may appear blasphemous or justified by human achievement. It is the essence
of this Victorian faith.

In the second place, although as Professor Willey will show,
the idea was not new (few ideas are !), its prevalence and popular
acceptance was profoundly original. For no other generation had
won the control over environment which gave rise to this
optimism, and no other civilisation had looked in to the future
with so much confidence, or set so much store by its duty to
posterity.

That idea (in spite of much disillusionment among intellectuals)
is still dominant today. We fight our wars, we organise our
welfare state, democratic or communist, for the benefit of
generations unborn. This outlook is still, in spite of the catastrophes of the last half century, spreading about the planet. It is
new in the history of mankind. It conditioned the outlook of
the Victorians.

If we cast back over history we find the thinkers of Antiquity
regarded the world with a predominantly pessimistic eye. The

beliefs of early Christianity were apocalyptic and salvationist; as the great ship of Greco-Roman civilisation settled and foundered, this pessimism grew.

With the rise of mediæval civilisation the confidence and vigour of a young society was expressed in terms fundamentally unworldly. With the Renaissance, and, in particular, the seventeenth century, Man takes the centre of the stage, while the boxlike mediæval cosmology gives place to the terrifying immensity of the Newtonian universe. In the reign of James I, Bacon defines knowledge as power. Above all, Descartes, in his *Discourse on Method*, formulates the principles of modern science. Here is the turning point, from which the Victorian idea of progress mainly derives. And Descartes knew what he was about. He could not, he writes, keep his principles concealed, "without sinning grievously against the Law whereby we are bound to promote the general good of mankind. For by them I perceive it to be possible to arrive at knowledge highly useful to life—to discover a practical, by means of which we might render ourselves the lords and possessors of nature". Here is the basis of the idea of progress—the new confidence, the determination to subdue environment, the most original characteristic of Western civilisation.

As the new method began to bring in its returns the ideas of Western man became increasingly confident. As is well known, Montesquieu, Voltaire, the Encyclopaedists—all believe in the capacity of reason to improve the world. The idea that Man makes himself was taking an increasing hold ; such was the eighteenth-century background to the Victorian Age.

Then came a series of the greatest material changes in history, collectively known as the Industrial Revolution. The penalties of these shattering events are familiar, but for the majority of the articulate classes and their Victorian descendants their advantages were overwhelming. And this revolution was predominantly an English achievement. Thomas Love Peacock might satirise the new Steam Intellect Society, but the masses understood—there got about by the mid-nineteenth century an increasing confidence in the future.

Further, the long-term influence of Adam Smith and Bentham conditioned the early Victorian mind. Bentham's reforming zeal with which he tackled the Hogarthian jungle of eighteenth-century poverty and maladministration and his belief in man's capacity for improvement produced formidable and familiar results. Notably what Professor Woodward has justly called "The organisation of a civilised social life".

All this is behind the Victorian Age. By the mid-century, then, the Great Exhibition symbolised a confidence and an achievement which enthralled even the conservative mind of the Duke of Wellington, whose interest in the enterprise was unbounded. He could, indeed, constantly be seen pottering round it, followed by an enthusiastic crowd.

Then another shattering event occurred—the culmination of a long and uneasy process, confirming the idea of evolution already in the air : Darwin's *Origin of Species* appeared. The concept of spontaneous evolution by natural selection came to dominate men's minds. Already St. Simon, Hegel and Comte had claimed to discover the laws of human society. Now this outlook seemed reinforced with scientific proof. Darwin's doctrines were capable of many interpretations, but Darwin himself was soberly optimistic. His book concludes : " As all the living forms of life are the lineal descendants of those which lived long before the Silurian epoch, we may feel certain that the ordinary succession by generation has never been broken, and that no cataclysm has desolated the whole world. Hence, we may look with some confidence to a secure future of equally unappreciable length. And as natural selection works solely for the good of each being, all corporal and mental environment will tend to progress towards perfection ".

Here, then, was opened up a vast vista of prehistoric time, a revelation of the immense antiquity of Man and of his kinship with all life. And a future too of incalculable possibilities. Man seemed not the disreputable descendant of fallen Adam but a surprisingly able descendant of something like an ape.

After the first shock the implications of the discovery began to sink in.

To those who had learnt to do without supernatural assumptions, the idea that over great stretches of time man had made himself could provide the basis of a guarded optimism. It could of course have different interpretations. To many Christians the idea was appalling. Already, before Darwin, Tennyson had written :

" And he, shall he,
Man, her last work, who seem'd so fair,
Such splendid purpose in his eyes,
Who roll'd the psalm to wintry skies,
Who built him fanes of fruitless prayer,

Who trusted God was love indeed
And love Creation's final law—
Tho' Nature, red in tooth and claw
With ravine, shriek'd against his creed—

. . . .

Who battled for the True, the Just,
Be blown about the desert dust
Or seal'd within the iron hills ? "

Some could adapt themselves, for there were already many followers of Paley's comfortable and admirably expressed argument from Design. Others lost their faith : Victorian literature is full of the agonising repercussions of this process, and of the domestic tension to which it gave rise.

For Darwin's hypothesis had coincided with the equally disconcerting results of German scientific Biblical criticism. For many of these mid-Victorians for whom the old certainties were swept away, and still more for their descendants, " vague half believers in their casual creeds ", the anthropocentric doctrine of man-made progress provided an emotional compensation. The critics, of course, were legion—Dickens, Carlyle, Ruskin, Matthew Arnold—but they were accepted, and somehow neutralised, as prophets, worthy additions to the Victorian scene. The great middle-class march to prosperity went on without them, though Thomas Hardy's sensibility was too keen for such consolation : man was " slighted but enduring ", the universe was not even consistently malignant—it was half witted.

Abroad the effect was more devastating. The concept of strength through struggle, the glorification of force, have a familiar pedigree. The Germanic perversions of the idea of evolution culminate in the demented utterances of Nietzsche— " God is dead : we will that the Superman live ". But in Victorian England the outlook remained predominantly hopeful— the discovery of the laws of human evolution seemed satisfactory. Even the critics of bourgeois society believed in the perfectability of man. Karl Marx's bitter indictment of class exploitation and his economic interpretation of history assume that the coming of the classless society is inevitable—albeit through the furnace of class war. For Marx claimed scientific authority for his beliefs. He had, he said " discovered the economic Law of motion " of modern society, as Darwin had discovered the laws of biological evolution. His whole thought is anthropocentric, his values such as they are, are man-made. And Marx was, and is, a very influential thinker.

Representative Victorian thought was thus profoundly conditioned by the idea of progress, whether interpreted as an aspect of Providential order by Liberal Anglican thinkers (the Catholics of course, with greater sophistication, remained uncompromising), or as the expression, as Spencer thought, of an inevitable overriding law of nature, or, more sensibly, as a manmade and precarious achievement in spite of surrounding chaos, the hard fulfilment of man's own being, realising the highest awareness of which the life force is capable in this world.

This enterprising and confident outlook, prevalent also in North America, was to dominate the thought of the most powerful nations of the earth into our own time, and today it has captured the Slav world as well. Against this background the Victorian Age must be understood. All I have been able to do is to try to set this unusual, original, and essentially Western European outlook in its intellectual frame ; we are dealing not with an antiquated manifestation of the Victorian Age, but with an outlook which has captured the minds of the masses, and in practice still determines the policy of governments.

How far, then, is this idea a delusion ? Is Max Beerbohm's satirical drawing just ? Was their optimism, in a world of armed sovereign nation states, a mere mockery ? Has the creative minority of our own generation, in its bitter disillusion, only a question-mark to contemplate against a murky sky ?

I would suggest, unfashionably perhaps, that this pessimism is overdone. The figure representing our age should be something far more alert and dynamic.

While the Victorian concept of steady, automatic progress is not sustained by modern knowledge, much new evidence, for example of anthropology and prehistory, sustains the belief that from the study of history, despite its setbacks and catastrophes, there are grounds for qualified optimism. The basis of spiritual and intellectual expansion is control over environment. There is reason to think, the archæologists tell us, that basic technological skills are seldom lost even in periods of retrogression. The Dark Ages, for example, were not in this aspect as dark as the sedentary monks (who had most to lose) who chronicled them maintain : in the *Völker wanderung* the barbarians, at any rate, were enjoying themselves. Incidentally they were providing a market for luxury goods—as witness the burial at Sutton Hoo. It may be historians, who judge by the literary evidence, are too pessimistic.

Further, man, having mastered so much of his external environment, may yet have time to turn the light of science on himself. The achievements of the last six thousand years—a short time span in the light of prehistory, have been stupendous. In spite of human suffering and cruelty there has been a recognisable, if chequered, expansion of that awareness and power—which was our original definition of progress. And that idea we inherit from the great Victorians.

BASIL WILLEY

Whatever opinion listeners may form of our two minds, Mr. Bowle and I have at least " thought alike " in one respect. For although my talk was concocted quite independently of his, I had designed to begin it exactly as he has done, with a reference to Sir Max Beerbohm's caricatures. And further, so inveterate is my habit of trespassing on other men's preserves, that I find my thoughts have followed somewhat the same track as Mr. Bowle's. In attempting to sketch the history of the idea of Progress, and to define its meaning for the Victorians, I am afraid I have followed the propensity of my own interests without sufficiently sticking to my own last. For this I crave forgiveness of him and of you. If I have anything to add to what he has said it may amount to something like this : that knowledge without wisdom brings sorrow, and control without repentance brings death. We have rightly learnt from the nineteenth century that man must make himself, and be the changer as well as the product of his own environment. But we must also learn that if man makes himself wholly in his own image, he may find that like Frankenstein he has created his own destroyer.

Max Beerbohm's comparison is, I think, more telling now than it was a generation ago. If Progress means the steady and indefinite increase in our own, our nation's, or even mankind's material wealth and prosperity, we have necessarily ceased to believe in it. Quite as necessarily, the Victorians did believe in this kind of Progress. The evidences of it simply stared them in the face : railways, steam navigation, gas-lighting, main drainage, the electric telegraph, anaesthetics—all these and other alleviations of the human plight had come within a generation. The dream of the great prophetic sage of science, Francis Bacon, was being realised : " The end of our foundation," he had said, " is the knowledge of causes and secret motions of things, and the enlarging of the bounds of human empire, to the effecting of all things possible ". Of the two aims which Bacon had proposed for science, the glory of God and the relief of man's estate, the latter at any rate seemed to be in process of attainment.

But that is not the whole story: for one thing, Victorians were not unique in holding an optimistic view of history ; for another, their idea of progress included ethical amelioration as well as material improvement ; and thirdly, many of their leading spirits believed that the conquest of nature was being achieved at too great a price—at the price, in fact, of moral and spiritual decline or paralysis. So perhaps we might briefly consider these three points.

The view that history means " change for the better " is older than the nineteenth century, though it *is* of comparatively recent origin. The ancients believed, on the whole, in recurring cycles or change, in the course of which the world's great age began anew at vast intervals,

> " When with the ever-circling years
> Comes round the age of gold."

In classical times the world-process was an orbit, not a trajectory, and if your lot was cast on the sinister curve of the circle there was no help for it. The mediæval world-view was static rather than progressive ; the temporal and spiritual hierarchies, culminating in Emperor and Pope, were divinely ordained for the discipline of fallen man ; and political, social and spiritual relationships were as fixed as the links in that great chain of being which extended from the worm to the seraph. The break-up of this order was brought about by the Copernican revolution, which shattered the crystal spheres of the old cosmology ; by the commercial developments, which undermined feudalism ; by the discovery of America, which opened up new worlds of profit and delight ; and by the scientific movement which displaced supernatural in favour of mechanical laws, and turned the Creator into an absentee First Cause. Even so, it took most of the seventeenth century to overcome two persistent anti-progressive notions. One was, that perfection had been attained in classical antiquity, and that everything modern must needs be inferior to the ancient models. With this was sometimes associated the idea that Nature herself was in her dotage, and had lost the vigour of her prime. The other obstacle was a legacy of Christianity : on the one hand man was a fallible, fallen creature who could not and must not seek any abiding city on earth, and whose only hope of perfection lay, through grace, in heavenly beatitude ; and, on the other hand, the Day of Judgment and the final conflagration were probably not far distant (according to the accepted chronology), so that Sir Thomas Browne could write, " The great mutations of the world are acted, or time may be too short for our designs ".

By the end of the eighteenth century, however, it had become widely accepted that progress, in the sense of intellectual enlightenment and a general advance towards greater happiness, justice and liberty, was not only possible but was actually taking place. To many ardent spirits the French Revolution seemed to be the dawn of a new millennium, and Wordsworth, recording his emotions at that time, could exclaim :

> " Bliss was it in that dawn to be alive,
>   But to be young was very heaven ! "

The teaching of Locke, the teaching, I mean, that the mind of man at birth is like a sheet of white paper, on which any kind of inscription may be stamped, now bore fruit in the writings of " perfectibilists " like Priestley, Condorcet and Godwin. If all men start from scratch in this way, the legacies of history and heredity can be ignored, and nurture matters more than nature. By wise education, by just and rational laws, and by free discussion, human nature can be indefinitely and rapidly changed for the better. " Perfectibility," said Godwin, " is one of the most unequivocal characteristics of the human species ". Men need only realise this, and the Jupiter of tyranny and superstition (as in Shelley's vision of perfection) would topple automatically from his throne.

Meanwhile science and philosophy were beginning to see in nature, and in the very essence of reality, not fixity but progressive development. Hegel taught that the world-process consisted in the gradual unfolding of the Divine Idea, the Absolute realising its own self-consciousness in history. Long before Darwin, it had dawned upon thinkers that evolutionary change, the development of ever higher and more perfect forms, was the all-explaining law of the universe. The solar systems had grown out of the original chaos of nebular gases ; the animal and vegetable kingdoms had developed from the primitive forms newly disclosed by the geological record. Men like Comte and Herbert Spencer believed that this evolutionary process was carrying human society also, and human nature itself, through ever-improving adaptations, towards greater perfection and happiness. What Darwin did was to prove how this evolutionary change actually took place in the biological field—namely by natural selection and the survival of the fittest. His work added the force of demonstration to an established evolutionary way of thought, and, coinciding with the spectacular material improvements of the time, helped to give the idea of progress the status of an unquestioned assumption.

But we must not forget those others who, while not denying the advantages of street-lamps, steam-locomotion and the like, yet felt that human well-being in the highest sense was not increasing at the same rate as wealth. Coleridge complained that we had " purchased a few brilliant inventions at the loss of all communion with life and the spirit of nature " ; Shelley, that " man, having enslaved the elements, remains himself a slave ". Carlyle denounced the infidel and mechanical trends of the age, its mammon-worship and machine-worship, its cash-nexus which had superseded human relationships, its ready surrender to political nostrums and cheap demagogy. The march of mind was all very well, but suppose it was marching into a desert instead of into the promised land ? Modern civilisation, typified by the Great Exhibition of 1851, might be very fine, but were men morally and intrinsically any the better for it ? Had it not produced the horrors of industrialism, a rootless proletariat, the dark Satanic mills, new diseases and new grievances ? Perhaps, as Rousseau and other primitivists had urged, civilisation was a monstrous aberration, and men were happier and better when fresh from the hands of God or Nature in some primeval Eden. Men like Burke, Sir Walter Scott, Cobbett, Carlyle, Newman, Ruskin and Morris stated or implied, in very varying accents, that the Middle Ages, in spite of Black Deaths or Wars of the Roses, were as far above the present in moral and spiritual stature as they were inferior in sanitation or mechanical skills. And Malthus had raised a spectre which haunted half the century ; Nature was niggardly rather than profuse, and, without stern measures, population would soon outrun means of subsistence.

In face of all this, some were for going back to the Middle Ages and trying to recapture thence what modernity had let slip : Faith, spiritual authority, chivalry, pride in craftsmanship, an ideal orientation. Some, like Spencer, were for letting things be, in secure confidence that if one trusted the laws of evolution, good would somehow be the final end of ill. Others, like the Socialists, Christian or un-Christian, favoured conscious planning, and the clearance of natural and human jungles by taking thought for the morrow.

One may say, perhaps, that the central problem of the time (it is still our problem today) was how to reconcile free growth with conscious contrivance ; how to retain the benefits of modern knowledge and modern enlightenment without sacrificing the values of an older and less self-conscious order ; how, in a word, to keep one's head without losing one's heart. The nineteenth century, for all its buoyancy and optimism, was homesick for an idealised but not wholly imaginary past, for the days " When life ran gaily as the sparkling Thames ", and for the " cool, flowery lap of earth ", where Nature " laid us at our birth ". The Victorians could often approve mentally of modern advances while their affections were still with things past or passing ; we can see this, for instance, in George Eliot's description of Shepperton Church after its restoration, and in her ensuing comment :

> " Immense improvement ! says the well-regulated mind,
> which unintermittingly rejoices in the New Police, the Tithe
> Commutation Act, the Penny Post and all guarantees of human

advancement, and has no moments when conservative-reforming intellect takes a nap, while imagination does a little Toryism by the sly, revelling in regret that dear, old brown, crumbling, picturesque inefficiency is everywhere giving place to spick-and-span, new-painted, new-varnished efficiency, which will yield endless diagrams, plans, elevations and sections, but alas ! no picture. Mine, I fear, is not a well-regulated mind ; it lingers with a certain fondness over the days of nasal clerks and top-booted parsons, and has a sigh for the departed shades of vulgar errors."

Or again, in *The Mill on the Floss*, this dialectic of progress and reaction, the head versus the heart, comes out clearly : " is not the striving after something better and better in our sur-roundings," she asks, " the grand characteristic that distin-guishes man from the brute . . . . ? But heaven knows where that striving might lead us, if our affections had not a trick of twining round those old inferior things—if the loves and sancti-ties of our life had no deep immovable roots in memory ". The dilemma may be thus expressed : Nature is wise (had not Wordsworth proclaimed it, and was not the Lake District still there to prove it ?), and Man, with his planning and contrivances, goes astray—his meddling intellect mis-shapes the beauteous forms of things. Yet what happens when man neglects to cultivate the garden ? Nature, left to herself, produces jungles ; human nature left to itself produces slums. So we must go on pruning and weeding. But then we are apt to construct geometrical patterns which are an offence to the eye and the soul. We plan for equality and justice in our social order, and in so doing (as J. S. Mill lamented in his essay *On Liberty*) we pro-duce mass-mediocrity and kill individuality and freedom. We plan a Brave New World, and find that we have produced unutterable ennui, and dried up the springs of joy.

The Victorians distinctly realised that there are many kinds of progress, and that these are not always mutually compatible. There is material progress, of which they had plenty ; there is intellectual progress, of which they were justly proud. But they knew that material progress often yields diminishing returns in happiness and in holiness. Increase comfort, and you decrease energy and resource ; increase amusement, and you decrease joy ; establish the kingdom of man, and you subvert the kingdom of heaven. Nevertheless when wealth, inventions and commerce are increasing, it is hard not to believe that human nature and happiness are also improving at the same time. And in spite of their misgivings and yearnings, the Victorians did on the whole believe, as we no longer can, that men were becoming less selfish, less unreasonable and less bellicose ; that free trade would promote international understanding and banish war ; that science and education would conquer error and superstition, and that in some not too distant future we should see " the Parliament of man, the Federation of the world ".

I agree with Mr. Bowle that man cannot now turn back ; that since he has eaten of the tree of knowledge he must push on to ever-greater mastery of nature and control of his own destiny. But I also think that unless this control is accompanied by *self*-control, unless knowledge (in Bacon's phrase) is " saved from the serpent " by charity and humility, unless—in a word, the kingdom of heaven is sought first, the kingdom of man will turn out to be built upon sand, and its ruin will come sooner than we may expect.

Macaulay and the Sense of Optimism

G. M. TREVELYAN

I HAVE been asked to talk tonight about the attitude of the mid-Victorians towards history and the past, with special reference to their belief in progress, taking Macaulay as the outstanding figure. But Macaulay's historical achievement is closely connected with the influence of Scott, though his idea of progress belongs to a generation later than Sir Walter's.

During the thirty years before the Queen's accession, Scott ruled the imaginations of men. The future leaders of thought among the early Victorians were as young people brought up on his writings, and derived from them a new view of history and of the past. Scott was a great antiquarian and historian, but his influence over men's conception of the past was exerted not by his regular histories, but by his lays, and still more by the *Waverley Novels.*

Scott, as I think, introduced into men's minds the idea of social history, the study of day-to-day life of various classes of the community in different ages and countries long ago. His pictures of the social past of Scotland were indeed far more accurate and valuable than his pictures of the Middle Ages, but although the *Heart of Midlothian* is much better social history than *Ivanhoe*, both caused people to think of their ancestors as real living people, not as stiff paste-board figures moved about by solemn historians.

The difference between Gibbon's view of the past and Macaulay's gives a measure of the influence of Scott. Gibbon's work comes near to perfection partly because of his limitations. He tells the truth, but he does not attempt to tell more than a small portion of the truth. Living as he did before Scott, Gibbon conceived of mankind as essentially the same in all ages and countries. The men of the fifteenth century in his handling are much the same as the men of the fifth. His history is like the procession on the Parthenon Frieze—classical and cold. But Scott's mind is the stained glass of a mediæval window, that breaks the white light into a hundred hues and flashes.

To Scott, each epoch, each profession, each country, each province had its own way of thinking, talking and fighting. Sir Walter showed mankind this new and richly variegated pattern of history, not as a mere narration of events, still less as a series of generalisations, but as a "fair field full of folk"; and without this view of the "folk", neither the narrative nor the generalisations can be very profound. The professional historians beginning with Macaulay took the hint from Scott.

When Macaulay, born in 1800, was himself a schoolboy, he knew Scott's lays by heart, and like every other young person of the Waterloo period, greedily devoured the *Waverley Novels*. Macaulay's *Lays of Ancient Rome* were suggested by Scott's lays. They were a very successful attempt to make the world of ancient republican Rome living and interesting to schoolboys and to their fathers, whose education in those days consisted chiefly of Latin taught in a very dry manner. *Lars Porsena* and *Lake Regillus,* rather remote themes in themselves, became as familiar names almost as Napoleon and Waterloo, to the Victorian mind, down to the end of the Queen's reign, a very remarkable feat on the part of the ballad maker.

But Macaulay's lays are imagination playing on history. What of his contribution to history itself? He aspired to write serious history that should be as popular as the most popular works of fiction, and he succeeded. Gibbon had been read by an aristocratic class and its appendages, but Macaulay was read by an enormous public in both hemispheres, including almost everyone who read any books at all, and this was true not only of his Essays, but to a scarcely less degree of his *History of England,* a very closely packed narrative of the last fifteen years of the seventeenth century, the only history of such length and detail that has ever been so widely read.

Macaulay and Carlyle created a popular interest in history which was continued in the last half of the reign by historians like Motley, Lecky, Froude and J. R. Green. History was a very important part of the intellectual make-up of Victorian England, scarcely less than science. History had a great effect on the political, philosophical and religious controversies of the day. Only in the last years of the century was there a reaction against popular or literary history, when history was declared to be a science for students, not a part of the national literature for the public. And it was so.

But to go back to Macaulay. One reason why his *History of England* was popular was because he had introduced into it so much social history. The third chapter, describing the economic and social state of England in 1685 was a new sort of thing, for Hume's attempt had not amounted to much. Nor is that famous third chapter the only part of his history that can be called economic and social. His account, in later parts of the book, of the East India Company, of the recoinage, of the Bank of England and its rivals, of the universities, of the emancipation of the press, and many other sections, paragraphs and sentences are social history, interwoven into the fabric of the political narrative with a skill that greatly enhances the interest and the value of the work.

Now that in our own day the study of economic and social history has taken on such large proportions, we are able to judge the value of Macaulay's pioneer work in this field. Viewed in these present-day lights, the economic and social parts of his *History of England* are still worth the attention of any modern student, and considered as pioneer work on what was then almost a new subject, they are very remarkable indeed. Of course his picture of England in 1685 had great faults and omissions, such as his very inadequate account of the various classes of country gentlemen, and of the state of agriculture. Macaulay was neither an aristocrat nor a countryman, but his interest in the middling and lower orders of society, as they were called, was very real, and his study of the condition of their lives past and present was made with sympathy and zeal. And here we come to the point on which I have been specially asked to talk tonight, Macaulay's belief in progress, typical of a large part of the thought of the early Victorians, though not of Carlyle's.

Macaulay was convinced by his studies that all classes of the community were better off than in the past, that these improvements had been going steadily on for a number of centuries, and he therefore thought it probable (here no doubt there was a defect in logic) that it would go on indefinitely in the future. I will let him speak for himself. The famous third chapter of his history, published in 1848, ended thus :—

" It is now the fashion to place the golden age of England in times when noblemen were destitute of comforts, the want of which would be intolerable to a modern footman ; when farmers and shopkeepers breakfasted on loaves, the very sight of which would raise a riot in a modern workhouse ; when to have a clean shirt once a week was a privilege reserved for the higher class of gentry ; when men died faster in the purest country air than they now die in the most pestilential lanes in our towns, and when men died faster in the lanes of our towns than they now die on the coast of Guiana. We too shall, in our turn, be outstripped, and in our turn be envied. It may well be, in the twentieth century, that the peasant of Dorsetshire may think himself miserably paid with twenty shillings a week, that the carpenter of Greenwich may receive ten shillings a day ; that labouring men may be as little used to dine without meat as they now are to eat rye bread ; that sanitary, police and medical discoveries may have added several more years to the average length of human life ; that numerous comforts and luxuries which are now unknown or confined to a few may be within the reach of every diligent and thrifty working man ".

These views he had already expressed a generation before, when as a young Edinburgh reviewer he attacked the pessimism of Southey's *Colloquies on Society,* as you can see in the last paragraphs of that essay. He believed in progress, mainly because he was certain that the ordinary man was far better off as regards material conditions than in times gone by. Speaking in the House of Commons on the Anatomy Bill in 1832, he said:—

" Does the honourable gentleman know from what cruel sufferings the improvement in surgical science has rescued our species ? I will tell one story, the first that comes into my head : You may have heard of Leopold, Duke of Austria, the same who imprisoned our Richard Coeur de Lion. Leopold's horse fell under him and crushed his leg. The surgeons said that the limb must be amputated, but none of them knew how to amputate it. Leopold in his agony laid a hatchet on his thigh, and ordered his servant to strike with a mallet. The leg was cut off, and the Duke died of the gush of blood. Such was the end of that powerful prince. Why, there is not now a brick-

4

layer who falls from a ladder in England who cannot obtain surgical assistance infinitely superior to that which the sovereign of Austria could command in the twelfth century."

This belief in progress he did not get from Sir Walter Scott, who loved the past too much to look forward with any enthusiasm to the future. Belief in progress was not symptomatic of the anti-Jacobin Tories in their desperate struggle with Napoleon, but it coloured the hopes of the following generation who passed the Reform Bill. This optimistic outlook on the course of human affairs was based not only on the evidence of material advance, but also on moral and intellectual grounds. Macaulay and many of his contemporaries, such as Dickens and Thackeray, saw that their own age was removing many abuses and cruelties that had not shocked their ancestors—negro slavery, cruel laws and punishments and much indifference to suffering. Macaulay, when he voted for factory legislation, observed that the employment of very small children in industry had been approved by the most enlightened philanthropists of the past, for they knew no better.

Now this belief in progress out of the past was not absurd, whether or not it afforded ground for confidence in the future. As regards material conditions of life, it was very largely true. The most authoritative of our economic historians, the late Sir John Clapham, recently showed that even in the first and worst half of the nineteenth century, the Industrial Revolution had not on the average lowered real wages, but raised them. Even in the "hungry forties", when Macaulay wrote, the working classes were on the average better fed and clothed than their grandfathers, and very large and prosperous new classes of mechanics and bourgeoisie had come into existence. Macaulay was not wrong in thinking that the English were better off materially, and were certainly more humane than in the past. The facts that escaped his notice, and escaped the notice of most of his contemporaries, were other evils that the machine age had brought—the destruction of craftsmanship and the intelligent joy of man in his daily work, the ugliness and depressing aspect of the great new cities which were taking the place of farm, village and country town as the scene of ordinary human existence ; the loss of rural tradition, which had been the real basis of our higher civilisation in England from the days of

Chaucer and Shakespeare onwards. In the last half of the century, Ruskin, William Morris and others denounced the whole tendency of modern industrial life on these grounds, and many of the principal writers of the Victorian Age—Carlyle, Matthew Arnold, Hardy, Meredith, to say nothing of Bernard Shaw, were severe critics of modern society.

At the same time, the advent of Darwinism and the theory of evolution complicated the issue. Evolution proved the doctrine of progress in one sense, for it showed that civilised man developed out of cave man, possibly out of monkey or jellyfish. But it saddened human thought by implying an ultimate end of no very joyous character. Some people indeed regarded the survival of the fittest as a splendid affair, but others remarked that it only meant the survival of the fittest to survive, not necessarily the survival of the best. Even as early as the 'forties, the era of Macaulay's limited historical optimism, Tennyson's *In Memoriam* shows us a young poet who had small joy in the prospects of the human race as indicated by modern science.

And so I think that the famous Victorian belief in progress was a very conditional affair. Times were improving in England, and people were glad of it, and gloried in it at the Exhibition of 1851 and again at the Jubilee of 1897. But they had no thought-out philosophic belief in progress as a universal law, true to all times and in all countries. Even Macaulay, in his essay on Von Ranke's *Popes* foresaw the New Zealander sketching the ruins of St. Paul's from a broken arch of London Bridge, and he never forgot that the great civilisation of ancient Greece and Rome had first stagnated and then fallen—in his own words, " It cost Europe a thousand years of barbarism to escape the fate of China ".

But though he never made a dogma or laid down an historical law about progress, he was thankful for the improvements that he saw in English life in the last few hundred years. He would not allow men to praise the seventeenth century at the expense of the nineteenth, nor did he expect that European civilisation would collapse as rapidly as it has in fact done. The Victorians had a sense of security that we have lost, but few of them had a philosophic belief in a progress that would go on for ever, and some of them, like Carlyle and Ruskin, thought the past had been better than the present. These pessimists were in a minority in

Macaulay's day, but their numbers had increased by the end of the century.

The answer that we each give to the question whether there has been progress or deterioration depends on what things each of us values most. Progress may be judged by purely material standards, by moral, by intellectual, or by artistic standards. The world has seldom or never progressed in all these ways at the same time, and there will never be agreement as to what constitutes progress or deterioration in morals, in intellect or in art. Talk about progress in the vague is therefore of little value. One must define the terms of the enquiry. The more the Victorians thought about the alleged progress of the human race, the more distinctions they made, and the less they agreed with one another.

The historical retrospect of the later Victorians was more subtle than Macaulay's, and his exuberant optimism irritated the intellectuals of the *fin de siècle*. Englishmen had by that time enjoyed so long an experience of material progress that they took it for granted and discounted it accordingly. In the earlier stages of the Industrial Revolution, it had been more of a novelty and it aroused more enthusiasm among thinking people. And now again in our own day, when material progress has met with a sharp reverse, we may, as we queue up with our coupons, be more able to understand why Macaulay, in the age of Peel and Cobden, rejoiced to see wealth accumulating so fast, supplying a rapidly increasing population with more food, better clothes, greater facilities for travel, and a more abundant supply of books old and new. Material progress is not to be despised. Not only does it make people more comfortable, but it gives freedom for a greater variety of intellectual life.

1851 and the Visibility of Progress

E. L. WOODWARD

SOMEONE—it may have been Lord Acton—is supposed to have said, in answer to a question about the Renaissance, that "the Renaissance existed only in prize essays". There was a time when historians would have inclined to say that the Victorian Age existed only in the writing of certain literary critics, and as a butt for ridicule, but most people who laugh at the past find the joke turning sooner or later against themselves. One need not worry therefore about writers who earn a rather dishonest penny by disparaging their great grandparents.

The real difficulty in talking about the Victorian Age is not so much to get clear of the trails of deliberate malice as to avoid the foreshortening which affects all historical judgments. There was not one Victorian Age, there were at least three, and each of them continually changed shape and colour like a display of the Northern lights. Moreover, nineteenth-century England was too free a country, and too rich in ideas, for men to tread the goose-step to the tunes provided by mass propaganda. Thus I could describe the year 1851, the climax of the early Victorian period, without reference to any of the qualities so confidently ascribed to it : a sense of political security, a belief in the inevitability of progress, a strong and dogmatic religious faith and trust in the Grand Design of Providence.

At the end of the year 1851 there was, in fact, not a sense of political security but a very considerable disturbance of mind over the possible designs of Louis Napoleon of France. Prince Albert wrote to the Prime Minister that it was " quite clear to the Queen that we were entering upon most dangerous times in which Military Despotism and Red Republicanism " (each word spelt with a capital letter) " will for some time be the only Powers on the Continent, to both of which the Constitutional Monarchy of England will be equally hateful. That the calm influence of our institutions, however, should succeed in assuaging the contest abroad must be the anxious wish of every Englishman ". The Queen and the Prince Consort were not alone in feeling disturbed. The new Poet Laureate, Alfred Tennyson, thought it his duty to awaken public opinion by writing patriotic poems on the need to prepare for invasion.

A year before the Great Exhibition, Tennyson had published *In Memoriam*. If this poem were the one surviving piece of early Victorian literature, what picture would it give of England ? The country would not appear as a great workshop. There would be no dark, Satanic mills, nothing to break the sound of bells in winter echoing from hamlet to hamlet, nothing to disturb the lovely summer dawns :

> " Till now the doubtful dusk reveal'd
>   The knolls once more, where, couch'd at ease,
>   The white kine glimmer'd, and the trees
> Laid their dark arms about the field."

The church bells might ring in this England—" four voices of four hamlets round, each voice four changes on the wind ", yet, for those who stayed to read and think, something had happened more disturbing than the rise of another Bonaparte to thoughts of security. Modern geology had already made it hard to accept the old belief in a special Providence for man. What interest did " Nature " show in man—and not in this man or that, but in all mankind ?

> " So careful of the type ?   But no.
>   From scarped cliff and quarried stone
>   She cries, ' A thousand types are gone :
> I care for nothing, all shall go.' "

Was there room left here for a belief in progress ?

> " The moanings of the homeless sea,
>   The sound of streams that swift or slow
>   Draw down Aeonian hills and sow
> The dust of continents to be."

Endless, indifferent change, but not progress. Even in the country garden is heard the voice : *Vanitas vanitatum, omnia vanitas*. Remember also that *In Memoriam* was not a poem

written for a small coterie. It became almost at once a best-
seller. The stanzas I have quoted must have been in the minds of
thousands as they moved among the temporal triumphs of the
Great Exhibition, and if they asked for consolation or for certainty
they were told that :

> " There lives more faith in honest doubt,
>   Believe me, than in half the creeds."

In Memoriam was as representative of mid-Victorian England
as the glass house of the Great Exhibition. I have spoken of
the one because I would wish you to keep it in mind when I
speak more at length of the other. One must not look for formal
consistency in an age any more than in a person. Yet there is a
real consistency, since behind the Exhibition, as behind the
poetry of Tennyson, lay the revolutionary effects of modern
scientific discovery.

The exhibits of 1851 have long been dispersed. The very
building which housed them has gone, but the sense of progress
made visible in the Great Exhibition of the Works of Industry
of all Nations—to give it its full title—this sense of progress
can be recovered by reading the printed catalogue. The
introduction to the catalogue explains the purpose of the Exhibition. The theme is reaffirmed in the opening address which
Prince Albert read to his wife Queen Victoria, and in the opening
prayer which the Archbishop of Canterbury offered to the
Almighty. Prince Albert pointed out that the Exhibition was
ready on the day originally named for opening it—that is to
say May 1st—and that this fact was itself evidence of what could
be done by "goodwill and cordial co-operation among nations,
aided by the means that modern science had placed at our command". In fact, the only exhibits which were late in arriving
were those from Russia.

The language used by the Archbishop was more remarkable.
It is curiously like that of Kipling's *Recessional*, written for
another celebration nearly half a century later. Consider these
words : " While we survey the works of art and industry which
surround us, let not our hearts be lifted up that we forget the
Lord our God, as if our own power and the might of our hands
had gotten in this wealth". A few sentences earlier the Archbishop and the assembly—you will have seen pictures of them

under this immense glass roof—summed up before Heaven their
" purpose of knitting together in the bonds of peace and concord
the different nations of the earth ". Then followed a sentiment
which has an English ring to it : " Of Thee it cometh that
violence is not heard in our land, wasting nor destruction within
its borders ". In other words, the revolutions of 1848 which had
swept over most of Europe had been stayed by the Almighty at
the cliffs of Dover. Yet there is more than insular satisfaction
at our escape from what Tennyson rashly called the " red fool
fury of the Seine ". Consider the next words of the Archbishop :
" It is of Thee, O Lord, that nations do not lift up the sword
against each other nor learn war any more ; it is of Thee that
peace is within our walls and plenteousness within our palaces ".
Here is the voice of a generation which had not known a great
war in Europe for thirty-six years. The phrases have that
blinkered optimism which so often distinguishes English isolation-
ist aspirations ; one wonders what the old Duke of Wellington
would have said about them. Everyone who heard them, and
certainly the Queen herself, knew that England would have been
in grave danger if her sea captains had not learned war any more.
The words also take an ironic meaning if they are considered in relation to the early blunders and mismanagement of
the expedition to the Crimea only three years later, and as the
prelude to the decade in which Germany was made by blood
and iron.

Yet it is certain that the Archbishop and the whole gathering
were saying something which they wished to think and which
did not appear a wild dream. As you read the immense list
of exhibits in the catalogue, you can see the grounds for this hope.
These exhibits were not just the latest gadgets—this year's new
models. They represented something novel in scale, if not in
idea ; similar exhibitions had been held in France, but not on a
plan commensurate with the stupendous increase in productive
power and in control over natural forces. Through its range
and through its completeness the English Exhibition of 1851
was symbolic of the raising of the standards of life for all classes.
Standards of life were being raised. Indeed there is a danger of
getting the fearful evils of early Victorian industrialism out of
focus. In saying this I am not trying to gloss over the
sufferings of the poor. It would be a low form of meanness to

pretend that these sufferings did not exist. They had always existed. The novelty of the Victorian Age was not its misery, but the realisation that urban and rural misery could be prevented by positive effort and not merely alleviated by private charity.

These possibilities of betterment were based upon the application of scientific knowledge to industry and agriculture. The Victorians who were excited by the new inventions and discoveries were not just giggling at machines. They knew well enough that material progress is the foundation of moral progress. Cheap cotton underclothing—not all of it the product of sweated labour—was among the preconditions of the spread of habits of personal cleanliness, and so also were the traps, gullies, glazed pipes and all the other devices of the engineers; filth and moral degradation went together, as a country parson like Charles Kingsley was always pointing out.

In retrospect it is perhaps less easy to explain why Mr. Gladstone, Mr. Cobden, and other Commissioners of the Exhibition thought that this increase in the *tempo* of material progress would make almost of itself for greater goodwill among nations and for the peaceful federation of mankind. A regime of peace, of general free trade and of open markets suited England; for this very reason it might appeal less readily to other nations. Yet even here logic and common sense were on the side of Mr. Gladstone and Mr. Cobden. They held that the spread of plenty through the profitable exchange of commodities would mean the disappearance of wars caused by the scramble for a limited number of prizes; war, like musical chairs, loses its *raison d'être* when there is *lebensraum* for everybody. At all events, if they trusted too much in human reason and in the beneficent " march of mind ", the Victorians, like their predecessors of the eighteenth century, erred on the right side. None the less they erred, and their mistakes, as far as they were English mistakes, were due to the English habit—it is not only an English habit—of deducing from one's own self interest general principles of behaviour. It may seem unfair to judge public opinion by the rather formal statements I have quoted. Official Catalogues, and still more, addresses to the sovereign and to the Almighty tend to put the best face on things. Let me therefore give you an unofficial view of the purposes and lessons of the Great Exhibition. A certain Mr. Robert Hunt, who describes himself as Keeper of Mining Records, wrote a Companion to the Official Catalogue from which I have quoted. He also began by a statement of the significance of the exhibits. He said—" we are in this Industrial Palace surrounded by the results of the efforts of thought in almost every direction in which the human mind has tried its powers. This opportunity, the grandest which has been offered in the world's history, must not be lost. It is for us to learn what through times past man has aimed at, what he has reached within the present, and what may be the powers of advancement which still remain for him ".

Mr. Hunt then dives into the Exhibition. He finds very soon that one question must be answered. What is the relation between these new achievements of thought and the older non-mechanical arts ? Mr. Hunt turns to the group of English sculpture ; a rather odd group including the Amazons, the Argonauts, Puck and Ariel, and the young King Alfred receiving from his mother a book of Anglo-Saxon poetry. This group gave Mr. Hunt his answer : " We have a satisfactory proof that practical England cultivates still the study of the beautiful and that the works of the hard-handed mechanic may be appropriately associated with the efforts of educated fancy to the advancement of the amenities of life ". This rather bloated phrase seems a long way from William Morris's definition of art as the expression of joy in work, but perhaps it is not as far as one might think. Men were not yet tired of machinery and the fatigue of the eye did not yet apply to the limited range of effects which machinery could produce. Mr. Hunt himself uses the term " beautiful " in speaking of the iron castings produced in what he calls " the rising town of Birmingham ", Limerick lace, the art of calico-printing, a slide-lathe, a steam printing press, glass chandeliers, a group of chemical salts, and an American grand piano. I must leave it to later speakers to disentangle the results of Mr. Hunt's " efforts of thought " in this direction, but I might quote another of his commendations to show the craftsman's pleasure in machine-made things. Mr. Hunt speaks of " an exquisitely carved trophy of birds, fruit and foliage, the remarkable feature of it being the application of steam machinery to produce such involved tracery and deep undercutting as is here displayed ". Now it is pretty clear that the workers who made this trophy, including the boy who oiled the steam-driven wheels, did not regard themselves as slaves of the machine. They had rather a new, exhilarating sense of mastery and of power. You notice it by contrast in the slightly patronising attitude of Mr. Hunt towards the " hand labour " which produced shawls and stockings in the Shetlands and Fair Island.

This power had been obtained by knowledge, by patient and resourceful enquiry into the principles and laws governing the forces of nature. Such enquiries brought a certain moral satisfaction ; for example, the calotypes (a now forgotten term used in the early days of photography) are praised not for beauty, but for accurate representation—for the " truthfulness " with which they represent forest scenery. Little wonder that all this evidence of the " march of mind " was interpreted in terms of progress.

Progress was not equated with increased and increasing comfort. Progress brought increased comfort, but the essence of it was something non-material ; an increase in intellectual control of the environment. Furthermore (though here one is on more difficult ground), progress seemed the result of individual effort, just as capital seemed the result of individual saving. I use the term " difficult ground " because it is not altogether easy to decide how the Victorians looked at themselves as individuals in relation to the community. It is easier to explain how they looked at the State, though even here much nonsense is talked today about Victorian *laissez-faire*. At least one can say that there was a strong belief in self-help. In his address to the Queen, Prince Albert says of the Commissioners : " We considered that it was a main characteristic of the national undertaking in which we were engaged that it should depend wholly upon the voluntary contributions of this country for success ".

Self-help was not necessarily selfishness. Indeed to the Victorians of 1851, self-help was the means by which the individual made his contribution to the community. " Private profit " was one of the yard-sticks by which the contribution of the individual to the community could be measured. And if this seems crude today, one should remember two things : first, that State or official control as an alternative to " private profit " was associated with the Bumbledom and jobbery, the inefficiency and incompetence which had been an obstacle to material advancement. It is relevant that admission to the Civil Service by competitive examination was not general until 1870. Secondly you must remember that the business world was still organised very much on "one-man" or "one-family" or "one-partnership" lines. Innovations in technique had come mainly through individuals or through small groups who had risked their own fortunes. The State had not built a single mile of English railways, and, if railway building had been left to the type of official whom Rowland Hill had to fight in trying to get Post Office reform, the pioneer work would have taken a generation.

This idea of harmony between the creative work of the individual seeking his own advantage and the needs of the community as a whole is brought out in another rather interesting contemporary reference to the Exhibition. In 1852, the Royal Society of Arts decided to give a series of lectures on the results of the Exhibition. These lectures were printed in a volume dedicated somewhat fulsomely to the Queen. The first lecture was a survey by Dr. Whewell, Master of Trinity, on the general bearing of the Exhibition on the progress of art and science. Dr. Whewell like Mr. Hunt, spoke of the "poetic" character of "machinery light as the breath of air which carries the flower dust to its appointed place". He too regarded the exhibits as "symbols, instruments, and manifestations of beauty and power", and as "articulate utterances of the human mind no less than if they had been audible words and melodious sentences". He too remarked on the uniqueness of the Exhibition; for the first time it had been possible to get a simultaneous view of the progress of the human race in industry and art.

Dr. Whewell used the term "progress" deliberately. He said that there might not always be "progress" in good government, but "there always is, except when very adverse influences roll back the common course of things, a progress in art, and generally in science". He took care to define what he meant by this statement. "Men," he said, "had always been artists and craftsmen; the transition in time was towards a more skilful, powerful, comprehensive and progressive form of art". And in what did this "progressiveness" consist? It consisted in the fact that at earlier stages of culture the arts were exercised mainly to gratify the tastes of the few, whereas, with us, they were used to supply the wants of the many.

Dr. Whewell took a curious illustration. He said that one

might expect "the most subtle and refined machinery" to be applied to the most delicate work, but in fact "the most exquisite and the most expensive machines were used where operations on the most common materials were to be performed, because they were to be executed on the widest scale ". Thus whereas in older civilisations thousands and tens of thousands worked for the pleasure and magnificence of the powerful military despot, "here (in Victorian England) the man who is powerful in the weapons of peace, capital and machinery, uses them to give comfort and enjoyment to the public, whose servant he is, and thus becomes rich while he enriches others with his goods ". So far here, almost to the border of rashness, is an academic blessing on mass production, even if it is in the form of a definition of progress in terms of the greatest good of the greatest number. It is also a blessing on the mass producer, and I think he sums up the ideas of the ordinary educated man in the year 1851 and 1852 not only about "progress" but about the relation between the individual and the community which allowed "progress" to attain its greatest speed and extension.

What was wrong with this Victorian view ? Something was wrong. The visibility of progress was undoubted, and, as I have said, the admiration of progress was not just a worship of comfort. It can hardly be said that the English poor, who formed the majority of the population, had in 1851 a superfluity of comfort to worship. Even the small upper class which could acquire luxuries was not coddled ; the professional class—perhaps the most important new social phenomenon of the age—was being educated by schoolmasters whose belief in toughness was at times almost pathological. Queen Victoria herself, as her court well knew, had the bleakest ideas of domestic comfort. Softness of living is at all events not mid-Victorian.

Nevertheless something is wrong, or I should say, something is missing from this vision of progress. For one thing, there is too little sense of mystery ; though here again Tennyson's poetry at its best was a corrective, a reminder that, after all, the wisest man does not know very much. This warning that the range of the known is and must remain far smaller than the range of the unknown recurs as something which could not be said too often in the writings of the greatest Victorians. For example, in Ruskin's *Sesame and Lilies*—a book once so popular and now forgotten

—suddenly in the midst of much lusciousness and sentimentality you come upon a warning against the dangers of spiritual pride ; the sin by which the angels fell.

The Archbishop of Canterbury, in the opening prayer which I have quoted, was humble before God, yet he assumed a considerable knowledge of the Divine plan. He seemed to know what song the sirens sang, and, if he could not himself bind the sweet influences of the Pleiades, at least some Fellow of the Royal Society would be able to tell him how it was done. The mysterious elements in life and history fell out of sight before the display of progress visible. The power conferred by accurate and measured knowledge within a limited field, distracted attention from the constant and overriding theme of tragedy. Thus the early Victorians forgot the fate of Oedipus, they forgot Virgil's *lacrimae rerum,* or Wordsworth's " still, sad music of humanity ". This spiritual pride, which the Greeks would have regarded as a foolish provocation of Heaven, accounts for the failure to see that progress itself did not mean increasing safety but increasing risks and that every step forward carried with it hidden and unexpected hazards.

The Victorians were living dangerously, far more dangerously than they knew. The world was much stranger than their machinery, and the nature of man much more fragile and at the same time more unfathomable. In the words of Sophocles:—

Πολλὰ τὰ δεινὰ κοὐδὲν ἀνθρώπου δεινότερον πέλει

An earlier Englishman understood these matters more clearly than the contemporaries of Macaulay. The great glass house of 1851 might contain all the evidence of progress visible in all the countries of the world. And yet :—

> " The cloud-capp'd towers, the gorgeous palaces,
> The solemn temples, the great globe itself,
> Yea, all which it inherit, shall dissolve ;
> And, like this insubstantial pageant faded,
> Leave not a rack behind."

1851—a New Age, a New Style

JOHN SUMMERSON

YOU REMEMBER the "Britain Can Make It" Exhibition, and you remember, of course, that it was held at South Kensington, in the Victoria and Albert Museum. Nobody seemed to think this location inappropriate, as I am quite sure they would have done if, say, the British Museum had been proposed. No, the Victoria and Albert seemed a natural enough setting for the display of modern industrial design. And why? Is there something about the soil of South Kensington, which favours the promotion of industrial art? Well, as it happens, that is very nearly the right answer. For the soil of South Kensington —a pretty large piece of it—was bought by the Commissioners for the Exhibition of 1851 ; it was bought with the very considerable surplus which the Exhibition earned ; and it was bought with a view to fostering the main object of the Exhibition—the Union of Art and Industry. So "Britain Can Make It" stood at the near end of a long tradition whose beginning was the Crystal Palace.

If you look round the Victoria and Albert Museum (I mean the actual building, not its contents) you will discover, tucked away behind the newer extensions, certain older galleries of a rather curious character ; built of iron, obviously bearing a rather close relationship to the Crystal Palace, and in a style which defies all attempts at classification—unless indeed you care to call it Victorian. "Style"—this subject played a considerable part in the thought of the 1830's, 40's and 50's, and was most pronounced in architecture and has, I think, a considerable general bearing on our enquiry into the Victorian idea of progress.

The seventeenth and eighteenth centuries had known, or at least revered, only one great architectural style of the past—that which prevailed in classical antiquity ; they were confident that all architectural improvement consisted in elaborating and refining on the great principles there embodied. The nineteenth century, however, discovered equally stirring truths in the architecture of the Middle Ages. The result of this was a division of loyalties and that rather childish rivalry which produced what came to be known as the Battle of the Styles. But this enthronement of two great styles of the past also produced something else—it produced the concept of a potential third Great Style ; in fact, of a *new* style. This notion of a new style, a style analogous to those of the past but different in constructive principle and in ornamental expression pervades the entire architectural history of the century. The circumstances attending the building of the Crystal Palace illustrate it with peculiar vividness.

The concept of a " new style ", had, it is true, emerged before the beginning of Victoria's reign. Architects and designers had been fidgeting with something of the sort for at least half a century. Their theories seemed—and were—merely academic and eccentric. But when the great portents of industrial civilisation began to arrive, when it appeared that a new age was indeed opening up before mankind, then the idea of a new style —and especially of a new architectural style—became imbued with strong emotional colouring. In the fourteen years between the Queen's accession and the opening of the Great Exhibition the feeling for a contemporary style grew rapidly in intensity. In 1845 a Mr. Vose Pickett produced a pamphlet called *A New System of Architecture, founded on the forms of Nature and developing the properties of Metals*. It is easy to see from that title, with its distinctly industrial ring, whither Mr. Vose Pickett's argument was leading him. Then in 1847, Professor Donaldson, speaking to the young men who were just founding the Architectural Association, voiced the challenge which was in all their minds :

> " The great question is are we to have an architecture of
> our period, a distinct, individual palpable style of the
> nineteenth century ? "

That was, indeed, the question, and young architects everywhere awaited the answer. Then, in 1851, came the Crystal Palace. It used, you remember, to be the fashion to consider the Crystal Palace ugly and ridiculous. Then, about 1935, a German architect came over here and praised it, after which, obedient sheep that we are, we ennobled it as a grand prototype of prefabricated modular design. Since the demise of the Palace in 1937 its canonisation has, of course, been made absolute.

It was certainly a very wonderful performance on the part of Joseph Paxton to take hold of the simple theme of the late Georgian iron conservatory and, after certain brilliant experiments at Chatsworth, to elaborate it on the vast scale required for the Exhibition. Paxton was an extremely able and imaginative organiser. As an artistic conception, however, the Crystal Palace really did not amount to very much. The original greenhouse was doctored by the architects and ornamentalists ; the architect of the Houses of Parliament was responsible for introducing the barrel-roofed transept. The final result was a very appropriate building for a very extraordinary occasion. New in its use of certain materials in a certain way, it was not essentially new or fruitful in the forms it adopted.

Nevertheless, many Victorians saw in the Crystal Palace the first glimpse of the new style which was to characterise the new age. The whole force of a most attractive analogy came into operation. We were to have crystal cathedrals and crystal homes. The appearance of our towns was to be transformed. Iron construction was to develop an ornamental system at least as elegant as that of the Middle Ages. Ferguson, the architectural critic, said how much better it would have been if the Houses of Parliament and British Museum (Paragons respectively of Greek and Gothic revivalism) could have been built on the principles so clearly enunciated in Hyde Park. " Once the people see," he said, " what can be done by common sense, they never again can be satisfied by copying." The analogy gained in force by the fact that the Palace had been designed not by a distinguished architect, nor even by a distinguished engineer, but by a man of the people—an artisan who by sheer industry and the development of his own inventive faculty had become rich and famous. Here was a type of creator as new and as characteristic of the age as the building he had designed. Paxton, the expert gardener, the observer of nature, the man of affairs, the engineer, the railway director, the promoter of newspapers and magazines, seemed as

5

much the "complete man" of Victorian England as Alberti had been of Renaissance Florence. (The fact, by the way, that he owed his opportunities directly to the patronage of a Duke, in true eighteenth-century fashion, was conveniently forgotten !)

When Paxton's design appeared, shouldering out at the last moment the deplorable brick mausoleum which had been sponsored by the building committee, there was an immense outburst of enthusiasm. The man and the building (no architect, I think, except Wren, has been so popularly identified with his work) were seen to constitute an almost miraculous answer to the doubts and enquiries as to the style proper to the Victorian Age.

But all this optimism was very short-lived ; it hardly survived the closing of the exhibition. Ruskin deluged it with scorn. Of the kind of architecture which the Crystal Palace suggested, he says in *Stones of Venice* that it is " eternally separated from all good and great things by a gulf which not all the tubular bridges, nor engineering of ten thousand nineteenth centuries cast into one great bronze-foreheaded century, will ever overpass one inch of". After that roll of thunder, he places Paxton's masterpiece with icy precision : " The quantity of thought it expresses is, I suppose, a single and very admirable thought of Mr. Paxton's, probably not a bit brighter than thousands of thoughts which pass through his active and intelligent brain every hour. . . . This thought, and some very ordinary algebra, are as much as all that glass can represent of human intellect. . . .

" The earth hath bubbles as the water hath
And this is of them."

And the great critic turned immediately to an excursus on Early English capitals.

All the more thoughtful artists and critics agreed more or less with Ruskin, and if we look for evidence of the influence of the Crystal Palace on English architecture we shall find it with great difficulty and we shall find it in the works of quite unknown architects of the second and third ranks. Look round the warehouse quarter of any industrial town and you will probably see, here and there, iron columns and ranges of iron windows which may derive some æsthetic support from Paxton's building—or rather from the myth which that building had engendered.

At South Kensington, as I have said, you can see iron halls which are a later experiment in the same direction.

The truth is that in 1851 artistic thought in England was being drawn irresistibly towards the past—and being drawn, in consequence, into an attitude of opposition. When A. W. Pugin, that total mediævalist, visited the rising Crystal Palace, he happened to meet Paxton who, very naturally, asked him what he thought of the building. "Think," said Pugin, "Think ! Why that you had better keep to building green-houses, and I will keep to my churches and cathedrals". To Pugin, progress in architecture meant one thing only—a bee-line for the fourteenth century. Inside the Crystal Palace there was a " mediæval court " where, with pointed incongruity, a font and font-cover, surrounded by altars, stained glass windows and encaustic tiles (nearly all designed by Pugin) stood as pro-testing witnesses against the new barbarism of glass and iron. Incongruous, archaic and barren these things may have seemed ; and yet, if one seeks to disentangle the threads of actual historic progress in nineteenth-century civilisation, here in this literal mediævalism is the beginning of one of them, a beginning which was to prove infinitely more fruitful than almost anything in the exhibition of 1851 or the building which housed it.

It is remarkable how profoundly true this is—how vastly more productive in the long run were the mediæval preoccupations of the 'forties and 'fifties than the hard, positive notions of material progress which, as it turned out, were nothing but the froth and foam of a great gush of optimism. Ruskin's patient dissection of mediæval Venice : out of that was born a whole philosophy of the relation of art to society, a philosophy which materially affects the policies and ideals of today. Morris's headlong passion for mediæval handiwork and the craftsman's ancient place in society ; could you assess the character of English political thought today without some acknowledgment to that source ? I think not. And these influences, spread all over the world, have already long outlasted those material conquests which, in 1851, seemed to give such emphatic reality to the sense of progress.

I said just now that Pugin's mediæval court was incongruous in its setting. But if that is true, it is necessary to add that it was no more incongruous than all the other art exhibits in the place.

Among these, Pugin's things were unique only in that they were works of scholarship and taste. I have searched in the catalogues and reports for any object not strictly utilitarian, which displayed some aspiration towards the modernity apparent in the Crystal Palace itself. I can find nothing. As soon as we leave pure engineering (which, by the way, retained some of the elegance of eighteenth-century machines) we are faced with pure bathos—the bastardization of eighteenth-century types, the senseless application of old styles to new purposes, the childish exploitation of the freakish and the insanely ingenious. The records leave one amazed that such an agglomeration of artistic corruption could ever have been regarded as yielding hope for the future of any age—let alone that they should be linked with the idea of progress. But here we must not be too impatient. To contemporary eyes, uninstructed eyes especially, a very vivid idea of progress did arise from all this confusion : it was the idea of conquest—absolute conquest of all styles, all materials, all techniques. No Buhl of the last century could compete (for intricacy) with the Buhl sideboard shown by Pratts of Bond Street. Few wood-carvers of any age could have produced the Rococo cot which Windfield of Birmingham produced in *cast brass* ; and it was enormously uplifting to see a gas-bracket rendered perfectly unrecognisable in a romantic group of marble nymphs and bronze lilies. Obviously, the nineteenth century could do anything—and in any material. Taste ? Well, after all, what was taste ? It didn't mean then what we mean today ; it didn't imply, for instance, the integration of a formal idea in the process of manufacture. It conveyed, rather, the sentiment evinced by the artist ; and the artists who gave us these elegant lilies, these modest nymphs, these touching allusions to English history and literature, engraved on or attached to even the most ordinary things of life, surely in such artists there was no lack of taste ? That, I think, was the broad, popular view and on the broad popular plane it gave much satisfaction—satisfaction of a purely sentimental and transitory kind. For the influence of all these peculiar objects, whether for good or for evil,was NIL.

I think the last word on the Great Exhibition must be the word Ruskin borrowed from Shakespeare to describe the building —a *bubble ;* a glorious bubble with the word " progress " written in fantastic characters on its rainbow surface. But there is this to be added : When, in October 1851, the bubble vanished, there was something left behind—there was, in fact, that comfortable surplus of £150,000 which, as I said at the beginning, was devoted to the purchase of land—the land on and around which the great South Kensington Group of Museums, Colleges and Institutes now stands.

From that day to this South Kensington has been the scene of a more or less continuous endeavour on the part of the State to encourage some sort of respectable union between industrial production and the arts. It has not, up to now, been notoriously successful, but the effort and its many by-products—great colleges of art and technology and superb museums of science and art, must be put down on the credit side of the Victorian balance-book. And these things were products, I believe, of the " idea of progress " ; the early South Kensington projects were endorsed by just that body of public opinion which had thought the Crystal Palace so wonderful, had thought that a great new style of design was just around the corner.

As we look back at 1851 we can see what a chimera the idea of progress is ; but we can see, too, that progress is real. Real, but utterly incalculable, as unpredictable as our own intuitions. If we look at the things of today which we cherish as being fine in design, to whom shall we say we are more indebted for them —to Prince Albert, Paxton and the promoters of the Great Exhibition, or to men like Ruskin and Morris who turned their backs on " progress " and ploughed their own eccentric furrows ?

Unquestionably to the latter. And yet it is the crude notion of progress in technics and the arts which has left that cumulative legacy of educational institutions at South Kensington without which our designers and technicians would fare very ill.

I wonder if the idea of progress in its most Victorian sense still exists in architecture and the arts ? I believe it does ; I believe it exists in the minds of those who like to distinguish certain types of modern architecture as being in the international style or who tend to glorify schools, hospital centres, or power stations as " the cathedrals of the twentieth century ". That sort of idiocy, to which I fear architects are more prone than painters, poets or musicians, is pure 1851, a curious vestige of our grandfathers' flights of optimism.

But progress is not a matter of crude analogy or of common sense. It is not the following of a track in the light of a head-lamp. It is a thing so intricate and obscure that only after a long interval can historians begin to define the multiple and labyrinthine courses it has taken. The Victorians thought they could put their finger on progress; they even thought, for a brief joyous moment, that it could be exhibited—in a glass case.

The Mood of Doubt

HUMPHRY HOUSE

VICTORIAN THOUGHT was dominated by the idea of
history as a sequence of events in time. The sequence was
imagined in terms of space. The whole human condition and
the whole condition of the Universe were imagined as either
being or following a horizontal line ever getting longer and
longer. Sometimes this line was thought of as ending at the
present moment, like the line of purple ink on a clockwork
recording barometer ; sometimes the line was more like railway
lines along which the human race or the Universe was travelling
—lines already laid down by Natural Law or by God.

I can best illustrate the preponderance of this horizontal spatial
imagery by two of the most hackneyed quotations from Tennyson :

> " The one far-off divine event,
> To which the whole creation moves "

clearly employs the figure of a spatial progression for the whole
cosmic process. And

> " Let the great world spin for ever down the ringing
> grooves of change "

was in fact an image taken from the railways ; for when Tennyson
first travelled by train he thought the wheels travelled in grooves
instead of on lines. Or again, Matthew Arnold writes in one
of his moments of agnostic determinism :

> " We, in some unknown Power's employ,
> Move on a rigorous line."

But he more often made the comparison with a stream or a
river : which is still the imagery of linear movement through
space.

This temporal, historical, linear habit of thought was on the whole shared by optimists and pessimists alike : it was common to religious thinkers and scientists, used by Newman in his *Development of Christian Doctrine* and by Jowett interpreting the Bible, as much as by Huxley defending Darwin. It is partly an accident of language that the word " Progress " has come to imply movement, while "Process" has remained neutral. Most of the significant Victorian writers, as well as ordinary educated people, were deeply involved in *processive* habits of thought, though they might not at all agree that a process in time always involved amelioration. One effect of this was that they were all acutely conscious of their own unique position in the linear sequence of time. They never could forget what John Stuart Mill called " the consciousness of living in a world of change ". The phrase has now been a piece of stock-in-trade with preachers for a century; but then it stood for a vivid and inescapable new mood. Tennyson caps the argument again :

> " I the heir of all the ages, in the foremost files
> of time."

The muddle of the image here does not destroy the proud consciousness of modernity. You find that consciousness just as plain in the first chapter of *A Tale of Two Cities* as in the third chapter of Macaulay's *History*. Dickens had a lot of dummy books to decorate his study, with facetious titles; among them was a series called *The Wisdom of our Ancestors;* the titles of the volumes included *Ignorance, Superstition, The Block, The Stake, The Rack, Dirt, Disease.*

This acute consciousness of modernity did not by any means lead to any assurance that the future was secure. During the years 1820–70 there were many moments when, for external reasons alone, the *future* seemed very insecure indeed : major epidemics of cholera in '32, '48–9, and other lesser outbreaks ; chances of revolution in '32, '39, '48 ; great disturbances in parts of the country in '50, and riots that thoroughly disturbed Matthew Arnold in '66 ; major scares of foreign invasion in the fifties, from Napoleon III, and in the seventies from Prussia. If anyone believes that ordinary life for the early- and mid-Victorians was safe, calm and secure, let him look up in the index of Irving's *Annals of our Time* the following heads : Colliery

Accidents, Collisions, Collisions at Sea, Railway Accidents, Riots and Shipwrecks.

And further, the tempo of life increased so much and so suddenly, and the multiplication of novelties and problems came so fast, that experience could not be quickly enough assimilated, assessed or related to other experience. This caused, both in the lives of individuals and in the political life of the nation, further difficulties and also discomfort, uncertainty, doubt and hysterical impatience leading almost to despair. The expression of these moods was not confined to the Cassandra-wailings of Carlyle or the melodious whine of Matthew Arnold. A hundred years ago this July, in the year of revolutions in Europe, just after the great Chartist demonstration had failed to become the English revolution, Thackeray wrote to his mother of " a society in the last stage of corruption, as ours is. I feel persuaded that there is an awful time coming for all of us ". The words are like those of Marx in his speech at the meeting called by *The People's Paper* in 1856.

I need not even recapitulate here the tale of horrors brought about in the new towns and factories by the developments of the industrial revolution, the tale of poverty, disease, lack of sanitation, child labour, overcrowding, long hours, barbarism, illiteracy, drunkenness. But I think those who have presented the Victorian case for Progress have minimised these evils and have minimised the degree of indifference to them. Computations of an average rise in real wages and a comparison of artisans' food and clothing with those of their grandfathers do not outweigh the evidence of contemporaries as various as Disraeli, Engels, Kingsley, Dickens, and Mrs. Gaskell, to name but a few. These writers either used or independently confirmed the huge reports of Commissioners, Inspectors and Doctors, and they add to that evidence a contemporary sense of moral horror both at the sufferings themselves and at the indifference so often shown to them. Even if real wages were higher, what was the quality of life which those who earned them could enjoy ? Cobbett, Wordsworth, Southey and Carlyle all saw and deplored the decay in the general quality of life before the beginning of Victoria's reign. Macaulay had the opportunity to see and understand what was involved, when he reviewed Southey's *Colloquies on the Progress and Prospects of Society* in 1830 ; but he did not even try to understand Southey's point of view. Southey, for instance, compares some country cottages with a row of new industrial cottages, and he asks : " How is it that everything which is connected with manufactures presents such features of unqualified deformity ? From the largest of Mammon's temples down to the poorest hovel in which his helotry are stalled, these edifices have all one character . . . and they will always remain as offensive to the eye as to the mind ". Macaulay either cannot or will not see the point ; he merely jeers : " Here is wisdom. Here are the principles on which nations are to be governed. Rose-bushes and poor-rates, rather than steam-engines and independence ". And he talks of an " enthusiast " who " makes the picturesque the test of political good ". I am not qualified to judge the merely statistical parts of this essay of Macaulay's, which read so convincingly ; but I am sure that with a prim and shallow confidence he has utterly missed the essential truth that Southey was trying to express—truths which Ruskin and William Morris laboriously recovered thirty years later.

In another essay, too, I think Macaulay failed to appreciate or deliberately shirked one of the greatest problems, one of the greatest causes of pessimism—in his essay on Sadler's *Law of Population*. Sadler's book was a hideously rhetorical and rather crazily argued attack on Malthus. Macaulay jeers Sadler out of court, but he never comes to grips with what lies behind him, the theory which overshadowed and darkened all English life for seventy years. Malthus's famous book was first published in 1798 as a direct counterblast to the anarchist optimism of Godwin's *Political Justice*. Even its author admitted that it cast over human affairs a " melancholy hue." In effect his doctrine boiled down to saying that poverty, squalor, disease, starvation and war were always necessary, and ordained by God, *unless* the lowest people in every society could be restrained from breeding ; it meant in application that a certain substratum of poverty was always necessary and incurable.

In an earlier letter of 1848, Thackeray pouring out his baffled complexities in face of the French Revolution said : " The question of poverty is that of death, disease, winter or that of any other natural phenomenon. I don't know how either is to stop." All the orthodox arguments of the time led to the same conclusion. Coleridge, Carlyle and Dickens launched attacks on the implications of Malthusianism. Mr. Micawber is a deliberately anti-Malthus character ; Dickens had another dummy book called *Malthus's Nursery Songs*. But emotional outbursts and jokes did no good ; the theory was never systematically disproved; the Poor Law of 1834 was based on it; and its acceptance underlay much of the dull, mournful acquiescence in misery which the age so freely produced.

Another common mood was that of frustration at men's bewildered incompetence to find answers to the age's countless problems both practical and speculative. I can take here only a few examples : faced with the problem of the relations between employers and employed, Dickens, at the end of *Hard Times* (1854) could offer no solution more hopeful than the re-iterated comment of Stephen Blackpool that " 'Tis a' a muddle." His treatment of the Trade Union in this book was neither dramatically nor factually convincing, for he was never prophetic, though in some things he did advocate what turned out to be the winning cause. He maintained with vigour over many years that it was useless to talk of education and morality to the poor until they had good houses, good drains, good water, light and air. A hundred years ago this year the first English Public Health Act was put on the Statute Book ; but it was totally inadequate ; it broke down on political disputes over centralised control, the use of public money (the old cry for economy !), and the propriety of compulsory powers. It failed. Dickens is still found in the 'fifties screaming still more shrilly for good houses, good water, good drains, light and air. He shows more clearly than any other man the frustrations caused by current political theory ; he set up a sort of plain man's cry for administrative responsibility and efficiency, by whatever means it was reached. On Public Health he shouted for centralisation and compulsion. But what would centralisation mean if there was nobody but the Tite Barnacles in Whitehall ? " 'Twas a' a muddle". Nothing is plainer than the growing despondency and bitterness of Dickens's later books. If progress was the rule of life, progress in Reform was abominably slow, in comparison with the progress in vulgar ostentation of the middle classes. Matthew Arnold took up where Dickens left off. Though the state may not be able to assimilate its indigestible problems of poverty, squalor and recurrent unemployment, there may perhaps be some hope if the Philistines can assimilate the best that has been thought and said in the world.

Arnold felt, fully and sensitively, the effects of the speculative problems of the time. As we look back now, one of these shows the Victorian dilemma more plainly than any other—the great problem of the Immortality of the Soul. This is utterly central ; for it raises the question whether life is worth living at all. The common approach was in the temporal linear habit of thought. Where are we going ? Where do the lines lead ? There were few men alive, whether utilitarians or religious people, who then thought of the goodness of an act as being in the act itself or in the will that willed it ; all was in the consequences, whether happiness tomorrow, or the " life hereafter " ; both were matters of future reward. *In Memoriam* was popular chiefly because it worried at the problem of immortality ; I will not quote the all-too-familiar passages in which doubts and fears work round to a faith that is a sort of desperate hope. But this is what Tennyson said in a talk about Immortality to Knowles and William Allingham in 1872 :

> " If I ceased to believe in any chance of another life, and of a great Personality somewhere in the Universe, I should not care a pin for anything."

This sentence is an appalling confession. Kingsley too wrote in 1850 that if God were a deceiver " I'd go and blow my dirty brains out, and be rid of the whole thing at once, I would indeed. " When irresponsible, suicidal cynicism is the other side of a religious medal, the religion is not now to us attractive ; and the war passages in *Maud* show again the moral irresponsibility to which the suicidal temptations of a great Victorian could lead.

But it is impossible now to sneer. We are in a position to begin to understand the depths of psychological disturbance which the whole change of human tempo, the change in the content of human experience, brought on. The more I read of the early- and mid-Victorians, the more I see anxiety and worry as a leading clue to understanding them. They were not complacent compromisers. They were trying to hold together incompatible opposites, and they worried because they failed. They clung to an immortality that should not include the possible

justice of Eternal Punishment ; they wanted a system of administration which should be efficient without expense ; in face of
repeated and ferocious strikes and riots they clung to the doctrine
that the interests of employers and employed were identical. They
knew such things as these were incompatibles. They worried
because they could neither reconcile them nor move on to other
terms of thought. They worried about immortality, they
worried about sex, they worried about politics and money.
They were indeed caught between two worlds. It fell to them
to begin the adjustment of the whole complex human organisation, personal and political ; it fell to them to adjust it to an
environment that was utterly new in the history of the race.
It is not surprising if, to support life at all, they turned to, among
other things, intensification of personal relationships and an
unbalanced exaggeration of domestic virtues :

> " Ah, love, let us be true
> To one another ! for the world, which seems
> To lie before us like a land of dreams,
> So various, so beautiful, so new,
> Hath really neither joy, nor love, nor light,
> Nor certitude, nor peace, nor help for pain ;
> And we are here as on a darkling plain
> Swept with confused alarms of struggle and flight,
> Where ignorant armies clash by night."

Fabian Socialism

H. J. LASKI

THE VICTORIAN Age never found an expression more characteristic than in the formation, in 1883-4, of the Fabian Society,
and in the evolution of its special doctrine. The Victorians had
the conviction that reason can bring man to see the need for
change, they assumed that the need for change once seen,
obligation to act upon it logically follows. They accepted the
Benthamite view that concrete reforms constantly achieved are
more acceptable, because more practical, than the sweeping
system-making which the contemporary followers of Marx and
Engels were trying to persuade the working class, especially
the undoctrinal trade unionists to embrace; it enlisted in its
service an amazing variety of talents : Sidney Webb, the
incomparably efficient civil servant, Bernard Shaw, the propagandist of genius, whose fantastic harlequinades never wholly
concealed the careful combination of stout common sense with
the ruthless cleansing power of profound wit. There were the
half-christian, half-æsthetic shame at evil ugliness which inspired
the anglican priest, Stewart Headlam, the moral earnestness
which gave the teacher's skill of Graham Wallas a special power
of enduring influence, the touch, though no more than the
touch, of Utopianism, of Mrs. Besant, all these are part of
the elements out of which Fabianism was originally compounded.
The Fabians had little money, they had fairly deep disagreement
over principles, they had temperaments not less obviously
Tory and Liberal than Socialist, and a warm conviction that
by hard work and consistent permeation, somehow they could
change the world.

Other elements in the Fabian habits admirably represent that
Indian summer of Victorian England into which they were
born. They were really uninterested in foreign nations and in
foreign doctrines ; not until the first World War did they ever

speak on issues of international policy, and though perhaps some half-dozen of them had seriously studied Marx, they obviously thought of him as a great prophet who denounced evil, like Carlyle or Ruskin, and in no sense as a great sociologist. Engels was living in London for the first twelve years of that existence ; but it no more occurred to them to establish contact with him, than, twenty years later, it occurred to the leaders of the Labour Party to seek out a shabby exile named Lenin, who had just won control over a Russian group hardly bigger than the then well-established Fabian Society. They were optimistic ; they may fairly be called secure—and even serene. Bernard Shaw has emphasised their profound Philistinism. To argue about art and literature one went out to Sunday night supper at William Morris's house, even though Morris thought the Fabians as blind in their insights as he thought Hyndman and his Social Democrats were fantastic in their methods. There is little evidence that they were interested in science, or that they saw with any depth, into the great issues of empire which were then being slowly shaped. But they had knowledge, energy and enthusiasm, at a moment in the Victorian Age when it began to have—though it hardly knew it had—one of its periodic attacks of social conscience. They gave a new clarity and a new precision to what Disraeli called the " Condition of England question " ; and they were able to make their socialist approach seem not only one which a practical man could respect, but one which had behind it English methods of analysis and expression, and the massive continuity of English traditions. These early Fabians did not seem to their generation anything so useless as dreamers, or as futile as artists, or as unsuccessful as refugees. They had a solid air about them, something of Hampstead, something of Westminster, not a little of the higher ranges of Fleet Street. There was not a trace of the exotic exhibitionism which led Lady Warwick to put her hope of salvation into the keeping of Mr. Hyndman—the General Booth of late Victorian Socialists.

Despite the charm of Edward Pease's volume of 1916, even despite the brilliance of one of Mr. Shaw's most famous pamphlets, an adequate history of the Fabian Society has still to be written. It could be immensely attractive. It would begin with the lectures of that remarkable wandering scholar, Thomas Davidson, with his plea for a " fellowship of the New Life " to a small number of young people gathered together in the room of Frank Podmore, a 27-year-old official in the Post Office. It would tell how Podmore and Pease, while they awaited a ghost in an empty but haunted house, at Notting Hill Gate, were led to discuss social questions by way of a common interest in Henry George—just then a new sensation in two continents. That led to the organisation of the group of the " New Hope " in the rooms of Pease, then a young member of the Stock Exchange, with an ex-officer, H. H. Champion, an Eton Master, J. L. Joynes, and that complex being, Havelock Ellis. Should they form a communistic fellowship ; should they, though staying within the world in which there were a Stock Exchange and an Eton, an army and government departments, still aim at " the reconstruction of society " in accordance with the highest moral principles. Should they do this after consultation with Robert Owen's grand-daughter, about to become Mrs. Laurence Oliphant, and herself a figure in one of the most fantastic stories of the nineteenth century. Clearly in the early 'eighties they were ready in Emerson's fashion to shoot their arrows at the stars.

They began to meet every Friday to perfect themselves, to subordinate the material to the spiritual, and to be single-minded, sincere and strenuous—these were words with hands and feet for the Victorians of true faith. The Fellowship of the New Life was divided into two different emphases and one of them, born on November 7th, 1883, became, and still remains, the Fabian Society. " It is a common experience ", writes Mr. Pease, with that slightly acid common sense which was itself a typical quality of the early Fabians, " that the higher the ideal, the fiercer the hostilities of the idealists ". I suspect that it would have taken exceptional resolution to work in persistent proximity to Henry S. Salt and Havelock Ellis and Edward Carpenter. No doubt they were all high-minded and ardent souls, but it is no longer cruel to suspect that they were a little lacking in the comic spirit.

The Fabian Society discovered itself to be an essentially socialist movement in the spring of 1884, though it is clear that its members lacked then, and for long years afterwards, the sense of being a part of a great international movement guided by the same objectives. In the first months of its life it was critical rather than constructive ; as its first leaflet showed, it was more inclined to define the evil than to propose the remedy. It is pretty obvious that we can date the day when it began to lose the ethereal qualities of its origin and to look more like the body we know. It was on September 5th, 1884, when a young critic named Bernard Shaw, his head full of ideas, and his lodgings full of unpublished novels, joined the Society. And it is characteristic of him that the Society's second pamphlet, which he wrote, should have been published only a fortnight later. Its authorship is unmistakable. Wealth cannot be enjoyed without dishonour or without misery under existing circumstances. It is the duty of each member of the State to provide for his or her wants by his or her own labour. It is everyone's birthright to have a life interest in the land and capital of the nation. The result of the present system, Mr. Shaw decides, has been the division of Society into hostile classes, with large appetites and no dinners at one extreme, and large dinners and no appetites at the other. It asks for the nationalisation of the land ; State competition with capitalist enterprise ; direction taxation ; State competition of parents to provide children with happy homes ; political equality for women ; a liberal education and an equal share in national industry for every citizen. It insists on the unrepresentative character of the government and it proclaims that we had rather face a civil war than such another century of suffering as the present one has been.

Early in 1885 the Fabians strode out into public notice. The occasion was that Industrial Remuneration Conference which is now forgotten, except by specialists, though it deserves to be remembered, partly for a striking tribute to the eminence of Karl Marx by the late Lord Balfour and partly for a speech by Mr. Shaw which was praised by John Wilson, a leader of Durham miners. But for still another year the Society was still mostly in that stage where large abstractions give rise to excited debate. It was on May 1st, 1885, that Sidney Webb, then a clerk in the Colonial Office, became a member, along with Sydney Olivier, later the Governor of Jamaica, and later still as Lord Olivier, the first Labour Secretary of State for India, in 1924. Just a year before, Hyndman had founded the Social Democratic Federation, and produced a momentary and even public alarm among liberals and conservatives by running two working-class socialists for Parliament—with money contributed by Tory headquarters.

Then came the great depression of 1886, and the famous trial of Hyndman, John Burns and two others for sedition; the jury acquitted them after a famous summing-up by the judge. So far, I think it is pretty accurate to say that the Society was finding itself. It has not yet discovered with any confidence either that anarchism was impossible or that the imminence of revolution was not even probable. In the summer of 1886 it had still only eighty-seven members, and its income was just on thirty-six pounds. Mrs. Besant was by far the best-known of its members, and her reputation was quite unrelated to the passing phase of socialism in the successive ardours of her tempestuous career.

What made the Society was the next three years. They saw the publication of the still famous *Facts for Socialists* and the now classic *Fabian Essays*, the inauguration of those public lectures, which, after sixty years still continue and the effective beginnings of that policy of permeation of which Sidney Webb was the chief exponent. The Fabians participated in elections to every sort of governing body, from the School Boards and the Vestries to the new London County Council and the House of Commons. They began to infiltrate into other bodies like the National Liberal Federation. They were advocates insistently of municipal socialism, of reforms like the eight-hour day and the humanisation of the poor law, the establishment of universal suffrage and of a decent system of higher education. There is a story of a meeting where the late Lord Haldane came to explain the "laws of economics" to the Fabians, and was operated upon with surgical precision by Webb and Shaw until there was only enough left of him, in an intellectual sense, to crawl home. There is the remarkable history of Webb's use of almost all contemporary periodicals of importance as a vehicle for the spread of Fabian doctrine, and of how Shaw used his position as musical critic of the *Star*, founded in 1888, to make that evening paper his personal platform for the exposition of his views. The *Daily Chronicle*, then edited by H. W. Massingham, asked for the support of the Liberal Party as the most likely instrument of Fabian realisation.

1892 is another notable year in Fabian annals. It saw the marriage of Sidney Webb and Beatrice Potter, not only one of the happiest in intellectual history, but the beginnings of that massive research which, one can really claim, has transformed almost every branch of social science all over the world. The Fabians were anticipating history, and then in 1899 came the judgment of Mr. Justice Farwell in the famous Taff Vale case. A year later, with effective participation by the Fabian Society, came the foundation of the Labour Representation Committee, and at the General Election of 1906, the Labour Party returned thirty members to the House of Commons. It was the beginning of a new era in the national life, one that implied not only hopes of change, but actual changes—changes the Victorian Age might have discussed, but I think it would have viewed with distaste. Collectivism was in the saddle ; a new Liberal Government did not see the implications of collectivism ; they prepared a disconnected body of measures of social reform ; they did not advance towards a socialist society. By choosing the former road it brought this Nation under the darkening clouds of civil war at home, and resistance to aggression abroad.

The Liberal Government brought the Nation towards that parting of the ways foreshadowed for all Europe in 1848. From the immense material before me, I can select three issues only for a brief annotation. First, what was the origin of Fabian philosophy, what shaped it ? Why did they reject Marx and revolution ? Why did they always remain as Fabians a small group, mostly of middle-class intellectuals ? Why did they make Engels not only hostile but also furiously angry ? And why was so large a proportion of its membership in a kind of omnibus relation so that there is a whiff of Fabian doctrine in Conservatives of the older generation like Mr. Amery, and of the middle generation like Mr. Walter Elliot ?

The main influences out of which Fabianism was born are, first, ethical revulsion from the social results of late Victorian capitalism. Secondly, the realisation that the classical doctrines of political economy failed to justify the systems they were supposed to prove. The third the validity of the supposed harmony of interest out of which a unified society emerged concealed a protective coloration from vital conflict which competitive industrialism could not prevent. Something came from John Stuart Mill, something from Cairnes, something from Jevons and Wicksteed. The historical chapters of Marx were of great importance, and they learned the important truth that is embedded in a good deal of Henry George's eloquent confusion.

They learned much from the historical investigation of Chartism by Graham Wallas ; and above all from the Webbs and their magistral examination of Trade Unionism. They learned something from Webb's incredible reading—omnivorous reading which made him acquainted with all the hints and insights that you can find in Saint Simon and Fourier. But above all, they knew all the institutions, political and economic, of Great Britain. The L.C.C. and the Stock Exchange ; Whitehall and the limited liability companies ; political parties, the trade unions, and the professions. Conventional social philosophy did not explain realistically how any of them worked—it was really a theology seeking to justify and not a science seeking by analysis and experiment to verify.

They rejected Marxist socialism because they thought his theory of value as dead as the classical economics out of which it was born. They doubted the validity of predictions which demanded a philosophy of history of the logic of which they were not sure. They disliked his narrow dogmatism ; they suspected his hostility to free enquiry ; they were more doubtful of a metaphysic which lacked the simplicity of straightforward analysis than the Marxians. They thought it confused the intuition of passion of prophecy with orderly inference from fact ; they saw the intrigues and expediences into which Hyndman was led, to the disgust of William Morris. No one who has read the writing of Webb or Shaw can fail to see that they admitted their debt to Marx, and acknowledged it fully, but they disliked the rigid and intolerant orthodoxy of the epigoni, and their fantastic combination of mechanical application with a reckless disregard between ends and means.

In the later years of the great figures of the Fabian Society, while they would have maintained their full faith in freedom of thought and the duty, where possible, to conquer by persuasion, it may be that they would have been less certain than they were in the Victorian Age that the transition from capitalist democracy to Socialist democracy can be made peacefully and painlessly. That was the view of Mr. and Mrs. Webb after 1931, and it is Mr. Shaw who has written that fifty years after the disputes of the 'eighties, it is possible that the poet's insight which led William Morris to accept revolution as a necessary method of change may have seen deeper than his Fabian critics.

A Socialist movement in its infancy is like a political emigration ; it splits into groups which dislike one another far more than they dislike the common enemy. Though Hyndman, for example, had great ability he was a vain and self-righteous person, full of large phrases. He couldn't run in harness with a man like Sidney Webb, selfless and exact and devoid of the yearning to sway the crowd, or Shaw who would have driven him mad by laughing at him. It is still less easy to think that there could have been a permanent union between the Fabians with their zest for facts and figures, and their careful analysis of actual problems, and the rhetorical mind like Ramsay MacDonald's, passionately ambitious, crafty in method, and secretive in temper. The conditions of intellectual unity were only born of the first World War in the Socialist Movement of Great Britain; and a generation later, it's still a good distance from being complete.

And why thirdly, did the Fabians devote so much effort to permeation ? When the Fabian Society was founded, the first great task was to bring into being great social reforms which convinced the working class that change can be made by driving home the rational implications of the facts. After the great dock strike the unions began to see that, if slowly ; they began to see too that they could use their power to make gains on the political as well as on the economic field, and that the main job of Fabianism was accomplished ; the supreme end that it set before itself was achieved since it had created a working-class Socialist Party.

The Fabians, like the Utilitarians, were inventive and full of practical sagacity, unresting in their resolution, and skilful enough never to be so far ahead of public opinion as to look like cranks or fanatics. They never said too much. They didn't rush to attack institutions like the churches or the family or go mad on currency, or, despite Mr. Shaw, vegetarianism or anti-vivisection, but they appeared before the world as sane and practical men and women, as well informed and perhaps better than most of their critics.

They did not cry for the moon ; they did not even confuse the public mind by some transcendental world-outlook. They did a creative and cleansing job by persuasion and intelligence in a sober and practical way. I think they deserved well of the Nation they served.

Herbert Spencer—Progress and Freedom

FREDERICK COPLESTON, S.J.

THERE ARE, I think, very few British philosophers who have enjoyed a worldwide reputation in their lifetime. But Herbert Spencer was certainly one of those few. He had no academic position (he hadn't even a university degree) ; but his writings won for him such fame abroad that more notice was taken of his death in certain foreign countries than in his own land. But it's probably true to say that he's now increasingly forgotten. I wonder how many people, even professional philosophers, could say that they had read the works of Herbert Spencer. Very few, I imagine. What is the explanation of this fact—of great fame, followed by comparative oblivion ? The explanation is easy enough to find. Spencer's lifetime (1820–1903) covered the whole reign of Queen Victoria, and he became the mouthpiece of his age in such a way that with the passing of the Victorian era his reputation has passed too. Like many broad generalisations this is not quite accurate. In the last thirty years or so of the nineteenth century new movements had started in philosophy and in the field of social legislation with which Spencer was not in sympathy ; but he was able to sum up and express as a philosophical system the " floating ideas " of the first two-thirds of the century. Spencer is a dated philosopher, closely wedded to his own time. All philosophers, of course, are dated to some extent ; but I hardly think anyone would seriously maintain that Spencer was a perennial philosopher in the same sense as Plato or Kant.

Herbert Spencer was one of the few British thinkers to attempt the construction of a philosophical system. Whatever one may think of system-making in itself, it certainly has not been the favourite pastime of the philosophers of this country, and many people, rightly or wrongly, would reckon this as a fact to their credit. However, in 1858 Spencer, who had already published, sketched out the plan for his system, which was to be based on the law of evolution, which he called the law of progress. This date is interesting because it was not until the following year that Charles Darwin's *Origin of Species* appeared. Spencer was, very naturally, influenced by Darwin ; but he didn't obtain the idea of evolution from Darwin ; he had already come to see in that idea the key of a systematic view of the world. Whether or not Spencer's philosophy would have won interest and popularity, had it not been for Darwin's scientific work, is another question ; but his anticipation of Darwin and his conception of a philosophical system based on evolution illustrate his ability to seize on and utilise to the full an idea which was, so to speak, in the air. Spencer certainly didn't *invent* the idea of evolution ; none the less his system was the first which we should probably recognise as a system based on evolution, in the sense in which most people now understand the word.

How did Spencer conceive evolution ? With his gift for fixing on and clinging to certain leading and unifying ideas he generalised what he had read in a book by a German author concerning the development of the embryo. According to von Baer, the course of embryonic development is from the homogeneous to the heterogeneous, from the indeterminate to the determinate, i.e. from the less complex and organised to the more complex and organised. Spencer generalised this principle. He maintained that the movement of evolution is towards differentiation and individualisation. Thus on the cosmic plane the movement of evolution proceeds from the nebula to the articulated and differentiated solar systems ; on the biological plane, from the lowest organisms or organic elements to the highest and most complicated organisms ; on the social plane, from the tribe to the industrial, liberal, and individualistic State. Once he had attained his general principle, Spencer tried to support and confirm it by examples ; but he was rather inclined to attend simply to those facts which appeared to confirm his general principle and to neglect or slur over inconvenient facts.

According to Spencer, the ultimate idea is that of force or energy. From the persistence of force, or conservation of energy, the ultimate principle, he tried to show how the process of evolution necessarily follows. Matter is indestructible, motion or energy is continuous, and the law of evolution is simply that of the continuous redistribution of matter and motion. This redistribution not only does, but must proceed in such a way that the homogeneous lead to the heterogenous, the less definite to the more definite, from the nebula to the solar systems, from the primitive living things to the human body, from the flint instrument to the modern specialised tool, from primitive languages to modern languages, from primitive communities to the highly organised and differentiated communities of today. It has been said that for Spencer the universe is simply a vast machine, and his system, under one aspect at least, would seem to imply this. He spoke, indeed, of a gulf between matter and mind ; but he also entertained the possibility of the transformation of physical into mental forces. If this idea is pressed, it follows, of course, that the universe is a material and mechanical machine.

Philosophy, for Spencer, must stand in close relation to science ; he had scant sympathy with any philosophy which seemed to him to pursue an airy path of its own, without a firm foundation in experience. Scientific knowledge unifies the more or less unrelated facts of ordinary experience, while philosophy discerns the most general principles which serve to unify the various branches of science. But this positivistic view of philosophy was combined by Spencer with an agnosticism which, he hopefully imagined, would satisfy the religious consciousness while not offending the scientist. To those accustomed to the thought of scientists like Eddington and Jeans or of philosophers like Bergson or Whitehead the so-called conflict between science and religion may seem a rather hoary topic ; but in Spencer's day this was not the case. It seemed to many minds that the doctrine of evolution was necessarily destructive of religion and belief in God. Spencer can hardly be called a religious man ; but he tempered his positivism and rationalism by admitting the sphere of what he called " the Unknowable ". Science is always extending her sphere ; but none the less human knowledge is necessarily limited and incomplete ; the ultimate reality, or Absolute, is inscrutable in itself, unknowable. It certainly seems paradoxical that Spencer devotes some hundred pages of his *First Principles* to the subject of " the unknowable " ; but the philosopher admitted that we can know that the Absolute exists, even if its essential nature remains inscrutable. If religious people were content to allow that the Power they worship is inscrutable and if scientists were to admit that the scientific explanation of the world is relative and incomplete, there need be no conflict, thought Spencer, between religion and science. But since for him the ultimate scientific ideas, particularly that of force, " pass all understanding ", there is little difference between the force or energy postulated by the scientific conception of the universe and the inscrutable Power postulated by the religious consciousness. In other words, Spencer's section on " the unknowable " which was a later addition to the system does not represent a genuinely religious element. Spencerian agnosticism may represent Victorian " decency " ; but it is a mistake to compare it (as it has been compared) with the Christian doctrine of God's incomprehensibility. It does, however, represent a compromise, for, while he finds no place in his system for any positive concept of God, Spencer refused to accept, as the religion of the future, that worship of man which was preached by Auguste Comte in France and by W. K. Clifford, the mathematician, and Frederick Harrison, the Positivist, in England. Spencer was untroubled by those religious problems which so exercised the mind of G. J. Romanes ; but he would not go all the way with the Positivists.

I have already mentioned that Spencer called the law of evolution the law of progress. In the social sphere (a sphere to which he gave great attention) he looked on the evolutionary process as moving towards the industrial, free and individualistic type of society, i.e. towards what we call the *laissez-faire* State. This type of society, he thought (or hoped), has a greater 'survival value ' than, for example, the militaristic type of society, which rests on force. In the moral sphere he utilised the very questionable notion that acquired environment (a peaceful, free society) can mould man to virtue. The highest standard of conduct, he said, is that of the completely adapted man in the completely evolved society. These ideas could, according to Spencer, be deduced from the principles of evolution ; but he later admitted that the doctrine of evolution had not furnished him the help in ethics which he had formerly expected. He tended to underestimate the less desirable elements in man, to give too much weight to ideas which he borrowed from the biological sphere and applied to the moral sphere. The principle of individual freedom, for instance, cannot be deduced from so-called ' animal justice '; it must be founded on the nature of man as such or it will never be founded at all.

Spencer never succeeded in showing that the cosmic processes necessarily favour human progress as he understood it ; nor, of course, could he show it. The Age of the French Revolution had laid stress on rational and moral progress ; but when the stress came to be laid on cosmic and organic evolution, it should have become clear to the philosopher that it was necessary to distinguish sharply the moral and social from the cosmic and biological spheres, human progress from cosmic and biological evolution.   T. H. Huxley saw this and maintained that the cosmic evolutionary process is non-moral and that social progress depends on moral factors, on repudiating the struggle for existence in favour of co-operation. But Spencer, sticking to his survival of the fittest principle, failed to see that the application of this principle in the social sphere could hardly lead to the type of society he wanted. Huxley, as I have said, distinguished the moral and amoral spheres ; Galton and Karl Pearson advocated eugenics to secure the survival of the fittest ; Nietzsche boldly claimed that what he considered to be the law of all life, the will to power, should operate in the human sphere as outside it ; Drummond, who attempted to show that theism and evolutionism are compatible, tried to trace altruistic behaviour in nature at large, in order to preserve the continuity of the evolutionary process postulated by Spencer, while avoiding the unfortunate consequences of over-emphasising the principle of the egoistic struggle for existence. But Spencer adopted none of these expedients ; he was content to assert the continuity of the moral and amoral spheres, while airily disregarding the consequences to which his premises would logically lead him.

However, Spencer was not simply a naïve optimist. There is, he thought, a rhythm in the evolutionary process ; what has been built up will one day be broken down. In fact, it is probable that there have been successive evolutionary processes in the past and that there will be successive evolutionary processes in the future. This is suggested, thought Spencer, by the laws of the distribution of motion. From this it follows that progress is only relative ; there is progress up to a point and then what one might call regress sets in. Finally, the whole process will be repeated in a variant form. From this point of view one might call Spencer's philosophy an up-to-date version of certain early Greek cosmologies, with their ideas of a cyclic process. It is probably not much more hope-inspiring than Nietzsche's idea of the Eternal Recurrence.

Nevertheless, Spencer certainly regarded the increase of freedom as the goal of evolution in its progressive phase. One may be inclined to see in his championship of individual freedom a reflection of his own independence of character and of his antipathy towards authoritarianism of any kind rather than a deduction from scientific principles, but the fact remains that he was one of the most resolute champions of individual liberty in recent times. This is apparent particularly in his doctrine of the State. All interference with the liberty of the individual by the State (apart, of course, from what was necessary for the preservation of peace and order) was abhorrent to him. His ideal was that of a society in which the individual would be everything and the State nothing, in contrast with the militaristic State in which the State is everything and the individual nothing. Prussia he reckoned as a type, and a particularly obnoxious type, of the militaristic State. Some of Spencer's views on this matter sound to us rather odd. That he upheld the rights of private property, of freedom of speech and of worship, is only what one would expect, but the fact that he condemned all factory legislation, sanitary inspection by government officials, State management of the Post Office, and poor relief on the part of the State, helps to surround him with the atmosphere of a bygone age. Several factors, of course, contributed to make him think along these lines ; for example, his personal enthusiasm for individual liberty, his conviction that private enterprise is more efficient than State enterprise, his notion that natural selection and survival of the fittest should be allowed to operate in social life. Given his idea of the essential function of the State, the protection of private rights, his practical conclusions might appear logical ; but this is questionable. It might obviously be argued that the worker's rights would not be protected in the kind of society he envisaged. The truth of the matter is that what Spencer liked to regard as the conclusions of philosophical premises were largely relics of a state of society which was already passing in his lifetime. One would certainly not expect Spencer to fall a victim to the type of pessimism represented by Hardy, the novelist ; but all the same his complacency is somewhat surprising. J. S. Mill also advocated *laissez-faire* ; but he saw the existence of social evils and nobly endeavoured to remedy them, even if without revising his premisses. Spencer, however, seemed oblivious to evils which were recognised by a philosopher like Mill, writers like Ruskin and Morris, politicians like Disraeli ; evils the recognition of which contributed to that revision of the liberal theory of the State by T. H. Greene and others which took place, or began to take place, in Spencer's own lifetime. The fact is that Spencer, one of the least metaphysical of philosophers, showed, perhaps paradoxically, a devotion to general theory at the expense of devotion to concrete facts.

Spencer applied his principles also to education. Education should be for life, utilitarian in character ; and liberty, absence of compulsion, should be aimed at as much as possible. In the spirit of the movement stemming from Rousseau Spencer advocated naturalness in education. In practice this means not only that the child's natural interests should be taken into account, but, in general, that the child's mind should be led from the concrete to the abstract. In the acquisition of a language, for example, the theoretical study of grammar should come last. Needless to say, Spencer stressed the value of science, not least because science takes no notice of authority but relies on experiment and reasoning. His educational ideas were not exactly new, but they harmonised with his emphasis on life, with his individualism and his anti-authoritarianism.

In Spencer's later years his ideas on evolution had either become common coin (in which case they were associated with the name of Darwin rather than with that of Spencer) or their truth was being disputed. Moreover, as his biographers have noted, many of his ideas in other fields had become or were tending to become platitudes, while his social principles were out of harmony with the new trend of thought and legislation which made itself apparent in the last thirty years of the century. In pure philosophy the thinkers of the neo-idealist movement, which had its roots in the thought of Hegel, were unsympathetic towards Spencer's system in general and his political ideas in particular. In addition, Spencer incurred unpopularity in Britain because of his attitude towards the Boer war ; he was never a man to conceal his opinions. Thus even if in positivistic circles abroad Spencer's reputation was still great, it was already on the wane in his own country. But he was undoubtedly one of the most powerful minds of the Victorian era, and even if one cannot agree with his exaggerated idea of the requirements of liberty, and even if the twentieth century, with its two great wars, has belied the optimistic hopes of the nineteenth one can but sympathise with his hatred of militarism and of political slavery. It is evident to us that the magic word " evolution " is no key to all truth, no panacea for all ills, and it is clear that man's rights and man's happiness are not best secured by the policy of *laissez-faire*; but if we pass over the manifest exaggerations of Spencer's thought, it is also clear that he has some message for us today. If Spencer were alive now, he would certainly add his voice to those which cry out against the political and ideological tyranny which has already engulfed a large part of the continent of Europe. His evolutionary philosophy was in many ways superficial, and he was not sufficiently alive to the deeper aspects of the human personality; but he certainly did not think that progress and the death of freedom are one and the same thing.

VICTORIAN

RELIGIOUS

BELIEF

and

CONTROVERSY

The Evangelical Discipline

CANON CHARLES SMYTH

IT IS one of the characteristics of popular, as distinct from learned, history that once a legend has become embedded in it, it is extraordinarily difficult to get it out. Such, for example, is the myth that Bishop Butler refused the Archbishopric of Canterbury on the ground that it was " too late for him to try to support a falling Church " : or, more material to our present purpose, the myth that William Wilberforce was so excited over the woes of Negro slaves that he exhibited a bland indifference to the miseries of the victims of the Industrial Revolution in his own country. Had Wilberforce indeed chosen to regard the Abolition of the Slave Trade and of Slavery as in itself a whole time job, that would have been a perfectly reasonable line : but in fact, being an exceptional man, he also found time to concern himself actively in prison reform, factory legislation, elementary education, the prevention of cruelty to children and to animals, the organisation of poor relief and the reform of the penal code : and he was one of the founders of the Society for Bettering the Condition and Increasing the Comforts of the Poor. The great Age of Evangelical Philanthropy at the end of the eighteenth century answered to the great Age of High Church Philanthropy at the beginning of that century, and it continued into the Victorian Era, and beyond. When in 1787 Wilberforce noted in his private journal : " God Almighty has set before me two great objects, the suppression of the Slave Trade and the refor- mation of manners ", it is to be observed that he was as much a traditionalist in his desire to reform manners as he was an inno- vator in his ambition to abolish slavery.

Wilberforce himself lies just outside our period, and his death in 1833 may be said to mark the close of the Heroic Age in the history of the Evangelical Movement in the Church of England. But the Evangelical Party in the nineteenth century, apart from its unnatural alliance with the Low Church Party which had once been its bitterest opponent, followed the broad lines of policy laid down for it by its Elder Statesmen, and consolidated the positions which they had established against heavier odds.

It is not too much to say that, more than any other single factor, the Evangelical Movement in the Church of England transformed the whole character of English society and imparted to the Victorian Age that moral earnestness which was its distinguishing characteristic : a moral earnestness which was perhaps especially conspicuous in the Victorian agnostics of the 1880's who inherited it from the Evangelical tradition itself against which they were in rebellion. The high seriousness of the Victorians may be traced back to the publication in 1797 of Wilberforce's best-seller : *A Practical View of the Prevailing Religious System of Professed Christians in the Higher and Middle Classes in this Country contrasted with Real Christianity.* " In it ", writes Michael Hennell, " he commented on the increase of prosperity, the growth of new cities, the splendour and luxury of the age, and the decline of religion, manners and morals ; he reminded the rich of their duties to the poor, and asserted that the only remedy for the selfishness which their wealth encouraged lay in Christianity ". To the amazement of his own publisher, 7,500 copies of the book were sold in the first six months alone : and the several editions through which it passed testify to its influence as well as to its popularity. A very old gentleman who near the middle of the nineteenth century made a tour of country houses, " told his friends on his return that he had found himself quite put out by the theological talk that prevailed in every house he had visited—except in that perfect gentleman's, the Bishop of ——'s, where the subject never occurred ".

The strength of the Evangelical Party in the Victorian Age lay in the well-to-do middle classes : but it did not neglect the poor, nor was it altogether neglected by the rich. Froude, in his life of Lord Beaconsfield, ventured upon the prophecy that " the students of English history in time to come, who would know what the nobles of England were like in the days of Queen Victoria, will read *Lothair* with the same interest with which they read Horace and Juvenal ". Froude was himself of course a student of history, and a distinguished one : but from that remark it may be doubted whether his acquaintance with

Victorian noblemen was very intimate or very extensive. The picture of ducal society in *Lothair* was indeed gloriously caricatured in Bret Harte's parody, which begins : " Gathered around the refined and sacred circle of the breakfast-table with their glittering coronets, which, in filial respect to their father's Tory instincts and their mother's Ritualistic tastes, they always wore upon their regal brows, the effect was dazzling as it was refined ". But very different from the privileged patricians of Disraeli's novel, in all their indolent magnificence, were the plain, pious, Evangelical, hard-working members of the aristocracy who are continually cropping up in the more homespun pages of the *Life and Friendships of Catherine Marsh* : Evangelical peers presiding, testifying, orating in Exeter Hall (the citadel of English Protestantism), Evangelical duchesses conducting family prayers for their domestic staffs, an Evangelical Lord Chancellor teaching in Sunday School, and Evangelical lords and ladies engaged in slumming, in sitting on committees, in starting soup-kitchens and night schools, in distributing Testaments and tracts, and in a manifold variety of philanthropic and missionary activities. But the greatest of them all was Anthony Ashley Cooper, seventh Lord Shaftesbury, " the Good Earl ", who, in the words of Mr. Gladstone, " during a public life of half a century devoted the influence of his station, the strong sympathies of his heart, and the great power of his mind, to serving God by honouring his fellow men—an example to his order, a blessing to his people and a name to be by them for ever gratefully remembered ".

The inspiration of Shaftesbury's philanthropy was his religion. " I am satisfied," he declared, " that most of the great philanthropic movements of the century have sprung from the Evangelicals " : and he was proud to count himself in that succession. Some men have become social reformers because they hated the rich ; others because they loved the poor. For Shaftesbury, the dominating motive was his strict sense of duty towards God. Had he not, as a young Member of Parliament, known himself called of God to labour for the disinherited of the Industrial Revolution, he would evidently have made politics his career and science his recreation. But this was not to be. He was too busy. Much of his success as a social reformer was due to the thoroughness of his personal investigations into social conditions. He never worked with second-hand facts, or left it to Commissions to carry out all the necessary enquiries. He never put forward a case which he had not himself thoroughly mastered by an unrelenting study of all the evidence available in blue-books and reports, as well as from personal contacts. And he was inexorable in his insistence that the rich must be made to realise the living conditions of the very poor. " Dirt and disrepair, such as ordinary folks can form no notion of ; darkness that may be felt ; odours that may be handled ; faintness that can hardly be resisted : hold despotic rule in these dens of despair ". "We owe to the poor of our land a mighty debt. We call them improvident and immoral, and many of them are so : but that improvidence and that immorality are the results, in a great measure, of our neglect, and not a little of our example ". Like the Evangelicals in general, Shaftesbury had but little notion of what we now call Christian Sociology, but his inspired compassion swept every dark corner of English social life. Lunacy Reform, Lodging-house Reform, Ragged Schools, Factory Reform, the Ten Hours Bill, the radical improvement of conditions in the Mines, the protection of Chimney Sweeps : these are but a few of his achievements in the sphere of Christian legislation.

George Jacob Holyoake, the Radical, said of him : " There are saints of the Church, and saints of humanity ; Shaftesbury was a saint of both churches ". Yet to the religious historian the real fascination and the true significance of Shaftesbury's life are to be found in the inward spiritual conflict behind the imposing façade of his public career. Had he not been an earnest Christian, he could have been a very bad man. For Shaftesbury's was a strong character, whether for good or for evil ; a character full of promise—and of danger. By temperament, he was as proud as Lucifer, imperious, dictatorial, sensitive, resentful, and intensely ambitious. His biography is the story of a man of almost ungovernable passions, but of passions gradually subdued and mastered by the constant, stubborn, unrelenting dedication of his life to God. Only Christianity could have made of Shaftesbury what, by God's mercy, he became. And his life-story is only a particularly signal example of the power of an Evangelical conversion in the history of a human soul.

It all ended gloriously, of course, with the public funeral in Westminster Abbey, a funeral such as England has never seen before or since ; with a wreath inscribed " The loving tribute of the Flower-girls of London " jostling another from a Princess of the Blood Royal ; with men in every walk of public life represented in the mourning crowd, while the band of the Costermongers' Temperance Association played " Safe in the arms of Jesus ". But the real secret of Lord Shaftesbury's life may be read in the three texts from Scripture which, by his own desire, were inscribed on his memorial tablet in the parish church in Dorset where he lies buried. " What hast thou that thou didst not receive ?—Let him that thinketh he standeth take heed lest he fall.—Surely I come quickly. Amen. Even so, come, Lord Jesus."

You have most of the picture there : except that it leaves out, of course, the œcumenical vision and the missionary enthusiasm which was also part of the Evangelical Inheritance. It was when Britain was engaged in a life-and-death struggle against a military power which had overrun the Continent and which was bent on her destruction, and when the complete extirpation of Christianity was a primary object of the French Revolution and of its sympathisers over here, that, for the first time for centuries, the Church of England, under the guidance of the Evangelicals, awoke to her vocation as a missionary church, charged with the propagation of the Gospel to the very ends of the known world. The foundation of the C.M.S.—the Church Missionary Society—in 1799 was one of the most significant events in the history of the Church of England, and the short sad life of Henry Martyn, missionary in India, almost the first Englishman to offer himself to the C.M.S. for service overseas, is among the most heroic in her annals. A very critical contemporary, who saw a good deal of him at Cawnpore, said of him : " No one could leave Mr. Martyn's company without feeling, more than before, the importance of the things of another world " ; and that, I think, explains very clearly the influence and the inspiration of the Evangelicals.

The two other outstanding achievements of the Evangelical Movement were the beginnings of Factory Legislation and Humanitarian Reform, and the Abolition of the Slave Trade and of Slavery. These signal triumphs were accomplished within a quite incredibly brief space of time—a bare half century or so —and by a minority party in the Church of England, a party which was unrepresented on the Episcopal Bench until 1815, and which owed more to the enthusiasm and the munificence of its faithful laity than to the leadership of a learned clergy. Yet, if you consider these two achievements together—the Abolition of Slavery and the beginnings of Humanitarian Reform—is it not remarkable that it should have been given to a minority party in the English Church, and really to a small " pressure group " within that party, to achieve more in this line in fifty years than the whole of Christendom had done in eighteen hundred ?

Where the Evangelical Party was weak, by comparison for example with the Tractarians, was on the intellectual side. This is the more surprising, because it always contained a number of individuals of outstanding intellectual ability among the clergy, and even more among the laity. The simplicity and the sincerity of the Evangelical piety captivated many extremely able men in every walk of life. It has also to be said, I think, that the quality of such scholarship as the Evangelical Party did in fact produce has been habitually under-estimated, whether because it is out of date or simply because it is forgotten. Nevertheless it remains true that, while the Evangelicals have always cared, and cared supremely, for individual souls and for their salvation, their contributions to positive theology have been almost negligible ; partly because the Movement had set too high a pace for the clergy in the discharge of their evangelising and personal duties to leave sufficient time for the work of study, of keeping abreast with the new intellectual currents of the age ; and partly also because the rank and file of the Evangelicals were inclined to shun secular learning, and even sacred knowledge of the academic kind, as a distraction and a snare. Conservative in politics, the Evangelical Party tended, from a variety of reasons, to become slightly obscurantist in its orthodoxy : it was averse from risky intellectual adventures. Mark Pattison wrote : " Its instinct was from the first against intelligence. No text found more favour with it than ' Not many wise, not many learned are called '." This, like most generalisations, is too sweeping. With greater subtlety, the Nonconformist leader, R. W. Dale of Birmingham, in his famous lecture on *The Old Evangelicalism and the New* (1889), put his finger on the real weakness of the

Party when he said that it was "wanting in a disinterested love of truth for its own sake, otherwise than as an instrument for converting men". In consequence, Evangelical preaching, which had once been a radical and revolutionary challenge to the formal piety of the age, itself became increasingly stereotyped and confined to the reiteration of a few leading themes : " the corruption of human nature, the utter inability of man to co-operate in the work of salvation, the all-sufficiency of faith, unconditional salvation, the wonders of grace, the ardour of the divine love, together with certain intangible and mystical representations respecting regeneration and religious feelings and experiences ".

Nevertheless, throughout the Victorian era, Evangelicalism remained a dynamic spiritual force, as it is still and always will be. I will not attempt to rehearse its roll of honour, resplendent with the names of famous soldiers such as Outram, Havelock and Gordon, of missionary bishops such as Daniel Wilson and the martyr Hannington, of English prelates such as Moule and Thorold, and of parish priests such as Champneys of Whitechapel, Cadman of Southwark, Christopher of St. Aldate's, Oxford, not to mention such pulpit orators as Melvill, the golden-tongued, or Close of Cheltenham, Stowell of Manchester, and McNeile of Liverpool, whose influence in their respective cities was comparable with that of the High Church Vicar of Leeds, Walter Farquhar Hook. But the real strength of Evangelicalism lay not in the pulpit or the platform, but in the home. To those who believe that the typical Evangelical sermon was about hell-fire, that the typical Evangelical layman is fairly represented by the father of Sir Edmund Gosse, and that the typical Victorian parent was Mr. Barrett of Wimpole Street, this may sound surprising. But, to judge from memoirs and biographies, the Evangelical families of England were conspicuously happy families, and it was in hearts of the Victorian mothers that the Evangelical piety won the most signal and the most gracious of its triumphs. The characteristic religious observance of the Victorian home was family prayers, which, as the then Archbishop of Canterbury reminded us ten years ago, brought the remembrance of God right into the heart of the home life from beginning to end. The Evangelical was not shy about his religion because he had grown up into it from his mother's knee. Puritanism, it has been said, was the religion of the State : Methodism the religion of the heart : the Oxford Movement the religion of the Church : but Evangelicalism was the religion of the home. And if we are ever to understand the quality of social life in the Victorian Era, we should do well to remember the tribute paid by G. W. E. Russell, himself an Anglo-Catholic, to his Evangelical upbringing. " The Evangelicals," he wrote, " were the most religious people whom I have ever met. . . . I recall an abiding sense of religious responsibility, a self-sacrificing energy in works of mercy, an evangelistic zeal, an aloofness from the world, and a level of saintliness in daily life, such as I do not expect again to see realised on earth. . . . *Sit anima mea cum Sanctis.* May my lot be with the Evangelical Saints from whose lips I first learned the doctrine of the Cross".

Evangelicalism of the Nonconformists

GORDON RUPP

" I very soon had enough of it,
The hot smell and the human noises,
And my neighbour's coat, the greasy cuff of it,
Were a pebble stone that a child's hand poises
Compared with the pig of lead-like pressure
Of the preaching man's immense stupidity
As he poured his doctrine forth, full measure
To meet his audience's avidity. . . .
My gorge rose at the nonsense and stuff of it,
I flung out of the little Chapel."

ROBERT BROWNING, dodging out of the rain into the frowsty glare of Zion Chapel in December 1849 could have been in no mood for dispassionate observation, but I think we know what he meant. Such places as Zion Chapel did exist, and even those humbugs and hypocrites, Stiggins and Chadband, like still more fantastic and repulsive characters, can be outpaced in fact. Read the pamphlets which Richard Oastler wrote in 1835 against certain Dissenters in the town of Huddersfield, watch him with scorching eloquence trace the slimy characters of Deacon X and Brother Y, as he says, " very covetous, very cruel, very pious ". There never has been a configuration of Christian piety which has not been susceptible of perversion into unlovely, even horrible forms, and Victorian Nonconformity is no exception.

But if Browning's Zion Chapel and Oastler's Dissenting Deacons are facts, Victorian Nonconformity also produced David Livingstone and Robert Moffat, John Bright, Dr. Barnardo and General Booth, and a thousand other noble men and women whose memory is still treasured by the churches.

Victorian Nonconformity was the product of the Evangelical revival and the Industrial Revolution, and for this reason, and because of certain civil disabilities and sundry social deprivations, it was confined within the limits of the middle and lower classes of society. Moreover, as in the seventeenth century the Puritan sects focused something in the very temper of the age, so there was in the Victorian era a strain of seriousness, a moral enthusiasm, of which Nonconformity was an intense but not an isolated expression. This was the bond which, despite ecclesiastical differences, joined Mr. Gladstone to his Nonconformist followers. This it was which led a Trades Union Congress in 1833 to propose a "Grand National Moral Union of the Productive Classes for establishing a new moral World". It bred a certain solemnity into our Victorian grandfathers. But if certain Victorian Christians appear dismal enough to our backward glance, we might remember that there was nothing ecstatically corybantic about the private life even of the disbeliever like John Stuart Mill. His utilitarian friends believed equally fervently in the importance of being earnest.

But the Nonconformists were much more than an aggregate of Mutual Improvement Societies, for they were sustained by deep spiritual impulses which persisted from the Evangelical revival. The transformation into sober citizens of Mad Margaret and the bad baronet of *Ruddigore* in Sullivan's opera is an authentic side-light on Victorian religion. The Victorian Nonconformists believed in conversion, in the transformation of character by the operation of Divine Grace, and they affirmed this, because their faith in God gave them a view of human nature more terrible than that of the sceptics and more glorious than that of the perfectibilians.

The proposal that the Methodists should celebrate in 1825 the Centenary of the ordination of John Wesley was defeated by Methodist public opinion on the ground that it was felt to be a strange inconsistency for the Methodist congregations to render thanks for the ordination of an unconverted man, when they would not knowingly tolerate such a man in one of their own pulpits. But when the Centenary was celebrated in August 1839, they crowded Brunswick Chapel, Liverpool, for the centenary sermon, and the preacher, Dr. Thomas Jackson, ex-President of the Methodist Conference, held a hushed and intent audience to the end of the two hours and fifty-three minutes of his discourse. It was a noble and scholarly oration. Yet the man who gave it was the son of a labourer ; he began by tending cattle, often crying for loneliness on the Yorkshire hills. Then he was converted, and of this he wrote long after : " The entire bent and habit of my nature was changed. My views and feelings, my apprehensions and inclinations, my desires, hopes and prospects were all new. The experience of nearly seventy years has served only to strengthen my conviction that the change I underwent was no delusion but a blessed reality."

Sidney Webb had said of the Primitive Methodists of Durham : " They did great work from village to village ; families were transformed ; and these men stood out as men of character gaining respect of their fellows. . . . Trade unionism was itself largely the result of the elevation of character brought about by religious conversion on individual leaders ".

They not only believed in conversion, but in Revival. In December 1849, the month when Browning flung out of the little Chapel, men and women crushed into the chapels in the town of Dudley, not like Browning to get out of the rain, but because of the deadly cholera. " Drunkards, prize fighters, thieves, harlots, in some cases whole families were converted, and gangs broken up ". When in 1838 a boy died in Wood-house Grove School, scenes occurred which outrival *Eric, or Little by Little.* Let me quote :—

" The boys were allowed to take a last look at their dying schoolfellow. The solemn march of the lads across the play-ground, their tremulous tiptoe tread as they moved round the crib where lay the gasping youth, the gentle word of solemn warning spoken to the deeply affected and astonished lads, formed a picture of touching interest. All play was by common consent suspended. Well nigh every boy seemed to be a suppliant at the mercy seat ".

At least twelve Nonconformist ministers came to mark that day as the turning point in their vocation. The religious life of the Nonconformist centred in his chapel. It might be some little Bethel along the village street, with coloured texts upon distempered walls, with gallery and rostrum and varnished pews and the inevitable aspidistra, often very ugly, but as has been well said " furnished with faces ". Or in the cities, some more pretentious edifice of heavy masonry and Corinthian pillars. Here the wealthy laymen drove up in their carriages, while their servants filed in at regular intervals in tidy processions, spaced with a nice exactitude of rank and dignity calculated to emphasise their proper station here below, and to prepare them for hierarchic bliss hereafter.

Here, men and women attended regularly and faithfully the ordinances of Word and Sacrament, sang their hymns, and met for prayer meetings, classes and the week-night services. E. E. Kellett has said : " It is almost impossible to exaggerate the part played by the Church or Chapel in the lives of its adherents. It took by itself the place now hardly filled by theatre, concert hall, cinema, ballroom, and circulating library together. It may have been a very small and narrow world, but it was one which pulsed with life ".

Nevertheless, religion was most assuredly also an affair of the family and of the home. Family prayer and devotional reading, and the common observance of Sunday were not by any means the meaningless and unwelcome discipline that they were to Samuel Butler. " Nothing contributed so strongly to awaken my spiritual sensibilities," wrote one, " as the daily gathering at the family altar, which was regular as the morning family meal. The solemn tender cadences of my father's and mother's voice were music to my ears. The reality of our home religion made the unseen and eternal world as real to me as home itself ". And the Victorian Sunday, though it might become a burdensome and irritating encumbrance to those outside the household of faith, was for many millions indeed a day of rest and gladness. For more than we can realise, cheerfulness kept breaking in. To quote E. E. Kellett again : " I never hope to see any human beings more uniformly cheerful than some saintly persons I came across in my youth. When we, their grandchildren, think of them as miserable, it is because we imagine that people can only be happy in our way ". Here is a mid-Victorian divine : " It would be a great mistake to suppose that my boyhood or my home was austere and sternly disciplined ; the religion with which my mind was imbued in childhood was essentially a religion of love and pleasantness and joy ".

The Nonconformists set a high value on their preachers, for debarred from the Universities and so from the learned professions, many of the most gifted entered the Ministry, and nowhere was the brotherhood of the preachers more strongly felt than among the Methodists. " Well my boy, what do you think of your Church ? " asked one preacher of a young man at his first Methodist conference, and he answered his own question : " It is a grand church, and it is an infinite mercy to belong to it. The men are good men, and some of them are great men. I remember my first Conference, and I have said so and thought so from that day to this ".

In the last decades came the great pulpiteers ; perhaps the chief of them Spurgeon, with his giant girth, his loud voice, his eloquence stemming from a mind steeped in the Bible and the Puritan divines.

In Birmingham, Dr. R. W. Dale lifted up his voice against a complacent and circumscribed pietism. He denounced " Christian ministers who, whenever a great calamity falls, preach to the people about the righteousness of God, and yet think there is someting like profanation in attempting to show from the pulpit by what political measures our legislation might be made more righteous ". Of his own magnificent application of the Christian gospel to the life of the great modern city, the *Birmingham Daily Post* said : " There was hardly any part of our life as a community which he did not strengthen and brighten and elevate ".

The Nonconformist conscience was pricked into a new awareness of the evils to be found in great cities, and a wave of humanitarian impulse found splendid practical expression ; the orphanages of Barnardo, Stephenson and Spurgeon were one result, the great city missions another, while the temperance and social purity campaigns were combined with devoted personal service in the slums of ' Darkest London '. These and a hundred other crusades burned in the heart of Hugh Price Hughes with an intense and devouring flame and led him to press for closer co-operation between the Free Churches, and indeed with all the Churches. " We Christians when we unite our forces are simply irresistible," he cried. " Let us then combine heartily to abolish slavery, drunkenness, lust, gambling, ignorance, pauperism, mammonism and war. After that is done we shall not have much difficulty in settling all our theological and ecclesiastical differences ".

I referred just now to the phrase "Nonconformist Conscience"; it symbolises the point at which the ideas and beliefs of the Nonconformists met the social and political structure of the Victorian Age.

At the beginning of the Victorian era, the dominant political tradition among the Methodists was Christian Toryism. Jabez Bunting was its redoubtable exponent. It would be superficial to write this off as mere reactionary fear of revolution or an other-worldly pietism. The enemies of Bunting complained that his politics were too definite, not that he had none, and they mocked him for haunting the House of Commons, pockets stuffed wide with newspapers and Parliamentary Reports, when he might have been reading his Bible. Bunting represents a classic Christian tradition of Christian Obedience, the tradition of the Duties as against the Rights of Man, the tradition from which Edmund Burke and John Wesley had impeached the revolution-ary and rationalist idealism of Priestley and of Price. In protes-ting against the swelling Liberalism, Bunting anticipated the Oxford Movement and the Papal Syllabus of 1864, though he would hardly thank us for putting him in such Popish company. The result was that a European-wide tension met inside Metho-dism in a grievous domestic conflict which cost it one hundred thousand members in a few months. But when the disciplinary counter attack of the Methodist Conference was denounced by all other Nonconformists, and the indignation of British opinion was voiced by the *Times,* it was in a letter to that journal (which they would not print) that a Methodist preacher upheld the " Crown Rights of the Redeemer " as surely as any John Knox or Hildebrand. " You forget," he said, " that we are a religious and not a secular society. We guard against those terms and usages which would assimilate us to the House of Commons or any other secular assembly ". Modern Christians have not always understood as well how to protest against that most subtle of all despotisms, the tyranny of an operative and national idealism, or to resist the most insidious of all temptations, to play to its own progressive gallery.

But it is as well that Wesleyan Toryism did not stand alone, that there were ebullient traditions of Christian liberty among the older Dissenting Churches, and that the Primitive Methodists combined evangelical fervour with a stubborn compassion which would break the yoke of any tyranny. The revival had been a good school for politics ; men learned to read their Bibles, then their newspapers ; they learned to pray and praise their Maker and turned their new found eloquence upon their fellows. A

Methodist wrote in alarm to Bunting, " If men are to be drilled at Missionary and Bible Meetings to face a multitude with recollection and an acquired facility of address and then begin to employ the mighty moral weapon thus gained to the endangering of the very existence of the Government of our country, we may certainly tremble for the consequences". That, in the event, those consequences were peacefully inscribed upon the Statute Book without dire and sanguinary convulsion of the body politic, owes something to men and women who emerged from the Dissenting Communities. Nobody can read the story of English Radicalism and the growth of the Labour Movement without noting how much some of its finest figures, from Thomas Cooper and the martyrs of Tolpuddle to Thomas Burt and Arthur Henderson, owed to their Nonconformist origin.

But it was the alliance of the Nonconformists with the Liberal Party under Bright and Gladstone that gave Dissent a political instrument such as it had never had since the seventeenth century Commonwealth. Its power was shown in 1890 when Hugh Price Hughes effectively voiced the demand that Parnell must resign as a result of the O'Shea divorce action. Amid a seething audience in St. James's Hall, while a gang of converted toughs acted as ' chuckers out ' to the very astonished Irish hecklers, Hughes made his devastating peroration :

" We stand immovably on this eternal rock : what is morally wrong can never be politically right." Hughes would have been a voice crying in the wilderness but for that moving weight of Nonconformist opinion stirred by a decade of humanitarian agitation for a moral reformation of public life. Yet was that fine phrase, " What is morally wrong can never be politically right" the prophetic word, or was it a dangerous catchword which evades the real problem of Christian politics ? Long before Lord Palmerston had said, " In the long run English politics will follow the conscience of the Dissenters ". He might have added, " But woe betide them if they try to force the pace ". There is an ominous exultation about the *Methodist Times* for October 1896 : " Sir Charles Dilke defied the Nonconformist conscience and is a political outcast today. Parnell despised the Nonconformist conscience and he destroyed himself and his party. Lord Rosebery ignored the Nonconformist Conscience for a racehorse, and the world sees the result ". For the greatest contribution of Nonconformity to English politics was made when it was " under the Cross " in the seventeenth century and not when, drunk with sight of power, it stooped to employ such boastings as the Gentiles use. In 1894, Hugh Price Hughes had uttered a genuinely prophetic warning : " We must not allow the Church to be identified with party politics. Woe to the Church which commits itself to either side. Our Churches must not take sides or they will be involved in disaster ". But that is another, not a Victorian story.

The primary achievement of Victorian Nonconformity was religious and it was not mean. If there is a strain of coarseness in its fibre to suggest the gibe at the " vulgarity of Dissent " (though " vulgarity " is a reproach which our age has slender right to fling) it was after all to a very coarse and vulgar world that the Victorian Nonconformists came, but a world with respect to the common people which they left a good deal tidier and cleaner and more mannered. They had great virtues : faith, and guts and moral passion, an impatience with cruelty and tyranny and injustice, an awareness that the supreme betrayal is to acquiesce in so called " necessary evils ". They had great limitations : a narrowness which shut out from religion whole realms of delight and beauty ; unlike the Puritans they produced no great literature, no intelligentsia. But they have something to say. They remind us that at the root of civilised life there are certain habits of right virtue, certain enormous moral platitudes by which nations live and apart from which they perish. They also knew that morality is not enough. In the end the witness of Victorian Nonconformity is that the great, lasting, ennobling traditions of the English people owe most to honest, decent, humble, believing men and women who loved justice, treasured mercy and were not ashamed to own their God.

The Tractarian Movement, Church Revival and Reform

ALEC VIDLER

THE TRACTARIAN movement, properly so-called, began about 1833 and ended in 1845 with the catastrophe—as it seemed at the time—of Newman's secession. "Tractarian" was originally a nickname that happened to stick. Archbishop Whately, of Dublin, who didn't like the movement at all, used to call the Tractarians "Tractites", which is certainly an uglier sounding word ; but happily that didn't stick. Anyhow, neither word is very revealing, for we have not learned much about a movement when we have been told that its ideas were spread by the publication of a series of tracts. The Tractarian movement, however, has another name which is more revealing.

When you hear it called " the Oxford movement ", that may at first do no more than convey to you the obvious information that it originated in Oxford. But when you recollect that it was the Oxford of about 1830, you will at once be prepared for the discovery that the movement was academic, clerical and conservative. For Oxford then meant the university. It was a purely academic place. So far from being an industrial city as it is today, no place in England was more remote from the industrialism that was then stretching itself rapidly over other parts of the country. And the university was at that time entirely identified with the Church of England, and was practically under the exclusive control of the clergy. And Oxford was ultra-conservative in politics. Only a few years before the Tractarian movement started, the university had demonstrated this fact by unseating its conservative M.P., Sir Robert Peel, because of the dangerous concession he had made to Liberalism in approving the Bill for Catholic Emancipation.

Now, there are more important things to be said about the

Tractarian movement than that it had these Oxford characteristics, but if you want to see it in perspective you must never forget them. The movement was academic. I don't mean in a bad sense. The point is that its appeal was restricted to the educated classes. Dr. Pusey might say (as he did say) : " The *Tracts* found an echo everywhere. Friends started up like armed men from the ground. I only dreaded our becoming too popular." But not many friends started up from the mills and factories and mines of England. There was no risk that the Tractarians would become too popular there.

Again, the Tractarian movement was a faithful reflection of Oxford in that it was predominantly clerical. It had to be clerical to begin with, since if the clergy did not accept and act upon its message, no one else would. It was Lord Melbourne who said that " the study of theology may be a very good thing, but it is not a thing that we want in these days ". Well, there was not much hope of convincing him that it was wanted, unless the universities and the clergy treated it as a subject of living interest. If the Tractarian movement did nothing else, it made theology a burning subject at Oxford, and it even succeeded in interesting the country clergy in theological questions and in church principles. This in itself was a considerable achievement, for the country clergy of the period were not unfairly described by a contemporary town parson as " constant readers of the *Gentleman's Magazine*, deep in the antiquities of the signs of inns, speculations as to what becomes of swallows in winter, and whether hedgehogs, or other urchins, are most justly accused of sucking cows dry at night."

Once more, it is important to remember that the Tractarian movement was occasioned, if not caused, by the passage of the Reform Act in 1832 and by the triumph of the Whigs. It is not easy for us to recapture the alarm to which these events gave rise in ecclesiastical and conservative circles. The Reform Act strikes us as an astonishingly mild and bourgeois measure, and who now would think of describing Lord Grey and his colleagues as revolutionaries ? They were, however, so regarded at the time. In 1830 there had been a second Revolution in France which had awakened all the slumbering horror of the original French Revolution. It was a signal that the period of reaction which had followed the Napoleonic wars was ending, and that all traditional institutions were again threatened with either demolition or radical reconstruction. It was the threat to the Church of England that particularly alarmed the Tractarians. "No time was to be lost," wrote Newman later, "for the Whigs had come to do their worst, and the rescue might come too late. Bishoprics were already in course of suppression ; church property was in course of confiscation ; sees would soon be receiving unsuitable occupants."

There was some exaggeration in all this. Nevertheless, churchmen had cause to be alarmed, indeed a good deal more cause than the Tractarians were ready to confess. For as the Church entered the Age of Reform it was in no condition to withstand the storms of criticism that were likely to blow up. The Church stood quite as much in need of reform as the old unreformed parliament had done. It was loaded with abuses that had lasted right through from the Middle Ages—pluralities, sinecures, nepotism, with all sorts of indefensible anomalies. The Tractarian movement would have accomplished more than it did, if its leaders had candidly acknowledged and boldly pressed the need for church reform. As it was, they met the attempt of parliament to do something about it with the cry of " National Apostasy ". If the Church survived the storms of the 1830's, and if Dr. Arnold's prophecy that " the Church, as it now stands, no human power can save " was not fulfilled, the credit was due not to the Tractarians but to statesmen and to churchmen of other schools. It was really the Ecclesiastical Commission, for which Sir Robert Peel and Bishop Blomfield of London were mainly responsible, that carried through large measures of over-due and indispensable reform, and so saved the Church.

The contribution of the Tractarians to the survival or revival of the Church was made at another level than that of the reform of the antiquated ecclesiastical machinery. The Church in the early nineteenth century, although it wasn't so desolate of spiritual life as has sometimes been alleged, was afflicted by a weakness that might have proved fatal if the Tractarians had not come to the rescue. The Church in the person of its bishops and other clergy, still more of its laity, had almost completely for-gotten what a Church really is. They were without any sense of its direct dependence on God or of its possessing a divine origin, mission and authority. Even high churchmen regarded the Church merely as a traditional part of the British constitution, and the bishops as the nation's ecclesiastical functionaries.

One of the Tractarians, who in 1833 attended the conference at Hadleigh in Suffolk where the movement was hatched, described the state of affairs by which they felt themselves confronted in these words : there was " no principle in the public mind to which we could appeal ; an utter ignorance of all rational grounds of attachment to the Church ; an oblivion of its spiritual character, as an institution not of man but of God ; the grossest Erastianism most widely prevalent, especially amongst all classes of politicians." It was, then, this ignorance of the A B C of churchmanship, among Englishmen generally and not least among the clergy, that the Tractarians set themselves to expose and to remedy.

Their method was to concentrate attention upon a single article of the Christian faith, "I believe in one Catholic Apostolic Church", and to unearth its forgotten meaning. They began in an even more limited way by emphasising a single doctrine, and a peculiarly provocative one at that, namely what is known as " the apostolic succession". It was startling and bewildering, not to say offensive, to bishops in the reign of William IV suddenly to be told that they were successors of the holy Apostles and that they ought to be acting as such, and even that they ought to be welcoming the prospect of martyrdom. " We could not wish our Bishops", wrote Newman in the first of the *Tracts*, " a more blessed termination of their course, than the spoiling of their goods, and martyrdom". It made the bishops, and other people, too, think and ask questions about the nature of the Church, which had never occurred to them, for there was very little in the appearance of the Church of England in 1833 to suggest its identity with the Apostolic Church of the New Testament.

It was as if the Tractarians had declared that on the drab, dirty and distempered walls within which English churchmen were accustomed to worship there were wonderful pictures that when uncovered would transform the whole building into something mysterious and sublime. That such a transformation of the Church might take place was at any rate the possibility that began to haunt and charm the minds of many who read the *Tracts for the Times*. And as the series advanced (ninety *Tracts* in all were published) one aspect after another of the Church's rites and institutions that had seemed dead or obsolete began to glow with new life and meaning. It has been said of Keble's *Christian Year* that it made the spirit of the Book of Common Prayer living to the men of his age, and of Newman's sermons in St. Mary's, Oxford, that " his power showed itself chiefly in the new and unlooked for way in which he touched into life old truths ". As they listened, men became aware of the marvels of glory and of awfulness amid which human life is passed.

For the Tractarians were much more than writers of tracts. Keble's verses and Newman's sermons made a more lasting impression, and most influential of all was the unobtrusive but profound spirituality which characterised the leaders of the movement and many of its followers. If the Tractarian movement had a powerful effect even on many who opposed it, it was because of the unmistakable holiness, austere, refined and almost fastidious, which it introduced into a society where virtue at its best had been of a very humdrum order.

Samuel Wilberforce, the son of William, had received of course a sound evangelical upbringing ; he was also a strong high churchman ; but he was critical of, and detached from, the Tractarians. In 1838 in the course of a letter to a friend he said this about them : " They hold up a glorious standard of holiness, and for us, my dear Charles, who know well the hopes of the Gospel, and can supply all they leave deficient, it is the very thing needful ; but there are ignorant and bowed-down souls who need a more welcoming treatment than their views of penitence will allow ". Wilberforce was right. There was something hard and forbidding in the holiness of the Tractarians, and also in their teaching, which contrasted unfavourably with the warmth and enthusiasm of the Evangelicals. Still, both movements were powerful because they brought holiness or godliness out of the pages of the Bible into the here and now of human life. No movement which does that will leave things as it found them. If the Evangelicals showed that personal conversion or a change of human nature is a thing that actually happens, the Tractarians showed that what the Bible calls "the fellowship of the mystery" or what the Prayer Book calls " the mystical body of Christ " is a thing that actually exists. These two discoveries are not incompatible, and there need never have been a cleavage between the Evangelicals and the Tractarians if both had been content to affirm their own principles.

What the Tractarians did, despite all the controversies in which their movement became embroiled, was to give substance once again to the great idea of the Church of Christ as a divine society and a sacred mystery. To have disinterred this idea of the Church and to have started it on a new course of life and development was a magnificent achievement. In fact, after the debâcle of 1845, it led directly to the remarkable revival of church life in England in the second half of the century. Indeed the forces which the Tractarians set in motion sooner or later revivified the teaching, the worship, the art and the architecture, not only of the whole Church of England, but of other Churches too. At the same time it must be confessed that the theology of Tractarianism was wooden, narrow, static, and altogether too backward-looking. It was " to the old times and the old paths ", as Pusey said, that they wished to lead people back, and by the old times they meant the seventeenth century, and still more the first four or five centuries of the Church's history.

The Tractarians did not, however, start out with a complete system of doctrine. They worked it out as the movement developed, and as we know the leaders of the movement eventually worked it out in different ways. Newman as well as Keble and Pusey could reasonably claim that they were following the original impulse of the movement, for that impulse was ambiguous. I should myself say that there was a contemporary of the Tractarians who saw more deeply into their discovery of the idea of the Church than they did themselves. I mean Frederick Denison Maurice, whose book *The Kingdom of Christ, or Hints on the Principles, Ordinances, and Constitution of the Catholic Church* was published in 1838. There is more to be learned from him about the nature of the Church than from all the *Tracts* put together. After being at first attracted, Maurice was finally repelled by Tractarianism. He perceived that the error of the Tractarians consisted, as he said, " in opposing to the spirit of the present age the spirit of a former age, instead of the ever-living and active Spirit of God ". He was a Catholic theologian in a larger sense than any of the writers of the *Tracts*.

It is a very partial view which equates the Catholic revival in England with Tractarianism. The names not only of Maurice but of Bishop Wilberforce, Dean Hook and Mr. Gladstone are sufficient to forbid such an equation. The Catholic revival was a bigger thing altogether. It had some features in common with the revival of Catholicism that occurred in France and Germany early in the nineteenth century, though it owed little or nothing to those external sources.

From one point of view the Catholic revival was part of the Romantic revival, that is of the return to romance and emotion, to mystery and adventure, after the cold and artificial rationalism of the eighteenth century. The Romantic movement in Britain which showed itself chiefly in the novels of Sir Walter Scott and in the poetry of Wordsworth, Southey and Coleridge, preceded the Tractarian movement, and to some extent prepared the ground for it. But Tractarianism was not merely a by-product of Romanticism. It was above all a sign that the idea of the Church as a divine society had again taken possession of the minds and imaginations of Englishmen, in such a way that everything to do with the Church, including its relation to the State, has for good or ill been different since. After 1845 it had not one sequel, but many, and they are with us to this day.

The Tractarians' Successors:
the Influence of the Contemporary Mood

T. M. PARKER

PRINCIPAL SHAIRP described the effect upon Oxford of the cessation of Newman's preaching in these words:

"It was as when, to one kneeling by night, in the silence of some vast cathedral, the great bell tolling solemnly overhead has suddenly gone still."

If that was the impression made upon one who did not share the principles of the Oxford Movement what must have been the impact upon those who did of that silence and of the parting of the ways which followed it? Indeed we know the effect upon some. Keble at Hursley walked about all day with a letter from Newman unopened in his pocket, dreading to read the news he foresaw. Dean Church was to head his chapter describing 1845 "The Catastrophe", and Isaac Williams wrote: "I see no chance of our recovery, or getting our heads above water from this, at least in England, for years to come. And it is a check which will one day be far greater than it is now".

It was in fact a double blow. The Movement was discredited in the minds of many as a possible intellectual position. At the same time it had lost its most eloquent voice, that of the most original mind among its first leaders. Though Pusey and Keble stood firm, and though Pusey was to be a tower of strength in Oxford until the eighties, though only Newman's closest followers went with him, yet the first enthusiasm of the Movement, already dulled by disappointment and opposition, was gone. And with it went all hope of any speedy conversion of the Church of England to Tractarian beliefs. Oxford itself was virtually lost. Dean Church says of the events culminating in Newman's departure that the "violent and apparently irretrievable discomfiture" of the Tractarians "as the rising force in Oxford" opened the way for the domination of the University by the theological Liberalism destined to be the prevailing influence for most of the rest of the century. The Oxford Movement was not to be the permanent theology of Oxford. Indeed, as Dean Church puts it : " After 1845 its field was at least as much out of Oxford as in it. As long as Mr. Newman remained, Oxford was necessarily its centre. . . .When he left his place vacant, the direction of it was not removed from Oxford, but it was largely shared by men in London and the country. It ceased to be strongly and prominently Academical ".

But that was not to prove wholly a source of weakness. Once more to quote Church : " The cause which Mr. Newman had given up in despair was found to be deeply interesting in ever new parts of the country ; and it passed gradually into the hands of new leaders more widely acquainted with English Society. It moved in fact into the parishes of England and so into the notice of the ordinary Englishman. To him it became no longer merely a fad of distant dons ; he saw its effects and heard its doctrines in his own parish church ".

What did he find there ? Increasingly a form of worship new to him, though claimed as the rightful heritage of the English Church. It used indeed the familiar words of the English Prayer Book, but it accompanied them by unfamiliar ceremonies, ceremonies which the layman was told were of primitive origin, and which were undoubtedly legal according to the true interpretation of Anglican formularies. They were meant to drive home a new teaching, a teaching justified on the same grounds, a teaching which stressed the identity of the English Church with the Catholic Church of the ages and gave prominence to such forgotten doctrines as the Apostolic succession of the priesthood, the vital importance of sacraments in general and of the Eucharist in particular. The Eucharist itself was regarded as a sacrifice in which Christ was really present in the elements. More significantly still in one sense, the layman was urged to develop his spiritual life upon a pattern very different from Evangelical piety. That had laid all the stress upon sudden emotional conversion and reading of the Bible. The Bible was not indeed disregarded by the Neo-Tractarians, but now it was recommended as a basis for systematic mental prayer of the Counter-Reformation type. The aspirant to piety was recommended to progress towards perfection by prayer of this kind, by self-examination, sacramental confession, frequent communion and ascetic self-conquest, instead of pinning his hopes to a conversion experienced once for all. Spiritual life appeared as a pilgrimage to God, not as the conscious realisation of salvation already received. For those who wished to develop their personal religion still more retreats for silence and prayer were provided, of longer or shorter duration. And finally—strangest of all to the Victorian Englishman, with his religion very firmly anchored in the everyday world—it was once again preached that for some men and women there might come the call of God to leave ordinary society. Monasteries and convents began to appear and Cowley Fathers and Sisters of Mercy in unwonted clothes were to be seen in churches and streets.

To all these developments the Victorian Englishman reacted according to his temperament. To some people this was a new revelation of what religion could be and was greeted with enthusiasm ; to others it was Popery invading the National Church and it was received with bewilderment and violent hostility. This last attitude rapidly led to a series of legal battles against what was termed " Ritualism ". At the opposite pole to the " Ritualist " there came into existence the Kensitite, who made public protests in church against ceremonial and prosecuted High Church clergymen. Nor were church services the only occasion of litigation ; a number of celebrated cases involving doctrinal disputes and the true sense of Anglican formularies of faith were fought out in the courts. In these, the High Church party were either struggling for the recognition of their beliefs as compatible with the principles of the Church of England, or attacking those of their opponents, which they believed to be irreconcilable with the true meaning of those principles. The issues involved were often technically theological, but the whole series of controversies, ceremonial or doctrinal, involved a matter of vital importance concerning the relation of religion to secular society. Through them all runs the attempt to maintain a principle inherent in the Oxford Movement from the beginning —namely the belief that the Church is a Divine Society and not a department of State. This necessitated a challenge to the claim of State-controlled courts to decide authoritatively questions of faith and worship. It was that claim, as much as anything else, which startled Victorians who had come to regard Erastianism as almost a principle of the Established Church.

What was the general effect of the theological and religious ferment induced by the later stages of the Oxford Movement upon Victorian life and opinion ? I should say, briefly, that the Movement challenged the insular early Victorian assumption that there could be only one expression of Christianity intellectually and emotionally acceptable, at least to Englishmen—namely Protestantism in one of its forms. Until the very end of the century Roman Catholicism was too weak and too much associated with foreign and Irish influences to shake this conviction in the mind of the ordinary man. The new High Church teaching and practice, however, entered too deeply into everyday English life to be dismissed in this way. Hence the bitter controversy it evoked and the searchings of heart it stirred. For some Victorians began to wonder whether a religion which could so obviously touch both the intelligentsia and the submerged population of the reeking city slums might not be at least as true to reality as the conventional or Evangelical Anglicanism of the prosperous classes or the stern Nonconformity of the trader and the artisan. I suggest that the greater cosmopolitanism of outlook noteworthy in the later Victorian Age owes something to a movement which claimed to be catholic in the full sense of the word.

But, if the later Oxford Movement influenced Victorian development, scarcely less did Victorian development influence that movement itself. This can be plainly seen in the sphere of theology. Tractarianism had been rigidly conservative theologically. It took as its authority the Bible, the early Fathers and the doctrinal decisions of the Councils of the undivided Church. It regarded deviations from these standards, as it understood them, as heresy. It cared at least as much for the general deposit of Christian faith in its traditional form as for the forgotten doctrines it felt bound to emphasise. It was suspicious of the philosophy of the day, which it thought to be rationalising secularist infidelity. What is more, it refused to make terms with most of the Biblical criticism, of German Protestant origin, which had been influencing England from before the middle of the century. That criticism seemed to the Tractarians to deny the idea of revelation and to pave the way for disbelief in the Creeds. Some of the second generation (such as Liddon, upon whom had fallen the mantle of Newman's superb preaching) held fast to this position to the end. But the publication in 1889 of a book of essays, *Lux Mundi*, showed a change in the attitude of some of the influential younger men. In intention as orthodox as their predecessors, the authors were thinking against a very different background from that of the original Movement. Liddon was especially grieved by Charles Gore's contribution, which accepted some of the views of biblical higher critics and asserted that they were compatible with a belief in inspiration. At the same time Gore adumbrated a view of Christ's Person he was to develop in later writings, a view which thought of the Incarnation as a process of Divine self-emptying in which the Godhead was circumscribed by human limitations. This was contrary to Tractarian orthodoxy and attacked as such. But, to the modern reader, far more significant is the general assumption of all the collaborators that the Christian revelation does not stand in sharp contrast to human wisdom, but is closely related to it. That assumption appears again and again in the book. " Revelation," said Aubrey Moore, " never advances for itself the claims which its apologists sometimes make for it, the claim to be something absolutely new. A truth revealed by God is never a truth out of relation with previous thought." Illingworth even claimed that " all great teachers of whatever kind are vehicles of revelation, each in his proper sphere ". Here we can see the influence of that immanentist philosophy characteristic of later Victorian England, a philosophy which seemed to fit in so well with biological evolution and the idea of inevitable progress. This was the real root of the antagonism between the old Oxford Movement and some of its later followers, and is evidence that a school of thought which began by questioning contemporary assumptions was by the 'nineties accommodating itself to a dominant framework of thought.

Connected subtly with this tendency is the change in High Church politics apparent in the latter half of the century. The Tractarians, though playing little part in active politics, inherited and for the most part maintained a Toryism of seventeenth century Anglican type. But the greatest layman of the Oxford Movement, Gladstone, progressed steadily from High Toryism to Liberalism and led with him such prominent High Churchmen as Church and Liddon. From this it was not too difficult a step to that Christian Socialism which had begun as a Broad Church movement, and some of the *Lux Mundi* school, such as Gore and Scott Holland, made that step. They would have claimed that their denial of a sharp distinction between reason and revelation, the natural and the supernatural, led them on to champion social reform in order to demonstrate the congruence of Christianity and social progress. They would have said too that it was this which had made them see the importance of a well-ordered natural society to the health of the soul. We, who have seen the exaltation of the natural over the supernatural made the basis of modern totalitarianism, may doubt whether there was such a necessary relation between their theology and their politics as they supposed. There is certainly no necessary connection between a high doctrine of revelation and social reaction. But that was the new men's claim, and we have here another, if rather different, example of High Church thought, as the century ends, conforming to one aspect of the contemporary mood.

Thus the end of the Victorian era found the heirs of the Tractarians divided and their movement in a phase of doubtful evolution, the issue of which is being worked out today. Though still held in general the clear-cut convictions of the Oxford Movement had, with the advent of forces not fully envisaged by the early leaders, lost their sharp outlines. In short, the pervasive mood of the times had invaded a movement which was originally in opposition to the prevailing pattern of thought around it. The effect of this was bound to be divisive, for the older ideas were not dead, though they were held by the rank and file rather than by most of the new leaders. The *Lux Mundi* school, in fact, were probably having more influence upon the Church of England as a whole than upon their own party. This need not surprise us if we reflect that the Oxford Movement, just because it was so uncharacteristic of most of what we mean by Victorianism, was bound to have only an indirect and diffused effect upon its century ; like most Fifth Columns it could penetrate deeply only in a disguised and modified form. By the end of our period it was, consciously or unconsciously, dressing in the contemporary style and using the contemporary passwords. For in one sense it was not a Victorian movement at all ; its roots lay farther back and its ideas are perhaps more comprehensible to the thought of our day than they ever were to that of its own.

Newman and Roman Catholicism

MONSIGNOR RONALD KNOX

I SUPPOSE it is my duty, in contributing to this series of talks, to discuss why a man of Newman's particular temperament should have changed his spiritual allegiance under the conditions of a particular moment in history. I am at a disadvantage, as being one who thinks that everybody who is in Newman's position, whatever be his temperament, ought to do what Newman did, no matter at what moment in history. But I will try to stick to my brief. I know many people will say I have got him wrong ; but then, Newman is one of those few people who have really opened their hearts to posterity—St. Paul and Dr. Johnson are in the same category—so that every fool thinks his Newman is the right one. *Cor ad cor loquitur* was his motto, and he must be content to be at the mercy of the receiving instrument.

The Oxford Movement began as a spiritual reaction to a political stimulus. And a " reaction " in the fullest sense ; it is no good pretending that the first Tractarians were not reactionaries. The whole situation which led up to the Reform Bill was seen by them, and condemned by them, as Liberalism. The intellectual challenge of Christianity, as we know it, had hardly begun. They lived in a world less than six thousand years old ; hints of an immemorial antiquity had been found, a few years earlier, in Kent's Cavern, but the man who discovered them, a Catholic priest, Father McEnery, was universally disbelieved. The *Origin of Species* did not appear till twenty years later. Destructive criticism of the Bible was becoming fashionable in Germany, but only well-informed men like Hugh Rose had yet heard of it. The Utilitarianism of Bentham and Mill was the enemy ; but this was seen as part of a general infiltration into England of Jacobin ideas, which the world at large called Liberalism, and Newman called Antichrist. Its most dreadful triumph, curiously, had been Catholic Emancipation ; Newman voted with gusto against the re-election of Sir Robert Peel, and wrote home to his mother, " We have proved the independence of the Church and of Oxford ". The suppression of ten Irish bishoprics put a match to the train of orthodox revolt, and Keble preached his sermon on National apostasy.

To meet the attack, Oxford, and through Oxford, England, must be kept safe as the preserve of Anglicanism. The old-fashioned High Churchmen, the two-bottle Orthodox, could not be entrusted with such a task ; the Church of England must be taught to realise herself as a spiritual body ; as a tree of independent growth, not a climbing plant which would come down among the ruins of the body politic, when Jacobinism should triumph. How Newman, an Evangelical at the roots of him and a Liberal by his early training, came to throw in his lot with the party of reaction, is (humanly speaking) a mystery ; not solved for us by the Apologia, or by Church's history of the Movement. Most probably it was due to the personal influence of Hurrell Froude, that infinitely attractive *enfant terrible* who so charmed and dazzled and shocked his contemporaries ; the man whose early death sets one's mind aching with the problem, " What line would he have taken in 1845 ? " Whatever the reason for it, Newman threw himself heart and soul into the cause ; that infinitely sensitive heart, that scrupulously disciplined soul. During the years of the Oxford Movement proper, from 1833 to 1845, his figure so dominated and dominates the scene that you are tempted to say he *was* the Oxford Movement.

From 1833 to 1845 ; strange that the passage of a dozen years should feel so long ! Yet in our own century the corresponding years mark the whole period between Hitler's accession to power and Hitler's death. The Assize Sermon, the *Tracts for the Times*, the preaching at St. Mary's, Hampden's professorship, the Martyrs' Memorial, the attack on Pusey, Ward's *Ideal of a Christian Church* and the condemnation of it—all this falls within the narrow space of those twelve years. And the process ended, so far as the direct object of the Movement was concerned, in a defeat ; instead of safeguarding the monopoly of Anglicanism in Oxford, it precipitated the secularisation of the University. In Tract Ninety, Newman was at pains to show that all his beliefs were reconcilable with the doctrine of the Thirty-nine Articles, and was widely denounced for his insincerity. W. G. Ward—

who was later to be the author of that inimitable phrase, " Shall I deny the fact, or defend the principle ? "—Ward was emboldened to take a more drastic line than his master. He admitted that he could not justify his views by a natural interpretation of the Articles ; but then, could any of the Liberals in Oxford justify theirs ? It was the hot-headedness of a born logician, not any instinct of sabotage, that led him thus to drive a wedge between the Pharisees and the Sadducees. But the effect was to discredit the Articles as a basis of subscription ; and the removal of tests, which was doubtless bound to come, came all the earlier for this unexpected attack.

Meanwhile, Newman was on his Anglican death-bed, in retirement at Littlemore. It has been customary to exclaim at the shortsightedness, the want of statesmanship on the part of the Anglican authorities which drove him to such a step ; if only they had tried to understand what the Tractarians really meant ! But such explanations are psychologically unsound. To a man like Dean Church, puzzled by the vagaries of conscience which led him to part from Newman at the cross-roads—" Oh hard destiny, except that the All-merciful so willed it, that such companions might not walk in the house of God as friends ! "—to a man like Church, it seemed necessary to suppose that the mind of his leader had somehow been wrought upon. But in fact, Newman had seen a ghost. It was not anything which happened in the nineteenth century, it was the theological controversies of the fifth century, that were exercising him. Had there ever been, effectively, a Universal Church without a Pope ? That question fatally disturbed the balance with which he trod the Via Media. Once your balance has been lost, disturbances from without count for nothing ; the confidence which has been shaken is irrecoverable. So, a man who is kept awake by indigestion will blame the financial worries which haunt his mind as the cause of his insomnia, but it is a false diagnosis.

It can be maintained more plausibly, that although Newman may not have been pushed over the line by his opponents, he was nevertheless pulled over it by his friends. It is true that he was always somewhat at the mercy of disciples who thought they saw the way more clearly than he did ; Faber and Dalgairns before his conversion, Simpson and Acton after it. But, in the first place it is not always a bad thing, at moments of decision, to have others dependent on you. It is sometimes easier to see what is the right course for another person, than for yourself. And in the second place, if personal motives beckoned Newman in the direction he took, how much stronger were the personal ties that held him back ! No, if ever a deliberate step was taken, it was the step Newman took in 1845. Criticise, if you will, the decision he made, but do not doubt that his whole self went to the making of it.

Newman himself has described that older Catholic world into which he graduated as " a race that shunned the light ". Perhaps all that would have changed, as the result of Emancipation, even without Newman. But I think that, as the result of his conversion, his coreligionists became more alive to the questions that were being agitated in the world around them—the questions with which this series of talks mainly deals. Hitherto, the Catholic body had been sealed off from its surroundings. And the Church itself, as Wilfred Ward has pointed out, suffered at that moment from an indifference to apologetic ; did not realise the difficulty of putting its message across. In England, at least, Newman sensitised it ; we could not go on in happy indifference to what was being said by Darwin, what was being said in *Essays and Reviews*. We were braced up beforehand to meet the challenge of Modernism which came with the dawn of the twentieth century.

Nobody, I imagine, would claim that Newman's *personal* influence was as great after his conversion as before it. His preaching, his writings, appealed to thousands of minds, thousands of souls ; he had a vast correspondence. But he was no longer at the head of an army. It was not only that he had cut himself off from the main stream of the national life, thrown in his lot with a minority, at that time an almost unregarded minority. He moreover consecrated himself to God's service in an Institute which, gracious and consoling as are its traditions, makes for immobility. Your Oratorian cultivates, no less than your Benedictine, the love of his own room ; his is an active vocation, but the parishioners of a single district have the first claim on him ; he is no student of Bradshaw. There are, of course, the high spots in Newman's life, the Achilli trial, the *Apologia*, the Cardinalate. But more and more as it went on his life was a hidden life ; he meant it to be.

Naturally, there was a constant agitation among his friends and admirers to bring him out into the limelight. The unfortunate issue of these attempts is notorious ; whether the unimaginative and sometimes unintelligible attitude of his superiors is wholly to blame, admits of doubt. It may be doubted, I mean, whether a position could have really been found, in that age, for a priest of those talents to exercise his talents with full advantage. The Irish University scheme, beyond question, was bungled ; but if it had been handled perfectly, would it have succeeded ? Neither Baines' attempt at Prior Park, nor Mannings' at Hammersmith, encourage the belief ; it is arguable that the whole scheme was too ambitious. Translating the Bible would have been a congenial task, but it is no recipe for securing popularity among your co-religionists. No, if there was any scheme that really held out hopes, it was that of sending Newman back to Oxford. What would have happened ? What would have happened if Newman and Jowett had faced one another across St. Giles' ? If there had been any religious figure in Oxford, these last forty years, with a tenth of Newman's influence, we might have some material for guessing.

Curiously, his influence belongs to our age, rather than to his own. We, who are apt to throw mud at the portraits of our grandfathers, refrain, somehow, when it comes to Newman ; we do not count him as part of that offensively prosperous world, on whose prizes he deliberately turned his back. But that is not all ; among his own coreligionists, in all the English-speaking countries, I think his fame stands higher today than it did half a century back. He, who so divided Catholic sympathies in his lifetime, unites them now that he is dead ; he has become the symbol of a living insipration. But among the Victorians, he does not fit in.

Others of the Oxford converts enjoyed, proportionately, more *réclame* : Manning as the typical embodiment of an ecclesiastic, Faber as a born revivalist, Ward in the incredible rôle of a seminary professor who came in for money. Only Manning, perhaps, achieved national importance ; history will at least remember the octogenarian who settled the dock strike of 1889. It is not easy to determine how much of Catholic progress in the fifty years that followed Emancipation is due to the conversions, how much to the rise of an Anglo-Irish body as the result of the Potato Famine. The Irish question itself does not, I think, fall within the scope of this talk. More and more it came to be seen as a racial, not a religious issue. Apart from that, did the Catholic body in England leave much mark on the history of the Victorian Age? On its gossip-columns, yes; we were in the news all the time, whether it were Lord Bute supplying the title-role for *Lothair*, or the Tichborne family fighting the Tichborne claimant. But when you have drawn up an imposing list of comparatively eminent Victorians who were also Catholics, you have not proved that their influence would have told differently if they had belonged to a different faith. Did Catholicism as such leave its mark on the annals of the day before yesterday?

The answer to that question is commonly forgotten; if only because the people concerned are not, and were not, in the habit of drawing attention to themselves. The really amazing thing those ancestors of ours did was to cover the whole of England with a net-work of charitable institutions—schools, hospitals, orphanages, rescue homes, and so on; almost entirely staffed by nuns. Whatever else we forget about the Victorians, let us remember the enormous voluntary effort they made to heal the wounds of a *laissez-faire* civilisation. It has been largely replaced, in our own day, by those Social Services which are its parricidal progeny; but in its time, it kept things going while the State did nothing. And Catholics, in proportion to their number and resources, did more than their share. Our English convents may have been founded, originally, from France, they may recruit, to some extent, from Ireland, but they are part of us. And if you could reckon up the volume of nun-power exercised, the number of nun-hours spent, between 1845 and the Diamond Jubilee, what a staggering total it would make! It accompanies, with a music not of this world, the story of our irrecoverable past.

The New Morality

H. G. NICHOLAS

THERE IS a remarkable paradox about mid-Victorian England, which marks it off not only from any earlier period of English history, but also from any contemporary society of the Western world. It is the intensity with which it sought to combine material development and public probity. The age of George Hudson, of Henry Bessemer, of Mr. Merdle and the House of Dombey is also the age of the Gladstonian conscience, the unbribable " peeler ", the dutiful civil servant. I don't want to say anything, tonight, about the warm uprush of public philanthropy which marked the early Victorian decades. Instead, I want to concentrate on an equally remarkable development of the middle of the century—what I might call the new institutional morality which went so strangely hand in hand with the new prosperity. Let me cite a few examples :

Entry into the Indian Civil Service, so long an almost hereditary perquisite of a few families, was made conditional upon competitive examination. The Northcote-Trevelyan Report advocated as much for the Home Civil Service, and by successive stages its recommendations won full adoption. Again, with the passage of the Oxford University Bill, sinecure and restricted Fellowships were abolished throughout the University. Florence Nightingale's *Notes on Nursing*—well described as " the burial service read over Mrs. Gamp—brought into being a new code for the most indispensable (and hitherto most despised) of professions. In the 'sixties, Gladstone established the Public Accounts Committee, following it with the Exchequer and Audits Departments Act : the two together were responsible for imposing new standards of rigid financial accountability upon all departments of government. Finally, the sale and purchase of army commissions was abolished and the way opened for entry and promotion by merit.

To all this the social and economic background was that of the great age of *laissez-faire*, of mounting prosperity, of new standards of comfort, of competition and of wealth—surely a surprising contrast? More remarkable still, this new probity spilt over into the very world of business and industry itself. Despite the impression sometimes conveyed of Victorian England as a kind of Janus-faced monster, moral in the parlour and in Parliament, but ruthless at the counter and in the counting-house, the full facts tell a different story. This is the age that, more than any other, built up in the eyes of the world the concept of the honest trader, the English merchant whose word is as good as his bond, on whose quality and price the nations who are his willing customers can implicitly rely.

The truth is that the Victorian philosophy of enterprise rested upon a conviction, in no wise a hypocritical one, that honesty *was* the best policy. Let Samuel Smiles, the Plutarch of the age, bear witness from the pages of his *Self-Help*. After all his exhortations to early rising and hard work and thrift comes this revealing passage :

" It is against the growth of this habit of inordinate saving that the wise man needs most carefully to guard himself ; else, what in youth was simple economy, may in old age grow into avarice, and what was a duty in the one case may become a vice in the other. . . . It is one of the defects of business too exclusively followed, that it insensibly tends to a mechanism of character. The businessman gets into a rut and often does not look beyond it. If he lives for himself he becomes apt to regard other human beings only in so far as they minister to his ends. Take a leaf from such men's ledgers and you have their life. . . . Though men of persevering, sharp, dexterous and unscrupulous habits, ever on the watch to push opportunities, may and do ' get on ' in the world, yet it is quite possible that they may not possess the slightest elevation of character, nor a particle of real goodness. . . . Money is power after its sort, it is true ; but intelligence, public spirit and moral virtue are powers too, and far nobler ones."

Can we perhaps probe a little way into the motive force behind this new public morality, indubitable in its vigour, though necessarily imperfect in its realisation? What made it possible to set these new standards of probity, and how were they main-

tained to such a remarkable degree in the face of an eighteenth-
century tradition of " respectable " jobbery and corruption, and
against the lure of unexampled material rewards ?

When Sir Stafford Northcote and Sir Charles Trevelyan
brought out their 1854 scheme for reforming the entry into the
Civil Service, they invited various persons to offer their comments. It was Sir James Stephen, late Under-Secretary of the
Colonial Office (no Decimus Barnacle, but a public servant of
the most exacting standards)—it was he who offered the most
devastating criticism. After various minor objections he attacked
the central feature of the report, its intention to eliminate the
large pockets of eighteenth century corruption which still hung
about the Civil Service. " The basis of the whole scheme," he
asked, "—that of government on principles of the strictest purity,
even so as to exclude all patronage whatever—is it as sound a
principle as at first sight it appears to be ? . . . It is at least a perfect
novelty. It is a rule never hitherto enforced in any commonwealth except that of Utopia. It does not prevail in the legal or
medical or sacerdotal or naval or military or mercantile professions. It is unknown to the great commercial and municipal
corporations among us. In every age, and land and calling, a
large share of success has hitherto always been awarded to the
possessors of interest, of connection, of favour, and of what we
call good luck. Can it be that all the world is and always has
been wrong about a matter so level, as it might seem, to the
capacity of the least wise, as well as of the wisest ? Or, if such
an error has become thus inveterate in our thoughts and habits,
is not the very fact of the inveteracy of it a serious obstacle to this
plan ? The lawgiver may keep ahead of the public virtue, but
he cannot shoot out of sight of the moral standard of his age and
his country. The world we live in is not, I think, half moralised
enough for the acceptance of a scheme of such stern morality as
this."

This was the objection, not of a cynical opponent, but of an
experienced well-wisher. Yet by 1870 the scheme was in full
operation. What had proved him wrong ?

I cannot pretend that there is any unanimity about the answers.
There is one school of historical thought which would contend
that Sir James Stephen was not proved wrong ; that his only
mistake was in misconceiving the nature of the innovation, that

what he scouted as a new morality was in fact merely a translation of power from an old ruling class to a new, with its appropriate trimming designed to disguise a continued subservience
of the public good to the interests of a dominant group. The
middle class were tired of corruption : first, because it produced
an inefficiency which hampered their trade, clogged their enterprise and raised their taxes, and secondly because it preserved the
fruits of office for the effete scions of a deposed oligarchy, a device,
as Dickens put it, for assisting the nobs in keeping off the snobs.

Certainly these reforms appealed to the new middle and
professional classes. Headmasters in the public schools, and
college tutors like the Rev. Benjamin Jowett, welcomed the
prospect opened to their charges. However, it wasn't quite so
simple as all that. It is significant that civil servants themselves
were worried lest the process would go too far. The Secretary
to the Board of Trade protested that the effect would be " to
fill the offices with the picked clever young men of the lower
ranks of society. . . . There would thus be a lower class of men
gradually introduced ". The truth was, that if the Jowetts and
the Macaulays were only interested in transferring patronage
from the class above them to their own, they were going a
dangerous way about it. They would have done better to drop
all talk of competitive examinations and simply imitate President
Andrew Jackson in the United States, with his forthright credo,
" To the victors belong the spoils ". Instead, they were establishing standards to which all men might repair, whether they
had been to Balliol or not, whether they favoured mid-Victorian
liberalism or late-Victorian Fabianism. For not only were they
going to admit without fear or favour, but also, inside the service
they were going to insist on scrupulous probity, anonymity,
political neutrality and public loyalty. While still themselves
inhabiting the sunny foothills of the ten-pound franchise, they
were constructing a vehicle of political and social locomotion
which was going to transport their children across the plains of
manhood suffrage. In the heyday of *laissez-faire* they were
forging the indispensable tools of the modern welfare state. Out
of the proceeds of a fourpenny income-tax they were fashioning
a most potent instrument—an instrument which in the hands of
a later age would effect the most ruthless and corruption-free
levelling of incomes that democracy has ever known.

To do all this required something more than a shrewd appraisal of class interest. The answer to Sir James Stephen's defeatism could only have been given by men who possessed to a remarkable degree the qualities both of administrative competence and moral conviction. To permeate entrenched professions and stubborn institutions with a new sense of probity and public service it was not enough to be a mere enthusiast, nor was it enough to be a mere administrative pedant like Trollope's Sir Gregory Hardlines. The new morality had to be served by a no less novel *expertise*. The High Church Gladstone had to go to school again with figures at the Board of Trade—as he bitterly put it : " The science of politics dealt with the government of men ; but I am set to govern packages ". The Evangelical Sir Charles Trevelyan had to work for nineteen years as Assistant Secretary to the Treasury ; the earnest Miss Nightingale had to serve her apprenticeship in every leading hospital in Europe.

Nevertheless, as one looks back on this Victorian achievement and marvels again at its range and thoroughness, what strikes one most is the vitality their public life drew from their private and personal convictions. Some no doubt were nourished on a strong religious orthodoxy ; others like the Utilitarian John Stuart Mill grazed on the paradoxical slopes of a sophisticated hedonism ; but all alike shared the conviction—and what's more exhibited the practice—of a morality which dictated equally their private, and their public, behaviour. Thus, while they seek, to a degree hitherto unprecedented, to give their morality an institutional expression, they don't suppose that it can long subsist if its fountains in the individual conscience dry up.

That, as I take it, is one of the central themes of *Middlemarch*, that novel into which George Eliot has poured her unsurpassed awareness of both the reality and the relativity of Victorian morals. Lydgate, the physician, you will remember, comes to Middlemarch determined to put into effect his ideas of medical reform. George Eliot says of him : " He carried the conviction that the medical profession as it might be was the finest in the world ; presenting the most perfect interchange between science and art ; offering the most direct alliance between intellectual conquest and social good. . . . He intended to begin in his own case with some particular reforms. One of these reforms was to act stoutly on the strength of a recent legal decision and simply prescribe, without dispensing drugs or taking a percentage from druggists". He meets criticism and opposition from his fellow-practitioners ; they are satisfied enough with existing standards, but nevertheless it is not this which wrecks his schemes. It is not even any professional inadequacies of his own. It is rather a sequence of events which are the by-products of a moral weakness within himself—the tacit deal with Bulstrode by which he trades his vote for the banker's support for his hospital, the marriage with Rosalind and the easy indulgence of her extravagance, his consequent debts and finally the too ready acceptance of Bulstrode's version of the death of his patient. He has committed no crime ; the material of his character simply proves insufficient to carry the strain of his intentions. So in the end he abandons his schemes, leaves Middlemarch, and gains instead an " excellent practice " where, says George Eliot, " his skill was relied on by many paying patients ". But, he concludes, " he regarded himself as a failure : he had not done what he once meant to do ".

In George Eliot's eyes Lydgate is the exemplar of the public man whose failure to realise his own new standards of public morality is rooted in the inadequacies of his own private character. Her Victorian readers would not have doubted the justice of her analysis. Sometimes, possibly this emphasis on the essential identity of public and private virtue would lead to a crude and Grundy-esque confusion of real and conventional values. Queen Victoria, not wanting Sir Charles Dilke in Gladstone's 1886 cabinet, recalls that he was cited as co-respondent in a divorce case. " Sir Charles Dilke, of course, I must and would never accept on account of his dreadful private character ". But fundamentally this idea rests on a conviction that character and behaviour are, in the last resort, all of one piece. It has turned its back on the Regency pretence that public life is, for most of the time, simply a kind of annexe to the card rooms at Brooks's, governed by no other principles than those that may be agreed upon by gentlemen of birth and breeding. Equally, it is too young to have gone to school with the mass-behaviourists, and to grow up in the presumption that (whatever cultivation may do for one's own garden) the outer world is a wilderness, given over to the inexorable and irrational instincts of the herd. Instead it is anchored in the belief that the totality of public life is, in the last analysis, nothing else than the individuals who compose it, and that its values and achievements are simply theirs reflected on a larger screen. The new morality of public institutions thus became, in effect, only the application to public life of a more rigorous code of personal behaviour. What John Stuart Mill had to say about government truly mirrored, in this respect, the sentiments of every institutional and professional reformer of his age. " Government," says Mill, " consists of acts done by human beings ; and if the agents, or those who choose the agents, or those to whom the agents are responsible, or the lookers-on whose opinion ought to influence and check all these, are mere masses of ignorance, stupidity, and baleful prejudice, every operation of government will go wrong ; while, in proportion as the men rise above this standard, so will the government improve in quality ; up to the point of excellence, attainable but nowhere attained, where the officers of government, themselves persons of superior virtue and intellect are surrounded by the atmosphere of a virtuous and enlightened public opinion ".

The Victorian Attitude to Evil and Personal Responsibility

D. M. MacKinnon

It is always dangerous in discussing any subject like the attitude of the Victorians towards evil and moral responsibility to concentrate too exclusively on men of ideas.

In a way, the subject belongs to the social historian rather than to the philosopher, who in the nature of the case can only see part of the game. Tonight, we are going to consider the views held on these matters by two opposing schools of thinkers—the Utilitarians and the Idealists.

Both belong to the Victorian Age, although the former had formulated their position before the Queen came to the throne. Both affected and were affected by the manners of their age. Their influence was, however, by no means limited to those who professed and developed their respective doctrines in their full form.

In a way, both tendencies matter less in their explicit expression than in their diffusion in the climate of the Victorian Age. But in order to take hold of them we are perhaps justified in looking at them briefly in abstraction, set over against one another.

On December 6th, 1817, James Mill in a letter to a friend expressed the wish that he had time to write a book which would make the human mind as plain as the road from Charing Cross to St. Paul's. If we take this quotation seriously, we must say that the older Mill thought he needed only time, only leisure, to lay bare all the mysteries of the human spirit.

He had the methods to his hand ; he had mastered them. All that he now required was the time to employ them. If the confidence of the quotation is a caricature of the utilitarian's attitude, it is at least a true caricature in that it throws into clear relief the underlying assumptions of the man.

Too often we think of the utilitarians simply as moral philosophers, as men concerned to put forward and then to modify, but never to abandon, one particular ethical position. A utilitarian is one who puts forward on *Erfolgsethik*—an ethic that judges actions simply by their consequences; and we contrast in moral philosophy his attitude with that of a *Gesinnungsethik*, or an ethic that judges actions by reference to the motive from which they are done.

Yet historically the " philosophical radicals "—Bentham, the Mills father and son, and their circle—were much more than mere moralists. It is a commonplace of history to point out that Bentham was primarily a legal reformer; but more than that, these men were all of them concerned to test out at all levels, I might even say to live out, the consequences of a certain attitude of mind.

The greatest of them, John Stuart Mill, has left us his testament in his *Autobiography*. No one can read that book without seeing the whole movement to which its author belonged in a new light. Mill's experience was in many ways a painful one, and I am not referring actually simply to his education, but it is an experience which reveals at the same time a great deal of the inwardness of what actually in the end its subject simply could not take of the utilitarian outlook.

Suppose we begin with the familiar characterisation of utilitarian ethics as an ethic of consequence. We must judge actions good or bad, right or wrong simply by these consequences. But why is this recipe commended to the ages ?

Fundamentally, I think, because it is thought that this way lies the road to the elimination of mystery—the kind of mystery that tends to gather round those notions of good and evil, of ought and ought not. You have only to read the polemical parts of the utilitarians' writings to see this. They sought an ethics not mysterious, and in such there could be no appeal to any intuitive insight or to any moral sense.

J. S. Mill assails the elder eighteenth-century naturalism on precisely the same grounds as he assails the doctrines of men like Richard Price and Immanuel Kant. Both Price and Kant, in Mill's view, were resisting the use of rational methods in the attempt to throw light on the nature of moral obligation, and those who talked of a moral sense were in no better case.

For Mill our traditionally accepted ethical rules were not indications of insight into the deeps of some Platonic intelligible world ; they were not deliverances of moral sense ; they were generalisations, however vague and inaccurate, however much in need of correction and revision, generalisations concerning the surest way to increase the sum of pleasure and diminish that of pain.

I say in frequent need of correction and revision, for of course Bentham insisted that codes of ethics as much as of laws required continual adjustment and revision. But provided we rid our minds of traditional prejudice, such adjustment should give rise to no problems.

An exploration of the phenomena of human consciousness revealed the tendency of the ideas or mental particles, of which it was ultimately composed, to associate together in all manner of ways. The skill of the best legislator would surely avail to attach the idea of pleasant feeling to the realisation of that state of affairs most likely to encourage and least likely to impede the satisfaction of the greatest number.

In his exhaustive study of the English Utilitarians, Leslie Stephen remarks their combination of a view of the phenomena of human consciousness as something fixed and given with a view of these phenomena as almost infinitely variable and plastic.

It was, of course, from this view of human nature as at once settled and malleable that their principles of legislative reform were derived. They were always inspired by the conviction that the study of human consciousness at once individual and social, only awaited its Newton : and this not simply that men should have guidance in finding their way through their actual problems and predicaments, but that the road might be opened towards a society wherein through beneficent legislation, conflict should be eliminated, and wealth and satisfaction increased.

Their characteristic position in moral philosophy was part and parcel of their general anxiety to liberate men's minds from the restraints of tradition, historical recollection and religion. To liberate men's minds in order that happiness, harmony and comfort should be extended and preserved.

All this may seem perhaps too simply to label the Utilitarians as mere Philistines and forget the magnitude of their achievement, but we are concerned here with their underlying outlook.

It is not quite enough simply to say that they aimed to be the Newtons of the moral sciences. We must try as far as we can to capture the inwardness of their assumptions. The technique of their psychology was introspective. Yet it was an introspection which altogether discarded the mysterious, and in some ways reminds us of the behaviourists, who, of course, have abandoned introspective technique altogether. The complex would always be shown as built up out of the simple and it was the simple which was the ultimately real. Thus it was no accident that Bentham judged Lush-pin the equal of poetry. All satisfactions were, as much, homogeneous and on a level. What mattered was not their quality but their harmony and their increase. Questions of good and evil were to be taken once and for all out of the context in which they were usually discussed, of morbid preoccupation with spiritual ultimates, and faced rationally in the light of practical concern with the promotion of human happiness and elimination of human distress. And no one could have any doubt where that happiness and where that distress was to be found. It is the marriage in the utilitarian of concern for reform with a conviction that the methods of exact science can be extended to the exploration of mental phenomena that shapes the utilitarian outlook ; impatience with the mysterious, hard-headed loyalty to the methods of mathematical physics in their Newtonian form, a disregard of history and tradition, a measure of ruthlessness, a desire to get things done, an assurance that no one will have any doubt when they had been done —all this we find in the utilitarians. The *Daily Worker* was perhaps right in its article, commemorating the second centenary of Bentham's birth, to claim his spiritual kinship with those who share the Communist impatience with contemporary concern with the so-called Western tradition ; and the similarities of Marxist to Benthamite ethics are actually much more pervasive than this.

I have said little or nothing so far of John Stuart Mill. Indeed to trace his intellectual pilgrimage would itself occupy a whole treatise. His *Autobiography* bears eloquent witness to the extent to which he broke with the doctrines in which he had been educated and to the influences which contributed to that liberation. His voluminous literary output gives further evidence of his extraordinary sensitivity to contemporary intellectual cross-currents. It also indicates the equally remarkable hold the strict utilitarian doctrine had on his mind till the end. Some of its emphases (for instance, its impatience with every appeal to intuition and ethics) he retained all through, even when, for instance, his acquaintance with Coleridge had opened his mind to the inadequacies of Bentham's political and social outlook, and even when he had become most deeply concerned with the threat to cultural values implicit in acceptance of the majority principle in government. To generalise about Mill would be fruitless, but it is perhaps unfortunate that his writings are so often regarded by the student simply as source-books of the most vulgar kind of fallacy. Collectively they form an extraordinarily interesting expression in one historical relative of the " progressive outlook ", and to the serious student of ethics as well as of logic and metaphysics, they provide abundant food for reflection and comment.

But Mill, of course, never achieved the " Copernican revolution " of questioning the entire utilitarian attitude to the extent of asking whether the order of their questions was the correct one. He was wise enough to query whether the performance of the Benthamite Utopia would be as satisfying as its promise was at one time attractive. But he failed to ask whether the treatment of good and evil, as if they were characteristics of objectively existing or realisable states of affairs, could ever hope to be adequate.

Although he had learnt Greek at the age of three, like others prematurely forced, he had been too young to reap the benefit of his studies. While recognising that " it was better to be Socrates dissatisfied than a fool satisfied " he had never precisely seen the implications of this recognition. He had never, that is to say, reached the point of questioning the extent to which the utilitarians were justified in treating such entities as satisfaction, idea and the rest as if they were substantial or self-existent ; as if they were, one might say, Cartesian simple natures. He never reached the point of querying the entire view of experience endorsed by the philosophical radicals, whether on its cognitive or its conative side. This work was actually carried through by a number of Oxford men of whom perhaps the most important for our purposes were Thomas Hill Green and Edward Caird. The former was best known as Fellow and Tutor of Balliol

College, Oxford ; the latter after a period as Professor in Glasgow returned to Oxford as Master of Balliol.

I select these two deliberately : although neither possessed the philosophical power of F. H. Bradley, their impact on their contemporaries was more direct and less restricted. They are commonly called " idealists " and it is certainly true that Caird owed much to Hegel and Green much to the study of Kant. But they were also students of the classics and it would be a justifiable exaggeration to say that their political theory owed as much to the study of Plato's *Republic* as to that of Rousseau's *Social Contract* and Hegel's *Philosophy of Right*. These men were before all else perhaps teachers, and as teachers their influence extended beyond the fields of technical philosophy. Politics, literature, the life of the non-Roman churches in England and Scotland all knew the influence of their outlook. For all the meticulousness of which they were capable in analysis, their doctrine had a generous streak that made it at once intelligible and congenial to a wider public.

But what of the doctrine in itself ? Like the Utilitarian it was a philosophy of experience, but it differed from the Utilitarian inasmuch as it refused to allow experience to be the simple thing the radicals had assumed it to be. For Green there was a real problem of knowledge. Something mysterious in the structure of the thing. You couldn't break up consciousness into a multitude of atomic psychical particles and then, so to speak, conjure the whole thing as we know it out of their mere aggregation. And what was true in this respect of intellect was also true of will. Green learnt from Kant the presence in experience, whether cognitive or conative, of an irreducible complexity : and although his work is now dated, there is no escape from the power of his thinking. One can imagine how young men, at once traditionally minded and intellectually curious, responded enthusiastically to this teaching. Here was meat from the eater with a vengeance. Green took the fact of scientific knowledge and out of it conjured a whole metaphysic. He dared to suggest that the scrutiny of the very experience on which the radicals had laid such emphasis was something which, if we only weighed its implications seriously enough, revealed the whole world as bound in unity by a spiritual principle.

Don't let us bother with the details either of Green's ethics or his metaphysics : although he died young, his output was large and he is not entirely consistent. But rather let us try to measure the revolution he effected. For the Utilitarian ultimately, Art, Religion, Culture, were all epiphenomena : bubbles thrown up by a process that was in itself indifferent to them. Politics, government itself served the need of a harmony that was sought primarily at the level of mere satisfaction and uncriticised enjoyment. Green stood this doctrine on its head : however these activities were related to the activity of the absolute mind which held the world together, they were at least continuous with it and expressive of its nature. Men like Green gave their students to think of the art of government, for instance, as something worth learning because ultimately politics was the expression of reason and the harmonies towards which it strove were not adjustments of interest but victories of spirit. It is easy to smile at these men : in some ways their high-mindedness is more remote from us than that of Mill. Yet one cannot deny either their intellectual power or their moral earnestness ; in them too we can trace a real unity of theory and practice ; for instance, in Green's concern for education and in Caird's dignified and sustained protest against the imperialistic vulgarity of the Boer War. From their sense of the world as the expression of an immanent spiritual principle, they called men to a new sense of the worth of the service of that world. Caird's sermons in Balliol College Chapel are as much concerned with human good as Mill's writings. But for Caird the service to which he summons his hearers is always to be sustained by the sense that it is not a struggle with some recalcitrant matter but an expression of the very nature of things. It is continuous with and expressive of that which in the end is the ground and sustainer for the world. You get this note struck right through Caird's sermons.

The later followers of the Tractarians, the men who wrote the famous essays in the famous volume *Lux Mundi,* embraced for the most part a metaphysic akin to that of Green or Caird, or rather, because they were also students of the early Fathers, they laid hold on such a metaphysic to baptise it by the name of the LOGOS theology. One can trace in *Lux Mundi* the same immanentism, the same readiness to trace a purpose working itself out in history, the same characteristically English translation of the Hegelian doctrine of the cunning of the historical idea. Gore himself, the editor of the volume, whose essay on Inspiration is the most notorious in the book, had too sharp a hold on moral distinctions ever to swallow the immanentist doctrine as whole as did some of his fellow essayists. But the bias of *Lux Mundi* is in the direction of a Christian reconstitution of the idea of progressive development, as the idealists entertained it. Again one must not smile at theologians of the stature of Aubrey Moore, Edward Talbert and J. R. Illingworth. Their problems after all were not quite those of contemporary theology. But in their enthusiasm they did certainly forget to ask just how far the religion they professed could be conceived in terms of the categories of a metaphysic which was ultimately a metaphysic of immanence. Again Gore was much wiser, but then, as I said, he never lost his grip on moral ultimates—the ultimacy of moral distinction.

It is odd that for all the sharpness and vigour of the idealist's critique of the radicals, to us it is the kinship of their positions that is most striking. In some of Mill's posthumously published essays on religion, essays in which the influence of Auguste Comte is clearly strong, he speaks language concerning the insignificance of personal immortality compared with the moral and spiritual advance of humanity that could be easily assimilated to some emphases of idealism. In their hostility to anything which might be called individualism, the idealists ultimately trivialised the tragedy of the individual. Their impatience with the vulgar notion of responsibility is notorious : for them moral freedom (and this is a subject they all discussed at length) lies in effect in the individual's acceptance, conscious and intelligent, of what he is. Freedom is in effect identified in the end with necessity—necessity recognised, affirmed and accepted. Obviously Green and Bradley too are incapable of understanding the obstinate irrational conviction of the individual that he is truly responsible in some sense for what he does and that there are times when he should and could do other than he actually does. Such discontinuity was scandalous in a world so ordered in its totality as always to bring truth out of error, good out of evil. And, of course, the world as the idealists saw it was a world so ordered.

The Utilitarians notoriously ignored the qualitative differences in human experience. Indeed it was just here their so-called materialism lay. They are blamed too for their identification of evil with physical pain. But the idealists who sought to answer them by revealing spiritual activity as the ground and very sense of the universe were in their turn faced with the question of the status of evil and error. And how, we may ask, did they face this question ? Sometimes in their enthusiasm for the level of spirit, they show an insensitivity to the sheer evil of physical pain, markedly less than that of the despised Mill. On this point Mill at least was refreshingly free from romantic illusion. He must always have the credit for the vigour with which he drives nails into the coffin lid of that hoariest and pious superstition, the superstition that pain ennobles. But when the idealists come to pain of spirit, to remorse, repentance, anguish of mind and the rest—are they any more successful ?

Some would say, with I think some justice, that in an idealist universe, Gethsemane would be a mere charade and the dereliction of Christ upon the Cross perhaps a confusion of mind, a mere imperfection of adherence to the sovereignty of universal rational good. There is in the end an impersonality in the idealist outlook as destructive of a true human seriousness, as trivialising as the grossest materialism. For them truth must be found in all error : and there is no evil that is not pregnant wth good. There is a steadfast refusal to acknowledge discontinuity in human life, to bear with its surd elements, to take those surd elements seriously in themselves and not simply by virtue of what is expressed and achieved in and through them.

For Green the self-differentiation of the universal mind into its finite centres was an insoluble metaphysical riddle. At one moment indeed he likens it to the old-fashioned theological puzzle, why God should create. But he never so plumbed the mysteries of personal existence as to query the adequacy of an impersonal reason to measure their immensity. Although he was no rationalist in the eighteenth-century manner, he remained unquestioning in his allegiance to the sovereignty and omnipresence of LOGOS. It is for this reason, I think, that as a moralist he ultimately fails.

The Utilitarian, of course, identifies the standpoint of the morally virtuous man with that of the reformer. His fallacy is, as Butler saw, long before Mill wrote his book, that of supposing benevolence to be the whole of virtue. The idealist critic, however, found a virtue in the power to discern and discerning, to express, immanent, rational order. He agreed with the Utilitarian, albeit perhaps unconsciously, in his indifference to the transcendent. Therefore, for all their learning, their achievement, their moral integrity and intellectual acuteness, the idealists never succeed in their writings at least in speaking to our most urgent and most intimate needs. They were men of their time who either ignored the eternal altogether or else had forgotten its infinite qualitative difference from the temporal. We smile at them in a way that we cannot smile at men like Coleridge or Hopkins or Kierkegaard, or to mention one who comes slightly later, Albert Schweitzer. Why is this so ? Because surely the idealists' enthusiasms are dated and there is perhaps nothing quite so stale as last year's political battles. One can never follow the antique drum, but the men who were not afraid to live out the relation of the temporal to the eternal, to endure its burden and its urgency, they still speak, even though to their day and generation they may sometimes have seemed awkward and out of place. One can no more label Coleridge than one can Pascal, and the burden of Hopkins' priesthood, while it tested him to the uttermost, makes him more our contemporary than the master of his college. And more recently, as I've said, Albert Schweitzer has reminded us how little comprehensive our frames of reference are ; how easily they can leave out what really matters.

Or is this question begging ? Such reflections as these inevitably raise in our mind how men can straddle the years. What there is in them as distinct from the ideas they entertained and partly served that gives them significance for us. The trouble with the convinced Utilitarian and with the thorough-going immanentist is that neither can complain if they are swallowed up and forgotten in the passage of years. For by the completeness of their absorption in the passing here and now, neither have allowed us to remember that in the end it is they and others like them (dare we say ourselves among them) that matter and not their ideas or ours. This is not, I hope, to advocate a fashionable contemporary " existential screaming " : it is rather to suggest that a truly humble anonymity is found less in the service of an impersonal idea than in the payment of the total cost of becoming human, with all that it involves of conversion from the bondage of the abstract and the general to the true service of the particular.

It involves men in ways as varied and multiple as there are human beings in the cultivation of a kind of receptivity which queries at once the facility of the reforming mentality and the immanentist's assurance of unbroken rational continuity. That there were such men among the Victorians we know : but what saddens us is the extent to which, when they are articulate, they seem to find no home on the broad highways of Victorian intellectual life. They were then awkward, outcast, at least, as I say, where their intellectual contemporaries were concerned. But perhaps we have to learn that in every age it must be so, or partly so. For it is certainly easier for the writer or thinker to abandon himself to the mood of an age than to live at the point where its passing moments are met by the urgent presence of the eternal. But only those who do live there can speak to us of good and evil, or of the ultimates of personal responsibility. And even then we must remember—and this is most important—it is sometimes the case that those whose experience is deepest, do not speak at all, for they are inarticulate.

The Strands of Unbelief

NOEL ANNAN

" CAN WE believe in Christianity if the Bible has been shown to
be partly compounded of allegory and pious myth ?   Can we
believe that God is good when His child Nature is shown by
Darwin to be cruel ?   If we can no longer believe in Heaven and
Hell, will men lose their moral sense, and will civilised society
perish ? " Open any serious periodical of the 'seventies and you
will find these questions being argued. I say the 'seventies,
because it was then that opinion became decisively secularised
with all the loss and gain that it entailed. But the change did
not come in a decade. Perhaps when we think of Victorian
rationalism we think first of the 'sixties—we think of *Essays and
Reviews* written by the Seven Against Christ ; or the social
ostracism of Bishop Colenso, or of Shaftesbury calling Seeley's
Ecce Homo " the most pestilential book ever vomited from the
jaws of Hell ". Most striking of all, we think of the famous
debate on Darwinism between Huxley and Wilberforce in the
Oxford Museum. The 'sixties would appear to be the crucial
decade—if of course we conveniently forget that *In Memoriam*,
Omar Khayyám, W. R. Greg's *The Creed of Christendom*, and
George Eliot's essays in the *Westminster Review* were published
in the 'fifties. And the decade before that, the 'forties was the
time of Mark Rutherford, the loss of faith by Froude and Clough
and others after Newman's secession to Rome, and it was also
the time of publication by Newman's brother, Francis, of an
open attack on Christianity—the *Phases of Faith*. At no time
during the Victorian Age are doubts stilled or unbelief suspended.
Can we, perhaps, for a few minutes try to unravel the strands of
unbelief ?

The first and oldest strand is political rather than intellectual.
I mean, the old working-class atheism, buttressed by Tom Paine's
and Owen's anti-clericalism and aided by the Philosophic Radicals.

These men argued that religion stood condemned, philosophically by the principle of utility, and politically as the creed of a persecuting middle class, who used Christianity to draw the teeth of popular discontent. Intellectually this cut no ice because it was evident that Evangelicalism was by the crudest Benthamite principles useful and daily changing the face of England, making men sober, respectable and humanitarian. Moreover, Chartism confirmed the prevailing belief that revolutionaries and atheists walk hand in hand, and that unbelief threatens the structure of society. The old atheism took a new form after the failure of the Chartists. George Jacob Holyoake, the great co-operator, who carried on the fight for free thought with Bradlaugh, propagated the creed of Secularism. Secularism was made out of scraps of popular science and positivism : its central tenet was that man could do good only by trying to serve his fellow men, not God. It had a marked effect on working-class education and opinion—and indeed Secularism is one of the parents of that Ethical Socialism which has distinguished the Labour Movement in this country and which has proved a barrier to a purely Marxist interpretation of Socialism. And do not let us forget that in this strand are to be found the martyrs of free thought —the men who were poor enough to be imprisoned and tried for propagating their beliefs.

But though Secularism influenced working-class opinion, it created no intellectual stir. What was it then that secularised middle-class beliefs ? The answer, I think, is the Sense of History, and the Call of Morality.

The nineteenth century made the mistake of worshipping the Muse of History as a goddess. Truth, they believed, was revealed in History, not in the Bible—but like every revelation it required interpretation. Carlyle, for instance, lost his faith in Calvinism and found it in an interpretation of history—remorseless Destiny shapes the Nations and her chains can be broken only by the Hero. Men began to see Truth no longer as absolute, philosophically static, revealed once and for all, but as relative, genetic and evolutionary. The birth of Christ became not *the* event in history, but *an* event on a globe on which Man was a transitory being. It was not Science itself, but Science interpreted *as History* which upset the orthodox Cosmology. Geology told us that the earth existed æons before man existed, and disproved the literal Genesis story of the Creation and the Flood. Darwin implicitly cast doubt on whether life had ever been created. He made one ask : At what precise moment in history had evolving man been given a soul accountable to God ? Moreover, he destroyed the old teleological proof of God which Paley taught : God did not give the duck webbed feet in order to swim, the duck evolved its feet or it would have perished. Physics suggested through the First Law of Thermodynamics that if energy was indestructible there was no need of an Energiser and Physics suggested through the Second Law that the Solar System, so far from being an ever-improving cosmos directed onwards and upwards by a wise God, would in fact run down and the earth would become a frozen lifeless globe when the sun had dissipated its heat. What science did was to offer a picture of history, both in the past before man was, and in the future when he should cease to be. You will have noticed how these scientific hypotheses were given an historical twist. Science repaid the compliment by giving history an added air of infallibility. The rules of weighing evidence, employed by scientists, were used by historians. Now if we can scientifically sift the evidence for the arrival of Julius Cæsar in Britain in 55 B.C., can we not apply the same methods in examining the evidence for certain events said to have occurred in Palestine in A.D. 33 ? Examined in this manner by German theologians, the Bible was found to be riddled with contradictions and uncertainties. It became a fallible record of human events not a God-dictated book. Nor was this all. Historians like Hegel and Marx began to claim that a scientific logic could be deduced from history. Indeed it was in the historiography of an obscure French Polytechnician, Auguste Comte, that Rationalism in England found its oracle. Comte produced an evolutionary interpretation of history, purporting to be deduced from a study of the mathematical and natural sciences. He argued that all thought went through three stages : theological, metaphysical and positive (or scientific). Only in our sociological conceptions do we still retain theological and metaphysical forms of thought —all other sciences have advanced to the positive stage. We must rid ourselves of these outworn creeds and transfer our worship of God to Humanity. Mill suggested that truth, like the species, evolves, and Comte suggested that it was evolving *away*

from Christianity. Thoughtful Victorians were being persuaded
by historians and scientists that the facts of Christianity as described
in the Bible might not be true. This in turn suggested something more. Is it not immoral to believe what the evidence
to hand shows to be false ? And if it is objected that Christianity
is too valuable as a moral system to cast aside, the answer is
plain : examine its central tenets and see if they do not strike
you as immoral.

This brings us to the third strand of Unbelief. Francis
Newman had found much of Christian dogma immoral and
rationalists love him. They found the doctrines of the Atonement, Predestination, Redemption by Grace—which can come
only from God—and Eternal Punishment as horrifying and
wicked. It was wrong of God the Father to demand the death
of His Son to placate his wrath against mankind. It was wrong
of Jesus to have been so evasive and obscure in His teaching.
It was wrong to bribe men to be good by promises of reward
in a world to come. Above all, how can Christians justify the
presence of evil in a God-created world—in a world where
Nature is cruel ; or rather where the laws of God in Nature
contravene human morality, and the laws of human society
discovered by Malthus and the Manchester economists are no
less harsh and revolting ? Mill said: " I will call no Being good
who is not what I mean when I apply that epithet to my fellow-
creatures ; and if such a Being can sentence me to Hell for not
so calling Him, to Hell I will go ". There was a higher belief
than Christianity. Let us be good for good's sake not for God's.
Listen to Huxley writing to Kingsley on the death of his small
son. " As I stood beside the coffin of my little son the other
day, with my mind bent on anything but disputation, the officiat-
ing minister read, as a part of his duty, the words, ' If the dead
rise not again, let us eat and drink for tomorrow we die '. I
cannot tell you how inexpressibly they shocked me. Paul had
neither wife nor child, or he must have known that his alternative
involved a blasphemy against all that was best and noblest in
human nature. I could have laughed with scorn. What !
because I am face to face with irreparable loss . . . I am to re-
nounce my manhood and, howling, grovel in bestiality ?
Why, the very apes know better, and if you shoot their young,
the poor brutes grieve their grief out and do not immediately

seek distraction in a gorge. Kicked into the world as a boy without guide or training, I confess to my shame that few men have drunk deeper of all kinds of sin than I. Happily my course was corrected . . . and for long years I have been slowly and painfully climbing, with many a fall, towards better things. And when I look back what do I find to have been the agents of my redemption ? the hope of immortality and future reward ? I can honestly say that for these fourteen years such a consideration has never entered my head. No, I can tell you what has been at work. *Sartor Resartus* led me to know that a deep sense of religion was compatible with the entire absence of theology. Secondly, science and her methods gave me a resting place, independent of authority and tradition. Thirdly, love opened up to me a view of the sanctity of human nature, and impressed me with a deep sense of responsibility."

Though men like Clough and Fitzgerald wrote of their loss of faith, the rationalists remained quiet until Darwin. But at the debate in Oxford the moral fervour of the Evangelicals passed in a flash from the son of William Wilberforce into the hands of the Agnostics and in the 'seventies the storm broke. For by the 'seventies a group of men, Huxley, Leslie Stephen, John Morley and the brilliant young geometer, W. K. Clifford, set about converting the public in the periodicals with an Evangelical zest. They called themselves Agnostics because they professed that no man could know what Herbert Spencer called the Unknowable—that is the whole realm of thought which lies outside the scientific sphere. If we can know nothing, why not admit it instead of quarrelling about the nature of grace or the relations which exist between the Trinity ? God may exist, or he may not—do not dogmatise. Stephen concentrated on the unreality of religion, Huxley asserted that miracles contravened the laws of nature. One and all stressed—and this is what the Victorians wished to be reassured about—that to give up religion does not mean giving up morality. A man can be moral and yet not acknowledge Christian dogma, and so can a society or nation. Above all, they propagated a theory of belief. Truth is the goal. "The longer I live," wrote Huxley, "the more obvious it is to me that the most sacred act of a man's life is to say and to feel 'I believe such and such to be true'". Truth is attainable in minute quantities if man will dig for it. Truth is protean, always changing her shape, but we can now and then nail her down. We can do this only if we do not chain our hands, fetter our intellect. " No one can be a great thinker," said Mill, " who does not recognise that as a thinker it is his first duty to follow his intellect to whatever conclusions it may lead." Life lays on us a duty, argued Clifford, to doubt and to ask questions—that is how knowledge advances. To stifle doubts is morally wrong ; to preach beliefs which cannot be inferred from the known facts of experience is morally wrong, for it is by our beliefs that we influence our fellow-men and create the world in which future generations will live.

These earnest assertions of faith drew various replies, for example : refined and scholarly Anglo-Catholicism, Matthew Arnold's defence of religion as morality touched by emotion, and William James's Pragmatism. James argued that in fact our beliefs are determined not by our intellect but by our will, which may either be a will to believe or to disbelieve. Quite obviously Agnosticism was not the last word. By the end of the century rationalist cosmos was being undermined. Science no longer admitted a purely mechanical interpretation and many of the scientific laws which Huxley took to be axioms were seen to be metaphysical speculations. Later still, Freudian and Marxist thought threw doubt on the premises of the rationalist. But let us never forget the moral and intellectual work of the Victorian rationalists. We should remember that they were opposing the bigotry and uncritical prejudice of their times. To all criticisms they would have replied that we must always form our beliefs on the best evidence available and that merely to believe what we want to believe and to appeal to the " heart " or to " intuition ", is to give in to a temptation and acquire a frame of mind which may be very dangerous when applied, say, to politics. Victorian rationalism was a faith, like any other kind of belief—a faith built on what were regarded as probabilities. The Agnostics in a sense, were a new Nonconformist sect. They believed that it was valuable to get rid of the concept of Original Sin since you could then frame your laws and order society on the assumption that man is capable of goodness. They believed this to be more healthy than a State run on the assumption that man is irrevocably bad and must be forced to be good. Some went even further like Winwood Reade, the author of *The Martyrdom of Man*, and argued that man was not only good but would get better—that is the old doctrine Shelley preached : the Perfectability of Man. The faith of the Agnostic was perhaps best expressed by W. K. Clifford, who said that we should try " to do as well as possible what we can do best ; to work for the improvement of the social organisation ; to seek earnestly after truth and only to accept provisionally opinions one has not enquired into ; to regard men as comrades in work and their freedom as a sacred thing ; in fact, to recognise the enormous and fearful difference between truth and falsehood, right and wrong, and how truth and right are to be got by free enquiry and the love of our comrades for their own sake and nobody else ". This may not be everyone's creed : but it is a noble confession of faith and worthy of praise.

Qualities of George Eliot's Unbelief

HUMPHRY HOUSE

THE VICTORIANS had a genius for getting themselves into memorable situations, and also for recording such moments—vivid and relevant, pathetic or funny—in the lives of themselves or others. Newman weeping over the gate at Littlemore ; Thomas Arnold the younger, on the eve of election to a Professorship that required him to be an Anglican, overheard by his family once more saying his prayers in Latin ; Mark Pattison meeting Newman in a train just after the publication of *Essays and Reviews ;* Digby Dolben mobbed in Birmingham for wearing a Benedictine habit and sandals ; Holman Hunt dressed like a nervous bandit painting by the shore of the Dead Sea a goat, to become " The Scapegoat" ; Margot Tennant on her knees in prayer with General Booth in a railway carriage ; the Prince of Wales riding into Jerusalem, under the guidance of Dr. Stanley, on the route of the Triumphal Entry ; Marian Evans toiling in her study at Coventry over the last chapters of Friedrich Strauss's *Life of Jesus,* distressed at the analysis of the story of the Crucifixion, looking up at an image of Christ to gather the endurance to go on with it.

Leslie Stephen, in telling the tale of Strauss and the Christ image, added : " To others the image might perhaps have suggested rather remonstrance than encouragement ". But it was entirely characteristic of Marian Evans that it gave her encouragement ; for she can scarcely be called typical in anything. Her skull measured $22\frac{1}{4}$ inches in circumference and was said to be broader from brow to ear than any other recorded skull except Napoleon's. She openly lived, right through the mid-Victorian age, with a man who was not her legal husband. The novels apart, she was not a typical person. Yet her history— her intellectual and spiritual and moral history—exemplifies so many trends and qualities of Victorian thought that she deserves to be considered alone.

It is characteristic of her that she lost her belief in dogmatic Christianity in rather a conservative style, in rather an old-fashioned context. The first phase of her infidelity was not brought on by Strauss or any other German Rationalist, nor by fossils and monkeys and shell-fish : it was rather brought on by the literary-historical tradition of the English eighteenth century. In spite of a few references to geology and to a reading of Mrs. Somerville's *Connexion of the Physical Sciences* it seems that there was very little in the sceptical side of her early thought that would have been unfamiliar to Hume or Gibbon. What would have been unfamiliar, and indeed uncongenial, to them was the intense laborious earnestness with which her scepticism was reached, the moral tone of it. Some causes of this different temper and tone, operative in the country as a whole, can be seen peculiarly active in her own early life.

Evangelicalism, more than anything else, changed the whole temper of society ; and though the religion of her immediate family was a tepid and conventional Church of Englandism, Marian Evans came under powerful Evangelical influence from three different directions; from an aunt, and from mistresses at her two schools. She developed very Puritanical habits and a strong sense of sin and justice and judgment: she abjured worldly pleasures and after reading a Life of Wilberforce determined upon a life of good works as well as good faith so that she should be " sanctified wholly ".

It is not quite clear whether in these years she herself held the typically Calvinist doctrine of Election : but it is certain that she lived much among Calvinists and that she often saw immoral consequences of this doctrine in persons of the Holy Willie and Justified Sinner kind. A woman convicted of lying said : " I do not feel that I have grieved the spirit much ". This not only turned her against Calvinism, but it intensified her own passionate love of truth and consistency. She carried the high moral purposes of her belief into the critique of it. In this, more than anything else, she differed from the eighteenth-century Rationalists. She was passionate and earnest and dutiful where they were amused and easy.

Her literary tastes removed her still further from their mood.

In her sternest religious phase she had rather ironically an admiration for that part of Young's *Night Thoughts* called *The Infidel Reclaimed*. But this was replaced at the age of 20 by a love for Wordsworth. She then bought the Collected Works and set herself down to read them through. " I never before," she said, " met with so many of my own feelings expressed just as I could like them ". This very sentence shows her unconscious stress on the importance of personal feeling. Years later, in the only full-length essay she ever published about a poet—it was in fact a merciless attack on the *Night Thoughts*—her judgment of Young proceeds by implicit reference to Wordsworthian standards. She focuses on Young's neglect of the true qualities of objects described or the emotion expressed ; on his lack of allusions that carry us " to the lanes, woods, or fields " ; and above all on the fact that he is not " true to his own sensibilities or inward vision ". There was a strong strain of Wordsworthianism in her earnestness and in her tendency to treat her own emotions as something sacred. She was never led into the Utilitarian error of underestimating the importance of feeling or into an estimate of ethics as a calculation of pleasure and pain : the inward claims of the sense of duty were overriding and paramount.

She was deeply affected by the sense of history prevailing in her youth. The view of history as linear in time was curiously expressed in a fashion for historical charts. Dr. Stanley made a chart of Early Church History at Christ Church and Marian Evans in Coventry was quite independently working on another, a thing of incredibly ambitious size in about eight parallel columns to cover a period of at least six hundred years ; she planned to publish it ; but long before it was done one was actually published which she thought far superior to her own : as she put it herself, such a chart was " thus evidenced to be a desideratum ". And indeed, if one was to read Joseph Milner's Evangelical *History of the Church of Christ* and the Oxford Tracts and Isaac Taylor's answer to them—all of which Marian Evans read or planned to read—some pictorial guide through the wilderness of Fathers and schisms and sects and heretics and councils and emperors was almost essential. And it seems quite clear that this study of early Christian History in a hunt for the true form of the visible Church, for pure and authentic original

Christianity, was the beginning of her religious doubts. She found that even the early Church was ambiguous and often corrupt.

This is a matter of the greatest importance for the history of the thirties and forties, because it shows how closely linked were the studies and frame of mind of those who became technically infidels and many of those who became technically Roman Catholics. The quickest way to appreciate the closeness of this link is to read Milman's review (reprinted in *Savonarola, Erasmus and Other Essays*) of Newman's *Development of Christian Doctrine*. Newman had stressed the silences, contradictions, imperfections of the early Fathers on vital matters of dogmatic theology in order to argue for the necessity of an infallible Church.

> " We are told that God has spoken. Where ? In a book ? We have tried it, and it *disappoints* ; it disappoints, that most holy and blessed gift, not from fault of its own, but because it is used for a purpose for which it was not given."

These are the words not of Francis Newman, but of John Henry. It is small wonder that Milman commented : " Not content with the Trinity, he fairly throws over the New Testament."

And so Marian Evans too, after getting bogged in the early Fathers, pushed further back to the critique of the Canon of Scripture. She had moved by this time with her father into the town of Coventry, and somehow there came into her hands a copy of Charles Hennell's book *An Enquiry concerning the Origin of Christianity*, which marked a turning-point in her life. It is of great interest that Hennell's book, first published in 1838, was written with little knowledge of the school of German Rationalist Protestants that had flourished for the past two generations. Their lines of thought had themselves in fact derived from Hume and the British Deists. In Britain itself this development had either been forestalled by the Biblical fervours of the Evangelicals, or had been driven, for political reasons and through the slumbrous Toryism of the Universities, into the by-ways of national life. The eighteenth-century rationalist tradition ran on through such men as Godwin, Tom Paine, Priestley, Richard Carlile and Shelley—most of all through the

Liberal Unitarians—and it was in this context that Marian Evans met it in Coventry with Hennell's book. Within a short time of reading it she met the author at the house of his brother-in-law Charles Bray. These two men and their wives and sisters and friends determined the main direction of her thought for life.

The two men were complementary. Hennell was primarily interested in history and Bray in philosophy. The main argument of Hennell's *Enquiry* is directed to meet the common orthodox theory that the rise of Christianity cannot be explained except on the supposition of its miraculous divine origin. He explains the life of Jesus in the religious context of the Essenes and the political hopes of Judas Maccabæus. Under the influence of the Messianic expectation, he says, Jesus came to believe that He was the Promised One ; He was put to death by the Romans for political reasons on the advice of the Jewish authorities anxious to preserve the public peace. The middle part of the book is a discussion of the dates and credibility of the Gospels, emphasising their " scantiness and mixed nature ". Underlying the statement that they are " loaded with miraculous additions " is the principle that " those miracles which cannot be resolved into natural events probably owe their miraculous part to the exaggeration or the invention of the narrators."

Now such a principle plainly implies not only a historical belief in the necessity of evidence but also a belief in the *a priori* unlikelihood of miracles ; and it seems improbable that Marian Evans would have fallen so easily to Hennell's history if Bray's philosophy had not been there to support it. Bray was a necessitarian who had been influenced by Shelley's notes to *Queen Mab*. His views on the connection between physical and mental behaviour had been much affected by a belief in the phrenology of George Coombe, a belief which Marian Evans for a time at least shared. Exactly how far she ever accepted his whole philosophy it is hardly possible to be sure ; but she seems to have accepted the principle of an " undeviating law ", that is an " invariability of sequence " in both the material and the moral world ; but such steps do not lead far towards a full philosophy.

At least she accepted once and for all the hypothesis that miraculous interventions do not occur in the course of Nature. With this, through the lines of argument developed by Hennell, fell the whole structure of dogmatic Christianity, Incarnation, Resurrection, Trinity, Atonement and all. Sitting on the bearskin under the acacia on the lawn at Rosehill, Coventry, a young Victorian had lost one faith. Her eyes glowed with the faith and hope that she had gained. For it was to her a great release, a great advance, a great moral triumph. It was victory for the virtue she held dearest of all—the love of truth, of truth dependent on the empirical study of evidence, of truth too dependent on fidelity to one's own feelings.

Before long the chance came to use her new-won experience for the benefit of others : in the cause of this truth she could employ her knowledge of German. She undertook to continue the translation of Strauss's *Leben Jesu,* which one of her new friends had begun. Strauss was then the latest representative of the German school of Rationalistic Protestantism in fear of which H. J. Rose and Pusey became in effect the founders of the Anglo-Catholic revival. He rejected as crude the theory that Jesus and his disciples were deliberate deceivers, because it failed to take into account the characteristics of the religious mind. He also rejected the theory (chiefly associated with Paulus of Heidelberg) that all the miracles can be explained on purely naturalistic grounds. He maintained that the Gospels contained a nucleus of historical fact, but that the miraculous elements had been imported in the spirit of the religious thought of the time in which they were written. The early disciples unconsciously attributed to Jesus miraculous powers and supernatural claims, in order to glorify Him as their teacher and vindicate Him as the fulfiller of prophecy. The Gospels thus showed the early stages of the growth of a great religious myth. The historical man Jesus was elevated into the Christ ; and Christianity was built on the " Christ Myth ". This thesis is plainly similar to Hennell's, and Strauss in fact arranged for Hennell's *Enquiry* to be translated into German, and he himself wrote a preface for it.

George Eliot, broadly speaking, accepted Strauss's view, however much she disliked the details and tone of his book. She found the relentless unemotional debunking of miracle after miracle unsympathetic to her sense of beauty and to the symbolic fitness of things. It upset the strain in her that loved Wordsworth and valued the feelings. In February 1846 she said she was

" Strauss-sick ", that it made her ill dissecting the beautiful story of the Crucifixion ; and that she could only endure it by looking at the Christ image. In the last hundred pages she felt that Strauss had had his say, and that even he himself was fagged. In March she wrote : " The Crucifixion and the Resurrection are at all events better than the bursting asunder of Judas ".

And then, in a letter dated July 30th, 1863, when Renan's *Life of Jesus* had just been published and she herself was a famous woman, she wrote :

> " For minds acquainted with the European culture of this last half century, Renan's book can furnish no new result ; and they are likely to set little store by the too facile construction of a life from the materials of which the biographical significance becomes more dubious as they are closely examined. It seems to me the soul of Christianity lies not at all in the facts of an individual life, but in the ideas of which that life was the meeting-point and the new starting-point. We can never have a satisfactory basis for the history of the man Jesus, but that negation does not affect the idea of the Christ either in its historical significance or in its great symbolic meanings."

The new Humanism had incorporated the world religions. For George Eliot, Christianity had lost its basis in history, and it had lost its claim to dogmatic certainty ; but it remained the most relevant and moving symbolism for the mysteries of life.

Unbelief and Science

J. BRONOWSKI

THE STRANDS of belief and unbelief in the Victorian conscience are bewildering in number and variety ; how did that age think of so many infinitesimal points of principle ? How did the sluggish waters of eighteenth century tolerance and even indifference become suddenly agitated in a hundred sectarian cross-currents ?

The answer is that the Victorian Age was above all else an age of enquiry : of enquiry and of decision. We picture the age by its family men, sleek, prosperous, and respectable, their every thought conventional. Nothing could be further from the truth. We have the appearance right, but we have missed the biography. Ricardo or Meredith, Pollock or Palmerston, known or unknown, these men had begun by being restless, adventurous and questioning. They differed from the doubters of our age because they not only looked for answers but found them, to their satisfaction ; and having once found them, they acted on them with assurance for the rest of their lives. Enquiry and decision : this is what made Edmund Gosse break with the Plymouth Brothers, yet made so great a scientist as Faraday a member of the obscure sect of Sandemannians. This made the strangely uniform pattern of steadfast nonconformity.

Enquiry made the Victorians restless, but decision made them as revolutionary as those earlier Nonconformists, the Puritans. The revolution which the Victorians perpetuated was of course the Industrial Revolution. The special form of that revolution in the Victorian Age was science. Enquiry and decision are in fact the method of science. At the end of the eighteenth century William Blake had raged on behalf of Tom Paine against the petty scientific carping of an eminent but unscrupulous chemist and divine, Richard Watson, the Bishop of Llandaff. That disreputable phase of rationalist enquiry in defence of the *status quo* was now past ; the Industrial Revolution had tipped it decisively with iron. Science had become experimental and empirical, the search for evidence as a basis for decision. The point is made by W. K. Clifford, the most lucid of all the Victorian expositors of science, and I will quote him :

> " Remember, then, that scientific thought is the guide of action ; that the truth at which it arrives is not that which we can ideally contemplate without error, but that which we may act upon without fear ; and you cannot fail to see that scientific thought is not an accompaniment or condition of human progress, but human progress itself."

Clifford's last words take the thought one step farther. When science becomes empirical, when it moves from enquiry to decision and so to fresh enquiry, then it ceases to be scholastic and becomes progressive.

These thoughts may now seem very abstract and remote. But they were actual to the Victorian man in the street, even though they were unspoken and largely unconscious. For he saw day by day science remaking the world about him. He saw it in steamers and in bridges, he saw it in gas light and the ticker tape. And though much of this spectacular growth was mere engineering work, the man in the street saw a great deal of real science too : electro-magnetism, anæsthetics, the discovery of the causes of infection, the synthesis of organic products, the prediction of the whereabouts of undiscovered planets, the first studies in inheritance and in population statistics ; and the brilliant work on sound and light and electricity and energy and the behaviour of fluids and many similar topics by the great English mathematicians—for mathematics in Victorian England had no truck with Continental finesse, and was confined solidly to work in practical physics. Finally, there were the two intellectual crises which no one could escape : geology and evolution.

These two issues, first the age of the earth and then the descent of man, have dominated the landscape of Victorian unbelief. But they were effective only because science as a whole had come to be respected and believed. They were the hammerhead ; the blow which they carried was the success of the whole of science. Out of the geological disputes of the beginning of the century had grown the British Association whose object was to make science understood by laymen. And it was at a British Association meeting that the famous showdown about evolution in Oxford in 1860 between Bishop Wilberforce and Thomas Huxley was fought and won. What was challenged there and what triumphed was not evolution alone but science. The age of the earth and the descent of man merely happened to be issues which laymen could grasp. Laymen and scientists seized them because here they shared what is usually the real lack between them, a common language of discussion.

This point is so important that I must stop to underline it. Noel Annan has remarked that the major issues of which we are speaking, say geology and evolution, were historical as well as scientific. And Humphry House has traced the influence of the historical enquiries by the German Bible critics on such people as George Eliot. This is entirely just. But George Eliot was not a typical Victorian. What impressed the typical Victorian was the achievement of science. Naturally, the ideas of science could touch him only where they met ideas which were already familiar to him, usually historical ideas about the Bible. History was the only language which he shared with the scientist. But as a form of knowledge, history was to the man in the street merely negative and critical, a method of enquiry. The doubts which it had held had been the leisurely, cynical, eighteenth-century doubts of Gibbon. By contrast the scientist spoke with authority, and the authority was conferred not by the historical language but by the success of science visible in a hundred solid practical fields. Science was positive, science was decision and action, science was on the offensive. Science might become the god to displace a god.

After the Oxford squabble, therefore, the believers realised that they must learn to understand the new ideas of science. For this purpose they founded in 1869 the Metaphysical Society, brilliant with almost every serious thinker of the time : Gladstone and Tennyson, Cardinal Manning and Ruskin, the Archbishop of York and Dr. Martineau. Clifford stood for atheism ; he was one of the young scientists who were giving distinction to the new London colleges because their unbelief had made them ill at ease at Oxford and Cambridge. The agnostics included Tyndall, John Morley and Leslie Stephen, and they were of course led by Huxley. Indeed, Huxley coined the word

" agnostic " to define his position in the Metaphysical Society.

The word " agnostic " has a negative air, so much less down-right than Clifford's atheism. But Clifford was a generation younger than Huxley, and his battle had been fought in that generation by Huxley. There was nothing negative about Huxley, who fought for whatever he believed to be true ; and who believed that his first duty was to demolish what he could demonstrate to be false. He never flinched from a challenge. At one of the first meetings of the Metaphysical Society it was proposed that everyone should avoid " expressions of moral disapprobation ". Thereupon W. G. Ward, the disciple of Newman and leader of the clerical party in the Society, said, " While acquiescing in this condition as a general rule, I think it cannot be expected that Christian thinkers shall give no sign of the horror with which they would view the spread of such extreme opinions as those advocated by Mr. Huxley ". Huxley's reply was characteristic : " As Dr. Ward has spoken, I must in fairness say that it will be very difficult for me to conceal my feeling as to the intellectual degradation which would come of the general acceptance of such views as Dr. Ward holds ".

Huxley spoke in this way not because he liked such battles— he did not ; he detested them, and they made him ill. But he felt himself to be the spokesman of all those who did not possess his gift of speech : whether they were shy like Charles Darwin, or inarticulate like the unbelievers in the Mechanics' Institutes. For we must never forget that below the bland and barbed exchanges of the Metaphysical Society was the anticlerical tradition of English working men since the days of Tom Paine. In ancient Rome, Christianity had once been a new hope to the dispossessed. Wesley had revived that hope in the eighteenth century. But Methodism in Victorian England had become what Wesley himself had feared, the religion of success. The men in the Mechanics' Institutes turned from it to unbelief.

Huxley and Tyndall spoke for these men, practical, rational, the new craftsmen of the machines. Both were themselves such men : born poor, without University education, and deliberately slighted by Universities and by society. But they spoke with the authority of science, and therefore made a deeper mark than propagandists like Bradlaugh. They made their mark on continental as well as English working men, because it happened that the outstanding German socialists, Marx and Engels, then lived in England. Engels in particular took up the new scientific ideas with gusto, and read avidly and very intelligently in such out-of-the-way subjects as anthropology.

Meanwhile, in respectable circles, the Metaphysical Society marked the end of the period of indignation among Victorian believers. After this, the new scientific attitude to belief became first tolerated, then accepted and in the end respectable. Unbelief did not triumph; it has not triumphed today, for in England and elsewhere eight or nine people out of ten still think of themselves as believers. But unbelief came to be recognised as an established and a reasonable way of looking at the world. Belief became what it is today, informal and little practised and rather negative. Under the showy to and fro of Victorian debate, Huxley and Clifford and Tyndall and their fellow-scientists had undermined the popular basis of belief almost unnoticed and left it hollow and ready for a landslide.

I have said that they made unbelief respectable, and I mean this quite literally. They had discovered that it was impossible to produce evidence, in the scientific sense, for let us say the Biblical miracles or the existence of God. Even when they persuaded believers of this, the believers replied that only God could define good and evil, and that only the fear of God could make men do good and shun evil. No, replied Huxley and John Stuart Mill and George Eliot and Bagehot; *we* are plainly all people of the highest rectitude; and therefore the moral sense must be inborn in every man. One consequence was that they felt personally bound to live lives of quite monumental dullness even when they sinned. This constraint made them martyrs to headache and indigestion and left them nervously exhausted, locked in a somewhat ridiculous posture of premature immortality.

More than anything else, this air of stuffed and embarrassed solemnity has made them strangers to us. We are ill at ease with the division between what Christopher Dawson at the beginning of this series called their social conformity and their intellectual non-conformity. This is ironical, because their moral dilemma has now grown to be the great ethical problem of our own age. For the fears of the believers within the Metaphysical Society have so far proved just. Science has destroyed the authority of the traditional moral codes and discovered them to be no more than social habits. As social habits they might have survived—as so eminently Victorian an agnostic as Bertrand Russell would have them survive—they might have survived, had not that very discovery set in motion profound changes in society and its habits. In the result, science has appeared to have nothing to offer in place of those fallen absolutes but claptrap : enlightened self-interest, the greatest happiness of the greatest number, the survival of the fittest, and the withering away of the State.

I believe that this is a critical but a temporary irresolution. It is the great ethical search of our day, and it has made many despair of science. They think of science only as a destroyer, and they ask, What positive values can it offer ? I believe that there are good answers to that question, and that these answers begin at Huxley's and Clifford's and Bagehot's faith in an innate, human moral sense. That is, I believe that we shall begin to find a source of value when we turn science to the scrutiny of man : when we build on an understanding of what makes him man and not some other kind of animal, and what makes his societies human and not animal packs. Only so, from the pangs of our generations, shall we isolate and re-create a body of human values.

Some belief of this kind sustained these uncompromising great men through their prophetic, personal pangs. They were confident of the outcome of the moral crisis, because they knew themselves to be honest, tolerant, searching and humble at once, men of good mind and good will. They knew themselves to be liberators in the widest sense, in the classroom, at Working Men's lectures, on public boards, in public health and comfort as well as education. They freed and liberalised and inspired men to be above everything men, unswerving, in enquiry and in decision together, the thought and the act of a piece. More than any other generation of scientists, they tried to make themselves not experts but whole men. That is how they brought science out of the laboratory into public affairs, and why they did not shirk the public clashes. The moral and the social problems which they thereby created are urgent today, but not more urgent and more challenging than their example.

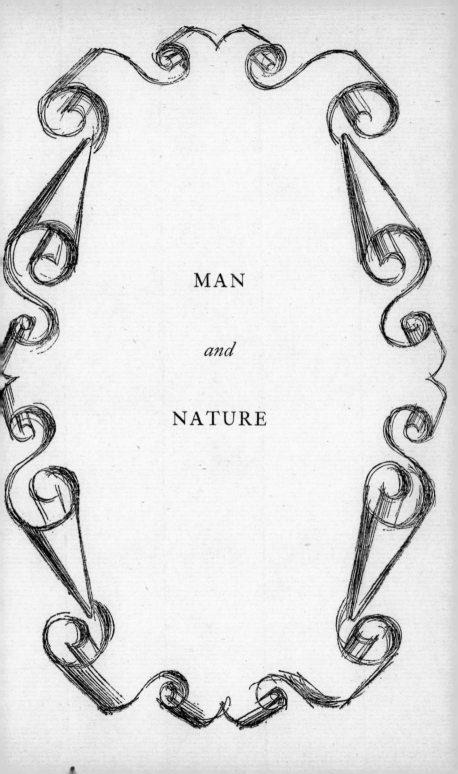

MAN

and

NATURE

Man and Nature

CANON C. E. RAVEN

THE MOST characteristic and, I suppose, still the most important of the "ideas and beliefs" of the Victorians are those which reveal the tensions created by the progress of science and concerning the relation of man to nature—those crises of which Dr. Bronowski spoke recently. We are all familiar with the controversies summed up in words like "Genesis or Geology", or dealing with the Origin of Species, or with Miracles and the Gadarene swine ; and we realise that these represent successive phases in the same basic problem. But here is something not so obvious. These particular and closely connected issues are themselves only the chief contemporary expressions of a development which had already been taking place for some three hundred years, and the end of which is not yet in sight. It is with this large issue, the relation of Man to Nature, that we are concerned this evening. To understand it we must go back far into the history of our Western civilisation.

All three sources of that civilisation bequeathed to it a strong conviction of the worth and significance of nature and of history ; the Hebrews emphasised its religious value, the Greeks its intellectual importance, the Romans its practical utility. In the earliest Christian thinkers as in the New Testament this was fully recognised. But, for causes which are easily discoverable, this joy in nature was replaced by an increasing tendency to contrast the natural with the supernatural, to treat this world as corrupt and worthless, and to see in it nothing but the stage on which the traditional drama of man's fall and redemption was being played out. The works of the Lord in which the psalmist had rejoiced, the study of plants and animals which Aristotle and Theophrastus had initiated, the concrete development of natural resources which the engineers of Rome had planned, these lost their interest ; and throughout the whole mediæval period they were almost wholly ignored. Natural history became mere fable, human history mere legend : nature was interpreted in terms of dogma and in the interest of edification.

It was the effort to recover a true appreciation of man's environment that inspired the great movement of human awakening of which the Renaissance, the Reformation and the beginnings of Science are the successive phases. It is wholly inadequate to ascribe the origin of science to pioneers like Copernicus or Vesalius, or to brilliant thinkers like Galileo or Newton. Science began when a multitude of obscure enquirers set themselves to recapture the ancient wisdom of Greece and of Rome, to test the mediæval tradition in the light of that wisdom and then to investigate afresh the world of nature. We can see the contrast between the classical and the mediæval in every department of life—in religion, in literature, in medicine, in politics, in the social order and in the individual's way of living. Science in the modern or narrow sense of the word is one aspect of a process vastly larger than the activities of astronomers or alchemists, mathematicians or biologists. What was happening was the replacement of one concept of man's environment by another ; and the concepts were so sharply contrasted that the change effected a revolution in all human affairs.

It was in the seventeenth century that the process became conscious and rapid ; but at the time (and indeed I think even down to our own enlightened epoch) the two outlooks existed side by side ; and for most men they were inextricably intertwined.

The cosmology of the mediæval tradition of *Paradise Lost*, and the cosmology of the *New Philosophy* or *Religio Medici* stood face to face. On the Continent they were too frequently at war. Fortunately in Britain there was no desire to persecute : indeed the best Christian men of the time, Wilkins and Boyle and Ray and Newton and a score of others, were champions of science : and by the end of the century it looked as if the conflict was over and the change to the new fully secured. The whole future of mankind would have been different if only that result had been achieved.

In the reaction—that curious failure of intellectual and moral quality which blighted the country in the 1720's—two far-reaching trends arose : first, science became increasingly mathematical, mechanistic, quantitative—as it still in large measure remains ; and secondly, religion failed to adjust its formularies to the new knowledge, fell back upon authoritarian and traditional beliefs, and tended to base its claims upon the contrast between nature and revelation. During the subsequent century science invented the steam-engine and produced the industrial revolution ; religion made almost no use of the new knowledge and little contribution to the new social order ; the intellectual life of the age strove to keep its seat upon two horses which, if not yet facing in opposite directions, were already moving along quite different roads. The Miltonic cosmology, with its doctrine of the " novity " of the world ; the definition of a species as " that which came in the beginning from the hand of God " ; the concept of creation as an act and of the universe as the theatre for the drama of man's fall and redemption—all these were increasingly inconsistent not only with the known data of astronomy, geology and biology, but with any worthy philosophy or satisfying faith.

To describe the issue so is, of course, to stress only its intellectual and academic aspect. Its poignancy for the Victorians was due to the mass of emotional and practical accompaniments which attached themselves to it, Science was beginning to mean industrialism ; and industrialism had captured the imagination of European man as a short-cut to Eldorado, an infinite source of power, an obvious and unquestionable beatitude. In spite of the defilement of the countryside, the proliferation of slumdom, the horrors of the mines and mills, the disillusionment of the " hungry 'forties ", industrialism and the machine claimed and received almost divine honours ; and science was the high-priest of the new religion. If the old religion had identified itself with a protest against such apostasy it might at least have been true to its mission. Unfortunately, it was concerned less with this world than with the next ; it was shocked and scared by the comparatively mild protests of Tom Paine or Francis Place or Lord Shaftesbury ; and it spent more time in stoning its prophets, Buckland or Maurice or Colenso, and disputing about its ceremonial, than in studying and interpreting the new world which was now its environment. Do not let me be misunderstood. I have no sympathy with the people who denounce industrialism as wholly evil or think that we can return to the hand-loom and the horse. Whatever its cost in human suffering, machine-power has at least broken down the barriers of geography, made mankind one, and enabled an immense increase and enlargement of all human life. Similarly, the religious debates about the validity of " orders " or the legality of ritual, trivial as they must seem in face of the huge issues which they tended to obscure, were in fact the shape in which protests were made against the abuse of mechanical power and on behalf of other than commercial values —a shape dictated by previous circumstances which, then as now, conditioned the form and fixed the arena of the conflict. That neither party was fully conscious of the real struggle, and that in consequence there was much wastage and much frustration, is hardly more true of the Victorian Age than of any other period of large-scale transition.

A new tension, however, was arising in regard to the scientific interpretation of nature. If nature was native to man, then man must be native to nature—and perhaps was nothing more than a specialised bit of matter, a transient animal, of the earth earthy. Until the Victorian Age this particular doubt had hardly arisen. Sir Thomas Browne and all his contemporaries in the seventeenth century had insisted that man was " the great Amphibium ", partly of earth, partly of heaven ; even Descartes had sharply distinguished him from the animals by providing him with a soul and a soul's appropriate instrument. Only when Lyell and the geologists of the Victorian Age began to suggest linkage between one order of creatures and another, and when ideas of evolution suggested that Adam had not been created literally by the hand of God and in God's own image, did the threat to human dignity and status become obvious. Even then it was slow in manifesting itself. Tennyson might hint in *In Memoriam* that nature " red in tooth and claw " claimed man as a subject of her own laws, and that his belief that he was more than dust might prove illusory. But when Wilberforce taunted Huxley with descent from an ape he evidently regarded the suggestion as in fact a *reductio ad absurdum* of the whole case for Darwinism. It is difficult for us to appreciate the full horror of the position when Darwin's *The Origin of Species* was followed by his *The Descent of Man*, and the " child of God "found himself not merely " a little lower than the angels " but a member of the brute creation, a monkey that had somehow developed an upright posture and a frontal cortex. Every doctrine of evolution has of course to provide not only for continuity of process but for the emergence of novelty. Of that we have now become aware. But it was difficult when science was triumphantly demonstrating the former, not to forget and ignore the necessity of the emergence of novelty.

But it is time to look at the effect which this deep antithesis in the basic outlook upon life had upon the character of the age. How did the great Victorians react to these two tensions ? If we take four typical exponents of Victorian biological science we shall see how diverse and how significant was their response.

Take first the veteran naturalist, source of these albums of seaweeds and collections of shells which some of us have inherited from our great-aunts, Philip Henry Gosse. His character alternately commended and condemned by his son, Edward, was deeply if narrowly religious, and genuinely and very energetically scientific. He was sufficiently competent as a geologist to know the testimony of the rocks ; as a working botanist and zoologist he had all the evidence for evolution under his own eyes. Yet to this he was not only blind but totally hostile. The perpetuity of specific characters was to him, so late as 1857, an axiom. In that year he published his " attempt to untie the geological knot "—so he described it—the book called *Omphalos*. In it he defined " the course of nature as a circle ", and creation as " the sudden bursting into a circle " ; and he dismissed all the evidence of stratification and fossils and vestigial organs as pointing to what he called a " prochronic " phase in which (presumably) the course of the world was proceeding in the mind of God. The details of his hypothesis are unimportant : the more so as he had collected in his first chapter a number of similar attempts to reconcile Genesis with geology. It is enough for us to note that since his time many more myths of this sort have been invented. Charles Kingsley disposed of this type of solution by saying that it " represented God as a sort of deceiver. "

If Gosse cut his knot by imagining a fantastic account of Creation, Charles Darwin, in the strenuous effort of elaborating his great theory, sacrificed his power of appreciation in any fields except those immediately related to his own researches. Few " Confessions " in all literature are more moving, I think, than the pages of his autobiography in which he recounts the price that he had had to pay for intense concentration upon his own scientific work. First his love of music, then his sense of wonder, then his consciousness of God—these had disappeared ; and with them, as his letters only too plainly reveal, had gone the power to see evidence which told against his own theory or to state a coherent argument against data which did not fit into his own case. To read his comments upon the objections raised against his theory by Asa Gray or J. A. Lowell is to realise the truth of his own saying : " It is an accursed evil for men to become so absorbed in any subject as I am in mine ".

These two, Gosse and Darwin, are typical of those who shut their eyes to one or other side of the evidence. More interesting in his reaction to the dilemma is Thomas Henry Huxley— Huxley the champion of Darwin and of Agnosticism, the hero of Dr. Bronowski's recent talk. Huxley was a man of strong though not very fully-trained mind and of equally strong ethical consciousness—one of those who, in an age of transition, could neither live with religion nor live without it. He saw far more clearly than most of his contemporaries that to reject religious faith would be to imperil if not to destroy sanctions for ethical conduct : his mind forced him to materialism, his conscience refused to let him behave like a beast or like a machine. The consequent tension expressed itself in his case in outbreaks of denunciation or outbreaks of self-pity ; and the effort to resolve it led to the inconsistencies of his Romanes lecture and the futilities of his controversy with Gladstone.

Yet a fourth type of response can be seen in another Victorian naturalist, Charles Kingsley. Kingsley was less technically expert in science than the other three, but he had a much wider outlook. As poet and novelist, philosopher and historian, reformer and preacher, he brought to the critical problem something of the integrative philosophy and profound insight of his friend, F. D. Maurice. His theology, though originally narrowly Protestant, developed under the influence of the great Christian Platonists of the early Greek Church, and of his friend, and of men who saw the whole cosmic process as evolutionary and educative, and who loved to trace the operation of the divine Reason through all the course of nature and history. Thus, unlike Gosse, he was able from the first to welcome Darwin's theory : it was nothing strange to him. " Men find," he wrote, " that now they have got rid of an interfering God—a master-magician, as I call it—they have to choose between the absolute empire of accident and a living, immanent, ever-working God ".

Although he had not the ability to formulate a complete statement of his position, it is clear that, just as he insisted that Christianity if true at all must be capable of supplying the principles of a righteous social order, so he was equally convinced that it must be consistent with the evidence supplied by the study of nature. To the study of nature he had been devoted from childhood ; in it he recognised a high educational and religious value ; to it he contributed very largely, both by his books and by initiating the foundation of the myriad Natural History Societies which were modelled upon that which he started at Chester. At a time when the conflict between religion and science was in danger of being accepted as axiomatic, no one did more than Kingsley to convince his fellow Christians and to testify to the world that science and religion, if rightly interpreted, " belonged together ".

The comparison of these four men, each to some degree an expert in biological science and each very certainly a man of education and influence, should express more vividly than abstract description the deep-seated perplexity of the Victorian Age. If its leaders were confused and self-contradictory, its common folk could hardly be expected to understand what was happening. "*Laissez-faire*," " muddle through," " it'll all come right in the end " : man's hopes are apt to rise in proportion as his powers to foresee and control events are weakened, especially if material prosperity accompanies intellectual and moral decline. Outwardly the growth of a purely materialistic outlook was promoted by the wealth, comfort and achievement of the Victorians ; inwardly the rebellion against it was not supported by any coherent philosophy or any religion which at once convinced men of its relevance and constrained them by its inspiration. They accepted the solid successes of science with complacency, and in their moments of exaltation either " faintly trusted the larger hope " or else assured one another rather loudly that the secret of England's greatness was still the Bible and the throne.

Evolution and Human Progress

JULIAN HUXLEY

THE IDEA of human progress took shape long before the discovery of biological evolution, but it was natural and inevitable that the two concepts should be brought into close relation, and each, in fact, has influenced the other. The naïve concept of the inevitability of human progress or at least its inevitability under certain simple conditions, such as a little more science and technology and a little more education for everybody, was carried over into biology, and made certain biologists and philosophers affirm that evolution was always, or essentially, progressive. Conversely, evolutionary facts, such as the steady development of the horse family from humble and insignificant ancestors into the noble and efficient forms of later geological times, or the gradual emergence on the evolutionary scene of ever higher forms of life—vertebrate later than invertebrate, mammal later than reptile, man latest of all—seem to be guarantees of the inevitability of biological progress : and this, of course, reinforced the optimistic point of view about human progress.

But there is another side to the picture, as we all know only too well—that disbelief in human progress, whether inevitable or otherwise, has been immensely strengthened by the events of the last few decades ; and meanwhile the spirit of criticism, even of denial, had raised its head among the evolutionists. Some went so far as to deny that any organism was either higher or lower than any other. Others pointed to the undoubted fact that most changes of type discovered by paleontologists, like that of the horses, although progressive in the restricted sense of giving improved efficiency, were only one-sided improvements, and also that they were limited since they eventually came to a stop. Still others stressed the equally undoubted fact that most evolutionary lines end in extinction ; and the most pessimistic of all have reminded us that our planet will eventually become less and less capable of supporting life, so that there will be an eventual extinction of animals and plants, beginning with the highest but eventually overtaking all. And these two negative points of view, of course, again reinforced each other : the disbelievers in human progress asking why we should believe in progress in man if it was absent in other organisms ; the disbelievers in biological progress pointing to the chaos and aggression of the period of the two great wars as a refutation of any idea of progress, biological or otherwise. The controversy, in fact, looked as if it were degenerating into a philosophical slanging match with no hope of a decision one way or the other. But philosophical slanging matches sometimes get resolved by the march of new scientific discoveries. Sometimes this cuts the ground from under the feet of both sides by showing that the question at issue is one which should never have been asked at all. Thus, when a plague or pestilence breaks out, we can no longer ask the question why God is angry, because we know that it is caused naturally by the spread of a bacterium or a louse. We no longer ask the question why God should have created venomous snakes or noxious insects, since we know that they were not deliberately created at all but have evolved through the automatic processes of natural selection.

In other cases, science may give irresistible arms to one side in the shape of previously unknown facts. Thus the dispute which once raged about the Golden Age could be settled by the demonstration, through the facts of paleontology and pre-history, that an original Golden Age never existed, and that the life of the first human beings must indeed have been, in Hobbes' words, " nasty, brutish and short ".

The progress controversy has now been settled in principle. As between the "pros" and the "cons", the "cons" have been beaten on the basic issue ; we now know that progress does occur. But on a secondary issue, the " pros ", or at least the most violent section among them, have also been beaten. Progress exists, yes, but it is neither universal nor unlimited nor, in any given case, inevitable. And finally a new slant has been given to the question—a new alignment forced upon the contending parties. Although human progress and biological progress are both parts of general evolution, yet we cannot transfer principles or conclusions directly from one field to the other ; for the mechanism of evolution differs as between animals and man, and therefore its results differ too.

The new scientific facts—mostly established during the last half-century—which have settled the Victorian controversy over progress, are drawn from many subjects and from many fields. There is first the actual course pursued by biological evolution, with facts drawn not only from geology and paleontology, but also from comparative anatomy and systematics. Then there is the mechanism of biological evolution, with facts drawn from genetics, psychology, and again systematics.

From the human side of the fence there is the same sort of division. First, the course of human evolution, with facts provided by paleontology, archæology, social anthropology, prehistory and, of course, history ; and then the method of human evolution, to which contributions have come not only from history and anthropology, but also many other disciplines in the human sciences, including psychology.

What then has science — recent science — to say on the question ? First, and most important for our purpose, is the establishment of progress as an evolutionary fact. We can today reconstruct, with a reasonable degree of certainty, the actual course of evolution, especially of animal evolution in its later phases, where abundant fossil documentation on the one hand, and, on the other, intensive taxonomic study of existing groups, have provided many accurate and detailed examples. As a result we can now distinguish three main kinds of evolution. One is the production of detailed variety; every generic type of animal or plant splits up into a number of separate species, as the units of evolution are called. The differences between these species of a given genus or family may be apparently fortuitous, or they may be adaptive—adaptations to local conditions or to a particular way of life ; but by and large they seem irrelevant to the longer-term trends of evolution—a sort of embroidery or frill of minor difference on themes of major significance. Of the long-range trends of evolution, the great majority are of the type to which I have already referred in the horse stock—trends towards improvement of efficiency in a particular one-sided way of life. We call them specialisations. The modern horse is better adapted than its ancestor to swift running and to eating grass, but less well adapted to life in forests or to skulking in herbage or to any other kind of diet ; and then they are limited in time—limited indeed by their very nature. There comes a moment when the stock is incapable of further improvement for its particular way of life. It has, by its very specialisation, cut itself off from other ways of life, and so it either persists in the same specialised form, sometimes for ten or even for hundreds of millions of years, or else becomes totally extinct.

But, finally, there is another, much rarer, type of long-term trend—in the direction of all-round instead of one-sided improvement. A very general example of this is the gradual adaptation of plants and animals to living on land instead of in water.

Perhaps a better illustration is provided by the evolution of land animals themselves. The moist-skinned amphibians, condemned to spend part of their life-history in the water, gave rise to one branch among many, which had dry hard skin, and produced tough-shelled eggs in which the embryos could develop safely, each in their own private pond, until ready to embark on a terrestrial existence. This was the ancestral branch of all the reptiles. It was not better fitted for one particular specialised way of life, but to land life in general.

The reptiles repeated the process. They branched out into specialisations of all sorts : pterosaurs specialised for the air, ichthyosaurs and plesiosaurs for the water ; tortoises specialised for protection ; dinosaurs specialised for every form of land existence ; and also to another branch which developed fur and warm blood, protection for the young inside the mother's body before birth, and milky nourishment after birth ; in fact, the ancestral mammals. These again were not specialised for any particular way of life, but represented an all-round improvement for the general business of living efficiently on land ; and just as the reptiles ousted the amphibian as dominant type in the Permian, so at the end of the Cretaceous the majority of reptile lines became extinct or much reduced in numbers and the mammals launched out on their dominant career.

It is such trends that have a right to be called " progressive ", and, by analysing their natures, we can today give a scientific definition of biological progress. Biological progress consists in the raising of the upper level attained by life in regard to certain of its properties, notably greater control over outer environment, greater independence of outer change, greater internal harmony and self-regulation, and greater capacity for experience, whether of knowing, feeling or willing. In other words, progress consists of all-round improvement in vital organisation. But—and the "but" is important—without shutting the door on further possibilities of progressive advance. Furthermore, this type of evolution is brought about (like all other evolutionary change) by the purely natural and automatic method of the natural selection of mutations and their combinations.

Here is something of great philosophic importance. Progress exists in the world quite apart from man. It is a rare phenomenon, but it appears to have been inevitable under certain definite conditions throughout the entire thousand million years of life's existence.

The second major contribution science has made to our problem in the last quarter-century is that evolution, in the sense in which it is usually applied—the changes undergone by animals and plants during geological time—is only one phase of a much more comprehensive and indeed perhaps an all-embracing evolutionary process. This process of general evolution can be divided into three main sectors : the inorganic, the organic and the human, each characterised by its own methods, its own tempo, and its own type of results.

Inorganic evolution is the story of the changes undergone by lifeless matter in the universe at large. Stars and galaxies evolve, but they do so with appalling slowness, over periods of time to be measured by thousands of millions of years. Furthermore, they reach only a very low degree of organisation. Indeed, only in isolated parts of the cosmos has matter ever been able to reach the molecular level, and only on our earth, and perhaps on a few other planetary specks, has matter reached that extremely high level of organisation at which it becomes self-producing or, in other words, alive, and so capable of organic evolution.

Organic or biological evolution is the sector about which science has the most to tell us. It is characterised by a wholly new method—what Darwin christened "natural selection" or, in modern parlance, the differential survival and differential reproduction of different variants. This immediately speeded up the possible tempo of evolution, so that in biological evolution we can obtain measurable changes, such as the formation of a new species, in a few thousands, or at most, tens of thousands of years ; important changes such as the full development of a new specialised order, such as the carnivores or the whales, in a few tens of millions of years ; and really major changes, such as the development and rise of a new dominant type, like flowering plants among plants or mammals among vertebrates, in one or two hundreds of millions of years.

The third sector is that of human evolution. In this, the tempo of change has again been immensely accelerated. This is especially so in its later phases, where, as we all know, major changes are occurring every few decades, or now, even every few years. But even in prehistory, from the time of the cave men with their art to that of the earliest civilisations, the rate of quite major change is to be measured in thousands of years instead of in tens or hundreds of millions of years. This difference in tempo was made possible by the introduction of a further new method, what we may call that of social evolution, operating by the transmission of ideas and institutions through the social heredity we call tradition : and this, in its turn, was made possible by the evolution of a new and exceedingly high form of organisation—that of the human brain—with true speech and conceptual thought among its functions.

The human sector of evolution emerged latest and is founded upon the biological, just as the biological emerged late in astronomical time and was founded upon the inorganic. It is interesting that in this process increasing importance becomes assigned to the individual and to the unlikely chance event. In the inorganic world, the individual electron, atom, or molecule does not count, but is submerged in the vastness of the mass ; so that the laws of physics and chemistry are in general statistical laws, applying merely to the average of immense numbers of individual units. In the biological sector, the unlikely and indeed fortuitous individual event of a favourable mutation can be preserved by natural selection and self-reproduction, and then can later be combined with similar and equally unlikely individual events to produce results, such as adaptations, which would, on the basis merely of statistical chance, be so astronomically improbable as the chance that the windows of a room should break owing to all the molecules inside the room happening to move in the same direction—in other words, impossible. Finally, in the human sector, the statistically rare or unique combination of genes giving rise to a genius can, through its influence on transmissible tradition, exercise a permanent and major effect on social evolution. And this, in combination with later effects of other equally rare and unlikely genetic events, can produce almost miraculously improbable results, such as a battleship, or a symphony, or the theory of relativity.

Another important trend as between the three sectors is the increasing importance of mind. In the organic sector, mind is either absent or at least undetectable ; and the same is true of the lowest forms of life, such as bacteria or viruses. But during biological evolution, mind becomes gradually more manifest, until in higher mammals a broad range of mental functions—knowledge, emotion and volition—is obviously available. Finally, with the evolution of man, a critical point is passed, and mind becomes the most important property of the new human organism.

It should now be clear that we cannot just take over the concept of progress as derived from the study of biological evolution and apply it directly and immediately to man and his affairs. Biological progress has consisted essentially in certain kinds of improvement in bodily structure and physiological function among organisms. Human progress largely consists in certain kinds of improvements in social structure and function, such as works of art, machines and manufactures, political institutions, moral codes, scientific theories, forms of entertainment or intellectual interest, and so on, which have been brought into being by contributions from the human mind to the stream of transmissible tradition. Biological progress can only be realised in a few lines among many. Human progress could best be realised through the development of one single line of tradition—one all-embracing common pool of human experience.

And finally, with the emergence of the human type of mind, intrinsic values emerge : in other words, certain things and activities come to be valued for their own sake, such as art, knowledge, moral behaviour, and certain types of spiritual experience : whereas biological progress is for the most part measurable only by material standards—the extent of control over external environment or the degree of internal self-regulation.

There remains also to be considered a strange evolutionary fact, mainly, that biological progress, in the restricted sense, appears to have come to an end during the Pleistocene with the emergence of *Homo sapiens*, the last form of man, as dominant evolutionary type. All existing types of animals and plants seem to be at the ends of specialised or one-sided trends, and these, as already mentioned, automatically come to a stop after a certain time. Even if the entire human species were to be exterminated tomorrow, it seems that it would be impossible for any other form of life now to evolve into a wholly new dominant type. But we can disregard this hypothetical situation, for man does exist, and even if it were possible for any animals now to begin to evolve into a higher type, man would certainly see to it that this new type was destroyed or rendered harmless as soon as it showed signs of becoming a rival to the human species in the control of the resources of our planet. Thus, just as the ancestral reptiles, and later the ancestral mammals, were once the only transmitters of progress, so now we men are its only repository.

There are, of course, a great many questions which arise with regard to the theory of human progress. There is, for instance, the relation between the general progress of the human species on the one hand, and individual progress in the development of the single human being on the other. There is the problem of the relation between all types of progressive process which take place in time and can never be finite or complete, and those mental and emotional and spiritual experiences like love and certain mystical states, which confer a sense of timelessness, of completeness, and utmost value. There is the question of one-sidedness, the laying of emphasis on one aspect only of human life ; the mechanical versus the æsthetic, or the military versus the mystical. Biological evolution, as we have seen, leads the one-sided type unavoidably up a blind alley of specialisation. In human affairs, where the mechanism of change is so entirely different, how serious is such one-sidedness ?

Unfortunately my space does not give me time to deal with them, important though they are. However, the most important of all does seem now to be established :—progress exists and can be localised in the universe. It exists quite apart from man, but, just as human evolution is a continuation of biological evolution, though by different methods and at a different speed, so human progress is the continuation, and indeed the crown of biological progress, though with somewhat different criteria, methods and results. For instance, we cannot transfer the idea of the struggle for existence directly from animal to human affairs, as some German militaristically-minded philosophers tried to do in the nineteenth century, for it is, in large measure, inoperative or inapplicable in that domain. Indeed, since biological progress has now come to an end, man is now the sole trustee for the future of all evolutionary progress, at least within our solar system. With this, morality and ethics receive a new sanction—a sanction from the universe at large, not one derived from purely human considerations. Furthermore, all moral and ethical problems have to be considered in a radically new way in which neither absolute value nor static level is important or essential, but right direction.

The foundation for all this was laid by Darwin and the nineteenth-century evolutionists, but it remained for the twentieth century to work out the details and frame a general theory of progress. This is, I think, a remarkable achievement, perhaps the most important contribution of science to general thought since Newton's day. It ties in man with all the rest of the cosmos and establishes the importance of mind and of values in evolution. It introduces the normative idea of right direction into the blind automatic processes of the universe as a whole, and has given the possibility of establishing certain external criteria for rightness or wrongness in human affairs.

Geology Changes the Outlook

F. SHERWOOD TAYLOR

" A ROSE-RED city, half as old as time ! " sang John William Burgon, of the city of Petra. That striking line was written in 1845 ; it serves to remind us that the generality of early Victorians believed that time had begun less than six thousand years ago. Moses had written it, and it was possible to believe that Moses was only separated by a few generations of oral tradition from the first man, from the creation in fact. As George Rawlinson gravely suggested in the Bampton lecture of 1859, Moses' mother, Jochebed, had probably met Jacob who could have known Noah's son Shem. Shem was probably acquainted with Methuselah, who had been for 243 years a contemporary of Adam—and Adam was made on the sixth day after the first day on which Time had begun.

Now, this was not a mere tradition, but was guaranteed as correct according to the very usual belief that every word of the Scriptures had the direct authority of the Holy Ghost. There was still, in fact, at the beginning of the reign of Queen Victoria an established and accepted history of the origins of the universe and particularly of man. It was a history based on the early chapters of Genesis, a little mixed with *Paradise Lost*—a history bound by a thousand sensitive roots to literature, to art, and above all to simple nursery piety. Its main features were the creation by God, about 4000 B.C., in six successive natural days, of the features of the earth—land, sea, hills, valleys and living organisms —resulting in a World substantially as we see it today, but perfect. That perfection was shattered by man's fall, which infected all creation and brought in its train the seeming imperfections of the world that man has always known.

With the exception of the one essential of an original Divine creation, concerning which science can say nothing, affirmative or negative, the whole of the account was apparently confuted by the advance of Geology. By the beginning of the reign of Queen Victoria the geologists had established the main outlines of the relative depths and relative ages of the earth's strata, together with their distinctive fossil content. They had discovered evidence, which seemed to them to demonstrate that a multitude of species of animals and plants had come into being and had been annihilated. The facts were clear and substantially undisputed, but controversy raged concerning the explanation. The two chief schools of geological thought were the catastrophist and the uniformitarian. The catastrophists supposed the extinction of the species found fossilised in the rocks to have been due to vast catastrophes—volcanoes, earthquakes, floods. Their view was the more readily accepted by those brought up on Moses' account of the creation and the history of the earth or the Mosaic cosmogony, as it is technically called. This was because it was possible to invoke the Biblical Deluge as the means of overwhelming and burying those organisms. But it soon became clear that one deluge could not alone have produced the whole of the strata and their contents, and catastrophes had to be multiplied to the point of absurdity. Moreover, from the end of the eighteenth century, the opposite or uniformitarian view had been gaining strength, and by the eighteen-forties was almost everywhere accepted. This view invoked as the causes of geological change only the processes which we see at work today—erosion by wind and water, the deposition of mud by rivers and the slow raising and lowering of land-masses. The rate of these changes today is almost imperceptibly slow, and, to quote words written some ten years before the beginning of the Victorian era :—

"Every step we take in the pursuit of geology forces us to make almost unlimited drafts upon antiquity. The leading idea which is present in all our researches and which accompanies every fresh observation, the sound which to the ear of the students of Nature seems continually echoed from every part of her works, is—Time ! "

Once uniformitarianism had established itself, the geologist began to extend the time scale. It rose from hundreds of thousands of years to millions, to tens of millions and, by the eighteen-sixties, to hundreds of millions of years. They saw

well enough the difficulty of reconciling this with the Mosaic
cosmogony, but most of them thought a geologist's business to
be the drawing of inferences from geological evidence, and not
the reconciling of them with the Biblical evidences. But the
professional geologists had a large popular audience. The
Victorians were great amateur scientists. They peered down
microscopes, pointed their telescopes to the heavens, and sallied
forth with their geological hammers. The popular reviews and
magazines of the period were full of first-class scientific articles,
far better than those that appear today. Indeed, geology became
an accomplishment. In 1845 Mr. Tennant's shop in the Strand
was characterised as "attractive to all who pursued and desired
to cultivate that favourite science of the day—Geology." Even
books for children inculcated geology in the form of dialogues
between governess and pupil. It seems that many, both of
laity and clergy, were prepared to study geology for its intense
interest, and to disregard its controversial possibility. Among
these were most of the well-known geologists themselves.
They were interested in the rocks and the history revealed therein,
and were by no means anxious to fight the battle of the evidences.

But there was a minority which was morbidly sensitive to
anything that might conflict with the view that the plain literal
sense of the Scriptures was the exact truth—that they were to be
read as a scientific text-book, without respect to the state of
knowledge or literary conventions of their human authors.
This minority was ready to cry "infidel" at the first murmur of
dissent, and their controversial writings accentuated the obvious
divergencies between the traditional and the geological account
of the early history of the world. The difficulties were many.
It was first obvious that the earth's reputed age of six thousand
years or so, arrived at by adding up the ages of the patriarchs,
the reigns of the Kings of Israel and the like, bore no relation to
the duration of the geological record. Furthermore, the order
of creation of the various living forms, as given in Genesis, did
not correspond exactly to the order in which these appeared in
the rocks.

Then came a fresh set of difficulties. They appeared in connection with the idea of the development of the earth, which the
geologists supposed to have originated from a barren globe of
igneous rock. To some it seemed blasphemous to suppose that

God had created an imperfect world, which had since been improved to its present state by mere natural causes, such as the action of wind and water, and the development of living beings. Then there was a formidable set of difficulties centred round the fall of man. In the earlier part of the Victorian era, many supposed that the Scriptures indicated that the world was perfect and without death until the Fall brought death into the world. The Fall could not have ante-dated man ; yet the fossil remains of some of the giant saurians showed that they were equipped for a carnivorous existence, and failed to fit into the picture of unfallen bliss.

It can well be imagined that an even greater difficulty occurred when the first remains of ancient man were discovered. In 1833 a human skull was found, in the valley of the Meuse, embedded amongst remains of the extinct mammoth and woolly rhinoceros ; it had to be inferred that all those creatures had lived at the same time. In 1857 the first remains of Neanderthal man came to light ; and the discovery of the stone implements and other remains of these ancient peoples added incontrovertible evidence that, long before the date which the natural interpretation of the Scriptures would assign to the Biblical Adam, there were beings on earth to whom the name of man could not reasonably be denied. Of course, the publication of Charles Darwin's *Origin of Species* in 1859, and of later works which specifically included man in the evolutionary scheme, added further difficulties. They gave an account of the origin of man, which not only differed from the Mosaic, but seemed to indicate that beast had become man by a change insensibly gradual, and that historically there was no clear line of demarcation between man and beast. It seemed very difficult, then, to assign to Adam and Eve any place in the world's history, for there were difficulties in either a remote or a recent date. But the origin of man, his fall, original sin, and the necessity of redemption— inseparable, it would seem, from Christian doctrine—were regarded as resulting from the acts of these very individuals, Adam and Eve.

During the whole of the reign of Queen Victoria our grandfathers were assimilating these ideas. At the outset the difficulties had been confronted by geologists, but not by many others. Owing to the clerical constitution of the universities, the Anglican clergy were then the leaders of opinion and very influential in public affairs. But their education was almost exclusively classical ; their view of history was truncated at the time of Homer, and, with the exception of a gifted minority, they were neither well-informed in scientific matters, nor disposed to become so. To quote Hugh Miller, the Scots stone-mason who had made himself a geologist :—

> " The clergy, as a class, suffer themselves to linger far in the rear of an intelligent and accomplished laity—a full age behind the requirements of the time."

The Anglican clergy were, at that time, it must be remembered, normally ordained without any formal theological training, and they were without scientific education. They did not, however, lack self-confidence. Throughout the nineteenth century there issued from the presses a stream of pamphlets, by men who were amateurs both in theology and geology. Their authors endeavoured to discuss the relation of Mosaic history, the criteria for the assessment of which they had not studied, to geological phenomena, of which they were totally incompetent to judge. This dreary and rancorous literature was still in full flood in the eighteen-nineties. The efforts to solve these difficulties fell into four chief classes.

The *fundamentalists*, as we call them today, continued to maintain the literal Mosaic account as against the scientific. It is enough to note their continued existence even to modern times. The *reconcilers* sought to find interpretations of Genesis and Geology that would not conflict. It was easy to extend the six days of creation to six periods of indefinite length, and to take a stand on the parallelism between the order of creation of the different classes of organism as given in Genesis I, and the order of appearance of these classes in geological strata. But as the order and content of the fossil-bearing strata became more certainly established, this view became untenable, as finally appeared in the Homeric contest between Gladstone and Huxley in the *Nineteenth Century Review* for 1885. The reconcilers came indeed to read Genesis in so figurative and unnatural a sense that their rationalist opponents felt aggrieved. "There must be *some* position from which the reconcilers of Genesis will not retreat", wrote Huxley, with something of the disappointed air with which the cat sees the half-stunned mouse creep into an inaccessible cranny.

The reconcilers were followed by those who frankly rejected the factual view of the Mosaic writings. Thus the famous, or notorious, *Essays and Reviews,* published in 1860, contained an essay on the *Mosaic Cosmogony* by C. W. Goodwin, wherein he expressed the view which follows : " It would have been well if theologians had made up their minds to accept frankly the principle that those things for the discovery of which man has faculties specially provided are not fit objects of a divine revelation." He rejected all attempts to reconcile the two accounts, Mosaic and scientific, and maintained that the former was simply a human utterance, containing, however, the great truth of the unity of the design of the world, and its subordination to one sole Maker and Lawgiver. After the fury occasioned by this and the other essays had somewhat subsided, Goodwin's view was generally favoured. Thus Frederick Temple (later Archbishop of Canterbury) said in 1884 : " There is no more reason for setting aside geology, because it does not agree in detail with Genesis, than there is for setting aside astronomy because all through the Old Testament the sun is spoken of as going round the earth. . . ." In his view Revelation intended to teach spiritual truth, but not physical truth. The problem is a serious one for Christians. Those who abandon the historical elements in the older parts of the Bible and treat its contents as Hebrew mythology, open the way to those who treat its revelations as of no higher authenticity.

The Roman Catholic Church took up a somewhat different position. The lesson of Galileo had been learnt by the hierarchy, and there was not the same violent reaction to geology as in Protestant circles : indeed on the Continent there was a certain amusement at our spiritual struggles. Cardinal Wiseman in 1859 applied to the geologists the words of Gamaliel : " Refrain from these men and let them alone ; for if the work be of men it will fall to nothing, but if it be of God, ye are not able to destroy it ". The Catholic Church had always clearly understood that the Bible was not to be read in a literal anthropomorphic sense, the belief in its total inspiration has always been firmly held. St. Augustine had made it clear that the words of Genesis conveyed a truth, but not necessarily that shown by the literal sense of the words : and that this truth, once elicited, could not disagree with the truths of Science, fully understood. Meanwhile judgment could be suspended.

For lack of clear thinking in these matters many, Catholic and Protestant, lost their faith completely. Some felt that the historicity of the Scriptural Adam was overthrown, and the doctrine of the Fall and the need of redemption with it ; and so came to lose belief in the Christian scheme. Others felt that the Bible had been shown to be untrue in some points and therefore no longer carried any assurance of authenticity. The causes of individual changes of opinion are impossible to trace, but I myself have little doubt that in England it was geology and the theory of evolution that changed us from a Christian to a pagan nation.

The overt reaction of the Victorian Age to geology was theological, but its influence extended to every phase of thought. It completed, in fact, the revolution that Copernicus began. The mediæval universe was small in space and short in life. The discoveries of the astronomers from the sixteenth century onwards had enlarged its dimensions, and the Victorians were fully conscious of man's spatial insignificance—though the universe they knew is but a small fraction of that which is known to us. The discoveries of geology enlarged their ideas of *time*. The sixty familiar centuries of Bishop Usher's seventeenth-century chronology could be easily visualised ; they were little more than three times the span of the Christian era. But a million years opened up a terrifying abyss of time : three hundred million or three thousand million meant but little more.

Now not only did there appear this terrifying desert of time, but also a most strange world which no human eye had seen, a world peopled by fierce, hideous and brainless beings. And these man had to acknowledge as blood-relations. His remote ancestors, he was told, were beasts, and the distinction between beast and man was but a matter of degree. Some could rejoice in the progress that had made beast into man. Some could find satisfaction in the solidarity of living beings implied by their evolutionary connection. But the most part felt lost, cut off from participation in the cultural life of the ages that had brought them into being.

The whole literature, art and philosophy of the past was based on the axioms that the changes of the world were a drama enacted on the unchanging scene of nature by unchanging man —a little lower than the angels and immeasurably above the beasts who had not understanding. The art and literature and morality of Europe were based on the Bible, understood in the old simple way. The later Victorians, isolated in vast deserts of space and time, with God seemingly removed to the dim status of a remote Architect of the Universe, could no longer feel themselves one with those who dwelt contentedly in the little universe of past centuries. They began to find the writings of the Middle Ages and antiquity to be strange and archaic ; they ceased to treat Homer, Plato or Isaiah as members of their own society, but only as objects of study—literary or anthropological specimens.

And so Victorians moved out of man's ancestral home, with its temples, palaces, cottages and cathedrals, golden with age, tenderly formed by the hands of the masters, into the fine new city of science—so convenient, so hygienic, so reasonably planned—but devoid of human tenderness and ancient beauty. The loss has never been repaired and man today is still a displaced person in a land that he has yet to make his home.

Archæology Links Geology to History

GLYN E. DAN EL

ARCHÆOLOGY, AS we know it, is the creation of the Victorians, and its growth was only possible because of the widespread acceptance of that geological doctrine of uniformitarianism which was one of the key beliefs of Victorian science. The effects of this doctrine of uniformitarianism on the Victorian antiquarians was tremendous. It meant that human bones buried under thick layers of earth must have been deposited there a very long time ago. The same conclusion had also to be drawn from the co-existence of humanly fashioned stone tools and the bones of extinct animals in sedimentary deposits. They must be very old—how old it was difficult to say, but certainly much older than 4004 B.C., the time of the creation of Man according to Archbishop Usher's interpretation of the Bible ; Lyell, himself, once hazarded 100,000 years for the antiquity of man. The proof of the antiquity of man rested on the discoveries made by Boucher de Perthes in the Somme Valley and by William Pengelly in South Devon. But these discoveries were only intelligible as proofs because of the widespread acceptance of the doctrines of the geologists.

The first impetus to the development of archæology in Victorian times came, then, from early Victorian geological science. With its proof of the great antiquity of man archæology helped to undermine the faith of the Victorians in the Mosaic chronology—a faith already so badly shaken by Biblical criticism and the new Geology. It is something of an irony, then, that the second factor which brought about the development of Victorian archæology—the discovery of the early Near Eastern civilisations—was at first welcomed because it seemed to strengthen faith in the Bible. This second source of Victorian interest in archæology was an historical one—the gradual pushing back of the frontiers of history by archæological means. In the Near East the history of the ancient Egyptians, Assyrians and Babylonians was being rediscovered by archæologists like Layard, Rawlinson and Mariette. Hitherto they had been seen only—and that very dimly—by the light of classical and Biblical histories.

And so, if the new technique of archæological history seemed at one moment, where it touched geology, to be refuting the Creation story, at another it seemed to be a great supporter of the Bible. In 1872 George Smith, an official in the British Museum, announced that he had deciphered on a broken clay tablet from Nineveh, a Chaldean account of the flood of Noah. The excitement caused by this announcement was tremendous. The *Daily Telegraph* offered a thousand pounds to equip an expedition led by Smith to look for the missing fragment of the tablet. Next year, by an amazing stroke of luck, Smith found the missing fragment on the fifth day of his work at Nineveh.

Knowledge of the discoveries in Mesopotamia and Egypt soon made the Victorians archæologically minded : even those Victorians who had at first thought archæology an impious discipline because of its association with the new geology. Certainly archæology was most popular in the mid-Victorian Age, and the joining of local archæological societies in the middle of the nineteenth century was very much the thing to do. Layard's *Nineveh,* first published in 1848, sold eight thousand copies in one year, which, as the author wrote, " will place it side by side with Mrs. Rundell's cookery ". Two years later an abridgement was published specially for the railway book-stalls. It was in John Murray's series called " Reading for the Rail, or Cheap Books in a large readable type published occasionally ". What better evidence that archæology was now considered suitable reading for the general public ? Equally popular were the works of the geological archæologists. Wherever Pengelly lectured, whether it be to the Mechanics Institute at Torquay or to the Sciences Lectures Association in Glasgow, and on whatever subject, his audiences were large and enthusiastic.

Archæology was certainly an element in the mid-Victorian climate of thought. Let us for a moment recall a lecture given at Oxford in 1870 by J. H. Parker, then Keeper of the Ashmolean. This is one of the things he said : " When archæology is made part of the system of Education in Oxford, as I trust it will be, with the help of this Museum, any educated man will feel it a disgrace to be ignorant of it. . . . The ladies are already taking the lead in this matter. Archæology is now part of the course of study in the education of young ladies, and I have frequently observed in society that to find out whether a young lady knows anything of archæology or not, is a test whether she has been highly educated or not. The daughters of our higher nobility, who have generally had the best education that can be obtained, are almost always well acquainted with archæology. Some of my most favourite pupils have been young ladies of this class, our future Duchesses or Countesses ".

Whatever might have been true for the future Duchesses and Countesses, it was certainly true that the Victorian scientists and historians of the 'seventies and afterwards were conscious of the ideas and beliefs of the archæologists. Scientific thought in the 'seventies, with its emphasis on uniformity and evolution, enabled the archæologists' proofs of the antiquity of man to be readily accepted. But the doctrine of evolution not only made people more ready to believe in the antiquity of man, it made the objects roughly chipped by early man, which were found in the river gravels and caves, not only credible but necessary. If man had gradually evolved from an uncultured prehuman ancestor to the cultured human beings of Egypt and Assyria, then there *must* be evidence of his primitive culture in the most recent geological levels. Evolutionary beliefs not only persuaded the reluctant to belief in the stone tools from Torquay and Brixham, they made it essential that more evidences of early human culture be found—and that traces should also be found of other stages of culture leading from these simple tools to the complex equipment and buildings of the known early historic civilisations. Although it did not grow out of the acceptance of evolution, it was impossible to believe in evolution without believing in archæology.

It is interesting to note the way in which the rôle of archæology in Victorian thought gradually changed. At first archæology seemed to be contributing to the destruction of the comfortable early nineteenth century belief in the Mosaic chronology and the verbal truth of the Genesis account. Then, at the same time, it seemed to be proving the truth of much of the Bible story.

Next, by revealing man's technological evolution, it seemed to provide a main support for the comfortable Victorian belief in progress. It was the French archæologists who first seized on the apparent demonstration of progress by archæology, but a great Victorian, Sir Augustine Woolaston Franks, was at Paris in 1867 arranging the British archæological collections in the Exposition. Franks shared the view that it was impossible to walk round the archæological collections in the Exposition and still doubt the great law of the progress of humanity. Chipped flint, polished flint, bronze, iron—these were, it would seem, the great stages through which man had slowly travelled before arriving at the historic civilisations. Swept away with the Mosaic chronology was any idea that civilisation was a fallen state to which man had come after an earlier perfection. Man's history was now seen to be a progressive technological development. The Victorians saw the Crystal Palace of 1851 and the Eiffel Tower of 1887 standing at the end of a great sequence going back to the hand-axes of the Devon caves and Somme gravels. "History," declared that remarkable Victorian, General Pitt Rivers, "is evolution, and science is just organised common sense". It was, thought General Pitt Rivers, by the organised common-sense methods of archæology that history could be demonstrated to be no more than a progressive evolution of man.

In a way, of course, the Victorians were right. Prehistoric archæology did reveal to them a gradual development from simple stone tools to complicated iron tools. But was this development inevitable ? Did it happen all over the world ? And could not archæology supply some facts about the non-technological development of man ? The French had ruthlessly applied what they took to be the lessons of archæology and constructed a single unilateral sequence of pre-historic periods leading from the first human tools to the Roman conquest. Into this scheme they tried to fit all the finds made of early man and his culture. They realised that this scheme would vary in its chronological details from one part of the world to another, but they felt that the scheme itself would remain true wherever applied. In a word they were treating prehistoric man as an animal.

It is to the great credit of many of the late Victorians that they began to have doubts about the validity and universality of this archæological succession. Boyd Dawkins, himself a geologist, could not bring himself to accept the progressive sequences of the French systematists. " There is no greater difference in the implements of any two of the French caves," he said, " than is to be observed between those of two different tribes of Eskimos. The principles of classification by relative rudeness assumes that rude implements are therefore the older. The difference, however, may have been due to different tribes or families having coexisted without intercourse with each other ". This was written in 1874. Boyd Dawkins was well ahead of his time. In the last quarter of the nineteenth century archæologists, together with other thinkers, were beginning to wonder whether the story of man was simply one of unadulterated, undisturbed progress. Gone was the crude assurance of the Paris Exposition. The wiser archæologists began to contemplate the phenomenon of retrogression. Archæology, which had, for a while, seemed to support the Victorian belief in progress, now began to sustain the late Victorian doubts regarding this doctrine.

William Pengelly had always been impressed by retrogression. He argued that there had been a great decline in culture in Britain in immediately post-Roman times. Could there, then, he said, not have been equally Dark Ages in prehistoric times ? Was the archæologist, in presenting his picture of technological progress, making objective observations which confirmed the Victorian belief in progress or was he merely projecting into prehistory his own belief in progress ? Did archæology really prove the cultural progress of man, or was it merely being used to demonstrate that cultural progress ? What made the later Victorians think again about prehistoric archæology was the discovery of hitherto unknown civilisations.

The civilisations of Egypt and Assyria had been known of from Biblical and classical sources. Now Schliemann was revealing the Mycenæan civilisation behind classical Greece, Petrie was revealing the pre-dynastic civilisation behind Dynastic Egypt, and excavators in Mesopotamia were bringing to light a hitherto quite unknown civilisation—that of the Sumerians. But perhaps the most surprising archæological discoveries were those of what we know now as Upper Palæolithic Cave Art. The later Victorians were much concerned with the dispute around the authenticity of this cave art. In the end they were satisfied with its genuineness. But it raised a great problem with regard to human history. Here was a remarkably naturalistic and competent art which flourished in South France and North Spain during the last glaciation of the Ice Age—at least ten and probably twenty thousand years ago, and which came to an end. The Upper Palæolithic artists had no successors, and their artistic impetus died out. Here was a tremendous example of retrogression, of degeneration, of decadence. It certainly worried Pitt Rivers, who had been an implicit believer in progress. He began to doubt whether progress—progressive evolution, gradual but persistent improvement—was the fact that emerged out of prehistory and early history. And he wrote : " Progress is like a game of dominoes. Like fits on to like. In neither case can we tell beforehand what will be the ultimate figure produced ; all we know is that the fundamental rule of the game is sequence".

Sequence—yes—but a sequence that might show retrogression as well as progression. That was the essential difference between late and early Victorian thought in so far as it related to early man. But was it, many asked, only technological sequences that archæology revealed ? Could this new discipline, to which they had turned so eagerly, speak only of the material development of man ? To many it seemed that this was so, and they turned away, disappointed, from the study of archæological relics. I think that much of the late nineteenth-century interest in anthropology—a very real interest to the late Victorians—derives from the disappointing answers which archæology gave regarding the mental, social and spiritual development of early man. The Victorians turned to a study of the modern primitives, to what we call the savage tribes, for many reasons. The acceptance or evolution made the study of primitive man a respectable and necessary one. The savage—the ' beastlie heathen '—was no longer a curiosity, or a degenerate ; he might represent an early stage in the evolutionary development which had led to the triumph which was Victorianism. For that reason alone he was worth studying.

Others studied the modern primitives because they refused to accept the apparent limitation of archæological method. They disagreed with those who argued that archæology could describe tombs, burial rites, temples, houses, but, from its very nature, could say nothing about prehistoric man's belief in God or an after-life, or the organisation of his society. They held that by comparing prehistoric people with existing preliterate peoples it was possible to postulate their spiritual and social culture. Briefly their argument was this : if a prehistoric people had the same artefacts as a modern primitive tribe, then perhaps we may infer that they had the same mental concepts as the modern primitive tribe. This was what has been described as the comparative ethnographic fallacy. It is, as all except Marxist prehistorians and anthropologists would now admit, improbable—to say the least of it—but it was very common in Victorian thought. Sir John Lubbock used it a great deal. So did Lewis Morgan, the American, whose fallacious equations of material and non-material culture were taken over by Engels and Marx and treated as though they were the facts of man's early development.

The use of the comparative ethnographical fallacy was in its way a reaction against the inadequacy of the archæological record. Archæology had, within the lifetime of one of the great Victorians like Sir John Evans, demonstrated the great antiquity of man, the nature of man's technological development, the existence of remarkable and vanished civilisations. Could it not somehow be made to tell more, could it not be made to tell the intellectual adventure of early man ? Could it not, with a longer perspective than that provided by the five thousand years of recorded history, tell us really what happened in history ? These were some of the ideas and questions which the late Victorians bequeathed to twentieth-century archæologists and pre-historians.

If, at the end of the nineteenth century, the Victorians were beginning to sense some of the limitations of archæology, they had not fully appreciated its contribution to the philosophy of history. In 1871 Edward Tylor, the father of English Anthropology, talked of prehistory as now taking its place in the general scheme of knowledge ; but this it never did in the minds of the Victorians. I think it has been left to us in the twentieth century to effect a synthesis of the facts of prehistoric archæology with history itself. The concept of human history is a twentieth-century one. The late Victorians were still talking of archæology *and* history. They had created archæology out of history, out of antiquarian studies, and out of geology. But it was this last element—the geological—that remained the strongest. So many of the Victorian archæologists were geologists. So many of the Victorian ideas and beliefs regarding archæology came from the natural sciences. The Victorians had mastered the essential technique of archæology, its teachings are mirrored in their thought ; they were proud of their creation and the millennia they had added to man's history. But they kept forgetting in their pioneer zeal that they were really historians and not scientists—historians of a special kind and using scientific techniques, but still historians. And they did not face up to the philosophical implications of prehistoric archæology—I mean the demonstration by archæology that what we term civilisation with the notions and religions which we regard as basic or normal, is an extremely late product in the life of *Homo sapiens,* the cultured animal. Perhaps we shouldn't be too hard on the Victorians for this, since we scarcely reflect an awareness of these philosophical implications in our own ideas and beliefs.

Science and Philosophy

A. J. AYER

JUST AS philosophers disagree with one another about the nature and method of their own subject, so they are divided in their attitude to science. Thus, some philosophers aim at constructing a speculative system, which is intended to be a picture of reality ; and of these there are some who try to take account in their system of the theories of the natural sciences, while others, as idealists or mystics, turn their backs on science altogether and arrive at their world-pictures by special methods of their own. On the other hand, there are the philosophers for whom logic and the application of logic is the essence of philosophy. Those who take this view are content to leave it to the scientists to discover what the world is like. Their own function, as they see it, is to carry out such purely critical activities as those of analysing concepts, examining assumptions, evaluating arguments, solving logical or quasi-logical problems and, in general, clarifying the uses of language.

But here again there is a division. Philosophers of this sort are seldom " malicious " towards science in the way that metaphysicians sometimes are, but they do in some cases ignore it. They may be content to apply their logical technique to the work of other philosophers, or to the notions of common sense. The problems they try to solve may be only those that arise in the use of everyday language. The problem of perception, for example, which has played so large a part in the history of philosophy during the last three hundred years, is a problem of analysis, which can be solved, if at all, at the common-sense level. And so long as a philosopher confines himself to questions of this sort, he can remain professionally indifferent to what the scientists are doing. But while this is the practice of some critical philosophers, there are others who regard the philosophical questions that arise out of the use of everyday language as of minor importance. In their view, the language to which the philosopher should devote his attention is the language of science. His work should be that of analysing scientific method, elucidating scientific concepts, revealing the structure and function of scientific theories. And indeed it is now becoming fashionable to say that philosophy is, or at any rate ought to be, nothing other than the logic of science.

If a philosopher is going to incorporate the scientific theories of his time into his world-picture, or if he is going to subject them to critical analysis, it is essential that he should understand them. And unless he is himself a working scientist this will not be easy. Until the nineteenth century it was not beyond the power of an intelligent layman to make himself familiar with at any rate the leading principles and the most important concepts of the various natural sciences. But with the rapid growth of science in the last hundred and fifty years, and with its ever-increasing specialisation, it becomes more and more difficult for anyone who is not a specialist in a given branch of science to have more than a superficial knowledge of it. In particular, it is very hard for anyone who is not a specialist to appreciate the significance of new scientific discoveries, at least in the cases where they involve far-reaching changes of theory. Once a theory is established, its import may come to be understood by the non-specialist, and perhaps even better understood by him than by some of the scientists who are working in the field in question. It does sometimes happen even in the domain of science that a certain type of onlooker comes to see more of the game. But what such an onlooker is apt to be watching is a game that it already played. What he is usually unable to do is to follow out the consequences of the decisive moves in the game at the moment that they actually occur. The result of this is that there tends to be a time-lag between the birth of a new scientific idea and its assimilation by philosophers. And this is particularly true of the relations between science and philosophy in the nineteenth century.

The nineteenth century, in England as elsewhere, was a period of great scientific expansion. Not only were great advances made in the application of science to industry, but highly important, one might say revolutionary, changes took place in the domain of scientific theory. Yet there is very little reflection of this in the work of nineteenth-century philosophers. For the most part they held to a conception of science which the scientists of their day were actually engaged in making untenable. This was all the more easy for them as the scientists themselves did not always realise how revolutionary they were. In many cases they went on trying to fit their new ideas into a conceptual scheme that had become inadequate to contain them. It is only in the twentieth century that the philosophical implications of nineteenth-century achievements in science come to be at all adequately understood.

In saying this, I am thinking especially of physics. I suppose that the most important developments in nineteenth-century physics were those that marked the breakaway from pure mechanism, as an all-embracing physical scheme, and the emergence of the field theory. The system of classical mechanics, which came to fruition in Newton's theory of gravitation, was remarkable for its simplicity. Its picture of the material world is that of a set of homogeneous particles endowed, as Locke expressed it, with the primary qualities of extension, figure, solidity, number, motion and rest. The fundamental type of change to which these particles are subject is change of position, and this is due to the attraction that they exercise upon one another. The strength of this attraction is governed by Newton's famous " inverse square " law from which it follows that once the masses of bodies are known, all that is needed to calculate their behaviour is knowledge of the distances between them. A body only changes its state when it is " compelled by force " to do so. Otherwise, according to Newton's first law of motion, " it continues in its state of rest or of uniform motion along a straight line ". The notion of force is at first sight somewhat anthropomorphic, but it can be defined quite innocently in terms of mass and acceleration and there is a simple law of composition for calculating the resultant of several forces acting together. It is easy to see that this scheme is entirely deterministic. Given complete knowledge of the state of the system at any one moment, it would be possible, by means of the laws of motion, to calculate precisely its state at any other.

So successful were these mechanistic hypotheses in accounting for physical phenomena, that it was still possible for a scientist, writing in the middle of the nineteenth century, to assert that " the problem of physical material science is to refer natural phenomena back to unchangeable attractive and repulsive forces whose intensity depend wholly upon distance ". " The solubility of this problem ", he continues, " is the condition of the complete comprehensibility of nature ". But it soon became clear that this claim could not be sustained. Thus, experiments carried out by Oersted and later by Rowland, in connection with phenomena of electro-magnetics, seemed to show the existence of forces which did not behave as mechanical forces should. Such experiments would not by themselves have been fatal to the mechanical view. It is nearly always possible to save a theory if you are prepared to make enough additional hypotheses. But difficulties arose also in connection with the phenomena of light. Newton's theory of light was corpuscular, but the experiments of Young and Fresnel on the diffraction of light favoured the wave theory. Now the wave theory can be brought within the mechanical picture provided that you can give a mechanistic account of the medium in which the waves are carried. This hypothetical medium was supposed to be the ether, but the attempt to endow the ether with the requisite mechanical properties did not succeed. One reason why it did not was that Clerk-Maxwell, continuing the work of Faraday, showed that the wave theory of light could be subsumed under a more general theory of electro-magnetism. And in the theory of electro-magnetism the whole concept of the ether becomes logically superfluous.

Clerk-Maxwell's theory was developed in the 'seventies. Its great advance on the Newtonian scheme was that it represented physical events not as occurring only at points at which matter is present, but as pervading the whole of space. Clerk-Maxwell's equations describe not the behaviour of particles but the structure of the electro-magnetic field. To quote Einstein and Infeld, " it is not the charges nor the particles but the field in the space between the charges and the particles which is essential for the description of physical phenomena ". This brings us a long way from the primitive simplicity of the mechanical picture. And when in the twentieth century the consequences of the field theory were developed by the theory of relativity, and so encroached upon the Newtonian system, it was Clerk-Maxwell's line of thought that prevailed.

If philosophy is to be regarded as the logic of science, then these developments in physical theory are certainly of philosophical importance. Thus the concept of mass loses its pre-eminence and its place is taken by the concept of energy. The laws of the conservation of energy, as established by the experiments of Joule and others, are in fact to be reckoned among the great nineteenth-century contributions to physical science. Again, the field theory gives rise, as we have seen, to the theory of relativity ; and this leads to a new conception of the space-time continuum. There is also a change in the notion of physical causation. Clerk-Maxwell's scheme is still indeed deterministic, but the causal laws take on a new form. What they enable us to predict, always assuming complete knowledge of the state of the system at any one instant, are the changes of the field. It was left to the quantum physicists in our own times to throw doubt upon the validity of the whole notion of physical determinism.

Turning now to the philosophers, we find that their conception of physical theory remains Newtonian. In the case of John Stuart Mill, who published his *System of Logic* as early as 1843, this could hardly have been otherwise. Yet of all the philosophers who come within our period, at any rate in this country, it is he who contributes most to the understanding of science. Since he was concerned with general questions of scientific method rather than the analysis of particular scientific theories, the value of his work is not destroyed by the fact that the science about which he writes is in many ways radically different from the science of today. The logical problems which he raises retain their interest, even though his own solution of them may not be entirely acceptable.

The principal aim of Mill's work was to establish a satisfactory logic of induction. Mistaking deductive logic for a method of proof, he argued that syllogistic reasoning was vitiated by a *petitio principii*. The conclusions did indeed follow validly from the premises ; but this brought no increase of knowledge, since in accepting the premises the truth of the conclusions had already been assumed. In inductive reasoning, on the other hand, we arrive at a conclusion which goes beyond the evidence on which it is based. We generalise from "some" to "all", we argue from one separate instance to another, we assume that we can successfully apply our hypotheses to events of which we have no previous knowledge. If these procedures are irrational, then all science is irrational. Thus Mill's attempt to provide a rationale of induction was essentially an attempt to give a logical justification of our faith in science.

Mill's solution of this problem was to make the validity of scientific laws depend upon the uniformity of nature, and to treat the uniformity of nature not as an *a priori* principle but as itself an empirical generalisation which is justified by the validity of scientific laws. Now as an argument this is plainly circular, and it does not justify induction. Indeed it is probably a mistake to try to justify induction. One inductive conclusion may be used to justify another, but it seems inevitable that any attempt to justify inductive reasoning in general will presuppose what it sets out to prove. And if this is so, it is not a fatal objection to Mill's " inductive logic " that it involves circularity, for this alone would not prevent it from being an accurate description of scientific method. The mistake would be that of confusing analysis with justification, or rather that of setting a standard of justification which could not logically be realised.

Mill defined the cause of a phenomenon as its invariable and unconditional antecedent, and accepted a Law of Universal Causation on the somewhat dubious ground that it was " but the familiar truth that invariability of succession is found by observation to obtain between every fact in nature and some other fact which has preceded it ". He then set out to give rules for the discovery of particular causes and effects. For this purpose he devised his " four experimental methods ", the method of agreement, the method of difference, the method of residues, and the method of concomitant variations. Of these the first two were the most important and were regarded by Mill as yielding a fifth method when used in combination. By the method of agreement it was laid down that if two or more instances of a phenomenon agreed only in one additional circumstance, that circumstance was the cause of the phenomenon, or its effect. According to the method of difference, if a situation in which a certain phenomenon occurs differs in only one other respect from a situation in which it does not occur, then this single circumstance, which is present in one case and absent in the other, is to be regarded as " the effect, or the cause, or an indispensable part of the cause of the phenomenon in question ". The method of difference, which is essentially a method of elimination, was regarded by Mill as the more powerful of the two and indeed as being capable, at least in principle, of yielding certainty in its results.

Even from this brief description it should be clear that Mill's methods are somewhat artificial. It is assumed that the field of possible causes is sharply differentiated like a list of candidates at an examination, and furthermore that the total number and quality of the candidates can be completely known. Now there is a sense in which this may be held to apply at an advanced stage of experiment, so that Mill's methods, when suitably interpreted, do in fact receive some practical corroboration. But they cannot be taken as general canons of scientific procedure. Nor, even in the cases where they apply, does any of them yield logical certainty. And indeed this is not to be expected of them. For Mill was concerned with establishing empirical hypotheses. And it is only when it acquires the status of a convention, and so ceases to be a hypothesis, that it can become logically certain.

In the latter half of the nineteenth century, there was a reaction among British philosophers against the empiricism of Mill and his school. And since this reaction took the form of adherence to the philosophy of Kant and Hegel, its effect was to widen the breach between philosophy and science. For the philosophy of Kant, which was written in the eighteenth century, was primarily an attempt to furnish an *a priori* justification of the Newtonian ideas of space and time and cause. And while the philosophy of Hegel was intended by him to be scientific, and did indeed contain a curiously "modern" element in its conception of process, it was its metaphysical aspect, the incomprehensible pilgrimage of the Absolute Idea, that fascinated his British disciples. It was only at the turn of the century that the connection between science and philosophy began to be re-established, on the one hand through the work of Bertrand Russell, Whitehead, and the mathematical logicians, and on the other through the interest aroused among philosophers by the science of biology.

In biology, the most striking nineteenth-century developments were the introduction of the cell theory, contemporaneously with, and in some respect paralleling, John Dalton's theory of chemical atoms ; and secondly, the Darwinian theory of evolution. The theory of evolution was at once seen as philosophically important. But philosophers like Herbert Spencer were more interested in drawing what they took to be its ethical implications than in making it the source of new philosophical ideas. Bergson, with his *élan vital,* did indeed acquire some following in England, but the most interesting offshoot philosophically of the theory of evolution was a theory developed in the twentieth century by Lloyd Morgan, and independently by Alexander—the theory of emergence. The fundamental assumption of this theory of emergence is that phenomena can be arranged in such a way that the laws which obtain at one level are not reducible to those which obtain at another. And from this it is inferred that when a set of elements falls into a suitable pattern, the pattern as a whole acquires properties that do not belong independently to any of its constituent parts. That is to say, new properties emerge from the arrangement and this is conceived not merely as a logical but also as a temporal process. Thus, in Alexander's system, the basic constituents of the world are point-instants. Point-instants form a pattern which has the physical qualities constituting the electron ; a certain arrangement of electrons forms the atom ; atoms have chemical qualities and combine to form the molecule ; and so throughout all the levels of matter, with each stage exhibiting qualities of a higher logical order. Out of matter emerges mind, and mind is evolving towards deity. Thus, in this system, there is no God who creates the World, but point-instants are eventually going to create God. This is a bold and interesting speculation but it takes us a long way from the original assumption about the interrelationship of scientific laws. And even this assumption is not certainly authenticated. It is by no means certain, for example, that biological phenomena cannot be accounted for by the laws of chemistry and physics, though it is true that this reduction of biology to physics has so far remained an ideal that some biologists aspire to, rather than an operation that they are actually able to carry out.

When nineteenth-century scientists themselves philosophised, they tended—with some notable exceptions, such as T. H. Huxley—to be mechanical materialists. Their materialism had indeed its romantic features ; it represented the pursuit of scientific knowledge as a wonderfully successful adventure ; but it also gave rise among the audience to which it was directed to a romantic hostility towards science, a hostility which arose from the idea that science was essentially dry and soulless, that it abstracted all the life and colour out of the world. Thus, it became fashionable to say that scientific method could yield at best only a fraction of the whole truth about reality. It was allowed that the scientists might succeed in constructing a reasonably accurate picture of the material universe. But what about the existence of mind ?

The obvious answer to this is that there is no reason in principle why mental phenomena should not be as much subject to natural law as anything else. Otherwise the development of the social sciences, which is also a feature of the nineteenth century, would hardly have been possible. But even when this is granted some difficulties remain. For if the physical world is to be regarded as a closed system, in the sense that the causes and effects of any physical event are to be found only among other physical events, then there is no place for any sort of interaction between mind and body. And this seems to contradict our ordinary experience. Furthermore, it appears fatal to the common-sense belief in the freedom of the will. This belief already seems to be threatened by the assumption of psychological determinism ; and it is for this reason that some philosophers have wished to deny that mental events are entirely subject to natural law. In the interests of human freedom, and consequently of morality, they have denied the possibility of deducing from causal laws how on any given occasion an individual will choose to act. But if there is an antithesis between freewill and determinism, the assumption of physical determinism is already sufficient to take away our freedom of action ; for all human actions issue in physical events. And once the freedom of action is gone there is not much point in insisting upon an empty freedom of choice.

These problems greatly troubled the Victorians, and well they might. The solution of them is, I think, to be found in a logical analysis of the notion of determinism, whereby it is made clear that the establishment of causal laws is ultimately only a way of correlating different elements of our experience, and that such correlations may take diverse forms. In this way we can get rid of the misleading picture of the mental and physical worlds as distinct causal systems, and also of the superstition that causes and effects are somehow joined together like members of a chain gang.

It may then be seen that there need be no opposition between freewill and determinism. For it is possible to give a satisfactory sense to freedom which is not incompatible with the hypothesis that human behaviour is systematic. And this is all that is required by the assumption of determinism. The germs of this solution are indeed to be found in the writings of John Stuart Mill, but with the philosophical reaction against empiricism the fruit of his insight was lost.

That scientific method could not yield the whole or final truth about reality was also the view taken by the idealist philosophers like Bradley, whose objection to science was that it did not make the world intelligible. But what these philosophers understood by the world's being made intelligible was that every true proposition should be shown to be logically necessary. And this is a demand which it is logically impossible to satisfy. However high we carry our explanations of events, we never wholly escape from fact into logic. The basic datum is always a matter of fact, the fact that things happen as they do. This being so, it is silly to ask more of any theory than that it should successfully apply to the world as we find it. The fact that the propositions of science are not logically necessary, so far from being an objection to them, is an indispensable condition of their giving us an understanding of nature. No doubt there will always be metaphysicians to whom the scientific type of answer is emotionally unsatisfying ; but there is no warrant in logic for putting anything else in its place. To quote an eighteenth-century philosopher, " Things are what they are, and their consequences will be what they will be ; why then should we seek to be deceived ? "

Physical Science and the Beliefs of the Victorians

N. F. MOTT

I AM talking to you tonight on the influence of physical science on Victorian thought. In the use of physical science for industry and manufacture, the Victorians were, of course, pioneers. The industrial revolution began in England; and the Englishmen in the nineteenth century were the first men to feel that exhilaration, that sense of power, that belief that everything is possible, that seems to come when a nation first learns to use machinery. Other countries have experienced something similar at later periods; for instance, in present-day Russia where it is probable that much of the energy and the self-confidence comes from the invigorating effects of industrialisation in its first stages. There is, however, one very striking contrast between the outlook of the modern Russians on the physical science that they use in their industry, and the outlook of the Victorians. As far as we can see, the ideas and beliefs of the Russians, their Marxist philosophy, are so well attuned to their industrial development that there is no conflict at all between them. But, with the Victorians, this was not so. Their religious beliefs frequently came into conflict with the findings of science, and their æsthetic senses conflicted with the results of industrialisation. It is mainly about this conflict, which seems so to have enriched Victorian thought, that I wish to talk tonight. Or rather, my thesis is with a part of this conflict, that part which was due to the impact on their way of thinking of physical science. There is no need for me to remind you that the scientific doctrine which impinged most directly on the thought of the era was Darwin's theory of evolution. But physical science supported Darwin in many ways; it also suggested mechanistic interpretations of natural phenomena, and its widespread use in industry was a constant reminder of its importance.

Now, in spite of the great advances that took place in the nineteenth century, the most striking thing about Victorian physics is the continuing validity right through the century of Newtonian mechanics. The whole edifice of nineteenth-century physics is based on Newton's laws of motion. It was only in the twentieth century that the theory of relativity, and still more the quantum theory, showed that the principles of Newtonian mechanics are not universally valid, and in fact break down for the particles of which the atom is built. But Victorian physics *is* essentially Newtonian. Now Newton died in 1727 ; yet in England, at any rate, it was not until the Victorian Age that much feeling of conflict arose between religion and the laws that scientists discover about the physical world. One sees the beginnings of the conflict in the writings of Godwin ; but its full development is to be found in the writings of Victorians such as John Stuart Mill and Huxley. To show you why this was so, I must remind you of the nature of Newton's laws.

Newton's laws of motion had their most striking success in astronomy. They were used already before the nineteenth century to predict the movements of planets, to predict eclipses for instance. Newton's laws make it possible to do this if you know just where every planet is, and just how fast and in what direction each one is moving. If you know that, the rest is calculation. But, apart from this, Newton's laws had great success in physics and engineering. And they were always of the same type. They always made it possible to calculate the future behaviour of any material system if only the position and velocity of all its parts were known. Such a system of laws is utterly deterministic. If they could be shown to be of universal validity, mankind would be forced into a mechanistic philosophy.

To the Victorians this conclusion raised questions of the utmost importance. They had to ask whether science really embraced all the phenomena of nature. The belief in freedom of will was strongly held, as was natural in an adventurous era which felt itself master of its fate. It was supported by religious ideas about personal responsibility. All these seemed antagonistic to the findings of science.

The men of the seventeenth and eighteenth centuries did not seem to feel this conflict. To them the rule of law was obviously in accord with the divine will. Their attitude was, I think, expressed by Descartes when he wrote : " God never changes His fashion of acting, and conserves the world in the same behaviour with which He has created it ". And he goes on to say that in order that they may continue to move with the laws originally given to them, God must keep matter moving with the motion that it originally had. And the same feeling of the essential rightness of matter moving according to preordained laws is shown in Addison's hymn :

> The spacious firmament on high
> With all the blue ethereal sky
> And spangled heavens a shining train
> Their great Original proclaim.
>
> In reason's ear they all rejoice
> And utter forth a glorious voice,
> For 'ever singing as they shine
> The hand that made us is divine.

The regularity of the planetary motions and of the laws which they obey are felt to be evidence of the existence of a divine lawgiver. Indeed no one who looks at eighteenth-century architecture, at the ordered terraces of Bath for instance, could believe that its creators would have any antipathy to the conceptions of natural law.

But to the Victorians the idea of the rule of law was far less attractive. It was replaced by the idea of progress. It was an era of opportunity, an era in which everything could be tried, any style of architecture, many philosophies, many movements in religion. And yet physical science continued to advance along mainly Newtonian lines, building up a more and more completely deterministic system based on law. I would like to illustrate this by mentioning two of the most important advances in Victorian physics : the discovery of electro-magnetic radiation, and the discovery of the nature of heat. The first is due to the great Cambridge mathematician Clerk-Maxwell. He found out the laws governing the behaviour of electro-magnetic waves, in other words the radio waves of broadcasting. He did this even before they were shown by experiment to exist. This was a discovery in the true Newtonian tradition. The laws of electro-magnetic radiation were just like Newton's laws. If one knows what a radio wave is doing now, one can calculate its behaviour in the future, as it travels out into space. Maxwell's theory was entirely deterministic, as was all the physics of that time.

More important in the history of thought was the discovery of the nature of heat. This began early in the century with the enunciation by the French engineer Sadi Carnot of what we now call the second law of thermodynamics. This was discovered by him through the study of heat engines and is a classic example of the debt owed by physics to engineering. Briefly it states that heat will not of its own accord flow from a cold place to a hot place ; or it puts in a quantitative form the obvious fact that if you leave a hot bath in a cold bathroom, the bath gets colder and the air of the bathroom gets warmer. Also it states that nothing you can do will reverse the process. The transference of heat from the bath to the air is, to use a technical expression, irreversible. And so Carnot's principle can be said to give a direction to time ; it makes a distinction between the past, when the bath was hot and the bathroom was cold, and the future, when they will both be tepid. There is nothing in Newton's laws at all like that ; there is nothing, for instance, to distinguish the future movement of the planets from the past. Carnot's principle in physics is like evolution in biology ; both are principles which emphasise change and the flow of time.

In the second half of the century, thanks to the work of Joule, Kelvin and particularly Maxwell, an explanation of Carnot's principle was given in terms of atomic theory. This we call the kinetic theory of matter, and most of its principles still retain their validity in the modern physics of the twentieth century. The kinetic theory shows that Carnot's principle is at any rate not at variance with Newtonian mechanics. The main ideas of the kinetic theory are as follows : Heat consists of the rapid motion of the atoms or molecules of which the hot body is made. Thus in a hot bath the molecules are moving faster than the molecules of cold air. Or, to be more exact, they have on the average more energy. So, in terms of the kinetic theory, when the bath gets cool and the air of the bathroom warm, it means that the molecules of water lose energy and the molecules of the air gain energy. In the end they will all have about the same energy. Why should this occur ? The answer is, that it is not absolutely certain, but it is extremely probable. If you spin a penny a thousand times, you would expect to get about as many heads as tails. You would think it a queer coincidence if you did not. The calculations of a life insurance company are of just this type ; although they do not know when any one man will die, they can be pretty that roughly so many will die in any one year. The arguments of the kinetic theory are statistical, in just this way ; although it is not absolutely certain that the bath will get cold, yet because of the very large number of molecules with which we have to deal, it has the same kind of virtual certainty as the predictions of an insurance company.

Maxwell's kinetic theory bears the same relations to Carnot's laws as the hypothesis of natural selection does to the theory of evolution. According to the principle of natural selection, we may suppose, the long-necked giraffe is very likely to survive at the expense of the shorter one, because he can get the leaves at the top of the tree. It is very likely that he will survive, but not quite certain ; the long-necked giraffes might have bad luck, and all get eaten by lions. But, in the long run, this would not be very likely, so the principle of natural selection would prevail. It is just like this with the kinetic theory.

So to the determinism of Newton's laws, Maxwell and the atomic theory added the tyranny of large numbers. Events are determined by the most probable behaviour of numerous particles. All these particles are exactly the same, just as if they were manufactured, as Maxwell put it. It would be easy to trace an analogy between the kinetic theory and the economic theory of *laissez-faire*. But, in fact, the heyday of *laissez-faire* was already passed when the kinetic theory was established, and I would prefer to show the impact of these ideas on the more humane spirits of the age. It is true that some scientists clung to an eighteenth-century way of thought. Faraday, for instance, writes in 1846, that when he perceives that certain natural pheno-mena follow " by virtue of powers in the molecule that are indestructible, and by laws of action the most simple and un-changeable, we may well, if I may say it without irreverence, join awe and trembling with joy and gladness ". But, to the later Victorians, there was much that was repellent in " the advancing tide of law and matter and the receding tide of spirit and spontaneity ". Thomas Henry Huxley expressed with great force the dilemma of the time. He writes in 1870 in his famous lecture on the physical basis of life: ". . . . I can find no intelligible ground for refusing to say that the properties of protoplasm result from the nature and disposition of its molecules.

"But I bid you beware that, in accepting these conclusions, you are placing your feet on the first rung of a ladder which, in most people's estimation, is the reverse of Jacob's, and leads to the antipodes of heaven. It may seem a small thing to admit that the dull vital actions of a fungus, or a foraminifer, are the properties of their protoplasm, and are the direct result of the nature of the matter of which they are composed. But if, as I have endeavoured to prove to you, their protoplasm is essentially identical with, and most readily converted into, that of any animal, I can discover no logical halting-place between the admission that such is the case, and the further concession that all vital action may, with equal propriety, be said to be the result of the molecular forces of the protoplasm which displays it. And if so, it must be true, in the same sense and to the same extent, that the thoughts to which I am now giving utterance, and your thoughts regarding them, are the expression of molecular changes in that matter of life which is the source of our other vital phenomena".

And later he says that the consciousness of this weighs like a nightmare on the best minds of the day.

John Stuart Mill writes in the same strain : ". . . the doctrine of what is called philosophical necessity," he says, "weighed on my existence like an incubus. I felt as if I were scientifically proved to be the helpless slave of antecedent circumstances ; as if my character and that of all others had been formed for us by agencies beyond our control, and was wholly out of our own power. I often said to myself, what a relief it would be if I could disbelieve the doctrine of the formation of character by circumstances. It would be a blessing if the doctrine of necessity could be believed by all about the character of others and disbelieved in regard to their own".

The robust desire of John Stuart Mill for belief in a free will of his own, at the least, in spite of the contradiction with the trend of scientific thought which that would imply, is, I think, typical of his age. But I do not think that the conflict felt by the Victorians between their deterministic science and their desire for individual freedom was a stultifying one, or one which inhibited their action in any way. I would like to finish by quoting Huxley's solution of the whole problem. " Permit me," he writes, " to enforce this most wise advice. Why trouble ourselves about matters about which, however important they may be, we know nothing and can know nothing ? We live in a world which is full of misery and ignorance, and the plain duty of all of us is to make the little corner he can influence somewhat less miserable and ignorant than it was before he entered it ".

Huxley, like Voltaire, would advise us to cultivate our own garden. But Huxley's is a wider garden than ever Voltaire knew—the garden of human progress.

Man and Nature : Some Artists' Views

HUMPHRY HOUSE

I WAS trying to write the script of this talk over Easter. I looked out of my windows at the plum-blossom fully out, and the pear not far behind, and the first green showing on the apple trees ; rooks carried twigs across my rectangles of clear sky ; the sun has been shining on the table. I have not wanted to think specially about the Victorians, still less make up a talk about them ; but the very things seen from the window brought scraps of their poems to mind ; and it's a love of fact like the Victorians' that has made me think what a ridiculous season this is, when all the poems belonging to April and May seem to belong simultaneously to the end of March. The blossomed pear-tree, the wise thrush ; the glassy pear-tree leaves and blooms, they brush the descending blue ; that blue is all in a rush with richness.

> " In Springtime when the leaves are young,
> Clear dewdrops gleam like jewels, hung
> On boughs the fair birds roost among."

Scraps of their descriptive poetry—what the Victorians called the poetry of " word-painting "—have been coming into my mind ; and it has been a shock to remember that " In the Spring a young man's fancy lightly turns to thoughts of love " is a line out of *Locksley Hall*. For a good deal to do with Man and Nature is implicit in that line ; and the word " lightly " is so curious.

And when my mind has wandered off to Darwin in the Galapagos Islands, where the volcanic landscape reminded him of the furnaces of Staffordshire ; to Diana Warwick walking on the Surrey hills ; to the Queen's life in the Highlands ; to Millais's *Scotch Firs,* and *The Deserted Garden* and *The North-West Passage.* And it was this picture in the end—*The North-*

West Passage—that gave me a clue about where this talk might, with all the bewildering stuff that could go into it, begin.

The love of fact is the clue. You will remember that the sub-title of the picture is " It might be done, and England ought to do it ". If there is a single fact about the geography of the globe still undiscovered, then something should be done to find it out, and it should be done by an Englishman. It is important that Darwin's work began on a naval survey voyage.

It was by means of the patient accumulation of fact that the Victorians domesticated mystery, made Romanticism res-pectable. From that point two attitudes developed : one was the purely scientific, for which the facts were all—as they were for Darwin—facts loved with a lingering passion. The other was a sentimental love of fact, for the sake of what could be easily attached to it in the way of belief and feeling. Both attitudes started from a common literalness of mind. Victorian senti-mentality is largely the imposition of feeling as an afterthought upon literalness.

Publications such as the *Penny Magazine* and Chambers's *Miscellany* and many others like them—some produced by The Society for the Diffusion of Useful Knowledge, and some by private enterprise—were designed to show that knowledge of fact about Nature and about History was of practical advantage. It was believed in the Early Victorian Age that the common man could keep pace with science and that the more he knew about botany and the rest, the better and the more useful man he would be. There was a spate of popular informative factual literature in the 'thirties and 'forties. The Exhibition of 1851 was the climax of this phase, the visible triumph of Useful Knowledge. From that time things tended to become less popular and more specialised. It was realised that the facts were too complicated for popular exposition in detail ; but the love of fact for its sentimental attachments remained.

The love of literalism and the love of exaggerated sentiment are two essential points for understanding Victorian art. The problem was either to avoid literalism and an extreme of senti-ment, or to reach a point of stability between them.

Nothing is more remarkable than the decay of the great Romantic tradition, the stifling of its grandeur ; Romanticism, as I have said, was made respectable. This was brought about partly by the narrow practical business manners of a rising bourgeoisie, partly by the pre-eminent intellectual insistence on the importance of fact. The cosmic visions of Blake or Shelley were brought to trial against the cosmic facts of astronomy and historical geology. Man was dwarfed by the new conception of time and had to exaggerate his morality and his sentiment in order to restore his self-esteem.

The abnormal consciousness of time is very apparent in all Victorian painting—not merely in the obvious love of historical themes and antiquarian detail, nor in the anecdotal *genre* pictures and the countless illustrations to eighteenth-century novels, but also in pictures with a minimum of anecdotal content. The world of their pictures is a world in which you expect things to happen. The pictures seem to refer to what has gone before or what will come after. This is achieved sometimes by the treatment of human figures who look as if they're going to walk out of the canvas in a moment ; sometimes by animals ; sometimes by wind or sea that blows and splashes in your eyes ; sometimes by an object like a sundial, or a mossy stone, or a falling leaf. Even a plain natural object looks like Tennyson's *Talking Oak* or his brook that babbles " Men may come and men may go, but I go on for ever ". If there is a picture of a rainy afternoon you start wondering what there will be for tea.

This is all partly because the style of vision is the vision of ordinary life. The world of Victorian art is the world of the plain, practical man, in which things happen and are done. It is an art to suit a practical age and be bought by practical patrons. This also helps to explain the appearance in the pictures of a " limitless " Nature : every effort is made to put everything in, as if the whole practical external world could be crowded into a canvas. The desire for this limitless effect was so strong that Henry Holliday actually made a special kind of huge stereoscope to increase his field of vision as widely as possible — a device with an exactly opposite purpose to that of the eighteenth-century landscape mirror which was designed to reduce the field of vision to a manageable composition.

The invention of photography did not, I believe, produce visual habits which the painters had not already begun to develop. One might almost argue that photography was invented to meet an existing demand for records of visual fact, rather than the other way round. There is little evidence that in its early days photography seriously influenced painting one way or another. Both camera and painter's eye were alike used to make all-inclusive visual records ; and in a sense the painter had an advantage because he could cheat : the photographers then chiefly cheated by trying to make their pictures look like paintings—a softened version of real life. Frith, who is often called a photographic painter, managed to get more clear detail into his pictures than any camera could achieve. He once tried to paint a portrait from a photograph, and gave it up as a failure. But Frith is the plainest example of all of a painter with the practical domestic vision.

In the attitude to Nature shown in Victorian art there is a lack of individual physical vision and also a lack of what one might call spiritual insight. Constable's highly personal vision of light almost died with him, at any rate in England; he seemed to teach few others anything. Turner had a few imitators, but a glance at a landscape by, say, Pyne, is enough to show that all the essential qualities are missing. With Samuel Palmer the loss of vision and insight occurred in the life and work of the one man ; in the Victoria and Albert Museum today one can see his glorious cherry-tree in the garden at Shoreham side by side with one of his later landscapes : the two pictures seem to belong to different worlds. In poetry, the imitators of Wordsworth either catch only the superficial aspects of his themes, or else they express their desire for a spiritual experience in the face of Nature, which they confess they do not directly achieve. One finds too that Wordsworth was often praised for the wrong reasons, especially for the minute fidelity of Natural description ; yet he was not particularly good at this nor very interested in it. The examples that Ruskin quotes in *Modern Painters* are only such as would strike the eye of a man who was himself concerned about such things. The details that were so much loved in Tennyson were of a different kind, and Mrs. Gaskell put her finger on the spot when she made the man in *Cranford* go and look at some ash-buds because Tennyson had said they were black. But they are only black to a literal vision in a particular kind of light. You will remember, too, all the controversy about whether the " sea-blue bird of March " was or was not a kingfisher. Chestnuts pattering to the ground, heavily hanging hollyhocks, rooks blown about the skies—these are the poetry of the period of literalism ; and the elm-tree bole in tiny leaf, of course.

Ruskin's *Modern Painters* is a valiant struggle—and one which has not even now lost its value—to reconcile the scientific consciousness, the fidelity to constant external fact, with the belief that Art was somehow concerned with individual vision and with mystery. It is more than an ephemeral tract against current academic conventions and the art criticism of John Eagles; its concern with Locke's theory of primary and secondary qualities, with the theory of light, with the structure of clouds and so on marks an attempt to incorporate within the world of Nature with which the artist deals the world of Nature with which the scientist deals. It is a plea that artists should *know*. To us the most surprising feature of the book is that of all modern painters the one constantly praised for his " pure straightforward rendering of fact " should be Turner ; the example is so wide of what we would expect either from the theory or from the other painters given faint praise.

"Details alone," said Ruskin in the Preface to the Second Edition, " Details alone, and unreferred to a final purpose, are the sign of a tyro's work ". " In landscape," he said, " botanical or geological details are not to be given as a matter of curiosity or subject of search, but as the ultimate elements of every species of expression and order of loveliness ". These last words are very obscure, but they show a common underlying problem for both painters and poets. Because the Romantic tradition said that Nature was somehow the source of important spiritual experience and because the habit of mind of the following generation, with an empirical scientific philosophy, was to dwell so lovingly on factual detail, a suspicion came about that perhaps the cause of the spiritual experience lay in the detail. I think this is how Ruskin read, or misread, Wordsworth. It also helps to explain the sentimentality which I have called the imposition of feeling as an afterthought upon literalness.

I can first illustrate this best from a description of the methods employed by Frederick Walker in his landscape painting, given by a friend of his called North :

" Walker painted direct from Nature, not from sketches. His ideal appeared to be to have suggestiveness in his work ;

not by leaving out, but by painting in, detail, and then partly erasing it. This was especially noticeable in his water-colour landscape work, which frequently passed through a stage of extreme elaboration of drawing, to be afterwards carefully worn away, so that a suggestiveness and softness resulted—not emptiness, but veiled detail. And there is scarcely an inch of his work that has not been at one time a careful, loving study of fact."

Lower down he writes of a possible reaction in Walker " from the somewhat unnatural clearness of definition in the early pictures of the Pre-Raphælite Brotherhood ".

A still more remarkable example of this mixture of sentiment and literalism occurs in a series of lectures *On the Poetic Interpretation of Nature,* which Principal Shairp gave in 1877. He says that the aim of a poet in observing the details of flowers :

" is to see and express the loveliness that is in the flower, not only the beauty of colour and of form, but the sentiment which, so to speak, looks out from it, and which is meant to awaken in us an answering emotion. For this end he must observe accurately, since the form and lines of the flower discerned by the eye are a large part of what gives it relation and meaning to the soul."

He says the poet must see the " outward facts of the wild-flowers " as they stand related " to the whole world, of which they are a part, and to the human heart, to which they tenderly appeal ".

To us these are very curious remarks. It is specially curious to find Shairp saying there is sentiment in the flower which *is meant* to awaken answering emotion in us. For his words do indeed seem to imply that this sentiment is verily in the flower, and is there for the poet to see. William Henry Hunt—" bird's nest Hunt " that is—said : " I feel frightened whenever I sit down to paint a flower ".

There was a very popular little book, reprinted by thousands, called *The Language of Flowers,* and I bought the other day a far more elaborate work which showed now the visible natural world is really packed with all the details of theology and ethics.

The best work of the Pre-Raphælites treats flowers with great particularity of detail in bright, clean colours : sentiment is not imputed to them ; the flowers are treated primarily for their own sake ; there may then also be an additional emblematic or symbolic meaning, but it does not distort the original directness. Holman Hunt always kept the emblematic purpose but unfortunately lost the directness of method. A whole series of sermons was preached on the botanical symbolism of *The Light of the World*. But if the flowers had been effectively symbolical the sermons ought not to have been necessary. There was no current convention in the matter. It has often been pointed out that it doesn't make two pins of difference poetically or ethically whether you say

> ' The lilies and languors of virtue, the roses and raptures
> of vice '

or

> ' The roses and raptures of virtue, the lilies and languors
> of vice.'

I don't think that these curiosities can be simply explained in terms of either " Anthropomorphism" or the " Pathetic Fallacy ".

One of Millais's most effective and satisfying Pre-Raphælite pictures, before his style went bad, is the drowning Ophelia ; and there there is a consciousness of reference to the symbolic use of flowers by Ophelia herself in the mad scene. Among many revealing critiques of Landseer's lions when they were added to the Nelson column was an article in *Art and Nature* which complained in one paragraph that they were not treated symbolically and heraldically enough, and in the next that they were not in detail naturalistic enough. The writer was evidently, like Holman Hunt, trying to have the best of both worlds.

The treatment of animals is, of course, another notable instance of the mixture of literalness and sentiment. Landseer was painting animals long before the Victorian Age ; but if you look, for instance, at his equestrian portrait of the Queen in 1839, which now hangs in Wyatt's huge Gothic hall at Ashridge, you will find still lingering traces of detached eighteenth-century treatment in the pony and dogs. Stubbs and others painted plenty of emotional animals, but they had animal emotions. Landseer in his later manner painted dogs, as John Piper has said, " with human eyes ". The habit of anthropomorphising animals spread outwards from dogs to horses and then to cattle. There is a picture by T. Sidney Cooper showing a number of cows at one side of a field, and at the other side, some distance from them, a single enormous bull. The title of the picture is *Separated but not Divorced.* The remarkable thing is that nobody seemed to think this funny.

In Landseer the process worked both ways. He made his dogs human : but he himself was quite prepared to go doggy.

" He was a brilliant talker, and could imitate to perfection the cry of any animal with which he was familiar. Being asked one day at Lord Rivers' to go and see a very savage dog that was tied up in the yard, he crawled up to the animal on his hands and knees, and snarled so alarmingly that the dog, overcome with terror, suddenly snapped his chain, jumped over the wall, and was never seen again."

All the anthropomorphism and the sentimental treatment of animals (as also the sentimental treatment of human beings themselves, especially children) was a means of infusing into what was otherwise a purely materialistic " scientific " representation of the external world some kind of " spirit ". It was, as I have already suggested, an afterthought. The effect of what we call sentimentality—that is of flabby and exaggerated sentiment— comes about partly because it is an afterthought, an added embellishment, extraneous to the first conception, and partly because the social and moral circumstances of the time required in art as well as in life the over-assertion of certain modes of feeling. The entirely novel stress on factual, measurable, statistical values and the expectation life offered of material gain— this called up in opposition an equally novel and self-indulgent stress on all those aspects of life which so obviously suffered from industrialism. Not all tenderness is sentimental, not even all Victorian tenderness. Mulready's picture *The Sonnet,* Madox Brown's *Autumn Afternoon* and some of Arthur Hughes's paint-ings, especially those of lovers meeting, are admirably tender. But such things as *Bubbles, The Mistletoe Gatherer, Hope* by Watts, illustrate the false tenderness of excess. No other art in the world, however bad, has ever been bad in quite this sort of way ; for its social context was unique. Both Nature and Art were being used as instruments for countering the obtrusive hardness of life.

In this process Art and natural scenery were thought of as partners whom the artist was to bring closer and closer together.

The countless landscapes which hung in the mansions of magnates who had made their fortunes in the hideous towns were a sort of propitiatory offering to make up for the squalor; they were also in the evenings thought of as sources of refreshment, light and peace. This had its counterpart in the cult of the actual country and the seaside. The railways made travel possible for thousands who could otherwise never have afforded to go so far ; the family summer holiday became an institution which was thought of as providing not merely rest from work but a spiritual regeneration from the sight of trees and fields and waves, and an education from collecting ferns and flowers and fossils and all the strangely curled and coloured creatures of the shore. Here is the beginning of Tennyson's *Sea Dreams* :

> " A city clerk, but gently born and bred ;
> His wife, an unknown artist's orphan child—
> One babe was theirs, a Margaret, three years old :
> They, thinking that her clear germander eye
> Droopt in the giant-factoried city-gloom,
> Came, with a month's leave given them, to the sea :
> For which his gains were dock'd, however small :
> Small were his gains, and hard his work . . . "

But there was something rather arid in all this uplift and in the belief that Nature by some sort of automatic alchemy could heal and restore both soul and body. Flowers might be capable of sentiment and dogs of tears; but man's place in Nature could not solely be that of a parasite on their virtues. He was, after all, a part of Nature in his own right : he was modifying Nature far more quickly than Nature was capable of modifying him : and besides, the biological link between man and dogs and sea urchins became at once more apparent after the publication of the *Origin of Species*. By the 'sixties the poets and novelists, though not the painters, were waking up to the essential link between man's sexuality and the productive vitality of nature, to the fact that when in spring a young man's fancy turned to thoughts of love it did so not lightly but with a solemn swing in time with beast and bird. Though Blake, Keats and Shelley fully understood this, it is curious that Wordsworth's intense consciousness of closeness between Man and Nature was so little sexual, or at least that he does not seem to be aware of it ; Tennyson was only faintly so ; it is with Swinburne and Meredith that we again find clearly both the explicit recognition of sexual affinities and also the use of sexual imagery in other places. They both give a new importance and a new quality to the idea of Earth as the Mother of man as well as of all other living things ; and in them, too, appears for the first time among the Victorians, openly confessed and worked out, the idea of sexual reproduction as the common principle of all Life—the idea which had been so magnificently stated by Lucretius. In Meredith it is most fully developed in the poems ; but in the novels too it is a main factor in the development of characters and also in the connection between the characters and their landscape. The following passage describes this sexual character in *Diana of the Crossways* :

> " She gave him comprehension of the meaning of love :
> a word in many mouths, not often explained. With her,
> wound in his idea of her, he perceived it to signify a new
> start in our existence, a finer shoot of the tree stoutly planted
> in good gross earth ; the senses running their live sap, and
> the minds companioned, and the spirits made one by the
> whole-natured conjunction. In sooth, a happy prospect for
> the sons and daughters of Earth, divinely indicating more
> than happiness : the speeding of us, compact of what we
> are, between the ascetic rocks and the sensual whirlpools, to
> the creation of certain nobler races, now very dimly
> imagined."

This is something that George Eliot for all her alertness to life and all her knowledge of contemporary thought, never expressed in her books. Emily Brontë had known it instinctively. Rossetti had indoor inklings of it which came out in some of his pictures. But it was with Meredith, Hardy and Jefferies that it became a primary theme.

The detailed method of description, whether in literature or painting, made it difficult to show passion for fear of being indecent ; and even the trees seemed to stand without sap and without growth. Even in such a picture as Holman Hunt's *The Hireling Shepherd*, of which the subject is nothing but pastoral lust, all passion is not spent but absent. It was only when the kind of selection used by the great Romantics came in again that the vital principle of Man and Nature could again become a theme of art. By the end of the century, not only were the arts affected, but life as well. In *Love's Coming of Age*, in 1896, Edward Carpenter was quoting Meredith in support of his campaign for sexual frankness and wrote of human love as belonging to the open air.

> " Sexual embraces themselves seldom receive the benison of Dame Nature, in whose presence alone, under the burning sun or the high canopy of the stars and surrounded by the fragrant atmosphere, their meaning can be fully understood : but take place in stuffy dens of dirty upholstery and are associated with all unbeautiful things."

At the beginning of this talk I mentioned the problem of avoiding altogether or striking a point of stability between literalness and sentiment. I should like to suggest that the virtues of—to take a few examples—Emily Brontë, Dickens at his greatest, Rossetti sometimes and Gerard Manley Hopkins lay either in the avoidance or in this stability.

Man and Nature

HERBERT DINGLE

MY THEME is the Victorian view of Man and Nature as it was related to the science of the time ; and to understand Victorian science we must return to the Renaissance. For this was no age of revolution but the reverse—a period of development and progressive confirmation of ideas already established by the time of Newton. The scientific revolution had occurred in the seventeenth century. In the year 1600 the mediæval universe, synthesising all thought, was still dominant : by the year 1700 it lay in ruins, and the Newtonian conception of rigorous mathematical law operating throughout a universe infinitely greater in extent but at first immeasurably poorer in variety, was firmly enthroned in its place. A problem was set before the coming generations. Could the Newtonian system of thought, which completely comprehended the large-scale movements of bodies —could that system be extended to cover all phenomena ? Galileo, who laid the foundations of the system, thought not. To him, all that we observed, except the shapes and movements of bodies, belonged not to the external world but to ourselves. The colours of things, their sounds, temperatures, tastes, smells— and, *a fortiori,* any aesthetic or mystical qualities they might seem to possess—were subjective ; the external world was simply a lot of moving shapes, completely describable in mathematical terms.

Newton later gave the complete description, but he was not satisfied as a true Galilean should have been. Like Alexander, he sighed for fresh worlds to conquer ; and so he projected some of Galileo's subjective qualities out into the external world again, and left it to his successors to see if the mathematical method could be applied to their description also. The eighteenth and nineteenth centuries took up the challenge. Their task was first to create suitable concepts for the representation of colour, temperature, magnetic actions and rest—concepts which would perform the same function with respect to these things as that performed by Newton's mass, space and time in the description of mechanical motion ; and secondly, to discover the laws exhibited by the phenomena and to express them in terms of such concepts.

Broadly speaking, the discovery of the concepts was the work of the eighteenth century and the early part of the nineteenth, and the statement of the laws in terms of them was the work of the Victorians. Slowly and laboriously the concepts of heat, temperature and entropy took definite shape for the study of thermal phenomena ; the concepts of ether and transverse light-waves were created for optics ; electric fluids competed with other concepts for electrical attractions and repulsions ; atoms and molecules were devised to deal with chemical reactions ; and so on, until by the time Victoria came to the throne the stage was set and the cast was chosen for the mathematical drama of exis-tence to be played in all its scenes.

The last scenes were never reached—and, as we now know, could not have been reached with the concepts adopted—but rarely has there been so magnificent a failure. For, as the play proceeded, the minor characters one by one turned out to be the protagonists in disguise. Heat, temperature and entropy were not independent existences; they were themselves expressible in terms of mass and motion. Light-waves became more and more like ordinary mechanical strains and stresses in a matter-like ether. Electric and magnetic, and even gravitational, forces also appeared as mechanical stresses in the ether ; and chemical affinity began to show itself amenable to description as Newtonian forces between the smallest bits of matter. Thus the whole of our experience seemed to be the product of the blind, inexorable interaction of masses moving according to mathe-matical laws. Some experiences, it is true, remained intractable —there was no mathematical account, for instance, of our sense of beauty, of awe, or of obligation—but since, one after another, the experiences which Galileo thought subjective had become objectively describable when the right concepts had been found, it was hard to avoid the conclusion that these too would fall into line in the fullness of time. As if to confirm this view came Darwin's theory of evolution, which brought the innumerable and seemingly unconnected species of living things into a single system by means of the one correlating concept of natural selection under changing physical conditions. Such conditions were fast becoming expressible in mechanical terms, our bodies took form under their influence, and our minds could be observed to depend on our bodies. Hence all our mental life, and whatever spiritual life we might consider we had as well, was ultimately reducible to the movements of masses according to strict mathematical laws. That was the apparently inevitable implication of Victorian science.

And yet none but a few were convinced. When we consider the scepticism of the time in relation to the strength and unanimity of the forces operating, I think we must count the Victorian epoch supreme among the ages of faith. For never has so much indisputable evidence and so overwhelming a weight of probability compelled so simple and compact a conclusion with so small an effect. In the Middle Ages the sea of faith was at the full because the Moon of knowledge and the Sun of reason combined to draw it upwards. The mediæval universe justified astronomer and theologian alike, and faith abounded because it was unchallenged ; indeed, it was less faith than sight—or imagined sight. But in the nineteenth century knowledge and reason demanded the uttermost ebb, but the waters obstinately refused to obey. The materialistic argument couldn't be answered, so it was evaded or assailed by invective. Honourable names, like "rationalist" and "free-thinker", became terms of abuse, synonymous with "infidel". The poet, James Thomson, expressed the inescapable conclusion :

> " I find no hint throughout the Universe
> Of good or ill, of blessing or of curse ;
> I find alone Necessity Supreme ;
> With infinite Mystery, abysmal, dark,
> Unlighted ever by the faintest spark
> For us, the flitting shadows of a dream."

This was indeed the impassioned expression in the countenance of Victorian science, but it glared unheeded. Thomson's verse ran, its publisher tells us, "counter to the current of popular opinion". Popular opinion ! What right had the current of popular opinion to flow uphill ?

Today I think we can see the matter more clearly. Science

asserted that the world had no purpose: faith replied that there was a purpose, though we couldn't see it. Both were wrong. The world of Victorian science has no purpose, but, though no illusion, it is not the world. Galileo saw a world of matter and motion only, and kept within himself his experiences of colours and sounds, of love and hate, of laughter and tears. The post-Newtonians projected all these things into the external world, and transformed them one by one into matter and motion. What the post-Victorians have done is not only to put them back again, but to put matter and motion back with them, so that what their description reveals to us is not an external world driving us blindly along in its inevitable course, but rather the structure of our own experience. The truth began to appear with Einstein's principle of relativity in 1905, shortly after Victoria's death. Motion was not an absolute thing; you could regard yourself as moving in any way you wished, or not at all, provided you preserved the relative motions of bodies. Furthermore, the mass of a body depended on its motion, and since the motion was at your choice you could make it as massive as you liked. The world of mass and motion, then, instead of being something that shaped us, was something that we could shape.

All this, of course, lies outside our period, and brief statements may mislead. I would only add that the new knowledge does not invalidate Victorian science, but changes our view of its relation to man; it remains a priceless part of the knowledge of all time.

CANON V. A. DEMANT

SOME OF the talks in this series have hinted at the strange paradox in the Victorian attitude to Man and Nature. In the conscious thought of the time—before the reactions at the end of the period—man, including his spirit, was, as it were, immersed in the stream of Nature.

That is one side of the paradox. The other is that while in his mind man was being told that he was a product of Nature, his dispositions were being formed rather by the fact that he was then taking his greatest steps in subduing natural forces to his will, in applied science and the industrial revolution.

Now I believe that the unstable combination of these two

things, the belief that Man is part of Nature and the fact that he has become a would-be tyrant of Nature, has been disastrous. It led to uncriticised assumptions that whatever direction our civilisation took was a direction of Nature herself. History was regarded as Nature's highest self, and then revolts against this crude naturalism in the name of humanity—the moral and social protests—these too were attributed to Nature. Thus we got the idea of Progress, a misapplication of biological development to man's social and moral history. The Victorians were so excited at what their scientific men taught about change as the underlying reality, and they were so convinced of the finality of their moral, social and intellectual positions, that they read their aims into the process of change itself.

Another result of a too easy resolution of the Victorian paradox is the habit of refusing to believe that men can, in fact, defy Nature—the earth's and their own—to the point at which human existence is threatened. It leads them to ignore the need for conscious obedience to Nature, for discipleship, as it were, in this sphere. I don't think that this is a highly materialistic epoch of ours ; it is rather a period of over-confidence in man's knowledge, ability and intention, which leads to a defiance of his limitations, and this defect I largely attribute to the heritage from the Victorians who were so impressed by man's participation in Nature that they thought *that* at any rate couldn't go wrong. The Victorian contribution did not in its outcome take man away from dependence upon God and remind him of his dependence upon Nature ; it emancipated him, in his consciousness, from obedience both to God and to Nature. Part of the trouble was that the Victorians were learning a great deal about continuity in the physical world and so they imagined that continuity was the only kind of unity in things. They found it hard to recognise a unity between such things as Nature and the inner life of man—a unity of polar opposites in the same field such as Christianity affirms by knowing God as the author of both Nature and the soul. The Victorians had perforce to bring them into continuity with one another, for apart from a religious interpretation of existence, with God as the source of unity, men will always have to choose between a complete lack of meaning or making continuous what reality—less tidy than the intellect— has made discreet.

The wiser and humbler of the Victorians did not force things into the category of continuity. T. H. Huxley, for instance, openly acknowledged that " the cosmic process had no sort of relation to moral ends " and that progress meant combating Nature. Huxley was content to leave this dualism an unresolved mystery and to work for the improvement of his own corner of the world without an answer. In this he was greater than his more consistent colleagues and descendants. The eighteenth century had, on the whole, turned with relief to the harmony of Nature away from the chaos of history and the human heart, just as the later romantics were to seek solace in Nature and in the Past from the aridities and emptiness of a utilitarian age. But the scientific Victorians were not satisfied to leave human affairs without sense or significance. In order to give them a meaning—that is to say to find a warrant for human aims in some more ultimate realm of reality—they tended to read human ideals into the natural process. For them it was the ascendancy of the nineteenth-century middle-classes that defined human ideals, and having read all this into Nature they said, so to speak, look what an intelligent and purposive thing this Nature is. You find that in the weaker sides of Macaulay and John Stuart Mill, both of them very great men. More critical spirits like Huxley could not find the key to human problems in sub-human Nature, and having no religious source of meaning, they paved the way for the pessimism of Bertrand Russell with its wistful picture of " Man's lofty thoughts ennobling his little day " finally extinguished by " the trampling march of unconscious power ", and also for the pessimism of Hardy and Housman in literature.

There was a fundamental instability about the alleged Naturalism of the Victorian Age. In these talks we are trying to see what we can learn from the Victorians—their contributions and their mistakes. That is a risky thing to do, for every epoch is sure that it knows the errors of its predecessors. But if we are self-critical we can modestly make the attempt.

I think the main error of the Victorian Age was to project its own greatness, its relative stability, its growing power, its rationalist inheritance from the eighteenth century, and its moral heritage from the European tradition—to project all this into Nature herself and so to assume that they are assured of survival.

This misplaced confidence ignored that these things—and science itself—came out of an historic development of a highly specialised kind, with a unique religious and cultural tradition ; it ignored the need for continuous or repeated tending and defending and renewal of that tradition ; it was blind to the destructive and explosive forces just below the surface, forces which could not be curbed by rational moralism as they had been curbed at the beginning of our era by a severely realistic religious discipline. The failure of the rational moralism of the Victorians has led in our day, on the one hand, to a sceptical opportunism and, on the other hand, to purely social interpretations of morality and the intolerant clash of peoples, cultures and classes each with absolute messianic pretensions.

A lesser man often tells us more about a period than its greatest representatives, for he exposes its unsolved problems more naïvely. One such Victorian was Henry Thomas Buckle who wrote a *History of Civilisation*. Without knowing what he did he summed up the whole paradox of the Victorian attitude to Man and Nature. On the one hand man is a child and product of Nature and cannot be understood in any other way ; but on the other hand man is also scientist, engineer and trader—the rational being who subdues Nature. Buckle finds a meaning for the whole human enterprise purely in terms of the future superseding the past : what man is going to be is good, what he has been is bad. European man, he says, is the bearer of humanity's destiny for, in his own words, " The tendency has been, in Europe, to subordinate Nature to man ; out of Europe to subordinate man to Nature . . . the great division therefore between European civilisation and non-European civilisation is the basis of the philosophy of history ". The terrifying simplicity and innocence of this typical Victorian view becomes even more clear to us when we notice that Buckle also sincerely held that war would disappear because the trained armies' desire for war would be overridden by the more intelligent and numerous civilians ; that the free market would overcome national jealousies, that increased communication and transport would dissolve hatreds and pre-judices. The history of our time has proved every one of these predictions to be wrong. But their significance is that they express so crudely some of the errors we have inherited from the Victorians. Two of these errors stand out : One is to identify the successes of a particular period with absolute and unconditional truth and goodness, at least in direction ; the other is to hold that the constructive forces are subduing the destructive ones by the mere process of Nature or the march of history. We have to learn that no age is nearer than its predecessors to a solution of these questions ; they have to be dealt with at each stage with a discipline which is realistic in the Christian sense, avoiding both a purely idealist and a purely naturalist interpretation of man—knowing that he is involved in Nature but yet is not entirely of it, for he lives and acts in Nature with a status and a power not given by it.

L. L. WHYTE

THE DOMINANT characteristic of Victorian thought, in relation to tonight's topic, was its emphasis on the view that physical man is part of the order of Nature, one organic species amongst many. But beside this development of an old idea, we find in the Victorian period newer ideas spreading which express a further stage in thought, the view that conscious man also is part of Nature, that his thoughts and feelings, as well as his body, belong to the natural order. The trend in both these aspects is towards the recognition of the complete man, conscious being as well as physical organism, as part of the order of nature.

But the prevalent scientific belief was that Nature is quantitative, obeying laws expressed in terms of numbers. So we may say that the Victorians tried to see man as part of quantitative Nature, but that in doing so they tended to neglect the human mind.

The view that physical man is a part of the order of Nature was an element both in ancient thought and in mediæval Christianity. What was novel in the later decades of the Victorian period was that scientific method had been applied by Darwin and Wallace to give a new precision and significance to an old idea, so that certain features of the traditional religious view of man were directly challenged. For if the human race was a biological species, then man was in the middle of his biological history, and all doctrines and values were, like man himself, subject to change and development. No ideas or ideals were absolute, for everything was in course of evolution.

That open challenge was grave enough, but the unconscious shock went deeper. Darwin had placed man in organic nature, but Nature was believed to be subject to Newtonian laws, and these laws were quantitative, atomic or mechanical, and expressed a determinism alien to the human mind, for it lacked any formative or developmental principle. Thus Darwin seemed to have imprisoned man in a Newtonian mechanical universe. The prestige of physical science was immense, and in viewing himself as part of Nature man unconsciously acknowledged the supremacy of quantity in all fields. The mind surrendered its true function, and entered the service of quantitative mechanism.

This is no hyperbole. The Victorian period owes its main characteristics to the fact that a great part of the energies of the community were devoted to the exploitation of quantitative techniques : to physical measurement, to developing increased horse-power and so increased production, and to the multiplication of bank balances. If Nature obeyed the laws of quantity—and the success of physics seemed to prove that— the Victorian *entrepreneur* had even less cause than his predecessors to question his impulse to express himself in some form of quantitative expansion. To him the growth of empire, of industry, of financial assets were all self-justifying activities even when, in the service of quantity, he neglected quality. The standard of living was being raised and knowledge steadily extended, but at a spiritual cost that would only later become evident.

Many leading Victorians thought that this increased knowledge and physical power justified the kind of rationalism current at the time. Reason was supreme, it had already established the fundamental mechanical laws, and using these it could go straight on to achieve Utopia—so it seemed to many ! But in surrendering to quantity, the representative man of the time had become unduly extrovert, he had largely forgotten his own mind and spirit—so the great integrating inheritance of Christianity began to fade, and national power politics and the personal ambitions of the *entrepreneur* increasingly dominated the social scene.

The universe seemed to be divided into two realms : the great practical realm of quantity and objective achievement, and the dwindling subjective realm of direct personal experience and religious, moral, and aesthetic values. On the one hand, expanding practical achievement, and on the other hand the wasting asset of a spiritual legacy operating mainly as a habit. This split gave rise to a yearning for harmony, shown, for example, in a romantic mood in literature which scarcely concealed the underlying sadism of dissociated and frustrated men, the cruelty born of the fear and conflict caused by this split in human nature that was to break out so disastrously in the present century.

But on the whole a superficial sense of optimism, of moral progress, and of security prevailed in Victorian England. Britannia was the workshop of the world and the mistress of the seas ; the Englishman of the upper and middle classes had little cause for fundamental doubt. The Continent began to listen to Schopenhauer, Marx, Dostoievsky and Nietzsche, with their premonitions of what was to come, and their suggestion that rational thought was a mere iridescence on the surface of life, and that beneath it lay the will to power, the economic class war, the a-rational divine purpose, or the vital impulse of man. But a utilitarian rationalist like John Stuart Mill was more suited to the experience of the fortunate English, who chiefly desired to have their optimism confirmed. Ruskin and Morris saw some of the dangers of mechanical industrialism, but their concern was beauty, and the expanding Victorian society in Britain remained blind to what lay ahead.

So much for the dominant feature, the service of quantity. But a deeper tendency, based on newer ideas was also at work. A few individuals were becoming more aware of the processes of their own thought, and were beginning to view human consciousness as a part of the order of Nature and therefore subject to inherent natural limitations. This new realisation took many forms. The historical interpretation of society implied that all thought was partly conditioned by its social context. Frazer, for example, was studying the social origins of human myths. Moreover the view was spreading that—I am quoting now—" It is our less conscious thoughts and our less conscious motives that mainly mould our lives ". That is Samuel Butler writing in 1872. In another field the study of language had led to the recognition that " the thoughts of men are limited by their forms of expression ", and that " language serves to perpetuate the errors as well as the truths of the preceding generations ".

That sounds like twentieth-century semantics, but it is from Stallo, an American, in a book published in London in 1885. Finally here is Bernard Shaw, writing in 1891 : " In our own century (the nineteenth, that is), the recognition of will, as distinct from the reasoning machinery began to spread ". That links straight on to the twentieth century, in which life, action, and the emotional aspects of experience are being widely valued above detached thought or pure reason.

You notice that all these ideas express the growing realisation that behind the experienced spontaneity of our conscious thoughts there lie social and organic tendencies, which we may neglect until we discover their importance through the scientific study of human beings and human history. In this way the Victorian period was beginning to view all the processes of consciousness, as well as human behaviour, as part of the order of nature, and the first steps were made towards a science of psychology.

That is how I see the Victorians' view of man's relation to Nature. They placed physical man squarely in organic nature, but the quantitative theories of the time held no place for the human mind. So the spiritual heritage was being dissipated without an adequate scientific picture of man being put in its place. The Victorians were largely unaware of the extent of the resulting damage, and few, if any, had an inkling of what lay ahead, or of the human capacity for conflict and cruelty. Today we have our eyes open to the failings of human nature, but the crucial problem is still unsolved. In an age when the prestige of science is so great, man cannot live properly, that is, in accordance with the potentialities of his nature, unless he has a valid scientific picture of himself. The human crisis today is due to the lack of a scientific conception of man so profoundly true that it can obtain general acceptance and promote health both in the individual and in society, as a unifying, healing, and developing tradition. Any such balanced picture of man must relate and integrate the human mind itself with Nature and the whole general order of things.

We certainly lack that comprehensive scientific conception of man, but we have made a step forward when we realise that that is our greatest need.

This talk was followed by a discussion.

THE

LIBERAL

IDEA

The Humanitarians

CHRISTOPHER DAWSON

THE NINETEENTH century was the classical age of humanitarianism, for it saw the development of a new sense of social responsibility and a new realisation of the evils which previous ages had either ignored or regarded as part of the order of nature. Above all it was an age of emotional sympathy for the under dog, whether the part of the under dog was taken by an oppressed nationality or exploited class or an unfortunate individual. But at the same time the nineteenth century was also an age of oppression and exploitation. It created slums as well as drains, and sweated industries as well as Factory Acts. And therefore the social consciousness of the age was also a guilty conscience, so that the concern for humanitarian reform and social justice was also a sign of repentance and a way of atonement.

This state of mind finds its most remarkable literary expression in Tolstoy's agonised search for a spiritual way of deliverance from the burden of social guilt. But we find a very similar attitude in Victorian England ; even such a sober observer as Beatrice Webb found the origin of the new ferment of social change in a " consciousness of sin among men of intellect and men of property."

But it is important to distinguish the particular responsibility of the Victorians from that of the nineteenth century as a whole. It is impossible to understand the Victorian Age unless we remember that the Victorians did not create the nineteenth-century world. That was the work of the preceding forty years, the age of industrial and political revolution ; and the Victorians inherited the task of gathering the harvest and paying off the debts which their fathers had left them.

The early nineteenth century was a hard and ruthless age, but it was not devoid of humanitarian idealism. Indeed it was during this age, more than at any other period of our history that English thinkers attempted to influence public opinion by organised ideological propaganda. The most famous example of this were the disciples of Bentham, the Utilitarians or philosophic Radicals who formed a regular sect during the early part of the century and produced a greater effect in a shorter time on English life than any other movement in our history.

Nor did the Utilitarians stand alone. There was also the school of William Godwin, the philosophic anarchist, which was represented by some of the greatest English writers of the age ; and there were the disciples of Robert Owen, the founder of English socialism, who carried on an intensive propaganda that lasted well into the Victorian Age.

All these people were humanitarian in the sense that they all accepted the principle of the greatest happiness of the greatest number and demanded the immediate and radical reform of the social system. All of them were liberals and almost all of them democrats who hated privilege and prejudice and possessed an unbounded faith in enlightenment and progress and the diffusion of knowledge. Unfortunately they differed so much in other respects that this community of ideals went for nothing ; the schism between the Utilitarians and the Utopians split the forces of the humanitarian movement for generations.

The effect of this schism was to strengthen the extreme tendencies on each side. The extremism of the idealists condemned them to ineffectiveness, with the result that the influence of Godwin and Owen has tended to be underestimated. But the extremism of the Utilitarians had just the contrary effect. It made them come to terms with much that was worse in contemporary society, so that their philosophy was used to cover the cruelties of early industrialism and the selfishness of middle-class morality. The reform of the Poor Law, which was the direct fruit of Utilitarian ideas and which was a sincere attempt to apply scientific principles to social problems, was at the same time felt by the common people an offence against humanity. " Rightly or wrongly," as a contemporary historian wrote, " the labourers of England believed that the New Poor Law was a law to punish poverty. It did more to sour the hearts of the labouring people than did all their privations "; nothing did more to create class hatred and popular revolt.

This was the situation of England at the beginning of the

Victorian Age, as seen by Engels in his *Condition of the English Working Classes* or by Disraeli in *Sybil, or The Two Nations*. Utilitarianism had become the philosophy of the new ruling class which turned a deaf ear and a stony face to the sufferings of the people. The idealists like Owen and Godwin and Southey were regarded as cranks or sentimentalists who had nothing to offer but quack remedies or moral exhortations. The only hope for the workers seemed to lie in class war and social revolution. Indeed it was the social condition of early Victorian England as seen by Engels which provided the background to the Communist Manifesto and the Marxian theory of the inevitability of revolution.

At this moment, however, a new factor intervened: it was the appearance of the Christian humanitarians, whose action cut across the existing division of ideological groups and political parties. These men had little in common with one another politically. They included a Tory land agent like Richard Oastler, a Methodist preacher like Joseph Rayner Stephens, a Radical factory owner like John Fielden, of Todmorden, and an Evangelical aristocrat like Lord Shaftesbury. They were not men of ideas, but they were men of great courage and integrity; they carried on an unequal fight against the strongest forces of the age—against the interests and prejudices of the new ruling class and the doctrines of the new political and economic fatalism which had created the hopeless misery of the Chartist period. Their action may be said to have ultimately changed the course of nineteenth-century history. Most of these men are forgotten today, many of them were forgotten in their own life time, but there is at least one who is still well enough known to rank as an Eminent Victorian and who is perhaps the most remarkable and influential of all the Christian humanitarians—I mean Anthony Ashley Cooper, the seventh Earl of Shaftesbury.

Shaftesbury took an active part in political life from 1827, when he was offered a place in Canning's government, down to his death in 1885, when Lord Salisbury was Prime Minister. He was not a good party man. In fact, he was a thorn in the side of successive governments owing to his disregard for political expediency and his unwearying persistence on behalf of unpopular causes. Charles Greville, who was a politician by instinct and

who did not like Shaftesbury at all, writes of his action over the
Factory Bill of 1844 : " The whole business is difficult and unpleasant. Government will carry their Bill now, and Ashley
will be able to do nothing, but he will go on agitating session
after session ; and a philanthropic agitator is more dangerous
than a repealer either of the Union or of the Corn Laws. We
are just now overrun with philanthropy, and God knows where
it will stop, or whither it will lead us".

Greville was right. That debate of 1844 marks a turning
point in our history. It cuts clean across the orthodox party
lines. The Conservative government was supported by Radicals
like Cobden and Bright and by Whigs like Lord Melbourne,
while Shaftesbury was supported by Whigs like Macaulay and
Palmerston as well as by extreme Radicals and extreme Tories.
Henceforward it was gradually recognised that the humanitarian
issue stood above party politics and that even the rigid dogmas
of nineteenth-century economic orthodoxy must yield when
they came into conflict with the elementary principles of justice
and humanity.

It was Shaftesbury who was primarily responsible for this
change in public opinion, for he did more than any other man
to break down the political and ideological barriers that separated
the different schools of humanitarian opinion. Thus immediately
after the battle of the Factory Law he became the ally of the most
active and uncompromising of the disciples of Bentham—Edwin
Chadwick—in the struggle for sanitary reform. Chadwick
stood at the opposite pole from Shaftesbury in temperament, in
tradition and in ideas. He more than any other man was
responsible for the New Poor Law which was the *bête noire* alike
of the Chartists and of the Tory humanitarians.

But though he was one of the most unpopular men of his time,
he was entirely single-minded in his hatred of dirt, disease and
selfish obstruction. He was the first and ablest of the new type of
Victorian official which created the social services—men like
Kay-Shuttleworth, R. A. Slaney and Southwood-Smith, all of
them in their way great servants of humanity as well as of the
State.

With Chadwick and Southwood-Smith Shaftesbury carried on
a crusade for six years against bad drains, bad housing and vested
interests. But these interests were too strong for the reformers.

The Board of Health was hunted to death, he wrote, by the press " the undertakers, the water companies, the Parliamentary agents and the whole tribe of jobbers who live on the miseries of mankind. The Commissioner of Sewers hated us with a perfect hatred'". The Board was broken up. Chadwick was shelved for the rest of his long life and Shaftesbury was offered the Garter, which he refused.

The whole episode illustrated both the strength and the weakness of the humanitarians. The religious humanitarians like Shaftesbury were able to co-operate with the scientific humanitarians like Chadwick. They were efficient and they got things done. But neither of them had much respect for public opinion and for the votes of the majority. Both in their own way were equally authoritarian, though the authoritarianism of Chadwick looked forward towards a centralised bureaucracy, while that of Shaftesbury looked back towards the paternal authority of a Christian state. If one must find a label for Shaftesbury's political views, I would describe him as a theocratic Conservative. Nor does he stand alone in this respect; the Victorian reaction against economic liberalism was to a great extent inspired by the same principles. Coleridge and Southey, Carlyle and Ruskin, F. D. Maurice and Cardinal Manning, even Gladstone in his earlier period, were all in their various ways Theocratic Conservatives, and these men contributed perhaps more than any other to the formation of the characteristic type of Victorian humanitarianism. No doubt Carlyle himself was far from being a humanitarian, but his influence on Ruskin and the Christian Socialists cannot be overestimated ; no one wrote more effective propaganda against the inhumanity of economic determinism. Moreover, it was this tradition that was responsible for the Socialist elements in Victorian thought. The earlier Socialism of the Owenites and the Chartists disappeared in the middle of the nineteenth century, leaving only a few isolated figures like Ernest Jones and Julian Harney. In its place there appeared the Christian Socialism of Maurice and Kingsley which was essentially a movement of religious humanitarianism inspired by the ideas of Coleridge and Carlyle.

So too with William Morris. Here the inspiration was definitely and confessedly that of Ruskin, and his Socialism had more in common with the spirit of Ruskin's Guild of St. George than with that of any political party. He was the most incorrigibly Utopian of all the English socialists, but though he was, as he says, "blankly ignorant of economics," he became one of the first English Marxians, because he saw the Social Revolution as the gateway to his Dream England of joy in work and fellowship in craftsmanship.

It is a long journey from James Mill to William Morris : and the whole world of Victorian humanitarianism lies between. If we attempt to find a central point, I should be inclined to see it in that alliance between the religious and the scientific humanitarians or between the Utilitarians and the Evangelicals, which we have seen in the case of Shaftesbury and Chadwick. This alliance lasted throughout the Victorian period. We see it at a later stage in the work of Canon Barnett and in the great social survey of Charles Booth under whom Beatrice Webb served her apprenticeship ; and it finally bore fruit in the social legislation of the early twentieth century.

It is easy to criticise this movement for its incompleteness and its inconsistencies ; but if we look back to the England of 1837 with its uncontrolled exploitation of labour, its cities without schools or drains or police, its cholera and its typhus, we shall be astonished not at what was left undone but by what was achieved by the energy and enthusiasm of a relatively small minority working against the interest and prejudices of an intensely individualistic society.

This success would not have been attained without the help of the Utilitarians and their disciples in the Civil Service and the parliamentary commissions who provided the detailed statistical knowledge and the new scientific technique which were the instruments of social reform. But Utilitarianism and science were not enough. Left to themselves they produced the bleak inhumanities of the New Poor Law and the anti-humanitarian philosophy of Herbert Spencer who regarded the miseries of the poor as part of the law of progress. The real driving force in Victorian humanitarianism came from religion. It came from men like Shaftesbury who did not believe in a natural law of progress or in the principle of enlightened selfishness, and who realised that all they had done and all they could do was little enough in comparison with the immensity of human suffering and the inhuman power of evil. Against these men Spencer wrote : " There is a notion always more or less prevalent and just now vociferously expressed that all social suffering is removable and that it is the duty of somebody or other to remove it. Both these beliefs are false. To separate pain from ill-doing is to fight against the constitution of things and will be followed by far more pain ". But Shaftesbury replies ," There is nothing that is so economical as justice and mercy towards all interests—social and spiritual—of all the human race ". " If St. Paul, calling our bodies the temples of the Holy Ghost, said that they must not be contaminated by sin, we also say that our bodies, the temples of the Holy Ghost, ought not to be contaminated by preventable disease, degraded by avoidable filth, and disabled for His service by unnecessary suffering." Here, I believe, it was Shaftesbury, the religious pessimist and the political reactionary, who voiced the humanitarian conscience of Victorian England better than Herbert Spencer the rational optimist and the philosophic liberal.

Emancipation of Women

R. GLYNN GRYLLS

EMANCIPATION IS another facet of progress : to many Victorians it was their emancipations—their new freedoms— that were the pride of the age, of which Charles Kingsley could exclaim : " I know no century which the world has yet seen so well worth living in ".

Science was emancipation from superstition : the expanding economy was emancipation from poverty ; each new invention and discovery was emancipation from discomfort. To an advanced thinker like John Stuart Mill the emancipation of women was a logical concomitant of the others ; to him the continued subjection of women was "the single relic of the past discordant with the future and must necessarily disappear ". And he recognised that to secure their rights, men's chivalry was not enough. The measure of the success of the campaign for emancipation is how much of his conception was taken for granted—and how generally—by the end of the epoch.

Although the votes for women which he advocated in 1868 was not to come until much later, it was bound to follow once economic and legal independence had been secured : what, going further back, Mary Wollstonecraft had called " women's private and proprietary rights ".

And here I should perhaps emphasise that we are dealing with the external conditions of emancipation: the emergence in any age of the really free man or woman—emancipated in spirit— is another matter.

The advance towards women's independence—emancipation —couldn't be made by outstanding individuals alone—an Elizabeth Fry or a Florence Nightingale—nor by leaders of ability and distinction, but had to come from the sustained efforts of an educated and disciplined rank and file. Mary Wollstonecraft had seen this in her plea for education. But, although she is the accepted forerunner, she is really not only outside the movement in dates, but also in personality. Her *Vindication of the Rights of Women*—so topical a title for its time —is an early statement of a case, but was not really influential in any practical accomplishment. As Godwin has to yield to Bentham as the significant ancestor of liberalism, so Mary Wollstonecraft has to yield in feminism to Harriet Martineau. Much more prolific in the production of spiritual daughters, it was she who set the standard of the objective outlook and the scientific approach in place of personal rebellion and political passion—and set at the same time an unfortunate standard of personal plainness to which it was a heresy not to conform.

The type of " the strong-minded woman ", caricatured itself in Mrs. Grote, the Egeria of the Philosophic Radicals, who used to sit with her feet on the mantelpiece in bright red stockings and was said by Fanny Kemble to look like Trelawny in petticoats. A worse caricature—which really set the cause back—was provided later in the century by the arrival from America of Mrs. Bloomer in what she hoped to get adopted as the garment of emancipation.

In so far as any one fact or action can ever be taken to mark a turning point in the tide of affairs, the capital event in women's emancipation may be said to be the foundation of the first college for women by F. D. Maurice in 1848 : Queen's College, Harley Street.

The need for an improved system of schooling for women had long been felt : the blue-stocking Mrs. Montagu had tried to persuade Mrs. Barbauld to undertake it but she declined on grounds that commanded general approval for a long time—that like the Spartans " the thefts of knowledge in our sex are only connived at while carefully concealed and, if displayed, punished with disgrace ". Mary Wollstonecraft had not the means to establish anything and Harriet Martineau's interests ran in other directions : in spite of other handicaps Harriet Martineau had been fortunate in being able to educate herself in the best way possible—the free run of a good library ; in that she was like Francis Power Cobbe (in spite of schools) or Beatrice Webb, or, in another sphere, Mary Kingsley—but while the girls who could avail themselves of these opportunities were rare, the changing conditions of the age made the opportunities rare also. The fathers of the now dominant middle class when asked where they kept their books replied, " in the office, of course ". Their wives and daughters living in the new provincial towns grown up round the factories no longer had the work to their hands that had occupied the great ladies of country houses or working women in their cottages. They made their idleness a virtue and the schools to which they were sent did what was expected of them, in providing a smattering of accomplishments with the sole object of catching a husband as soon as possible after leaving. " Girls have been educated," wrote T. H. Huxley, " to be either drudges or toys beneath man, or a sort of angel above him ", or, in Ruskin's words " you bring up your girls as if they were meant for sideboard ornaments and then complain of their frivolity ".

No wonder that with this attitude the head of a prosperous middle-class household looked askance at the girl whose menfolk had fallen by the wayside in the competitive race. In the Governess, he saw, but for the grace of God, his own daughters. Usually he turned not to training the girl but to making yet more money. But as a man who liked to get good value he was not unwilling for the teachers in his household to have improved qualifications—and for his womenfolk to bring more intelligence to their listening—and so it came about that one of the most revolutionary of the single actions in the campaign was in-augurated with every blessing of respectability.

The governing body of the Governesses' Benevolent Institution proposed conducting an examination for a diploma but when they found that the candidates had no knowledge on which to be examined, a course of lectures (out of working hours) was proposed for them at the instigation of Frederick Denison Maurice. This idea he soon enlarged to include other women beside governesses for, as he proclaimed, " we were asked how we dared to deny that every lady is and must be a teacher of some person or other, children, sisters, the poor ". (The frequent use of the word " dare " by the Victorians is by no means a sign of spiritual diffidence.)

The school was founded in entire accord with the spirit to which an introductory speaker in this series referred—" a spirit of moral idealism, social conformity and intellectual noncon-formity ". The teachers were all men—professors that Maurice had enlisted from King's College—for there were no women with the necessary qualifications, but the proprieties were ensured by chaperones known as Lady Visitors, described in a committee minute so aptly as " ladies of rank and talent "—terms for which we have to go a long way round to find equivalents. In the classrooms two generations met : the cultivated women of an age that was passing and the girls who were to be the professional workers and public figures of the future.

Of particular significance was not only the spirit of religious vocation that Maurice and his colleagues brought to the teaching, " all the studies are concerned with the life and acts of a spiritual creature ", but what they taught : pre-eminently mathematics. This put the subjects which girls learnt on an equality with boys and established the essential foundation for earning a living. It was an incident destined to be momentous when Sophia Jex-Blake was first appointed assistant to the mathematical professor and offered the rate for the job. Her father protested that it was unladylike for her to accept ; her brother's case " was different ; as a man he had just taken the plain path of duty ".

These young women growing up in the 'fifties were not daughters of a sturdy, successfully competitive middle class for nothing. Clough's maxim fell on ready ears :

" Away, if to teach be your calling,
   It's no play, but a business. Off, go teach and be paid
     for it."

Even Charlotte M. Yonge, no " new woman " but a survivor of the best of the Big House tradition on a small scale, urged the importance of keeping household accounts properly and deprecated sending to Church Bazaars inferior articles or underselling those made by people working for a living. Handiwork that was uneconomic was best confined to the embroidery of altar cloths.

There are dates and events—and personalities—that provide landmarks, although they must always seem to be arbitrarily chosen : directly from the foundation of Queen's College comes the first girls' public school in Cheltenham Ladies College, of which Dorothea Beale was Headmistress, and the beginning of University education by the decision of Miss Llewellyn Davies in 1869 to take a house at Hitchin, and—again directly—

comes the opening of the medical profession from Sophia Jex-Blake's attempt to get a degree at Edinburgh, also in 1869. The community life at school was also teaching a new sense of solidarity as important as any subject in a curriculum.

And from the influence of F. D. Maurice springs all ensuing social service—whether Victorian slumming or modern sociological research.

As Aurora Leigh put it :

> " My right hand teaching in the Ragged Schools,
> My left hand washing in the Public Baths."

Indiscriminate charity was to go out with Octavia Hill—or Beatrice Webb—or Mrs. Nassau Senior, the sister of Tom Hughes, that ideal of muscular Christian socialism. As the first woman inspector of workhouses and pauper schools, Mrs. Nassau managed to bring humanity, as well as efficiency, into the Poor Law. Less spectacular than such an appointment, but as significant, was the establishment of girl clerks as civil servants in 1870 when the electric telegraphs were taken over by the Government; it showed that a department expected—and got—from women, trained and efficient service. That is the economic side of emancipation.

There is another major aspect : the struggle for women's rights at law—for possession of her own property, her own children, her own person. One of these was in some measure secured by the passage of the Custody of Infants Act as early as 1839—due to the political " petticoat " influence of Caroline Norton—(like Mary Wollstonecraft she was disapproved of by Harriet Martineau and not counted in the legitimate feminist succession). Also through her was incorporated into the Matrimonial Causes Act of 1857 some protection of women's own money, although the Married Woman's Property Act was not passed until 1882. A notable contribution to legal reform was the publication of a list of the laws relating to women drawn up in 1846 by Barbara Leigh Smith, later Madame Bodichon—and she, with Bessie Belloc, was also responsible for the first woman's paper with a serious outlook—the *Englishwoman's Journal* in 1858. That these two young women both had considerable personal charm and were not to remain unmarried shows how the movement was developing. It was not to be restricted to the strong-minded, the plain, though worthy, spinster who wore her Mission like a fringe across her forehead, who, like

> "Miss Buss and Miss Beale
> Cupid's darts do not feel,
> How different from us
> Miss Beale and Miss Buss."

Children and property, had been partly secured; there was still to come Josephine Butler's fight against the Contagious Diseases Act and W. T. Stead's heroic exposure of the legal sale of children into prostitution, for the part played by men of progressive views sympathetic to the cause must not be ignored.

The landmark dates do not rise in a steady curve of positions achieved or public opinion converted : in some cases the further a woman's step forward brought her, the sooner was she sent back two—as in the case of Elizabeth Garrett Anderson's medical degree from the Society of Apothecaries or the prizes won by the women at Edinburgh. In 1835, for instance, Mary Somerville had been elected to the Royal Astronomical Society with the words " that the time has gone by when either prejudice or feeling should be allowed to interfere with the payment of a well-earned tribute of respect ", but it was in 1893 that a proposal to admit women to the fellowship of the Royal Geographical Society was defeated : George Nathaniel Curzon declaring that " it would have been not so much injurious to men as disastrous to women ".

The same attitude of what was really economic fear disguised as chivalry is reflected in the hostility of the Controller of the Savings Bank department when it was proposed to introduce girl clerks there as well as in the Telegraphs. He felt " in common with the entire staff, the grievous dangers, moral and official, which are likely to follow the adoption of so extraordinary a course ".

He hadn't complained when women worked side by side with men in the factories—or in the mines, but such a view was generally considered less eccentric than the logic of Professor Lorimer at Edinburgh who couldn't see why it was worse for girls and young men to " meet at their occupations than at their amusements—such as croquet and riding parties ".

But by the end of the reign of Queen Victoria—and the fact that a woman was making a competent sovereign (far more worthy of respect than her immediate masculine predecessors) had its effect indirectly on public opinion even if she did not favour the New Woman herself—by the end of her reign, the ideas that were new and revolutionary at the beginning had been largely accepted. New heroines appear in fiction, and in fashion plates : the voluminous skirts, tight waists and unwieldy hats only meant for carriage wear give place to the trim blue serge coat and skirt and the straw sailor of the woman who has to get about in public conveyances to her job : common sense has taken over from sensibility ; the doll has walked out of the Doll's House.

The Emancipation of Women:
Its Motives and Achievements

VIOLA KLEIN

THERE ARE people who explain everything in economic terms. Ideas are, to them, the products of social and economic conditions and revolutions the necessary outcome of an intolerable economic situation. The more impoverished a social class—so they believe—the riper it is for a revolution.

Such economic determinists will have difficulty in doing full justice to the particular revolution called the Emancipation of Women. A revolution it certainly was—and it involved radical changes both of social conditions and of mental outlook.

It was very much the child of its time, but it might be said to have sprung, like Pallas Athene, from its father's head rather than to have been born in the more natural way of revolutions. It was the product of the spiritual climate of its age, and it bears all the characteristics of its age : the optimism, the faith in progress, the zeal for social reform, the moral enthusiasm, the iconoclastic fervour and the self-confident assumption that all that was needed was the removal of restrictions.

It was the creed of a vigorous and resolute people who had taken it upon themselves, as Jack Tanner says in *Man and Superman*, " to take in hand all the work they used to shirk with an idle prayer. Man must, in effect," adds Tanner, " change himself into the political Providence which he formerly conceived as god ".

The people of this age were unwilling to accept anomalies and sufferings as necessary or beyond remedy and they were profoundly convinced that of all the evils which beset mankind and all the dangers which threatened it, none was beyond the reach of human intelligence to analyse or of human resolve to cure. And they felt sure enough in their righteousness to say : " We have never done the Creator the wrong of doubting that the world is so constituted that if we are morally right we shall be socially and physically happy ". (These are the words of one of the most confident critics of the Victorian social scene, W. R. Greg.)

The women who attempted to improve their lot and to reform their position were not an exploited class in the sense of suffering material hardships—unless the putting out of action of an otherwise healthy limb of the body politic be considered a privation. If they were ' dispossessed ', they were dispossessed of their sense of purpose and social usefulness. For the place in which the Feminist Movement was born was not the factory, nor the mine, but the Victorian middle-class drawing-room.

You only have to visualise it in order to gauge the meaning of this radical departure and to appreciate the courage it needed to step out of these physically and emotionally secure surroundings into the rough wind of public life : The comfortable drawing-room—overstuffed with furniture and relics of all kinds and crowded with children of all ages—one playing the piano, another doing some dainty needle-work or water-colour painting; the governess supervising some others ; and, in the corner, just beneath the aspidistra, the eldest daughter bashfully receiving the attention of her suitor. All this presided over by the mother of the family, whose children must always be seen but not heard, and who, at the age of forty an awe-inspiring matron, held the organisation of the household as firmly in her hand as she kept the bunch of keys on her belt. This drawing-room was the one point of stability in a rapidly expanding, changing world and to preserve this sanctuary men took great care to exclude from it all the harsh realities of life.

This rosy and much-romanticised picture of domestic bliss and security was broken—not by the exploited slave, the servant or the governess, but, if one may say so, by a spectre : the spectre of the governess and of the maiden aunt.

The fate of the " redundant " woman was very much on people's minds and the unmarriageable surplus of the female population formed a constantly recurrent topic of discussion. It was felt to be an acute problem, although in actual figures it was not more, but rather less, alarming than in previous times. It was, however, accentuated by the emigration of able-bodied men of marriageable age to America and the Colonies. Between 1830 and 1875 about five million young people left this country.

The problem was aggravated even more by the disappearance of the family as an economic unit. As long as the family was the centre of production, the question of redundancy did not arise. There was plenty of work for all available hands and each member of the family had its share in providing for the needs of the whole.

The Industrial Revolution changed this situation profoundly. It transferred an increasing number of productive activities from the home to the factory and thereby relieved women of many household burdens. It compelled the women of the newly-formed proletariat to accept work as sweated labour — so that they neglected their homes and children to an extent which assumed appalling proportions as the century went on. At the same time it excluded the women of the middle class from the economic process and made their lives idle and futile.

Beatrice Webb gives a graphic description of the effects of this transformation in her autobiography : " Commodities of all sorts and kinds rolled out from the new factories at an always accelerating speed with an always falling cost of production, thereby promoting what Adam Smith had idealised as the *Wealth of Nations*. On the other hand, the same revolution had deprived the manual workers, that is four-fifths of the people of England, of their opportunity for spontaneity and freedom of initiative in production. It had transformed such of them as had been independent producers into hirelings and servants of another social class ; and, as the East End of London in my time only too vividly demonstrated, it had thrust hundreds of thousands of families into the physical horrors and moral debasement of chronic destitution in crowded tenements in the midst of mean streets."

The social problem of the working-class woman therefore was essentially different from that of the middle- and upper-class woman. While the women of the working class wanted protection, those of the bourgeoisie claimed equality.

The need of women in industry for differential treatment was widely recognised and, in fact, legislation for the protection of women and children affords the first historical example of State interference in private enterprise and was enacted at various stages from 1802 onwards.

But it is one thing to grant protection to the weak and another to concede to claims to equality. Besides, those claims were not raised either at once or generally. The needs of the bourgeois women did not make themselves felt so immediately. They were of a subtler and, above all, a psychological nature.

It's one of the charms of idleness that you can bear quite a lot of it before it starts palling on you. There are so many little things with which it is agreeable to fritter away one's leisure that it takes a long time and some strength of character to realise the futility of it all. Not many women would have reacted like Millicent Fawcett, who was shocked into revolt when she over-heard a conversation between two clergymen's wives busy making small articles of lace to be sold for the benefit of charity —" What do you find sells best ? " asked the first. The other replied : "Oh, things that are really useful, such as butterflies for the hair ".

The rising middle class had put a premium on the idleness of their women. It attached a definite prestige value to it. Apart from bearing children, the social function of the bourgeois woman was to be a living testimony to her husband's social status. Accordingly, her virtues were chastity and a sense of propriety. They did not include either industry or intelligence.

Feminine education conformed to these standards. Francis Power Cobbe, the social and educational reformer, writes in her memoirs : " Nobody dreamed that any of us could, in later life, be more or less than an ornament to society. That a pupil in that school should become an artist or authoress would have been regarded as a deplorable dereliction. Not that which was good and useful to the community, or even that which would be delightful to ourselves, but that which would make us admired in society was the *raison d'être* of such requirement. The education of women was probably at its lowest ebb about half a century ago ", she writes in 1904. " It was at that period more pretentious than it had ever been before, and infinitely more costly, and it was likewise more shallow and senseless than can easily be believed ".

Innocence and inexperience and a cultivated fragility were the characteristic attributes of the Victorian girl. Delicacy, as a sign of refinement, was widely upheld by polite fiction. To be put on a pedestal was apparently the only cure for a disease, called " decline ", a disease which threatened the young women of that period and made an astonishing number of them helpless invalids for no manifest reason. It was not only the imitation of literary models which made the young ladies waste away their lives pathetically prostrate. It was also an excellent way of catching attention without overstepping the very strict confines of maidenly reserve. Moreover, it was the result of a situation which had made matrimony the only possible means for a woman to provide for herself, while at the same time minimising her positive contribution to marriage to such an extent as to make her feel a burden rather than an active partner in a common enterprise. Last, but not least, the extravagant Victorian idea of " propriety " made any natural social intercourse between the sexes almost impossible. It put terrific obstacles in woman's only way to achieve her object in life : to attract a husband.

In the circumstances it was chiefly from the classes immediately above the " labouring poor "—those who had to maintain a position and to keep up appearances on insufficient funds—that the ranks of the old maids were recruited. Daughters of unfortunate tradesmen, of poor clerks or parsons who were unable to secure a husband and who were forced to fall back on their own resources found their equipment badly wanting. The " distressed needlewomen " and governesses were a social as well as a psychological problem.

It was the urgency of this practical question which very effectively underlined the arguments of feminists. But the consequence was that, for a very long time to come, women's work bore—for women as well as men—the odium of a second-best solution, of a pale substitute for human affection.

But the fortress of social disapproval was breached largely by women of the upper social strata, by the daughters of professional men and wealthy merchants. Their intellectual weapons were forged in the fire of the democratic, individualist philosophy which spread ever more widely as time went on. They made their practical entry through a loophole provided for them by the increasing awareness of social evils and of the need for effective remedies. So we find women in rising numbers entering all fields of social work : Prison reform, nursing and hospital administration, social investigations, and charitable organisations of all kinds. In fact, it might be maintained that Social Services and Women's Emancipation were twin sisters, born of the same reforming spirit and in the same circumstances of social change.

The breaking up of the masculine monopoly was made possible because the work undertaken by women was of a charitable nature and therefore not in conflict with the prevailing ideas of femininity ; it was in a new field and therefore did not, at first, mean an intrusion into masculine spheres ; and in most cases it was not connected with remunerative reward and therefore did not imply a loss of caste.

Feminist claims can be summarised under four main headings : 1, Education ; 2, Professional and industrial liberty ; 3, Political status ; and 4, Equal moral standards for men and women.

Advances were made in all these fields—though at various rates of progress differing widely according to the emotional resistance offered by public opinion.

Miss Grylls has outlined the main milestones on this road : From her account it can be seen that success was speediest and most comprehensive in the sphere of education. It was slowest, I believe, with regard to moral standards—though this point is debatable. Certainly complete advance in the sphere of employment was almost as slow.

Generally speaking, it seems easier to set up new institutions or reform legislation than to change popular opinion. From our present vantage point, we see that those reforms—so vigorously and passionately fought for—cover only part of the picture. To make it complete we have to take human attitudes into account. And they lag a step or two behind. Thus, for example, we have to correct an impression which arises from the fact that so many educational facilities are now open to women. To complete the picture we ought to add that to send a daughter to the university is, in most cases, still considered a luxury by the same class which takes a university degree as a matter of course for its sons. Equally, in the field of employment, we have to supplement the fact that there are today hardly any exclusively masculine domains of occupation left, by the fact that women are mostly to be found in the lower grades and are not paid at an equal rate. And feminine achievements—although widespread in many fields—have not yet lost their news-value and their somewhat sensational character. Women's achievements are still considered comparable—in Dr. Johnson's phrase —to the feats of a poodle who can walk on his hind legs.

The emotional opposition against women's coming-of-age was gigantic. The defence of masculine prerogatives and its prejudices was clothed in moral uplift and a patronising benevolence. Gladstone's public letter to an anti-suffragist M.P. is one example of this. Gladstone wrote that he feared voting would injure women, "it would trespass upon their delicacy, their purity, their refinement, the elevation of their whole nature".

This emotional attitude was, however, not confined to the sex which had a vested interest in the *status quo*. It was shared by the majority of women, some outstanding ones, such as Hannah More, Caroline Norton or—for sometime at least— Beatrice Webb amongst them. Queen Victoria herself was an outstanding case in point.

In fairness, I think, we ought not to overlook the point that among the generation which reaped but did not sow the harvest of Emancipation—that is to say, the generation which inherited the spoils of the fight but not its moral fervour, there are quite a number who don't regard their heritage as an undivided blessing. They are either those women to whom the right to work does not seem nearly as attractive as to their grandmothers who fought tooth and nail for it ; or else those girls who had to discover that, outside the drawing-room, men do not always behave like gentlemen.

The eventual victory of what is usually called " the Woman's Cause " was—as far as it goes—brought about by the gradual development of a new type of woman : The woman to whom competent work had given self-confidence and strength and whose claims to be treated as a full-grown person, regardless of her sex, could no longer easily be dismissed. And an age that had freed the slaves, enfranchised the working classes and abolished the disabilities of religion couldn't, in the long run, remain deaf to the protests against the disqualification of one half of the human race on account of its sex.

Toleration

BERTRAND RUSSELL

THE VICTORIAN Age was in most respects less tolerant than the present, so far as our own country is concerned. It was remarkable not for the actual amount of its tolerance, but for the vigour and eloquence of the advocates of toleration, and the rapidity of their success in amending the laws.

Perhaps it will be well to consider separately what the Victorians said on the theory of toleration, and what they did as regards the practice. Let us begin with the theory.

At the time of the wars of religion, there were two grounds for persecution : first that theological error entailed damnation, second that those who differed from the Government were apt to be disloyal.

In England, both grounds persisted in unenlightened opinion until after the Napoleonic wars, chiefly, as regards disloyalty, because the Catholics concerned were mainly Irish. But the Broad Churchmen and freethinkers of the Victorian Age had doubts about damnation, and Ireland it was hoped could be rendered loyal by conciliation.

A general sense of security and stability, reinforced by the fact that England had no revolution in 1848, diminished the general fierceness of opinion and produced a state of affairs in which advocates of general toleration could obtain a hearing. Mill, the most philosophical of the advocates of toleration, based his arguments upon a principle which never had as much scope as he thought and now has hardly any. This principle was that a man should be free as regards actions which have little effect upon others, but not necessarily where the interests of others are seriously involved.

One might give as an example, though he does not give this illustration, that, on his principle, suicide should be tolerated but not murder. But quite other arguments and principles are needed to justify the standard freedoms for which Liberalism has stood, such as free speech, freedom of opinion, and freedom of political propaganda.

This was perceived in one matter, namely freedom of combination, as to which Liberal opinion was divided. In fact, Mill had other and more valid grounds for toleration, of which the most important perhaps was the argument that intolerance involves an unjustifiable assumption of infallibility on the part of the intolerant Government.

But even so, there were questions which his maxims could not answer. Should a man be free to assassinate the Sovereign? Clearly not. Should a man be free to advocate tyrannicide? The fashionable British answer was somewhat unphilosophical. It was : yes, if the tyrant is a foreigner.

Supposing tyrannicide condemned, should it be legal to advocate Republicanism so vehemently that hot heads would pretty certainly be led to attempt assassination? It is clear that in deciding such questions, common sense as applied to the actual situation must supplement general principles.

Two general principles, however, remain, both of which are found in Mill. The first is that governments may err and may suppress opinions which are in fact desirable. The second is that free discussion is to a certain limited extent a method of combating error and promoting rational opinion.

We may add, as deductions from those principles, that love of power would always cause governments, if unrestrained by public opinion, to go too far in enforcing their own views, and that uniformity of opinion is one of the most insuperable barriers to progress, not only in theoretical matters, but even in such as are purely technical.

For example, the Duke of Wellington objected to rifles. If he had been the head of a totalitarian State, he would presumably have made it illegal to argue in favour of them. Such considerations still retain their validity, but the world has grown rapidly more organic so that everybody's action and opinions have more effect on everybody else than they had in Mill's day, and this is raising new problems for the advocates of toleration.

For example : the political opinions of a handful of atomic scientists may conceivably decide the issue of a world war ;

the general public, therefore, cannot be indifferent to their opinions, though it may still hold that they should be influenced by persuasion rather than force.

I come now to the nineteenth-century practice in matters of toleration. To a limited extent, toleration had been established at the end of the seventeenth century. William the Third brought the practice from Holland, and Locke supplied the theoretical basis by pointing out the fallibility of all human opinion.

By the Act of Toleration it ceased to be criminal to be a practising Catholic or Nonconformist, except such as denied the Trinity. But all who were not Anglican were still subject to various disabilities, of which the most important were exclusion from Office and from the Parliamentary franchise. Only Anglicans could hold Fellowships at Oxford or Cambridge, or be members of municipal corporations.

Eighteenth-century complacency saw no reason to reform in any way a Constitution which was considered to have become utterly perfect in 1688. Then came the French Revolution, the fear of Jacobinism, the long war and the appalling conditions of early industrialism.

In these circumstances the Government naturally became persecuting. Almost any Liberal opinion, unless uttered by an aristocrat, could be construed as seditious libel, or as an aid and comfort to the French. Fortunately for England there have always been some liberal-minded aristocrats who took advantage of their privileged position to keep alive the sentiment of toleration.

As I was brought up in the atmosphere and tradition of Victorian liberal aristocracy, and am myself, as kind friends like to inform me, a Victorian fossil, I shall illustrate the reforming sentiments of these times as far as I am able by means of personal and family reminiscences, which could be paralleled by anyone else who had grown up in the same milieu.

My great-grandfather, the first Lord Stanley of Alderley, a quiet country gentleman, described by his daughter as a " true friend during his whole long life to truth and freedom, and yet not in the least in the world of a democrat ", was among those who were shocked by the conduct of the authorities at Peterloo in 1819. When a dinner was arranged in honour of the troops who had fired on the crowd, he would have nothing to do with it. His daughter's journal of that date says : "Papa cannot think of giving his aid and countenance to this dinner, which is to express gratitude for the admirable conduct of these very men who Papa regards as having behaved most shamefully. He is in an unpleasant position, for he cannot write a formal letter expressing his feelings on the subject without his meaning being liable to be misunderstood, and to his being called a friend of the mob and an approver of such seditious and dangerous meetings."

Men of this temper, especially Fox and his followers among the Whigs, served a purpose which men of less social standing could not serve. Indeed their influence was so powerful that it overcame completely the reactionary panic of the Napoleonic period, and led to a steady growth of reform.

From 1822 onwards, under the guidance first of Canning, and then of the Whigs, the Government moved further and further towards abolishing the remnants of bigotry which defaced the statute book, and the country gradually forgot its fears, both of the Vatican and of revolution.

At the beginning of this Liberal movement, legal intolerance was chiefly theological. The two most important steps towards religious equality had already been taken when Victoria became Queen : the emancipation of Nonconformists in 1828 and of Catholics in 1829. The former of these measures is associated with one of the most vivid of my childish recollections. In 1878, a few days before the death of my grandfather, Lord John Russell, with whom I lived, a crowd assembled on the lawn in front of the house and proceeded to cheer. When I asked for an explanation, I was told that they were Nonconformists come to express their gratitude to my grandfather for the removal of their disabilities fifty years ago.

It was in fact he who, by an unexpected success, had carried the measure through the House of Commons, although he was at the time in Opposition.

It was many years before Parliament did equal justice to the Jews. The measure of 1828 as it passed the Commons would have applied to them, but in the Lords the Bishops carried an amendment, insisting on a declaration containing the words : " On the true faith of a Christian ". The objection to Jews was religious, not racial. Those who were Christian, like Disraeli, encountered no obstacles.

Modern readers of Trollope must be struck by his obvious belief that anti-Semitism was not a weakness to be confessed with shame but a religious duty. The record of the Upper House as regards Jews is a bad one. In 1848 they again defeated a measure for Jewish enfranchisement which had passed the Commons. Baron Lionel de Rothschild, who had been elected to Parliament in 1847, was not allowed to take his seat. It was not till 1858 that Jewish disabilities were removed, largely as the result of the persistent efforts of Sir Moses Montefiore, a man who retired from business in 1824, and devoted his ample fortune and long life—he lived to be 101—to securing justice for Jews in many lands. Here also I have a vivid personal recollection. In 1877 I was taken to see him, after it had been explained to me that he was a Jew and also a man deserving of the highest admiration. Until then, I had not known that there were any Jews except in the Bible. It was partly for this reason, and partly because of his great age and long beard, that he made an impression upon me as a five-year-old boy which seventy years have not effaced.

One very noxious piece of religious bigotry survived till 1871. Until that year, no one could be admitted to a Fellowship at Oxford or Cambridge until he had signed the Thirty-Nine Articles. The majority of the Dons saw no reason to change this system which, but for the intervention of Parliament, might have persisted to the present day. Many regarded the matter as a mere form ; most of those concerned thought that if the Articles had originally been signed in good faith, it did not matter if a Fellow's opinions subsequently became less orthodox.

This, however, was not the opinion of Henry Sidgwick, who though originally a good Anglican, gradually became a free-thinker. His conscience consequently led him to resign his Fellowship in 1869, and this action did much to precipitate the reforming legislation.

Twenty-four years later, I had the good fortune to be his pupil when I began the study of philosophy at Cambridge. There was not a single one of my philosophical teachers at that time who could conscientiously have signed the thirty-nine Articles.

The last remnant of religious intolerance was the refusal of the Parliament of 1880 to allow Bradlaugh to take his seat. As an atheist, he at first asked to be allowed to affirm, which was already legal in the Law Courts. When this was refused, he expressed willingness to take the oath, but was not allowed to do so. At last he entered the House with a Bible, and administered the oath to himself, but this was not considered valid. However, in 1886, the Speaker of the next Parliament gave way and allowed him to take his seat.

The growth of religious toleration throughout the Victorian age was balanced by an intensification of intolerance in all matters connected with sex. During the 'twenties, John Stuart Mill was sent to prison for suggesting that birth control might be a preventive of infanticide. My father, Lord Amberley, in 1868, was held up to obloquy because at a private gathering he had said that birth control was a matter deserving of the consideration of the medical profession. The scurrility and offensiveness of the election campaign against him were such as are hardly credible to those accustomed to modern contests. He was called " Vice-Count A. B. Lie " and was represented in leaflets and on posters as a man of immoral habits, which he was not, and an advocate of infanticide.

The Conservatives took full advantage of this outburst of obscenity in defence of morals. The whole incident when contrasted with elections nowadays shows the close connection between toleration and decent manners.

Whoever took up the cause of birth control was made to suffer. Bradlaugh and Mrs. Besant were condemned to a fine and imprisonment for publishing a birth control pamphlet, though the sentence was not carried out. The social consequences of unconventional sexual behaviour, however conscientious, were far worse than the legal penalties.

For example, a completely innocent woman, who left an intolerable husband, ceased thereby to be respectable. Intolerance on this subject lasted till long after the Queen's death, and was so bitter as to force acquiescence in conduct and expressed opinion even on those to whom it seemed unjustified and cruel.

It is remarkable that Mill, in his book on liberty, never mentions the restrictions which law and public opinion in his day imposed upon even the most serious discussion of topics which the Victorians preferred to ignore. In view of his own early experience this must have been from fear of losing the readers' sympathy for his general principles.

In one respect the Victorian Age was more tolerant than our

own because it was less democratic. There was a respect for eminence of whatever kind, and a toleration for the eccentricities of the eminent which was not extended to the vulgar herd. Darwin and Huxley were unmolested when they proclaimed opinions which would have been considered intolerable in a village blacksmith. George Eliot was widely received, although a village girl who indulged in similar conduct would have been an outcast. On similar grounds, distinguished foreigners who were obnoxious to the authorities in their own countries, were permitted without question to live in England. When, as sometimes happened, difficulties with foreign governments resulted, a very vigorous sentiment in favour of the right of asylum made itself felt. On one occasion, to please Austria, the British Government took to opening and reading Mazzini's letters, but there was such an outcry that the practice had to be quickly dropped. When, in 1858, there was an attempt on the life of Napoleon III. and it was proved that the bombs employed had been manufactured in England, the French Government vehemently demanded that we should make stricter laws for the control of revolutionary refugees. Palmerston's Government agreed, and introduced a Bill for this purpose. My Grandfather, in a speech opposing the Bill, said : " Let those who will support the Bill of the Government ; in that shame and humiliation I am determined not to share ". The Bill was defeated, and the Government fell.

Kropotkin, though an anarchist, was allowed to give propagandist addresses wherever he could find audiences willing to listen. In this respect we have become less liberal than the Victorians. Kropotkin's disciple, Emma Goldman, who in 1917 returned to Russia from America, found the Communist regime unendurable and sought permission to settle in England. The Foreign Office refused permission, giving as their reason the belief that she was a Bolshevik, a belief which two minutes' attention to the matter would have shown them to be false, as was proved by the fact that when later she was allowed to pay a visit to England, she devoted herself to a campaign against the Soviet Government.

The growth of Democracy since the Victorian Age has in fact led to a shift of toleration. The opinions of the few are less revered and the opinions of the many more respected, and since the opinion of the general public on political questions has now

become of vital importance in deciding or controlling the outbreak of wars, our intolerant impulses are more readily aroused
by opinions which seem dangerous to our safety in this world,
than by those which appear to threaten a remoter future.

Unusual political opinions, and particularly fanatical opinions,
are generally suspect ; in each lurks the danger of war. It must
be admitted that there is some rational basis for intolerance of
opinions which may have relatively immediate unpleasant effects
If our house is on fire we do not feel it our duty to be tolerant of
anyone who recommends petrol as a fire extinguisher, but the
question of how far political toleration should be carried is one
of the most urgent problems of our day. We have to decide
how far to tolerate intolerance, and give liberty to those who aim
at the abolition of liberty.

I do not find, in the writings of Mill or any other Victorian,
any precept applicable to this problem.

Intolerance, speaking generally, has two main sources : First,
fear of a threat to the power of the privileged ; second, fear of
loss of cherished convictions. Both existed in Victorian times,
but the former has been very greatly diminished by the growth of
democracy. The latter, however, is quite compatible with
democracy and may even be strengthened by it. There is, I
think, less of this kind of intolerance in Britain than in any other
large country, but in America there is a great deal, and democracy
does nothing to prevent it. Any opinion which is unusual in
the United States, particularly if it is common in some European
country, is regarded as un-American, and on this ground is both
feared and disliked. De Tocqueville, in his book on democracy in
America, remarked, what is still true, that in that country,
opinions disapproved by the majority bring, if expressed, social
penalties which are visited upon even the most able and eloquent.
In America, he says, " the majority lays rigid bounds to thought ;
within these limits a writer is free, but woe to him if he dares to
pass beyond them. It is not that he has to fear an auto-da-fé,
but he is exposed to unpleasantness of all sorts and trivial perse-
cutions. A political career is closed to him ; he has offended the
only power which can open it to him. Everything is denied to
him, even fame. Before publishing his opinions, he had believed
that he had allies, but when he has revealed himself to all it
seems that he no longer has any. For those who condemn him

express themselves loudly, while those who think as he does, lacking his courage, are silent and leave him. He yields, he bends at last under the daily pressure and relapses into silence as if he felt remorse for having spoken out ".

All this, which de Tocqueville says of America in his day, might equally well be said of America in the present day. This danger to freedom rather than those of the Victorian Age in England still needs to be combated, especially as, in its extreme forms, it leads to totalitarianism.

Philosophically, the fundamental argument for toleration is that no human institution is perfect and no human belief is infallible. Where there is not tolerance, there is either no progress or progress only by violence. Nineteenth-century Britain is so far the most noteworthy example in history of progress without violence, and it is to the fortunate influence of its apostles of tolerance that it owes this enviable pre-eminence.

The Social Conscience and the Ideas of Ruskin

LORD LINDSAY OF BIRKER

I AM to talk tonight about the ways in which Ruskin's ideas affected the social conscience of England. But to say his ideas is not enough. The change in the climate of English thinking on social questions which Ruskin brought about was due to the passion with which he held and proclaimed those ideas and acted on them.

There are some lines of the American poet Vaughan Moody which always remind me of Ruskin and the social conscience which was a passion in him :

> " To be out of the moiling street
> With its swelter and its sin !
> Who hath given to me this sweet,
> And given my brother dust to eat ?
> And when will his wage come in ? "

From the publication of *Unto This Last* in 1860 till the last letters of *Fors Clavigera* before his final breakdown in 1883, he gave all his powers and time and much of his fortune and his health to rousing the people of England to realise how evil were the doctrines they were believing, and how horrible the practices they were allowing. This passage in the first letter of *Fors Clavigera*, published on the 1st of January, 1871, is typical of what he reaffirms again and again with the same passionate conviction :

" I have listened to many ingenious persons who say we are better off now than ever we were before. I do not know how well we were off before ; but I know positively that very many deserving persons of my acquaintance have great difficulty in living under these improved circumstances ; also that my desk is full of begging letters elegantly written either by distressed or dishonest people ; and that we cannot be called, as a nation, well off, while so many of us are either living in honest or in villainous beggary. For my own part, I will put up with this state of things, passively, not an hour longer. I am not an unselfish person nor an evangelical one ; I have no particular pleasure in doing good. Neither do I dislike doing it so much as to expect to be rewarded for it in another world. But I simply cannot paint, nor read, nor look at minerals nor do anything else that I like, and the very light of the morning sky, when there is any—which is seldom nowadays near London— has become hateful to me, because of this misery that I know of, and see signs of when I know it not, which no imagination can interpret too bitterly."

He seemed to himself to have failed. *Cornhill* stopped the publication of *Unto This Last*. The outcry against it was so great. The articles in *Frasers's Magazine,* which were afterwards published as *Munera Pulveris,* raised a similar outcry and though Froude, the editor, was prepared to go on with them, the publishers stopped their further publication. *Time and Tide* and *Fors Clavigera* were not subject to such veto, but the scorn of almost all economists, the regrets of leader-writers that Mr. Ruskin should waste his time on sentimental nonsense continued for at least ten years.

At last the tide turned. The change he had brought about in economic teaching was slowly recognised. In 1885, twenty-five years after the publication of *Unto This Last,* he was presented with an address signed by many of the foremost men of the day, including professors and teachers of Political Economy. This —among other things—is what it said :

" Those of us who have made a special study of economic and social questions desire to convey to you their deep sense of the value of your work in these subjects, pre-eminently in its enforcement of the doctrines :

" That Political Economy can furnish sound laws of national life and work only when it respects the dignity and moral destiny of man.

" That the wise use of wealth, in developing a complete human life, is of incomparably greater moment both to men and nations than its production or accumulation, and can alone give these any vital significance.

" That honourable performance of duty is more truly just than rigid enforcement of right ; and that not in competition but in helpfulness, not in self-assertion but in reverence, is to be found the power of life ".

The change which Ruskin's work made in economic thinking has been so far-reaching that today it is difficult for us to realise the perversity and the power of the economic teaching which he fought. The Webbs in their *Industrial Democracy* quote a passage from Harriet Martineau where she gives her opinion about a Factory Bill which proposed to limit the working hours in factories of children under 14, and after saying that legislation cannot interfere effectually between parents and children in the present state of the labour market, ends with this extraordinary statement : " The case of those wretched factory children seems desperate ; the only hope seems to be that the race will die out in two or three generations, by which time machinery may be found to do their work better than their miserable selves ". And yet Miss Martineau was an able and public-spirited woman. She was not wicked but blind—blinded by the economic doctrine of her time. A perverted theory corrupted a capable mind and she could more easily believe that defenceless children under fourteen are a race which might die out than doubt the pronouncements of orthodox theory about labour and capital. It is an additional proof of Ruskin's insight that he calls her not a villain but a goose.

Classical economics as taught in those days was indeed a perverted theory. It had started with a complacent optimism that if everyone were allowed to pursue their own economic interest without interference, the result would be completely harmonious. When the horrors of the early factory system gradually destroyed that optimism economic theory settled down into the complacent pessimism so evident in Miss Martineau. It was Bentham's foolish psychology (the doctrine that men were moved only by fear of loss or by hope of gain), which was responsible for the fundamental perversity of the economics of the day, and for the attempt to regard all social facts in terms of buying and selling. The " Devils' and Fools' Political Economy ", says Ruskin, " maintains that good things are only good if they can be turned into money, and that all human prosperity must be founded in the vices of human nature, because those are the essential power of human nature, and its virtues are accidental and impotent ".

Perhaps the greatest contribution which Ruskin made to political economy was this enlargement of its scope. It was not to be confined to exchange : it was not to ignore the real goodness or badness of men's choices : " The essential work of the political economist ", he says in *Munera Pulveris,* " is to determine what are in reality useful or life-giving things and by what degrees and kinds of labour they are attainable and distributable ". The political economists of his time would have stoutly denied that it was their business to determine what things are in reality useful, and many economists would still be of the same opinion. By the economist demand must be taken for granted—whatever it was a demand for. Whether the object demanded was good or evil, would do good or harm was not the economists' business. Ruskin refused to accept this abstraction—for an abstraction it surely is, and by his refusal often saw things to which the professionals were blind. Consider, for example, this passage from *A Joy for Ever* where he perceives the fundamental facts about unemployment, not perceived by the professional economists till Keynes :

" You complain of the difficulty of finding work for your men. Depend upon it, the real difficulty rather is to find men for your work. The serious question for you is not how many you have to feed but how much you have to do ; it is our inactivity, not our hunger that ruins us : let us never fear that our servants should have a good appetite " . . . " Our wealth is in their strength, not in their starvation. Look round this island of yours and see what you have to do in it. . . . Precisely the same laws of economy which apply to the cultivation of a farm or an estate apply to the cultivation of a province or an island. Whatever rebuke you would address to the improvident master of an ill-managed patrimony, precisely that rebuke we should address to ourselves, so far as we leave the population in idleness and our country in disorder. "

There follows from Ruskin's wider conception of the scope of political economy a different conception of value. As he says : "Value signifies the strength, or availing of anything toward the sustaining of life. The production of effectual value always involves two means : first the production of a thing essentially useful ; then the production of the capacity to use it. A horse is not wealth to us if we cannot ride, nor a picture if we cannot see, nor can any noble thing be wealth except to a noble person ".

Bentham in a foolish endeavour to make the study of man conform to the methods of physics had tried to make it ethically neutral. He said in an oft-quoted passage : " Push-pin (what we now call shove-halfpenny) is as good as poetry ".

An economics which knows its strict limitations may take moral values for granted, may regard them as the concern of the legislator and itself appear to be ethically neutral. But the reigning economics of Ruskin's time did not know its limitations, told legislators what they must not do, and thought that that melancholy abstraction the economic man was real. Ruskin with a remarkable power of analysis and a lively sense of concrete values cut through all those abstractions to recall man to the realities the economists are supposed to be talking about. His fundamental doctrine that Wealth is Life ; and that some things create, restore and maintain life ; and that other things, however much money they may cost or be sold for, destroy and corrupt life and should be called not wealth but illth, is surely practical common sense. Consider these passages :

" The material wealth of any country is the portion of its possessions which feeds and educates good men and women in it ; the connected principle of national policy being that the strength and power of a country depends absolutely on the quantity of good men and women in the territory of it and not at all on the extent of the territory—still less on the number of vile or stupid inhabitants. Following out these two principles I have found and always taught that, briefly, the wealth of a country is in its good men and women and in nothing else : that the riches of England are good Englishmen ; of Scotland good Scotsmen ; of Ireland good Irishmen ". In another passage in *Fors,* after speaking appreciatively of some earnestly-minded employers whom he had met he goes on : " But all they showed me, and told me, of good, involved yet the main British modern idea that the master and his men should belong to two entirely different classes ; perhaps loyally related to and assisting each other ; but yet—this one, on the whole, living in hardship—the other, in ease ; the one uncomfortable—the other in comfort ; the one supported in its dishonourable condition by the hope of labouring through it to the higher one, the other honourably distinguished by their success, and rejoicing in their escape from a life which must nevertheless be always, as they suppose, led by a thousand to one of the British people ". This from a man who called himself a Tory and who despised and poured scorn on many democratic slogans ! Yet, even now, have we learnt that profoundly democratic teaching ? Or again, " Servants and artists and splendour of habitations and retinue, have all their use and propriety and office. But I am determined that the reader shall understand clearly what they cost ; and see that the condition of having them is the subjection to us of a certain number of improvident and unfortunate persons over whose destinies we exercise a boundless control ".

I am far from holding that Ruskin never made mistakes and should be blindly followed. He so revolted against the economists' glorification of exchange that he never took the trouble to understand it properly ; and against their bad defences of the taking of interest that he thought interest indefensible. His views on the position and functions of women are deplorable. He could be petulant and opinionated. He had had a lonely childhood and he never, I think, learnt the give and take which is learnt only in the companionship of equals in early years. Therefore, though he understood profoundly the relation of master and servant or teacher and pupil and what made such relationships beautiful or corrupting, yet the co-operation of equals in a fellowship, which is the basis of democracy, he never experienced and hardly appreciated. His practical proposals for what he called the Guild of St. George were ineffective and deserved to be so. But for all that he was a great social prophet. He taught his generation much and there is much which our generation can learn from him. His longest and latest book with the strange name *Fors Clavigera* is a curious book. Those who like tidiness and system and moderation and are put off by occasional extravagant and indefensible statements had better leave it alone. But those who do not mind being in turn exasperated and illumined, delighted and puzzled, will find in it, for all its turns and twistings, the messages of a prophet, though a sore and disillusioned and exasperated prophet.

Of the earlier books *Munera Pulveris* and *Time and Tide* are well worth reading, but *Unto This Last* is the greatest of all these books of Ruskin's social teachings. Sir Kenneth Clark in a recent broadcast called it " one of the great prophetic books of the nineteenth century ". So it is, for Ruskin had the great gift of a prophet, a direct and simple vision of fundamental truths to which his contemporaries were blind.

The Aristocratic Idea

DOUGLAS WOODRUFF

"WE ENGLISH," said Mr. Podsnap, "are very proud of our Constitution, Sir. It was bestowed upon us by providence. No other country is so favoured as this country." "And other countries," said the foreign gentleman, "they do how?" "They do, Sir," said Mr. Podsnap, gravely shaking his head, "they do, I am sorry to be obliged to say it, as they do. For this island was blessed, Sir, to the direct exclusion of such other countries as there may happen to be."

What was this Constitution—the "glorious Constitution" of many Toasts—on which the Victorians prided themselves so much? Magna Charta and Habeas Corpus came into it, but the historical event to which it really looked back was the glorious Revolution of 1688, by which the English had saved themselves from the absolutism that still, in the nineteenth century, was so much in evidence on the Continent. After the French Revolution most Englishmen were more than ever convinced of the great superiority of their system, for France was a vivid object-lesson of the evils of the two extremes of what happened if the King had too much power, and what happened if the demagogues had too much power. Power must be divided, distributed and limited, and a glorious Constitution was one with three elements, Crown and Lords and Commons, each with a great part to play, but none supreme. The idea that a majority vote in the lower chamber, perhaps on something where public opinion was certainly divided and had not been consulted, the idea that such a vote automatically became the law of the land, regardless of other parts of the Constitution, would have seemed to most of the Victorians a bad and not a good notion of government.

The aristocratic element in Victorian government represented pre-eminently the land, and life on the land—the landed interest, as we meet it for example in Trollope's novels, thought of itself as maintaining the framework of life. Their main business, as they saw it, was not with innovation or repair on the farm but with security of tenure, to prevent disturbance while the seasons and the years fulfilled themselves in orderly progression. Severe laws protected the rights of property.

So the government of the nation was looked at in agricultural terms by men formed through long generations of life close to nature. The Englishman, Chesterton once said, is not interested in the equality of man but in the inequality of horses. It is an inequality deliberately sought by breeding for it, and we most easily enter into the spirit of the pre-democratic age when we think of it as the philosophy of countrymen, continually living in the presence of slow growth, respecting the nature of things, and understanding the importance of nurture, and of nurture extended through more than one generation, both expecting and rejoicing in the existence of widely different varieties of men as of stocks and crops. The government of England was in essence the wise management of a varied estate, a contrivance by which all the innumerable private homes and families from castle to cottage might all live secure from external or internal threat. The pride of public service and public servants, was to protect private life. The State existed for and served the nation, and the pride of Englishmen was not public architecture but domestic architecture, not town halls but country seats. And if the supremacy of private over public concerns was the fundamental notion, and the opposite of that maintained both in theory and practice in so much of the mainland, who could be better trusted to express and fulfil this conception of government than those who had the greatest personal interest in maintaining the structure, in keeping the executive limited, the oldest as well as the wealthiest families.

If it was pointed out that the Victorian aristocracy was in great part quite modern and much of its heraldry was really like Victorian Gothic, that only reinforced the conviction that those must be good social conventions which could so easily absorb and tame so much new blood. When a Victorian lady of a county family was reproached for not having called on neighbours who had been settled nearby for seven years, she replied, "We never rush in Rutland". Newcomers, with money made in the Black Country or in Asia, could buy great houses, but they had to wait for social acceptance for the profound reason that a society which does not exact conformity, impose its standards and scrutinise its would-be recruits, soon loses its own standards and dissolves. A very great deal of money was being made quickly in Victorian England, in the North, in the City and abroad, and it had to be taught to behave, to be shown what a pleasant social life its possessors and their children could have provided they learnt and kept the code. " It takes three genera-tions," said the Victorians, " to make a gentleman." They also said (noting what in fact happened often enough), " shirt sleeves to shirt sleeves in three generations ". In the business life of the country there was a fierce competition between individuals for the money that then qualified men for the next round, to enter the social world, a field where families and not individuals became the effective realities ; the old, or cooked money, judging and the raw or new money awaiting judgment. Who is she ? Who was his father ? From what family pursuits and back-grounds did he come ? These were the questions considered of the greatest relevance by men who would have had little patience with the modern idea that there is an abstract quality of ability to be looked for in children ; able to do what, they said ? And they thought that for a great many public employ-ments the man best able to perform them was the man with the appropriate birth and upbringing. There were technical forms of skill which secretaries, interpreters or accountants could supply if a man could not write grammatically, follow French or do figures, but the man himself must possess the qualities no secre-taries could supply in his stead, of which the chief was being who he was. So Napoleon, the supreme example of the parvenu, exclaimed, " What could I not do if only I were my own grand-son ? " If, that is, custom and familiarity had only made his rule natural and familiar to his subjects and to himself, he could even have afforded failures. A hereditary king of a long dynasty could sign an unfavourable peace and still go on reigning, and a settled governing class could follow out long term national policies without having to ask whether they were immediately popular or widely understood. So a better peace was made in 1815 than in 1918, by men much less afraid of public opinion at home as well as better educated.

The aristocratic rulers, the scions of the families of whom Mr. Belloc has written :

> " It happened to Lord Lundy then,
> As happens to so many men,
> About the age of twenty-six,
> They shoved him into politics "

these seldom became whole-time professionals. We are so much wiser than you, Burke had explained to a young French lord, because we take our politics so much less intensely, are continually standing back and seeing what we are doing, for our parliament only sits a few days each week, and besides we take four or five months holiday in the country in the Summer. There is, indeed, a great deal to be said for the principle that great powers should only be entrusted to men who would rather not be exercising them, and would be rather doing something else, or so it seemed to men who were continually comparing, like Mr. Podsnap, their advantages with those of the nations of whom " Rule, Britannia " speaks, the nations not so blessed as we, who in their turn to tyrants fall. Like the founders of the American Republic, Englishmen had an abiding dread of the executive, of arbitrary power, so the nobility and gentry left their agricultural pursuits and pleasant seats, where they would much rather be, and sat through long speeches which they would much rather neither make nor hear, not for the sake of governing, but to protect themselves and the nation from being governed by anybody else.

A critic can say that they were so busy congratulating themselves that they lived free from any fear of the Star Chamber or *lettres de cachet*, or the Inquisition, that they failed to perceive, or to scotch when there was time, the great evils that grew up in early nineteenth-century Britain. They let the industrial proletariat come into existence under conditions that made it almost certain that its members would be drawn away from the national tradition rooted in the countryside ; the dogged Yorkshire Tory, Richard Oastler, fighting his lifelong battle for the limitation of factory hours, defined his Toryism to the Duke of Wellington as " A place for everything and everything in its place ", but too much was coming into the national life, via the industrial revolution, for which there should not have been any place. And men who thought of themselves as the natural leaders of society did not lead enough, they were too supine, took life too easily, till suddenly aroused. Consider for a moment a man so truly representative of aristocratic government as that Lord George Bentinck whose life Disraeli wrote. His first love was the turf, his second politics. He boasted that he understood horses and men and little else and he was a very successful breeder of racehorses and better on them, until he suddenly woke up to politics to fight the repeal of the Corn Laws. He threw himself into this struggle, mugging up statistics, working, says Disraeli, eighteen hours a day, killing himself in two intense years of uncongenial and unhealthy activity, driven to it by a genuine patriotic desire to save England from what he regarded as a tragic mistake. He inspired a great deal of confidence and his fellow countrymen liked him the better because he preferred horses to men and expressed his mind with difficulty. The English have always felt reassured by inarticulateness, looking for practical men of affairs who will make a good practical judgment. But this was in the event the great weakness, and the final undoing of the English aristocratic politicians as a political force, that they were intellectually indolent, were content to improvise—which meant in fact, letting themselves be driven by currents of opinion brought here from the Continent. They shirked fundamental reading.

Nor were they really and consistently Conservatives ; in their European policies they were Liberal, on the side of change, and so they saw themselves as progressive, taking a leading part, and adventuring their money cheerfully, all over the world. The traditionalist writers of the Continent, such men as De Maistre, and de Bonald and Balmez were not even names to them, and like the French aristocracy of the eighteenth century, they imagined they could keep their own special position while agreeably watching, and very often cheering on, the growth of a general scepticism. They were only too ready, abroad, to christen all change as progress, especially if it was change that increased the wealth of Britain. It might be said that when the Victorian age began they had just made one prudent concession to new forces, the great Reform Act of 1832, and that when the Queen celebrated her Jubilee fifty years later they were still very strongly entrenched socially and politically. They had conducted a very orderly retreat for half a century. What really undid them was the continual broadening of the suffrage towards the universal franchise. There was nothing in the least inevitable about this doctrine in England. Consider the views of so representative a man as Lord John Russell, a progressive Whig, whose name was intimately associated not only with the great Reform Bill but with many other reforms like those of the criminal law. He thought it just as absurd to say that the only method to follow, to secure a government responsive to public opinion, is to give everybody the vote, as it would be to say that the whole people, whether it studied the facts or not, must be the jury and must give judgment in civil and criminal trials. No, he said, we select—and not by vote but by nomination—a small representative group, the twelve jurymen, to do this special work for the rest of us. The right to vote, he said, " is not a universal and personal right, but an artificial right given by society for the good of society ". What society needs is good government, constitutional, moderate, enlightened, and the great question is whether universal suffrage is the best way to secure a good government. No, he said, " it is manifest that universal suffrage is calculated to produce and nourish violent opinions and servile dependents, to give in times of quiet a great preponderance to wealth and in times of disturbance additional power to ambitious demagogues. It is the grave of all temperate liberty and the parent of tyranny and licence ; this is not a dream but the recorded result of the experiment in France, and every Frenchman who loves liberty speaks with horror of universal suffrage". Even Fox could be quoted in this sense, saying " that was the best system of representation which called into activity the largest number of electors whose circumstances rendered them independent, and on the contrary, that system was the most defective which called into activity those who by circumstances were not capable of deliberation ". Parliamentary reform was discussed in 1832 and 1885 by men with the full courage of their conviction that the important thing to do was to represent property, stakes in the country, and that the French example showed the madness and misery of any other course or of giving political power to those who would only use it to despoil the possessors and enrich themselves. They wanted the political structure to reflect and express the economic structure. But they failed signally to maintain or establish their view of what the government and the constitution ought to be, against the advocates of the French doctrines.

Yet they had immense advantages. Victorian Englishmen all the way down the social scale loved a lord, brought a fund of goodwill, liked them the better for doing themselves very well. Look at Victorian aristocracy in the light of Lenin's three conditions for a small minority to rule over millions, that they must possess the army, the police, and the *mythus* or official orthodoxy about the meaning and purpose of the national life and the story why the government is to be obeyed, honoured and loved. The Victorian aristocracy had them, all three. It officered the army, and kept it rigorously subordinate to the civil power. It created a good, efficient police force. It controlled the church patronage of the Establishment and the Universities. For its own survival it only needed to impress upon the middle classes and to reach the artisans with the conviction that government ought to be approached as the Courts of Justice were approached, with the conviction that it was a matter of mixing and blending elements, that the Pocket Boroughs were perfectly sound samples and that the elections before 1832 provided quite genuine opportunities for the expression of public feeling, but that public feeling was only one element in the life, and one factor in the government of the nation, which was a partnership of the living, both with the dead and with the unborn, looking before and aft. Such a view and a belief in the value of estates of the realm was congenial enough to the English ; it went with their grain. They understood difference and quality and European critics said of them that they were the only people in Europe with an active dislike for equality. But the landed aristocracy was not naturally fitted to undertake higher education, and its propaganda was more unconscious and instinctive and was soon left behind. An elementary education was provided with the three R's, but secondary and university education, and still more the education men could give themselves, was left all too completely to other and hostile hands, to men like the young H. G. Wells, burning with the resentments first formed in the housekeeper's room on the humbler side of a green baize door in a south of England country house. The Press was left to men outside and often very hostile to all this side of English tradition. Yet the landed aristocracy in late Victorian England possessed immense financial resources, wielded immense influence, could so very easily have staked and asserted its claims, so much more powerfully and impressively than it ever attempted to do.

But this kind of education they failed to impart, for the propagation of political doctrine was not work that came easily to them ; their strength was in what was unquestioned and customary. When they drifted into accepting the leadership of an exotic adventurer, like Disraeli, and let him enter into a competition with the Liberals in rapid extensions of the franchise, an astute observer could have forecast that their days were numbered. "We must educate our masters", said the intelligent Robert Lowe (later Lord Sherbrooke), at the time of that 1867 Act ; but it was already very late, education should have long preceded enfranchisement ; within a generation Sir William Harcourt would be saying, "we are all Socialists now", an admission that if there had been education and a moulding of the mind the landed aristocracy had not given it, but had accepted it at other hands. Perhaps that was their weakness, perhaps their virtue : it was certainly their epitaph.

Victorian Democracy: Good Luck or Good Management

K. B. SMELLIE

" SOME PARTS of it are rotten, and some parts of it are sound. If it were all sound, it would break by its own obstinate stiffness : the soundness is checked by the rottenness and the stiffness is balanced by the elasticity ". Now this passage comes out of one of Peacock's novels and he was talking about a river bank, but I want you to think of it as applied to the Constitution of England in Victorian times. It does illustrate what I mean when I ask myself, Victorian democracy, was it good luck or was it good management ?

We must begin by being quite clear that if we are a democracy to day we have become one since the first World War. We were not a democracy between the battle of Waterloo and the battle of the Somme. Queen Victoria knew that well enough. In 1880 she was exasperated by her Prime Minister, Mr. Gladstone, and a Cabinet which seemed to her to have, as she said " no respect for kings or princes or any of the landmarks of the constitution ". She wrote then that she could not and would not be the Queen of a " *democratic monarchy* ".

And, of course, she never had to be. The Victorians were not entirely free from humbug, but they never humbugged themselves into thinking that they were democrats. Politically they were never democrats, if by a political democracy is meant a form of government controlled by a numerical majority of the population. We know how reluctantly the franchise was extended by the three Reform Acts of 1832, 1867 and 1884, only one person in every twenty-four having the vote in 1832, one in twelve in 1867 and one in seven in 1884. Socially they were never democrats, if by a social democracy we mean that air of social equality which we breathe in France or which blows around you in the United States. The Victorians may have believed, some of them, in a common good but they had not much faith in the common man—except, of course, on Sunday. I think that only a modern Dante could do justice to the Victorian social scene—that Secular Comedy where the terraced slope of property swept upward from the odorous and groaning masses to the circles of nobility encircling the glory of the Crown, *Victoria Beata*. It was an Oxford don, T. H. Green, who said in 1867 that " the flunkeyism which pervades English society from top to bottom was incompatible with any healthy life. " Matthew Arnold thought that " a religion of inequality " had so material-ised our upper class, vulgarised our middle and brutalised the lower that we had failed in civilisation.

There were, of course, supporters of political democracy. John Stuart Mill believed that if every adult were given the right to vote it would be possible for the reason of the middle classes to hold the balance between the conflicting interests of capital and of labour. He believed, too, that the sharing of political responsi-bility would create a democratic society. We find the same idea in T. H. Green : " The enfranchisement of the people," he said, " is an end in itself ". Only citizenship, he thought, could give a " basis of respect for others . . . without which there is no lasting social order or real morality ".

Furthermore, these democrats of the study were supported by Mr. Gladstone. In 1859, when he was Chancellor of the Ex-chequer in the Cabinet of Lord Palmerston, he said that less than one fiftieth of the working men were in possession of the fran-chise, and asked how anyone could defend a system that let in the lower stratum of the middle class and shut out the upper stratum of the working class. " Every man," said Gladstone, " every man who is not presumably incapacitated by some constitutional consideration of personal unfitness or of political danger, is morally entitled to come within the pale of the con-stitution ". It was in vain to explain to his astonished chief that all he had meant was that all persons ought to be admitted to the franchise who could be so with safety. The latent meaning of his words became manifest in 1878. It was then that he asked : " Did Scribes and Pharisees or did shepherds and fishermen yield the first, most and readiest converts to our Saviour and the company of His Apostles ? . . . in judging of the great questions of policy which appeal to the primal truths and laws of our nature, those classes may excel who, if they lack opportunities, yet escape the subtle trials of the wealthy state ".

To Conservatives, this was indeed an almost devilish use of Scripture. For they quite frankly feared the effect which the lower classes might have on the conduct of business. The *Economist* newspaper said in 1848 : " Granting to them the best intentions and the most unselfish views, their haste, their impressibility, their openness to deception and their inevitable ignorance, must ever make, and has ever made the government of the lower classes fatal beyond all others to freedom, to prosperity, to peace ". Disraeli himself thought that the fruits of democracy must be extravagant expenditure, discontent in meeting it, rash wars and humiliating treaties, insecurity of property and liberty—the whole culminating in a reaction to despotism. He hoped that it would never be the fate of the country to live under a democracy. That was his opinion before, in 1867, he himself gave the vote to the sceptical and thinking artisan. And listen to Lord Salisbury, who had the greatest contempt for what he called the radical belief in the divine right of the multitude : " There is nothing in the nature of things to make us suppose that the freedom of those who are not on the side of government will be better observed where the government is the creature of a multitude than where it is the possession of one ".

These points for and against the " lower classes ", " the masses " or the " working classes " may seem trivial and almost vulgar to a modern ear. But they were part of a debate about the very nature of a people and the proper functions of the state in a period of unprecedented change. The Victorian Age lasted from 1837 to 1901 (that is barely twice the period from 1914 to now). But in that period the new forces of nature which men had harnessed—the beginnings of that control over the very structure of matter which is now our fear—had swept this country to a brief period of power and of glory before they revealed their threat to the very life of man. To us, looking back from amid the rapids which are hurrying us we know not where, that Victorian age may appear a calm before the storm. Bitter as were the struggles of the Bleak Age—the hungry and the dirty 'forties— they were a storm in a teacup compared with what has happened since or is yet to come. It is the comparative simplicity, one could almost say the comparative naïvety of the discussion which is so fascinating to us, . We have seen these issues—the nature of a people and the proper functions of the State, transferred from these islands to the frontiers of the world itself.

Now politically the Victorian period falls into two parts, before and after 1867. All chronological divisions are approximate. It is misleading to write about the nineteenth or the twentieth centuries as though they were separate rooms in a museum. No gong reverberates in the skies when one century gives place to another. Instead of speaking of the Victorian Age from 1837 to 1901 it would better mark the forces at play if we were to speak of a nineteenth century which began in 1832 and of a twentieth century which began in 1870. In the generation before 1870 England had become the workshop of the world, its shipper and its banker. By luck or good management she had avoided a revolution in 1848. This was in spite of the fact that she had taken the first impact of the new and strange changes in production and distribution caused by the use of scientific methods— her landscape was the first to be covered with dark Satanic mills. Her island security and her historic unity meant that she had no frontiers to be shaped by blood and iron and that her constitution, unlike that of the United States, had not to be remade by civil war. She developed almost unhindered by war or revolution her many inventions for the supply of manufactured goods to a world which was not yet industrialised. That her peace and plenty were not entirely the result of good management we know from the tragedy of Ireland which was to bring England to the verge of civil war in 1914. But there was before 1870 a hope that free trade might become a grand panacea which would— Cobden hoped it might—" inoculate with the healthy and saving taste for civilisation all the nations of the world ".

Before 1870 also there was influential in all political thinking an eighteenth-century belief in a natural order in human affairs. Between the English revolution of 1689 and the French revolution of 1789, it was thought that governments might restore society to its natural working as a doctor brings his patient back to health. This subtle idea of nature was a lure both to radical and to conservative interests and temperaments, and survived deep into the nineteenth century. Tom Paine had written that

" the great part of that order which reigns among mankind is not the effect of government . . . society performs for itself almost everything which is ascribed to government . . . government is no further necessary than to supply the few cases to which society and civilisation are not conveniently competent ". This idea of a natural order seemed to be confirmed by the vitality of the swift advance of industry and the hopes of international free trade which were the bases of the optimism of the 1860's. It made possible a belief in a form of democratic government which would avoid the seeming absurdity of the control by the masses of their betters. It was believed by the philosophical radicals that industrial progress was producing a form of society in which governments would have less and less to do. A harmonious natural order was being woven by the economic loom. If most of men's needs could be met by the initiative of the captains of industry, the functions of the State might be limited to enforcing the proper rules of the game. If the functions of government were merely to umpire the economic game, even the most common men might take their turn of power. A liberal state might be based on popular votes because it would have so little to do.

Nevertheless, even before 1870 neither the socialists nor the conservatives were much taken with this liberal theme of the umpire state. The socialists because they felt that the rules of the game were of too great antiquity and that many players were unfairly handicapped ; the conservatives because they too felt that the rules of the game were more subtle and needed more care than the liberals supposed ; and also because they thought that no government which was popularly elected would long keep to umpiring and not itself join in the game.

After 1870 the hopes of the liberals themselves that the government might be the umpire in this way and not itself take sides were to be destroyed. The more swiftly the pace of industry moved beneath the spur of advancing scientific knowledge, the more in fact were governments called upon to do. The failure of the Cobden hope of international free trade meant that every government in the world was to become indirectly responsible for the pattern of its people's economic life. It was found that the swifter grew the pace of economic change, as the spirit and techniques of the natural sciences entered more and more subtly into every fibre of our social life, the wider and more penetrating had to be the influence of the state. The discovery of the microbe brought in its train the health, the housing and the town planning services. The arrival of the internal combustion engine meant state control of roads and fuel, the understanding of the causes of the trade cycle brought unemployment insurance and the social service state. Many of these changes fall outside the Victorian chronicle. But they were all implicit in the generation after 1870.

The great issue of the proper functions of the state has not yet been settled. Part of the fascination of the Victorian scene is that we can see the issue emerging, and hear it debated in comparatively simple form. Moreover, it was intertwined with the other fundamental question of the nature of a people or the character of citizenship. Both questions were interwoven in the changing fabric of the Constitution. The slow merging of its early gothic lines into the machinelike precision of the modern bureaucratic state is one of the miracles of political history. It was in the alchemy of that transformation that the English people won the unity which they were so desperately to need when the *Pax Britannica* had gone.

So it must be with rather a shock that we turn from the sweep of the great debate about the proper functions of the state and the tradition that the English state was so well organised to the technical and dusty details in which that system moved and had its being.

At the accession of Queen Victoria in 1837 the first effects of the Reform Act of 1832 had appeared. In theory that Act had been a skilful blend of the representation of property and the representation of intelligence—or so the Whigs who had sponsored it liked to think. The influence of land and the influence of numbers had been so blended that it was hoped that Kings, Lords and Commons would continue an elastic trinity of power. An open system of voting (there was no secret ballot until 1872) safeguarded the legitimate interests of property—the heads of colleges and of cathedrals influenced their tradespeople, employers their workers and landowners their farmers—and men were excluded from the House of Commons who might be uncongenial to the spirit of our institutions. In practice this meant that before 1867 it was impossible for any working man to be a member. Nor was direct corruption entirely eliminated. The Parliament of 1841 was called the bribery parliament.

From the point of view of a believer in the control of government by a numerical majority of the population there is no end to the anomalies of the working constitution from 1837 to the Second Reform Act of 1867. But in that period of privilege the groundwork of a democratic order had been laid. " Political democracy," Santayana, our most sympathetic critic, has written, " is a late and artificial product. It arises by a gradual extension of aristocratic privileges, through rebellion against abuses, and in answer to restlessness on the people's part. . . . It is compatible with a very complex government, great empire and an aristocratic society ". It was because the extension of the suffrage was so gradual that every fibre of the constitution was strong to meet the demands which were to be made upon it. In the development of the constitution the democratic idea was given a tough and technical reality which no theory of the right of the majority and no criticism of the stupidity of the masses could have anticipated. Which is to say that the Victorians had the luck to build more wisely than they knew.

Those who opposed a radical revision of the constitution by the abolition of the monarchy or the abolition of all property qualifications for the vote were right when they sensed that :

" our stability is but balance, and wisdom lies in masterful administration of the unforeseen ".

They did not realise the effect of the revolutions in industrial methods and the attendant changes in the structure of society on the power of the people to think and plan for themselves. In every town council, every trade union and in every church and chapel there had developed a self-restraint and an ability to decide and work for common aims. Not only at Westminster and in Whitehall, but in every town and village a web of thought and action was being woven to cope with the problems which after 1870 marked the transition from the Victorian Age to our own.

Radical Democracy in the Victorian Era

H. N. BRAILSFORD

THE LONG Victorian reign got in sight of democracy only in its last years, if then. Indeed, as Mr. Smellie has stated, truly democratic institutions were half a generation away when the great Queen died. The ascendancy of the Whig aristocrats had first to fade out and then it was the industrial middle class that succeeded them as the dominant power. What, meanwhile, was going on in the mind of the working class ?

It is a complicated story that begins with Chartism and ends with Keir Hardie. When the long reign started in 1837, the factory worker was still a peasant at heart. He remembered how he or his father had suffered under the cruel process of enclosure, which drove them from the common land and turned them into proletarians, with nothing to lose but their chains. He remembered the brutality of Peterloo and the fate of the Tolpuddle martyrs : he counted in their hundreds the comrades transported to Botany Bay. Two recent events had fixed his attitude to politics. By the Reform Act of 1832 he felt that he and his class had been betrayed. They had borne the brunt of the long struggle for reform ; only to find themselves at its end voteless and impotent. Two years later the new Poor Law taught them what they had to expect from a middle-class Parliament. The cold inhumanity of this Act so infuriated the masses that in some parts of England three years passed before it could be enforced. It ended all outdoor relief and imprisoned the destitute in " bastilles ", as the workhouses were called, in which families were broken up and wives separated from husbands.

And so the workers turned away from politics, completely disillusioned. They were now for direct action. They discovered a leader in Robert Owen, the brilliantly successful cotton manufacturer of New Lanark, a leader as dynamic as he was original. The older generation had drawn its political inspiration from Godwin, Tom Paine and Cobbett. None of these three had understood or accepted the new age of machine production. The significance of Owen, the socialist, was that while he fought against its barbarism, he also saw its promise. His active leadership of the Trade Unions came to an end in 1834, but Owenism lived on as a vital influence in the new reign, above all in the co-operative movement. He was, I think, the first man who clearly realised that the periodical crises and slumps in the capitalist system are caused by under-consumption—in other words by the wrong division of the product of labour.

Robert Owen was an enlightened pioneer in popular education, and a decided rationalist. Nothing came of his Utopian plan for settling the unemployed and eventually the whole working population in self-governing and co-operative village communities, half agricultural, half industrial, but for a time it fired the imagination of the workers. They believed that they could create a Socialist England by their own efforts and sacrifices, without the help of Parliament. The earliest co-operative societies aimed at using the profits they made from the sale of groceries to finance the creation of co-operative villages. The Trade Unions tried to dispense with the capitalist employer, by creating their own co-operative markets to which craftsmen brought their products for exchange, while the builders set up their own working guild, which here and there had its momentary successes.

During two hectic years, Owen, who did nothing in a small way, succeeded in uniting the whole workers' movement, trade unions, co-operatives and friendly societies in a single organisation, the Grand National Consolidated Trade Union. Two parliaments, the Owenites declared, met simultaneously in London, and theirs, they said, was the more important and the more democratic of the two, for it spoke for nearly a million members. Their aim was to organise a general strike, a national holiday, through which they hoped to win first of all an eight-hours' day and eventually their ideal, the co-operative commonwealth. The overgrown Leviathan collapsed, chiefly because the employers met it with a determined counter-offensive, partly because of internal dissensions. Infidels were ranged against believers. It was Owen and the infidels who stood for charity and persuasion and opposed the spirit of class-war. The Owenite myth of the general strike lived on till 1926, and Continental Socialists saw in it a means for preventing the outbreak of international war.

So Owenism failed and once again the pendulum swung to political action. The workers' demand for a charter of political rights revived the movement for parliamentary reform. The Chartists were far from being academic democrats who wanted the vote for its own sake. They were desperate proletarians, who valued the vote in order to get a humane Poor Law and an eight-hour or at least a ten-hour day. In other words, their aims were economic. Many of them, like Lovett, their upright and capable secretary, and Ernest Jones, who wrote their songs, were Owenites who wanted Socialism. Attwood, the Birmingham banker, who led their few middle-class adherents, had views about credit and currency which anticipated those of Major Douglas. Others, like Feargus O'Connor, the magnetic but muddle-headed orator who led them to the fiasco of 1848, were individualists who wanted to recover the land for the dispossessed peasantry. As one of their incidental activities, they settled colonies of small-holders on the land, notably on a big estate near Rickmansworth, which they called O'Connorville. They were agreed only on the six points of their Charter.

There was nothing new in these six points. Manhood suffrage and annual parliaments were the demands of the Levellers and the Agitators in Cromwell's New Model army; only the secret ballot and payment of Members were modern additions. Their three monster petitions, of which the last received two million signatures, were also a traditional expedient. As Parliament rejected one after the other of these petitions, they were confronted with the question what form of pressure they were next to use. The moderates talked of organising a run on the banks; the majority favoured the Owenite strategy of a general strike; a minority believed in physical force. It tried to collect arms; it did a little drilling, but its only attempt at an armed rising was the pitiable effort of the Welsh miners at Newport in 1839. This sufficed to alienate such support as the Chartists had among middle-class radicals.

Passionate and prolonged though the Chartist agitation was, it never had a chance of success; the middle-class was firmly entrenched in Parliament and its affairs moved forward on a high tide of prosperity. Why should it surrender its monopoly of power ? The case of the middle class in Vienna, Berlin and even in Paris in the year of revolution 1848, was wholly different. On the Continent it had to fight monarchy and the Police State and it needed the alliance of the masses. In Britain it was already in the saddle.

But it was not the Duke of Wellington's troops nor even the legendary shower of rain that defeated the assembled Chartists on Kennington Common. The Chartist movement had been undermined by the Anti-Corn Law agitation. A large part of the working class had come to accept the middle-class leadership of Cobden and Bright, though both of them were stubborn opponents of the Factory Acts. It bartered for a cheap loaf its dream of winning political power. Its acceptance of the ideology of Free Trade meant that it was reconciled at last to the capitalist industrial system.

There now began, round about 1850, a long and humdrum phase of the working-class movement which lasted into the 'eighties. It had had enough of adventures. It saw no visions and dreamed no dreams. It had ceased to think of the conquest of power. It adopted the liberal and individualistic outlook of the master class, and sought to raise its own standard of life, family by family, and trade by trade. The virtues it cultivated were thrift and temperance. It struggled hard to educate itself by poring over primers of useful knowledge and attending lectures and discussions in Mechanics' Institutions. Much of its mental life centred in Nonconformist chapels and many of its leaders were lay preachers.

There was, however, a rationalist Left Wing, which followed Holyoake or Bradlaugh, and sought its intellectual food in Halls of Science, Secularist Societies and ethical churches. It was evolving a new type of Trade Union, which organised the skilled men in closely-knit craft unions, and secured valuable benefits for their members. These unions tilted no longer against the capitalist system : their aim was to get for their members the best conditions combination could secure within it. They had a considerable measure of success, for, in spite of the terrible slump of the 'seventies, real wages were rising during the latter half of the century.

Meanwhile the Friendly Societies flourished, and the Co-operative Movement entered on a new phase, when the Rochdale pioneers in 1844 invented the dividend. They were at the start Owenite idealists, but the millennial dreams of the movement grew dimmer, as it expanded into an immense and successful trading concern. It is easy to say that the workers lacked vision during this sober generation : certainly they did no fresh thinking. But they became adult ; they gained education and experience ; they learned to organise ; they acquired a new self-confidence and self-respect. By thrift and organisation they left behind them the abysmal poverty of the Industrial Revolution. The main body of the workers were ceasing to feel and think like a desperate proletariat. They had at last a little to lose besides their chains. Statisticians now spoke of a submerged tenth, but it was only a tenth.

In politics the urban workers, who got their votes at last in 1867, were content to follow the Liberals, with a preference for their radical wing. They still had to fight hard for the right of combination, but though in this matter and some others they owed more to the Tories, their allegiance to the Liberals was not yet shaken. The few Trade Union leaders who got into the House stood as Liberals and two of them were rewarded with minor offices. Like the middle-class radicals, even these men stuck to *laissez-faire*.

The radicals and devotees of Free Trade, individualists in their outlook, had a genius for evading fundamental social issues that touched the condition of the people. They were republicans ; they aimed at disestablishing the Church of England ; they struggled manfully for secular education and against the Blasphemy Acts and the tithes. They stood for economy and disliked indirect taxation. At bottom their radicalism was a traditional hatred of the surviving remnants of feudalism. Their class enemies were still the parson, the squire and the House of Lords. After reading Henry George's *Progress and Poverty* they were keener than ever on the taxation of land values, but their nearest approach to socialist thinking was that their more daring spirits called for the nationalisation of the land.

Socialism during this individualistic generation had ceased to be an organised movement. Owen was forgotten and the continuity was broken. However, the Christian Socialists, with Ruskin and Carlyle, had kept alive an ethical and aesthetic criticism of the triumphant capitalist system. Marx had a few half-convinced English associates in the First International, but their influence was negligible. But in the last decade of the century two new tendencies began to make history, the new Trade Unionism and the new capitalism.

After the London Dock Strike of 1889, trade unionism took a new form ; it organised the unskilled workers and created the big nation-wide industrial unions. The psychological and political consequence was that the workers, gathered in their Trade Union Congress, became conscious of a new and wider loyalty, not merely to their fellow-craftsmen but to their class. The second of these new tendencies revealed itself in the structure of the capitalist system. Visibly and rapidly, it was moving from competition to combination. The self-made man who really did take a risk and practised abstinence—to accumulate capital— was now a thing of the past. First the limited liability company and then the price-ring, the cartel and the trust, were shattering the theoretical defences of capitalism erected by the classical economists. The consumer as well as the workers faced a new phenomenon, monopolistic capitalism.

It was no accident, therefore, that Socialism as an organised movement sprang into life again in the 'eighties. It took two forms, one of them revolutionary and Marxist, the other gradualist and Fabian. The first of them, the Social Democratic Federation, which took that name in 1884, owed its existence to H. M. Hyndman, a wealthy stockbroker, able but rather pompous, who lacked the instinctive sympathy to grasp the English workers' habits of thought. He never translated the peculiar technical terminology of Marxism into work-a-day language. This elaborate theoretical system was alien to the empirical English mind. Much of it struck the average worker as out-of-date. He did not feel that steadily increasing misery was driving him fatally towards revolution. This party was uniformly unsuccessful in elections and suffered from internal dissensions, which soon cost it the support of its most distinguished recruit, William Morris.

That Morris believed himself to be a Marxist is a fact, but a very puzzling fact, for in his own daring and virile way he drew all the consequences from Ruskin's opposition of welfare to wealth. He stood for fellowship, for the joy in good craftsman ship, and looked back with nostalgia on the art and the guilds of the Middle Ages. Beloved and admired as man and poet, his *News from Nowhere* had an immense influence in turning the minds of the younger generation, both workers and intellectuals, away from the complacency and philistinism of Victorian commercialism.

The publication of *Fabian Essays* in 1889 marked a new epoch, while from 1891 onwards Blatchford's *Clarion* was winning working-class converts for socialism. The mainspring of the Fabian attack upon capitalism was an intellectual revolt against disorder and waste of an unplanned society. Wells in his early writings never tired of describing the untidiness and meanness of the world in which he was brought up. The Christian Socialists dwelt on the selfishness and cruelty of an acquisitive society : the Fabians assailed it for its stupidity and inefficiency. Like Owen, they were optimists who argued that we had hardly begun to realise the potential benefits of machinery, but this we could do only in a planned society, based on the collective ownership of the means of production. They all aimed at a class-less society and Shaw with his remorseless logic preached literal economic equality.

The Fabians had no use for Marx, but I have often wondered whether they had ever studied him seriously. Wells, who poured ridicule upon him, certainly had not. The Webbs did monumental work as social historians : but had even they learned all that Marx and Engels had to teach about history, the class basis of the state, and the causation of social changes? The Fabians devoted themselves to service for the interests of the working class. But they never idealised it, as Marxists often did, nor did they regard it as the class whose unique historic mission it was to realise socialism. On the contrary, in their early years, they hoped to get socialism, in gradual instalments, by permeating the Liberal party. These coldly reasonable people, with their mastery of statistics and their faith in the expert, rendered an immeasurable service to the evolution of the Welfare State and the definition of socialist techniques, but they were not the men to inspire a socialist mass movement.

That phase was reached in 1892, when Keir Hardie as the independent Labour Member for South-West Ham took his seat in the Commons with a worker's cloth cap on his head. This man was a miner who had faced in his own person all the vicissitudes of a worker's lot—hunger, overcrowding, unemployment and victimisation. A moral genius whose courage and integrity were apparent in all he said and did, he fought not only for the workers' material interests, but above all for their self-respect. His socialism recalled Owen's in that it was primarily ethical in its inspiration, though he understood clearly enough, as Owen did, the economic causes of the trade cycle fatally rooted in the capitalist system. The rest of the story we all remember—how Hardie founded the Independent Labour Party in 1893 and how that led in the last months of Queen Victoria's reign to the formation of the Labour Representation Committee, out of which in the Edwardian era the Labour Party evolved. It was a new and startling apparition, to end the middle-class monopoly of power. Yet in its singularity—for its structure resembles nothing on the Continent—it followed tradition and bore an odd resemblance to Owen's prematurely-born Leviathan, for it too was a federation of Trade Unions, Socialist societies and eventually of co-operatives also.

Was it, as Hardie conceived it, a class party? Yes and No. Against the class that lives by owning, he preached the solidarity of the workers. The Owenites called them " the industrious and useful classes "; the modern phrase is " workers by hand and brain ". But the opposition was never absolute. The British Socialist movement never thrust its opponents, as the extremer Marxists did, beyond the pale of a common social organism, that included all its fellow-men. In short, it never proclaimed the revolutionary class-war. It believed that a common ethical code bound socialists and their opponents alike. To this, through argument and persuasion, it made its appeal. Our social conscience is for it the root and foundation of democracy.

The Development of Education

E. SALTER DAVIES

HENRY BROUGHAM said that at the beginning of the nineteenth century England was the worst-educated country of
Europe. Yet in 1902, Balfour's Education Act built our present
educational system upon the foundations laid in the previous
century.

During the Victorian Age there was, in fact, an immense turbu-
lence of ideas and beliefs, and a solid practical effort throughout
the whole field of educational reform—primary, secondary,
and University. Two questions need an answer ;—first, in
what way *did* the ideas and efforts of the Victorians move us
from the situation on which Brougham commented to that
created by Balfour's Act : and second, to what extent did those
ideas provide an adequate response to the educational requirements
of the nineteenth century ?

In considering this process of development, it is impossible
not to be impressed by certain tendencies—and by two in particular, which appear as a fairly constant element in educational
thought. One is the emphasis which has always been placed in
this country—and will, I hope, always be placed—on the moral
and religious aspects of education : the other the desire, almost
non-existent at first but growing stronger as time went on, to
create a national system of education free from the disabilities
caused by difference of religion, class, or sex.

The religious over-tones of education were at once a source
of strength and weakness. It was to the religious bodies that
almost all early attempts at reform were due—in particular,
the movement to bring the influences of religious education to
bear on " the children of the poor " in which Hannah More and
the Evangelicals were so prominent. On the other hand, the
fierce sectarian differences of the Victorians were a heavy brake
on thorough-going educational progress. As G. M. Trevelyan

has said : " The main reason why English Education lagged behind in the mid-Victorian period was that no government, Whig or Tory, could conceive a means of setting up a national system at the public expense that would not have given the bitterest offence either to the Dissenters or to the Established Church ".

At the beginning of the Victorian Age, the urge to reform still came mainly from the religious groups, and the State kept carefully aloof, only too happy to leave popular education in their hands. The first State grant was indeed made in 1833 : but that amounted only to £20,000. It was " in aid of Private Subscriptions for the Erection of School Houses for the Education of the Children of the Poorer Classes in Great Britain ". The rate of acceleration from that point may be judged from two further figures : in 1859, the grant had risen to nearly £840,000 ; for the year 1948-9 the net expenditure of the State on education is estimated at over £162½ million.

With the increase of State expenditure on education came of necessity an increase in State control, exercised partly through Government Regulations and Circulars and partly through the appointment of an Inspectorate. The duties of Her Majesty's Inspectors were " to collect facts and information and to report the results of their inspections to the Committee of Council ". One of Matthew Arnold's reports attacked the unfortunate system of assessing the amount of school grant by the result of an examination by these Inspectors. The nearer the pupil gets to the top of the school, he said, " the more does his examination in itself become an inadequate means of testing the real attainments and intellectual life of the scholars ". But the system was not brought to an end until the introduction of the Block Grant in 1900.

What were the causes which induced the State to assume, with increasing momentum, so great a part in the provision of education ? The basic reasons were the enormous growth in the urban population caused by the Industrial Revolution and the need for skilled workmen and executives which that Revolution created. In addition, the gradual extension of the franchise during the Victorian period demanded an informed electorate, fitted for its responsibilities. " We must educate our masters," said Robert Lowe after 1867. This was a great change from the old call—" we must educate the poorer classes ". In one sense, the story of the development of education in Victorian England is the story how the State came to realise and answer this challenge.

In the field of elementary education, the realisation and the answer came slowly. It was not until 1870 that Forster's Act was passed, setting up Schools Boards empowered to provide schools (with the aid of Government grants, local rates, and fees) wherever the provision made by the voluntary bodies was inadequate. Earlier in the century Factory Acts had been passed, limiting the hours of labour of children working in factories, and requiring them to attend school for part-time. Here too the principle of State intervention was implicit. But all this was merely to scratch the surface, and in 1870 the situation was as Forster described it to the House of Commons. " On the speedy provision of elementary education," he said, "depend our industrial prosperity, the safe working of our constitutional system, and our national power. . . . If we are to hold our position among men of our own race or among the nations of the world, we must make up for the smallness of our numbers by increasing the intellectual force of the individual ".

The Act of 1870 set elementary education on its feet by making a compromise on the religious issue : for by it the existing denominational schools had their State grants doubled, while in the newly-created Board Schools any distinctive denominational teaching was forbidden. It is sometimes said that State schools are forbidden to teach religion : the only restriction is that they must not use a formulary distinctive of a particular denomination. Within six years a million and a half new school places were provided. This was a very great achievement, paralleled only by the development of secondary schools which followed the passing of the Act of 1902. Soon some of the elementary schools, not content with the ordinary curriculum, converted themselves into higher grade schools providing classes in science and art. A court judgment in 1899 decided that State-aided elementary schools could teach only elementary subjects ; and this decision paved the way for the Act of 1902 by which the Board Schools were abolished and the local control of education was placed in the hands of local authorities. The new wine, in fact, had burst the old bottles.

Forster's observations on foreign competition in 1870 were

merely an echo of fears which the Great Exhibition of 1851 had brought home to those interested in English industrial development. The progress which certain countries, especially Germany, were making in the application of science to industry, and the planning of their scientific education, brought home to the nation the need for increased attention to technical training, if British trade was to hold its own. This " increased attention " was marked, for example, by the formation of the " City and Guilds of London Institute " in 1880, followed by a number of polytechnics and technical colleges. And, towards the end of the century, any county or borough or urban sanitary authority was empowered to aid and promote technical education up to a penny rate. But, as Mr. G. M. Young has observed, " no real or solid progress could be made until the great Victorian omission had been made good, and the executive class educated up to the level of the demands now made on it in a trained and scientific world ". Through all these years hovers the spirit of Matthew Arnold as School Inspector repeating again and again : " You must organise your secondary education " ; but the call was not fully answered until the beginning of the twentieth century.

If the Victorians failed to answer the full demand for secondary education, they did make a well-defined progress with their public schools. But the improvement was accompanied by some decline in the old-established grammar schools. Though there were hundreds of these in existence at the beginning of the century, many had fallen into disuse. As late as 1866, for example, Whitgift's School, Croydon, for a generation had not been attended by a single pupil.

At the beginning of the century the public schools, too, had fallen on evil days ; we have lurid accounts of constant floggings and the tyranny exerted by the older boys. In 1818, at one famous school, soldiers with fixed bayonets had to be called in to quell the rebellious boys. But, before the century's end, certain enlightened headmasters brought about notable reforms, in particular Butler and Kennedy at Shrewsbury and Thomas Arnold at Rugby. Arnold took his stand on the principle that Christianity should be the basis of all public education. Here, indeed, lies the distinctive quality of the Victorian public school —the stress laid on moral standards, on "tone", on the ethical virtues stimulated on the playing-field. It might be argued that this breeding of character was not a wholly unsatisfactory answer to the Teutonic concentration on technical skill. Before the end of the eighteenth century the real English public boarding school was represented by but a few examples, such as Eton and Winchester. The Victorian schools which followed them, and in which Arnold's tradition was worked out, were developed either from religious foundations (like Westminster) or from town grammar schools (like Rugby). Their curriculum—like that of the endowed grammar schools—consisted almost entirely of Greek and Latin, though English, mathematics, and modern languages were occasionally added as "extras". And to them were added a number of private schools, though we may hope that not all of them were like Dr. Blimber's Academy as described in *Dombey and Son* :—

" Dr. Blimber's establishment was a great hot-house in which there was a forcing apparatus incessantly at work. All the boys blew before their time. Mental green peas were produced at Christmas and intellectual asparagus all the year round. Mental gooseberries—very sour ones too—were common at untimely seasons and from mere sprouts of bushes under Dr. Blimber's cultivation. Every description of Greek and Latin vegetable was got off the driest twigs of boys under the frostiest circumstances."

At the beginning of the century neither Oxford nor Cambridge University was open to any but members of the Established Church. Moreover, their curriculum consisted almost solely of classics and mathematics, and most of their students were preparing for one of the liberal professions—the Church, Teaching, the Law, or Public Life. Many manufacturers and business-men felt that this sort of education was out of touch with modern needs, and sought for something like the curriculum of the Mechanics Institutes, the aim of which was " to instruct the members in the principles of the arts they practised, and in the various branches of science and useful knowledge ". Moreover, a number of undergraduates at both universities did little or no work, and discipline was lax in the extreme. According to one critic—the headmaster of a public school and a former Fellow of an Oxford College—many of the Colleges were becoming " sinks of ignorance, infidelity, corruption, and debauchery ". In these circumstances, a number of Nonconformist Academies had sprung up, free from the restrictions imposed at Oxford and Cambridge. In 1828 London University had been established, free from religious tests and with a broad curriculum. The fact that the new University—unlike Durham founded four years later—was non-residential was felt by many to be a great drawback, but this fact made it possible for students to enter at a fraction of the cost at Oxford or Cambridge.

The movement for reform spread slowly to the older universities, in fact it was not until 1871 that religious tests were abolished at Oxford for all degrees other than Divinity. Further reforms followed the report of the Royal Commission on Oxford and Cambridge in 1874. These changes had the effect of converting Oxford and Cambridge from close professional and denominational academies into modern universities.

Provision for the education of girls and women had lagged far behind that for boys and men. In all ages some women have been able to overcome such handicaps : in the sixteenth century, for example, Queen Elizabeth and Lady Jane Grey were highly educated. But in Victorian times the idea was prevalent that in intellect women were the inferior sex, that in their case the purpose of education was to fit them for marriage and the home. The ordinary curriculum for girls, therefore, consisted mainly of " accomplishments "—perhaps some French, with drawing and painting, needlework, singing, dancing, and instrumental music, and sometimes a subject called " the use of the globes ". In order that the pupils might be able to play an intelligent part in social life they often received some instruction in general knowledge, through such a text-book as Mangnall's *Questions,* which retained its popularity throughout the whole of the century. There were a number of private schools for girls like Miss Pinkerton's Academy in *Vanity Fair* and Mrs. Goddard's school in *Emma,* and a number of the daughters of the well-to-do were under the care of governesses. One such in fiction, Mrs. General, is memorable because of her reproof to Little Dorrit : " Papa is a preferable mode of address. Father is rather vulgar, my dear. The word Papa, besides, gives a pretty form to the lips. Papa, potatoes, poultry, prunes, and prism, are all very good words for the lips ; especially prunes and prism ".

In 1869 the Endowed Schools Act laid it down that the benefits of endowments should be so far as possible extended to girls, and recommended that in every town capable of supporting a grammar school there should also be a day school for girls under proper management and at a moderate fee. A number of good schools were started in the large towns, particularly by the Girls Public Day School Trust, though the provision remained most inadequate and indeed towards the end of the century, when the School Enquiry Commission investigated the provision of girls' education, they still had some scathing things to say.

Women, too, successfully invaded the universities. Women's colleges were established in London and at Oxford and Cambridge, though it was some years before women were allowed to take their degrees. And so, largely owing to the public spirit and devotion of a few women, Miss Beale and Miss Buss and others, the education of girls and women was brought nearer to an equality with that of boys and men, and the aspirations expressed by Thomas Becon nearly 400 years ago were at least partially realised : " It is expedient that by public authority schools for women-children be erected and set up in every Christian Commonweal. Is not the woman the creature of God as well as the man ? And as dear unto God as the man ? Is not the woman a necessary member of the commonweal ? "

I have surveyed some of the main achievements of the Victorians in the development of education : and, though—as I have suggested—they had their limitations as well as their successes, one is compelled to admit the immense progress for which they were responsible. It was progress, and a progress which, at its best, was animated by the spirit described by Ruskin in a private letter to a friend which was shown to me by a Headmistress and which, so far as I know, has never been published :—" Sir, the first law of all Education is to teach our youth to love truth and speak it, and to love work and thoroughly do it, and to love knowledge and seek it—not in novels but in fields and seas. And, only so far as we love all these three things ourselves, can we teach the love of them to others ".

The Victorian Conception of Wealth

GRAHAM HUTTON

MOST PEOPLE today think of the Victorians as prone to sweeping generalisations on good and evil, wealth and capital, the duty of the individual and the duty of the State. But the generalisations of our Victorian ancestors are as nothing to our own emotional and unfounded generalisations about the Victorians. First, *which* Victorians? Those of 1837 to 1870—the first half of the Queen's reign? Or those of 1870 to 1901 in the second half? There is a clear division somewhere around the years 1865 and 1875. Nowhere is this " great divide " more apparent than in economics. And by economics here I mean the ways of thinking about the nation's wealth : how individuals and the State were to behave in making and sharing wealth, and how all other institutions and ways of thinking—religious, social, political and international— influenced, or were in their turn influenced by, the new and revolutionary economic affairs.

It was the first time in human history that machines overcame human and animal power. This is what the so-called industrial revolution really meant. But the machines had to be made, first, before they could help human hands to turn out for the same effort far more consumable goods than had ever been turned out. The new steam engines, looms and other machines gave an entirely new meaning to the words " wealth and capital ". You see the resulting confusion in economic thinking all the way from Adam Smith, in 1776, to John Stuart Mill, who died in 1873, the time of the " great divide " in Victorian thought. No one was quite prepared to think of wealth as a yearly *flow*, instead of a fixed amount of capital. All production, all communications, depended until the nineteenth century on simple static forms of wealth. All that was violently upset between 1776 and Victoria's accession in 1837. So that first Victorian era, between, say, 1830 and 1870—one lifetime—was the great age of a great transition.

I do not think, even now, we realise how similar was that age to our own—similar in its sweeping challenges to established and inherited ways of social and economic thought.

The implications of this early-Victorian industrial revolution were difficult to understand because the old historical basis of British agriculture remained much as it had been before. Indeed, despite the import duties on foreign corn, which were swept away by Peel in 1846, British agriculture became more efficient and profitable right down to 1873—the " great divide " I mentioned earlier. The yield of British cornfields down to 1873 was the envy of the world. So for the first half of Victoria's reign, the landed gentry of England remained on their fields, and in the Lords and Commons, as a strong and profitable " estate ". And all that time the new commercial and industrial "estate" was developing alongside them ; saving, investing in new machinery, demanding cheap imports of foreign foodstuffs for their workers, and financing the rapid economic development of the world overseas out of fabulous profits made at home. Ostentatious wealth and spending, on personal consumption, was in fact—whatever we think today—less obvious between 1837 and 1870 than it was *before* Victoria became queen, or than it was *after* 1870, when the sons of the early-Victorian thrifty businessmen began to spend the profits of their fathers' investments. And that's what you would expect ; for the period of the Regency and George IV, with its vulgar ostentation and lavish personal spending, had more affinity with the *fin de siècle* than it had with the early-Victorian period of religious earnestness, abstinence and thrift.

It is very important to remember this background as we look back on the Victorian Age as a whole, for most of our current thinking, with its troubled heart-searchings and deep animosities, stems from that " great divide " in Victorian thinking between 1865 and 1875, when Britain finally turned her back on her own agriculture and became one hundred per cent dependent on world trade for her living. What the early-Victorian economists did was to concentrate—perhaps over-concentrate—their thinking about capital and national wealth upon mechanical adjuncts to industrial production. True, they still kept to the eighteenth-century conceptions of land and agriculture, since it was still profitable, and still unmechanised. But their social, political and economic thinking was, naturally enough, permeated with a deep sense of responsibility for the informing of the people, and their Governments, of the wonderful (but serious) implications of this industrial revolution. To them it was no time for easy living, wide social benefits. It was, on the contrary, a time for austerity, saving, investment, so that within a generation all the machines, railways, ships, and other remarkable inventions should get built and start turning out consumable goods. *Then*, they thought, would come what Americans call " the pay-off ". Well, they were right. The bad times, the forlorn years, were the 'thirties, the " hungry 'forties ", the diseased 'fifties, and the 'sixties of the cotton famine and so on. But between 1865 and 1875 came the biggest and quickest accumulation of British capital investment in history and from 1865 onwards the British people began to reap the material benefits of a generation of thrift and investment. There, again, is the " great divide " of the Victorian Age.

So the changed conception of wealth and capital first became clear in the 'sixties. After 1865 Limited Liability divorced the ownership of industrial capital from the business administration of capital. After 1865 capital and wealth became less individual, more social, impersonal, and a matter for State supervision and State action. Therefore after 1865 we come, in the later Victorian epoch, to the climate of opinion still prevailing in our own day. Lord Keynes, better than anyone else, made this point clear in his brilliant pamphlet in 1926 entitled *The End of Laissez-Faire*. It ought to be re-read by all of us, today.

Yet we would be wrong if we concluded, as so many still conclude, that *laissez-faire* and Mill's economic man, *homo economicus*, were cast-iron beliefs of the early-Victorian economists. As Keynes said, the early-Victorian economists were far more catholic, far more human, than most of the new manufacturers. Ricardo was a stockbroker; Mill was a famous administrator in the East India Company; Nassau Senior— perhaps the most brilliant of them all—was the reformer of the Poor Laws of England and Ireland, a Master in Chancery, the first Professor of Political Economy at Oxford, and an international authority on European politics and diplomacy. (Just as Grote, the great historian of ancient Greece, was a banker.) Not one of the early-Victorian economists was *against* intervention by Government for the bettering of social conditions.

Anyone who thinks that ought to read their works first—as Keynes recommended—or just look at the numerous and efficient Government bodies for social improvements on which they all sat. Despite the definition of Economy as Political, Professor Senior said that the realm of politics and legislation was not, and should not be, the economist's sphere. The economist ought *only* to study. His work should end with his making available to others his discoveries. Theirs was the responsibility.

The landed gentry, and many of the economists themselves—particularly John Stuart Mill and Nassau Senior—were the critics of unbridled *laissez-faire*. Early-Victorian economists believed, at worst, in an austere view of the need for capital, machinery, investment, and thrift—but only as the prerequisites for greater output with less human labour later, for the benefit of the workers as well as anyone else.

The trouble was that the New Wealth, the capital sunk in the new machines, became the New Property—not landed property, as wealth used to be, but property in the means of production. This it was which Karl Marx duly noted as the New Danger to the workers; and the publication of Marx's *Das Kapital* coincided with the " great divide ". The first volume was published in 1867. The later-Victorian Age after 1865 is the epoch of the impersonal capital, of the increasing importance of this industrial capital, and the waning importance of land and agriculture, *throughout Western Europe*. Oddly enough, it was in Russia at one extreme, and in America at the other, that agriculture continued to be important; but America, meanwhile, became industrialised and Russia not. So today the Russian Communist experiment, reared upon Marx's foundations, is making the Russian consumers go without consumer's goods in order that industrialisation shall go forward more rapidly. In other words, an early-Victorian thrift and abstinence in Russia today is being forced through by the State for better standards of living sometime in the future, just as it was forced through by economists and businessmen in Britain a century ago, and just as we in Britain today are again having to force it through under the State for different reasons. So do economic principles (which the Victorian economists correctly discovered) work out, despite all differences of time, government, politics and ideologies.

The Victorians rightly saw that quick accumulation of the new capital and the new machinery meant great benefits to the people, *in time*. For the moment, however, they meant thrift and austerity, before they could all be built. This made the new businessmen use the economists' arguments for more selfish reasons, and brought the term *laissez-faire* into such disrepute. It also led to the revolt of Carlyle and Ruskin and others against "the dark Satanic mills", the "hard-faced businessmen", the grime and disease, long hours of work, and low standards of living. It led to Chartism. But it also led to the best housing for the workers in the world at that time—houses which later Governments allowed to become slums; but they weren't slums when they were built, adjoining green fields. Later it led to Communism and Marxism—yet only when the private capitalist system had already begun to "pay off" to Britain's working class.

The revolutionary protests of Marx, Engels, Veblen and others were the materialistic counterpart of Victorian businessmen's materialism itself : thesis provoked anti-thesis ! And in the non-material sphere, the Victorian businessmen's materialism provoked another antithesis—that of Ruskin and William Morris, who sighed for the rural and Gothic England which was vanishing, but which did not finally vanish till, after 1873, the Great Agricultural Depression broke Britain's landed gentry. Both protests—the materialistic by Marxism and the aesthetic by Ruskin—largely failed to have a revolutionary effect in Britain, because the material results of early-Victorian economic and social thought were realised by the later-Victorian economists, politicians and reformers. Thus, though there was truly a "great divide" between the era up to 1870 and the period following it, it was not a fixed gulf. It was simply a turning-point, at which all the implications, already drawn by the humane (if stern and austere) early-Victorian thinkers, were able to be carried out thereafter. The formative early-Victorian Age thus gave place to the later-Victorian Age ; freedoms of the franchise, trade unions, of women and the workers, shorter hours, greater well-being and better health. Late-Victorian England lived well, on the austerity of early-Victorian England. If the problems of early-Victorian England were those of hard and unhealthy work for a pittance, those of late-Victorian England already fore-shadowed those of the twentieth century—the problems arising from greater leisure for the masses. In our own day, since the old Queen's death, the era of the World Wars has made us, all over Europe (including Russian Europe), relearn the lessons not of the late-Victorians, but of the far greater men and thinkers, the early-Victorians, who also had to think fast and furiously in the face of the greatest challenge to thought which had ever been presented up till then. The issue is simply : how much austerity are we prepared to advocate, and shoulder, for sometime—luckily it need not be as long as the generation between 1837 and 1865—in order to overcome shortages, and save and invest in new capital wealth, in order to turn out later on greater amounts of consumable goods and pleasures ?

No economist today ought to conclude without a tribute to the far-sightedness, the humaneness, the strict logic, the facing of unpalatable issues, by the economic thinkers of the great Victorian epoch. Not one of them could ever have said such a thing as *tant pis pour les faits*. The facts were sacred, however unpalatable their implications for social policy or governments. Economics, for them, was *not* the whole truth and nothing but the truth. It was only a small, if helpful, part of the new study of a newly developing technical society. The men who first systematised what we now call Economics were not economists. They were churchmen, like Archbishop Whately or Malthus ; lawyers like Senior ; philosophers like Mill ; bankers like Ricardo or Bagehot ; businessmen like Cobden and Bright. They fearlessly drew the conclusions from the facts of their time, and they tirelessly dug out the facts, and forced governments to get them dug out. But they were never hard-hearted. They admitted their errors in their own lifetime. They conceded where their opponents were right. They thought and worked in a climate of belief which bound them to render to every man his due, as a child of God, and to render to Cæsar the things that were Cæsar's. They were neither petty-minded, nor even party-minded. They were not narrowly nationalistic or imperialistic like the late-Victorians. They saw what was happening around them as the working-out of principles which could be discovered and systematised, in England as well as abroad, within the limits of a broad liberal humanitarianism. They were certainly not fatalists, either about what the British people could achieve, if properly led, or about what humanity could achieve, once leisure and education could be gained for all, by the help of the new Capital. They were therefore not merely materialists. They saw large possibilities before humanity, if only humanity would endure for a little, and be patient, and work for a better morrow. Their late-Victorian and Edwardian children enjoyed the sunshine of that morrow. We today can learn much from that lesson.

The Idea of Empire

J. W. DAVIDSON

WHAT WAS the Victorian idea of empire? Probably few
people would find much difficulty in giving an answer. It was,
they would say, the idea of " painting the map red ", of " trade
following the flag ", of " the white man's burden ", of an
" empire upon which the sun never sets ". This is, indeed, a
part of the answer which cannot be ignored. But it is not the
whole answer, nor even the most important part. The ideas of
the late-Victorian imperialists—of Seeley and Froude, Disraeli
and Joseph Chamberlain, Rudyard Kipling and Cecil Rhodes—
are a spectacular deviation from the settled tradition of British
thinking upon empire. They are not an integral part of it.

To find the ideas which guided our policy and our action over
most of the nineteenth century (and which largely guide it
today) we must go back to the first half of Queen Victoria's
reign, to a time before that typically Victorian figure the " gentle
reader " had begun to murmur the lines :

> " Take up the White Man's Burden—
> Send forth the best ye breed—
> Go bind your sons to exile
> To serve your captive's need . . ."

In those earlier years we shall find an idea of empire more modest
and less condescending, more respectful of genuine human
values and less tinged with delusions of grandeur.

Such a mode of thought fits more readily into our ordinary
way of political thinking. It stems from the philosophy of which
Edmund Burke was the most forceful exponent. It argues that
societies evolve organically, upon the basis of their own traditions
and necessities, and that to impose alien institutions and controls
undermines stability and the restraining force of the moral code.
If such ideas are true of England—and of European countries—

they are obviously true of colonies as well. But how have they actually formed our idea of empire, and been worked out in our imperial policy? Even now the ordinary Englishman—even the politician or the political philosopher—knows very little about the colonies. Least of all has he that intimate acquaintance with them which is needed for an understanding of their ways of thought—of the subtle changes of outlook which make Australians and New Zealanders something other than " transplanted British " ; or of the alien cultures of non-European peoples. In Victorian times ignorance was, certainly, no less.

The answer is, of course, that our imperial thinking has always been done for us by a small minority of men who were specially concerned, men who had lived in the colonies or served at the Colonial Office, missionaries in the field or humanitarians at home, and a few persistent travellers in distant parts of the world. Among the Victorians we have to look to men like James Stephen, Edward Gibbon Wakefield, David Livingstone, Goldwin Smith, Charles Dilke, and Arthur Gordon. They are a diverse group—Stephen, the evangelical who entered the Colonial Office to fight slavery and remained to become its permanent head ; Wakefield, the associate in Canada of Lord Durham, and leader in the colonisation of South Australia and New Zealand ; Livingstone, the missionary turned explorer ; Charles Dilke, the republican who travelled round the world soon after going down from Cambridge and took England by storm on his return with his book *Greater Britain* ; Arthur Gordon, the Earl of Aberdeen's youngest son, who abandoned a political career at home for one in colonial administration. Perhaps the most interesting of them all is the penetrating and pungent Goldwin Smith. He gave up the Regius Professorship of Modern History at Oxford, became one of the foundation professors at Cornell, and finally settled in Toronto. He was described by Roundell Palmer (later Lord Selborne), one of his Oxford seniors, as having more of the quality of personality which he supposed Milton to have had than anyone else he had ever met. And Matthew Arnold considered that Parliament suffered its greatest loss by his absence from it.

In earlier times it would not have been easy to apply the Burkian philosophy to colonial policy. For the colonies had formerly been valued as privileged sources of raw materials,

protected markets for British manufactures, and exclusive preserves for English shipping. They had been hedged round with
a mass of laws and regulations, imposed in the interests of Great
Britain. But the Victorians completed the destruction of these
Mercantilist controls, which had begun before their time. Mid-
Victorian Britain could buy or sell where it would ; and the
colonies could go their own way. As Goldwin Smith wrote :
" The time was when the universal prevalence of commercial
monopoly made it well worth our while to hold colonies in
dependence for the sake of commanding their trade. But that
time has gone. Trade is everywhere free, or becoming free. . ."

With the fall of Mercantilism, the state itself began to seem
less important. In relation to empire, the Victorians were concerned with the spread of English civilisation, rather than with
the extension of political control. This was the idea behind the
theory of Wakefield and the Colonial Reformers of the eighteen-
thirties and 'forties. They believed in " systematic colonisation ",
by which they meant the creation of new societies abroad repro-
ducing, so far as possible, the characteristics of England. This
was what interested Goldwin Smith and Dilke, too. It was at
the root of their affection for the United States ; for there millions
of immigrants—not only from Great Britain but from all
Europe—were becoming assimilated to English civilisation.

If Canada, Australia and New Zealand were to emulate the
United States, they must be given a fair chance. Political
dependence made colonists irresponsible, it prevented the full
use of their energies. " We are keeping the colonies in a perpetual state of political infancy, and preventing the gristle of
their frames from being matured and hardened into bone ".
Goldwin Smith wrote that sentence in 1862. He was scarcely
just to Durham and Wakefield and their friends, for their work
had made the idea of responsible government a form of political
orthodoxy. The powers which were retained over the major
colonies were fairly narrowly restricted. But even this was not
enough : responsible government, as it was then conceived, was
still a form of dependency. If the colonies were to become new
nations they must be completely free ; they must be given their
independence.

To men like Goldwin Smith and Dilke a belief in colonial
separation did not mean a dislike of colonies as such. As Goldwin

Smith wrote : " I am no more against colonies than I am against the solar system. I am against dependencies, when nations are fit to be independent ". Nor, as we have seen, was independence a purely negative conception. It would enable the former colonies to develop, and at the same time it would ensure the preservation of friendly relations with England, on a basis of common interests and sympathies. There was everything to gain and nothing, really, to lose. " After all," to quote Dilke, " the strongest of the arguments in favour of separation is the somewhat paradoxical one that it would bring us a step nearer to the virtual confederation of the English race ". The colonial separatists were the first to foresee the modern Commonwealth.

For the colonies of European settlement, the future seemed clear. But what of the dependencies with a non-European population—India, Ceylon, the West Indies, the settlements in West Africa ? Ultimately, they too would become free nations, when their people had adjusted themselves to Western civilisation and learnt how to work a modern constitutional system. But in the meantime they needed active help.

The Victorians had, indeed, inherited a strong sense of obligation towards backward peoples. Missionary expansion and the long struggle against slavery had produced a conviction that it was our duty to convey the benefits of our civilisation to those who did not possess them. David Livingstone, for example, in his lectures at Oxford and Cambridge in 1857, pressed upon his hearers the duty of spreading among the Africans " those two pioneers of civilisation—Christianity and commerce ". Such an extension of trade and missions did not necessarily, of course, involve the acquisition of territory and the setting up of a colonial government. In fact, it was best if this step could be avoided ; for then native society could adapt itself gradually to the changing needs of a new age. But sometimes annexation became unavoidable ; native rulers ceased to be able to maintain law and order in the face of growing European activity. It was so in regard to New Zealand in 1840, to Lagos in 1861, and to Fiji in 1874.

But if non-European people came under British rule, how were they to be governed ? Obviously it was not sufficient either to transfer British representative institutions or to establish some form of despotism. Both methods had been adopted in practice, but they could not satisfy an intelligent observer.

Charles Dilke was greatly troubled by the problem after travelling in India ; but—like most writers on the empire—he had not the experience to attempt a solution. It was left largely to men who had actually served as colonial administrators to work out this part of our imperial creed.

We may take as one of the most distinguished examples the contribution of Sir Arthur Gordon. He had gone to Fiji in 1875 as the first Governor of that new colony. His ideas were already formed by experience in previous Governorships. In Fiji he had the task of creating a whole system of government. When he was in England on leave in 1879 he explained and justified what he had done in an address to the Royal Colonial Institute. He pointed out how rule by even the best-intentioned of outsiders was often characterised by " a want of imagination on the part of the dominant race which prevents any conception by them of matters from the native point of view ". This lack of imagination produced friction, which in its turn often led on to actual injustice. " Indeed it is probable," he said, " that as much real wrong has been inflicted by the conscientious but narrow-minded desire to act in accordance with maxims in themselves generally sound, but not of universal application, as by violence and consequent tyranny ". From this analysis, it is not difficult to deduce the solution. It was the same, in essence, as that which had long been advocated for the colonies of European settlement. The people must be given responsibility, and their institutions must be in accord with their own ideas. Changes must come about in response to local demand, not to the whim of a European Governor or his home government. Upon those lines he founded his system of native administration, and it has survived, in its main outlines, to the present day.

Gordon's contribution to colonial theory was made, of course, when the mid-Victorian tradition in imperial matters was being temporarily overthrown. In 1872 Disraeli had committed the Conservative Party to a policy of imperialism. In 1876 he had, by the Royal Titles Act, made Queen Victoria Empress of India—or, in the words of a contemporary, he had " changed the sign of the Queen's Inn to Empress Hotel Ltd. ". Before 1890 we were to be involved in the " scramble " for Africa. The causes of the change were complex, but they were mainly economic. From the late 'sixties onwards Britain experienced a series of depressions. It began to be realised that our industrial predominance was likely to be a temporary phenomenon. Colonies became increasingly attractive as markets and fields of investment. Fresh annexations were welcomed, and a prolonged attempt was made to tighten relations with the existing self-governing colonies. It was hoped by many that the colonies would abandon the right to make their own tariffs. And much labour was spent in drawing up paper constitutions for the federation of the empire.

It is obvious from these projects how wrongly the new Imperialists had gauged the temper of opinion in the colonies. But at home they had great success : and they bespattered their predecessors in the field with a liberal stream of abuse. Goldwin Smith, in particular, became the victim of a conventional anti-radical witch hunt. When he left Oxford one London paper had declared its satisfaction that no longer would young men of " the Higher Orders " be exposed to the corrupting influence of his teaching. Disraeli had greeted one of his earlier utterances with a description of him as a pedant and a prig ; later he called him, amongst much else, " an itinerant spouter of stale sedition ". Even in his old age, in Toronto, the Imperialists didn't forget him. Perhaps it was only to be expected that a man who possessed both wit and integrity in such a high degree should have almost as many permanent enemies as Disraeli had temporary friends.

Even in our own time we have not been willing to give full recognition to the contribution of the mid-Victorians to imperial thinking. We have slowly learnt again through experience nearly all the lessons which they taught. But we still feel that—like the writers of history books—we should reserve the topmost places in our hierarchy of honour for the leaders of the generation which followed. We seldom possess the courage to repeat G. K. Chesterton's observation on Cecil Rhodes. " There is nothing large," said Chesterton, " about painting the map red. It is an innocent game for children. It is just as easy to think in continents as to think in cobblestones. The difficulty comes in when we seek to know the substance of either of them ".

But today, looking back on a year which has seen the establishment of the Dominions of India and Pakistan, the grant of independence to Burma, and the attainment of dominion status by Ceylon, does it not seem that the opinions of Rhodes and his contemporaries have less to offer us than a passage such as this which Anthony Trollope wrote in 1872 ?

" We are called upon to rule them (the colonies)—as far as we do rule them, not for our glory, but for their happiness. If we keep them, we should keep them—not because they add prestige to the name of Great Britain, not because they are gems in our diadem, not in order that we may boast that the sun never sets on our dependencies, but because by keeping them we may assist them in developing their own resources. And when we part with them, as part with them we shall, let us do so with neither smothered jealousy nor open hostility, but with a proud feeling that we are sending a son out into the world able to take his place among men."

ALFRED COBBAN

THE EMPIRE Theatre in Leicester Square opened its doors in 1884. Its name was a new one, calculated to appeal to a new generation. The Empire, evidently now entering into the public consciousness, was not so new. It is not the Empire, however, as an outstanding fact of the reign of Queen Victoria, but late-Victorian imperialism which I want to talk about. And I must begin by admitting that while it was *in* the Victorian Age, it was not quite *of* it.

What had the Empire meant to Cobden or Bright, to Dickens and Trollope and their readers, to the young Victoria and Albert ? But then the Empire in *their* day had been different—pioneer settlements in the empty lands, a net-work of trading-stations and forts, strung along the coasts and water-ways of the world. It could not be more, until it became possible to open up the interiors of the great continents and link them together by new methods of transport. Steam started the wheels of Empire turning. Power created power. Technical inventions, in fact, made the new imperialism possible. At the same time, increasing foreign competition with Britain made it desirable, because by the fourth quarter of the nineteenth century British industrial supremacy was being challenged. Economic rivalry stimulated a search for new sources of raw materials, new markets, and more profitable outlets for investment, and in this way the new imperialism was born.

The economic motivation is plain, though at the same time imperialism had to be presented in a form capable of appealing to the moral and religious conscience of Victorian England. " There are forty millions of people beyond the gateway of the Congo," declared the explorer Stanley to the Manchester Chamber of Commerce, " and the cotton spinners of Manchester are waiting to clothe them. Birmingham foundries are gleaming with the red metal that will presently be made into ironwork for them and the trinkets that shall adorn those dusky bosoms, and the ministers of Christ are zealous to bring them, the poor benighted heathen, into the Christian fold ".

Other countries, unfortunately, were also moved by the desire to extend the blessings of civilisation, so that political rivalry complicated the economic drive towards empire. Many forward steps were taken by late-Victorian statesmen for the purpose of forestalling or counteracting the extension of other empires, themselves moving forward under the impulsion of the same hopes and fears. When the Russians occupied Merv in North-west Afghanistan in 1884, or again when they moved into the Pamirs, though the country still separating them from India was rather difficult military terrain, alarm in England went as far as talk of war.

If one date is to be given for the beginning of imperialism as an effective force in British politics, it is June 24th, 1872, when Disraeli, in a speech at the Crystal Palace, adopted imperialism as one of the three main planks in the Conservative platform. Two years later he became Prime Minister. The Suez Canal shares and the Imperial Crown of India, peace with honour, Cyprus, the annexation of the Transvaal, the Zulu and Afghan Wars, redeemed his pledge. Why did Victorian pacifism and the cult of " little England " give way to this bellicose imperialism ? Before attempting a fuller explanation, it is necessary to ask what imperialism was, apart from being a term of abuse. Economic and political rivalries may explain the *fact* of Empire. But every important political fact demands its theory. Imperialism was an assertion of the right of Government over other lands and peoples, and behind this assertion, in the last resort, lay a theory of human destiny, an interpretation of history.

Yet if we look to the historians of the nineteenth century for a clue to the nature of the new imperialism we shall not at first sight find one. History has to be the history of something. The nineteenth century being an age of nationalism, historians naturally wrote the history of nations. The historian was the schoolmaster of nationalism, which seems to be the very opposite of imperialism. But opposites sometimes turn into one another. Nationalism involved a belief in the identification of the nation, as a community with a traditional culture of its own, and the state. Where the identity was not perfect, it had to be made so. Hence the attempts by ruling nations to assimilate by force any minorities unhappy enough to find themselves in their power. In movements such as Germanisation, Russification, Magyarisation and so on, European nationalism developed into a kind of petty imperialism. Empires have existed in many periods, and taken many different forms. I want to suggest that, paradoxical as it may seem, the imperialism of the late nineteenth century, for all its economic origins, acquired its peculiar colour and tone from the emotional nationalism which prevailed in the Europe of that day.

England inevitably was affected by this trend towards national aggrandisement, but with a difference. England was not in a situation, and did not inherit traditions, for which nationalist ideas had much practical significance. Her unity had been achieved long ago. She had no memories of foreign oppression, no *irredenta* beyond her own boundaries to rescue. Moreover, England was only a part of the United Kingdom, which was not, and never had been, even in idea, a real nation-state. The existence of the Channel Isles, of the conquered but not assimilated principalities of Wales, the freely united Kingdom of Scotland, with its own laws and institutions, the subject but unreconciled Irish, forbade any attempt to conceive of the British Isles as the home of a single nation. There was *no* British nation. Hence the intensification of emotion resulting when nation and state coincide, when political loyalty and cultural inheritance reinforce one another, could not be more than a temporary aberration in British conditions. The national enthusiasm of English historians could not, therefore, have quite the effect such enthusiasms produced elsewhere.

This is not to say that it had no effect. But it did mean that the kind of bastard imperialism which is merely nationalism writ large, was a peculiarly artificial and temporary phenomenon in Great Britain. Certainly there was an Empire, and economic and political circumstances were promoting its growth. Late-Victorian imperialism might be interpreted as an attempt to translate this empire into terms of nationalism. The point I am trying to make is that it was a hopeless attempt.

To take a specific example. Seeley, in 1883, wrote the history of the Empire under the title *The Expansion of England*. His book sold 80,000 copies in two years, and is said to have converted Lord Rosebery to imperialism. Excluding India, the Empire, Seeley said, "is a vast English nation", with "a population which is English throughout". This was a little difficult to reconcile with the facts. Scots, Welsh and Irish, even if they were regarded as junior partners in the Empire, and this might hardly have stood the test of statistics, were in any case there to protest against the conception of an English Empire : it had to be British. Even this was not very satisfactory. What was a Briton ? A barbarian, dressed in skins and supplying their inadequacy with large quantities of blue dye, waving a battle-axe, and perishing heroically, but rather inefficiently, at the hands of the Roman legions. Definitely not a ruling nation. Born to be conquered—by Romans, by Angles and Saxons, by Danes, by Normans—and not even speaking English. But one had to stop somewhere. Language was the favourite test of nationality. Anglo-Saxon attitudes prevailed in art and literature. The Norman conquest could be explained away. Kingsley had written of the great deeds of Hereward, the historian Freeman of Godwin and Harold. Later, Kipling's Norman knight, by marrying a fair Saxon, showed the way to redress the balance.

> "But now this game is the other way over—
> But now England hath taken me!"

The term Anglo-Saxon therefore came into fashion as a more convenient adjective for the new imperialism than English. It had the advantage of being jargon. It fitted in with the new racial ideas. "I believe in this race", proclaimed Joseph Chamberlain, "the greatest governing race the world has ever seen ; in this Anglo-Saxon race, so proud, tenacious, self-confident and determined, this race which neither climate nor change can degenerate, which will infallibly be the predominant force of future history and universal civilisation".

Pseudo-Darwinian conceptions of the struggle for existence and the survival of the fittest helped to promote this interpretation of imperialism as an expression of racial conflict, and the new trend of thought won widespread acceptance, although it involved a breach with earlier Victorian ideas of political morality. Force and fraud were perhaps now a little more respectable, required rather less decent veiling. If trade followed the flag, did it bring a more commercial morality with it ? A Stanley trod in the steps of a Livingstone. Something was gained, doubtless, but something else was lost, when the generation of Henry Lawrence of Lucknow was replaced by that of Cecil Rhodes.

There was always, of course, a current of opposition. Gladstone strove against the flowing tide unceasingly. But by 1895 the voice that had so long been Britain's conscience was soon to be heard no more. In 1895 Joseph Chamberlain went to the Colonial Office. The new imperialism, of which he was the chief spokesman, made its appeal to all sections of society. The ruling classes found an outlet for their sons in conquering and governing India, or administering the new lands. The rapidly growing Public Schools provided a training which specially fitted their pupils for the governing of " lesser breeds without the law ". The great financial houses of the City of London shifted their allegiance to the Conservative Party, or attached themselves to the Liberal imperialists. For the lower middle classes the idea of Empire provided an emotional satisfaction and an assertion of their status as members of an imperial nation.

Imperialism, indeed, was a peculiarly urban though hardly urbane phenomenon. Something in the gathering of large agglomerations of individuals in the big cities, for the very reason that it destroyed the traditional social groupings, seemed to create a need for newer and more artificial stimuli. The political parties had not yet become big mass movements. Organised sport was only in its beginnings. Imperialism filled a gap in the social development of the masses. Its voice was the voice of the music halls. " We don't want to fight, but by Jingo if we do ", gave a name to the new movement. A long series of popular songs followed, with ennobling invocations of " Tommy Atkins ", the " dear old flag ", and the " Soldiers of the Queen ".

But imperialism did not reach its heights in the music-halls, or in the politics of trade and territorial aggrandisement. If, as I believe is true, it was partly a response to an emotional need, its most revealing manifestations are more likely to be found in literature than in politics. In the later decades of the century the literary possibilities of the Empire were discovered by popular writers. The call of the wild was heard in City office and country rectory. Even before Kipling, romance was bringing up the nine-fifteen. Scott's Highlanders and Crusaders were too remote, Tennyson's Knights of the Round Table too unreal. The Empire was a fact. One could throw up one's job and join the Canadian Mounted Police, explore the Congo with Stanley, relieve Lucknow with Havelock, sit, with imagined nostalgia, in the shade of the old Moulmein Pagoda, or adventure in search of a Treasure Island or King Solomon's Mines.

There is no time to elaborate this theme. It will be best to concentrate for a moment on the writer who was the Poet Laureate of Empire, Rudyard Kipling. Time is winnowing his writings. Phrases like " the White Man's Burden ", and a certain streak of brutality, led critics of his own day, and later, to identify him with the crudest jingoism. Let me read you a passage from the most distinguished literary journal of his day—" Mr. Kipling only voices a drift of ethical speculation which is becoming articulate at more than one point. . . . Such speculations attempt to translate into ethical language the biological formula of the " struggle for existence " ; and although they do not commend themselves to minds which have enjoyed the advantages of a philosophical training, they certainly do to a group of brilliant, persistent, but, so far as philosophy is concerned, somewhat shallow journalists of whom Mr. Kipling is the most striking representative ". That was the *Athenaeum*.

If this were all there is in Kipling, his books would now be gathering dust in the back shelves and cellars of Charing Cross Road. But there is an India in *Kim* which Birmingham never knew. When we read *On the City Wall* or *Without Benefit of Clergy* we are a long way from the Simla of Mrs. Hawksbee. Old Testament morality is much in evidence in Kipling, but the racial theory, and the Chosen People, the Anglo-Saxons, do not make as frequent an appearance as might have been expected. His jungle is one which at least is ruled by law. His state is the servant, not the master of man. In Kipling's stories we meet soldiers, administrators, doctors, nurses : the economic motive is conspicuously lacking.

There is something in Kipling's imperialism which reaches beyond the jingoism of the age. When, in *Puck of Pook's Hill*, he tries to recover the spirit of the greatest empire of the past, he looks for it, not in the records of a great cosmopolitan capital, but in the lonely garrisons scattered along the Wall, the thin line behind which the settled populations teemed, and civilisation flourished and declined. And the maturer Kipling chooses not the moment of triumph but that of decay, when Rome is falling.

> " Cities and Thrones and Powers
>   Stand in Time's eye,
>   Almost as long as flowers,
>   Which daily die."

When Kipling wrote this, and when he wrote *Recessional*, was he already writing, in advance, the epitaph on the aggressive imperialism he had seemed to embody ? It *was* the epitaph. For jingoist imperialism did not last. The Diamond Jubilee of 1897 was the grand parade of Empire ; the Boer War its most characteristic achievement ; its last political triumph, the General Election of 1900.

The trend of the public mind was soon to change. The Boer War proved to be rather more than the military picnic so lightheartedly anticipated. It was not a masterpiece of political or military art, and it delivered a shock to the public conscience from which jingoism never really recovered. It was difficult to represent the victory of a great Empire over a tiny nation as a glorious triumph. The strong vein of humanitarianism in the country made any permanent acceptance of the doctrine of blood and iron impossible. Mafeking was a popular but transient outburst of emotion. The *Annual Register* for the same year wrote that " the outlook at the end of the year which closed the nineteenth century could hardly fail to arouse misgivings as to the future in all but the imperviously self-satisfied ".

The Imperialism of the jingos, then, illuminated the last days of the Victorian Age, but only with an evanescent coruscation. It shot up like a rocket, and went out as soon. If the only inspiration of Empire had been this, it would have been dead within a few years of the ending of the Boer War, with the ending of the social and political conditions which had made jingoism possible. For all its popularity and nation-wide influence, late-Victorian imperialism was an abnormal growth, alien to the deeper political habits of thought of the country. As Mr. Davidson has shown, there was something different, and something more permanent in the idea of the Empire and Commonwealth, which outlived jingoism, something which, being a living force, grew and changed, in ways remote from the imaginings of those who had nursed or neglected its infant years, which had its roots far deeper in the traditions of the British nations, and which survived storms to which the Boer War had been a summer breeze.

The Liberal Mind in Victorian England

G. M. YOUNG

THIS EVENING we are to think for a while about the Liberal mind in Victorian England. But may I first remind you of something which we are all apt to forget—I mean that the Victorian Age, as we call it, is the insular phase of a movement common to the whole of Western Europe and its offshoots beyond the seas. When we lift our eyes from our own country, our own ancestors, and look across the Channel, or across the Atlantic, constantly we find that ways and habits, fashions and prejudices, doctrines, ideas, and even phrases, which we think of as typically Victorian, are really part of a general European pattern. Let me give you one instance : you know how hotly our Victorian moralists and satirists inveigh against the shortcomings of women's education, the silliness and shallowness of the boarding school, the time wasted on trivial accomplishments. Well, then, which of them wrote this passage ?

> " She had been brought up in one of the most exclusive establishments, where three objects are regarded as of the highest importance. First comes French, then the piano, that she shall be able to amuse and soothe her husband, and lastly a thorough acquaintance with the principles of household economy in its highest and most aesthetic sense, including the art of knitting purses."

Is it Thackeray, or Dickens, or George Eliot ? It is none of them : it is not English at all. It comes from Gogol's *Dead Souls*, I suppose the most intensely Russian book ever written. But it was an age when thoughtful men, and women, were deeply concerned with this question of women's education, and so you find Gogol at the far end of Europe writing a sentence which you would not be surprised to meet in any English book of the time, while, if you searched, I have no doubt you would encounter the same ideas in much the same language, in Swedish books and Portuguese books. It is part of what I called just now, the European pattern : just as Gothic architecture was part of the pattern before the Renaissance and classical architecture after the Renaissance. But as we travel about Europe we soon learn to distinguish French Gothic from English Gothic, or Spanish baroque from German baroque. They are the same but with a difference : and you might perhaps say that the difference is more interesting than the identity, and the identity is more significant than the difference. That I think is the right way to look at any of these great European patterns, and I shall try this evening to show what I believe to be the fundamental unity of Liberal thought in the Victorian Age, and to set off against it the English variations from the common type, and the English contributions to the common stock.

Now, take that word Liberal. In England, before the French Revolution, it meant magnanimous, open-handed, open-hearted, and—just note the change which is setting in—open-minded, free from prejudice, ready to judge things on their merits. What things ? Everything! The State and its institutions, the Church and its doctrines. You see there is something rather explosive in that word *liberal*, because if the State is oppressive or the Church corrupt, if the laws of the State are unreasonable or the teaching of the Church incredible, then your Liberal man will tend to be a revolutionary and a free thinker. So you may understand why Sir Robert Peel called *liberal* an odious word, and why some people were careful in speaking of liberals to call them by their French name, *les libéraux*, or their Spanish name, *los liberales*, just to show that Liberalism was one of those hateful foreign doctrines, immoral and irreligious, which had brought about one Revolution in France, and might bring about another, perhaps, in England.

The Liberals were, in fact, the disappointed heirs of the Revolution, and when, after Waterloo, the dynasts returned to their thrones, the Liberals in Spain and Italy and in France were the opposition, the resistance, ready to overthrow the restored order of things whenever occasion offered, and if necessary by force. In this sense Byron and Shelley were Liberals—in Italy. But in England the word lost its subversive sense, partly because we had a much more expressive word of our own : *Radical* ; and partly because, with our long political experience and education, our reformers knew very much better than the foreign *liberales* what they wanted and how to get it. So in England, the wide-sweeping liberalism of Europe was canalized, so to speak, towards one object, the reform of the House of Commons and an extended franchise. And when that was achieved, and the decision loyally accepted by the Tory opposition, liberalism in England, became respectable. If a man had called himself a Liberal in 1837 no one would have concluded that he wanted to dethrone the Queen or plunder the bishops. He was certainly a loyal subject and very likely a devout churchman—as Mr. Gladstone was, and Mr. Gladstone, destined as we know to become the greatest Liberal of all time, never for a moment abated his reverence for monarchy, aristocracy and the Church.

You see how difficult it is to pin the liberal mind within the four corners of a definition. But I think we can get a little nearer if we consider this. Before the French Revolution, even intelligent men seem to have taken it for granted that the world would always be very much what it was. It would improve no doubt : civilisation would spread to the Pacific islands, superstition would make way for reason, science would be cultivated in Siberia and the Far West of America, and the nations, if they were wise, would live in harmony under free constitutions like that which had made England so great and so happy. That was about as far as the most far-sighted man could look. Then came the French Revolution, which showed that institutions which had lasted for generations might be destroyed in a few months, and that Europe, so far from being stable could, if revolutionary principles prevailed, be turned upside down. The nations might indeed defend themselves against the French armies. But could they defend themselves against French ideas ?

But that is only one half of the story ; because even if there had been no French Revolution, a great change in men's ways of thinking would have come about, simply from the development of science, or, as they called it, Natural Philosophy. And to that there was no end in sight. If a train could run thirty miles an hour, why not three hundred ? If a Lancashire mill could turn out ten thousand yards a day, why not a hundred thousand ? If science could master smallpox, why not all other diseases ? And so, in place of the old notion of society as something static and gently improving itself, you get the new notion of society as something dynamic and constantly transforming itself, by processes to which no limit could be assigned.

Now bring these two ideas together, the French idea of Liberty, Fraternity and Equality, and the English idea of Progress by means of Science. What shape will the compound take ? Something like this, I think : " Frame your institutions so as to give the utmost scope to these new pioneers and this new power. Throw down everything that may obstruct the progress of industry and the march of mind. And that means, bring your laws and your administration by means of free discussion into accordance with the findings of Public Opinion. Then there will be no subversion, no revolution, because the people will be on the side of the law ; the Government will govern with their consent : and the process of improvement will be working everywhere and all the time, because political freedom and material progress are two sides of the same medal ". That, one may say, is standard, mid-Victorian Liberalism. But here we must just remember, though we have no time to dwell upon it, that in England public opinion and discussion were bound by conventions—moral, social and religious—stricter, I should reckon, than in any European country enjoying the same amount of political freedom. Now the Liberal, we remember, is the man who claims the right to judge everything on its merits, without prejudice or dogma, and English society was, we may say, dogmatic all through. A man did take a risk if he discussed too freely certain religious questions or certain social questions, if he criticised our divorce laws, or asked whether God really commanded the Israelites to put the people of Canaan to the sword. Mill's *Essay on Liberty* is really a plea for freer discussion of serious matters, and there is a phrase dropped casually by Darwin which throws a flash of light on the world that Mill and he lived in. When the *Origin of Species* came out, Lyell, one of the greatest names in English science, first hesitated and then announced his support. And Darwin writes : " In view of his age *and his position in society* his conduct is heroic ". *His position in society*, you notice, might have been shaken by his adoption of a doctrine contrary to the orthodox faith. No wonder thoughtful men looked wistfully to the Continent—to the universities of France and Germany and Holland, where you could believe what you liked, and the only question was " What reason have you for believing it ?" And the breaking down of these conventions in England was one of the greatest services, and most lasting, of the Liberal mind.

But, whether here or abroad, the central conception of Liberalism is political : it means government in accordance with opinion elicited by discussion, and so it was possible to divide the nations of the world quite simply into the *liberal* who were our natural friends and the *despotic* who were our natural enemies. " There are two parties in Europe," Palmerston once said, " one party considers nations to be the property of their governors, the other holds that governments are established for the good of the many, and that is the principle on which our government was founded in 1688 ". And the good of the many means what they think good for themselves not what someone else, however wise and benevolent, thinks good for them. Hence comes the Liberal watchword : Self-government is better than good government. But notice once more how the concept has to be adapted to fit our island circumstances, and our long tradition of government by a Parliamentary aristocracy which the Continent did not possess. What, for example, is the essence of Gladstonian Liberalism ? I should say, a detestation of all authority, from Empires to Trade Unions, not omitting Parliaments, which does not rest on the consent of the governed, *habitual* or expressed ; and note that word *habitual* because it is the dividing line between the Liberal and the Radical, between, say, Gladstone and Bright. The Liberal makes allowances for the fact that the people still respect, admire and trust the old governing class, so long as it acknowledges the power and final judgment of Public Opinion. And so in the mid-Victorian years, we settled down into an easy genial compromise between progress and tradition—years when a candidate, being asked about his political opinions might reply, and very often did reply : " Sir, I am a Liberal Conservative," which meant " our old institutions have served us well, and I see no reason to change them. But I have an open mind, and if there are any improvements which Public Opinion demands then I am ready to consider them ".

Now what are the improvements which Public Opinion demands, and the Liberal will support ? I think you can bring them under one head and say—the removal of any unfair advantage, social, political, national or racial. To introduce competitive examination for the Civil Service : to disestablish the

Irish Church : to abolish the purchase of commissions in the Army : to admit Dissenters to the Universities, and Jews to Parliament : to give self-government to the South African States after the peace of 1902—these are all typically Liberal measures. But when you come to economic inequality, to the advantage which the rich man has over the poor man, then you feel that Liberalism, political Liberalism, is coming to the end of its programme : it is passing the torch on to a new competitor in the race for power. Socialism in late-Victorian England has not begun to make itself felt. But it has begun to make itself heard. And what it is saying is that neither party, Liberal or Conservative, has any answer to the great problem of modern life— poverty in the midst of plenty. You tell us, these newcomers say, that our old institutions have served us well. We reply that they are serving us very ill today. You tell us that you are prepared to improve them. We reply that your Education Acts, your Trade Union Acts, your County Council Acts, none of them goes to the root of things. We do not want improvements. We want change.

And now you see the tide turning. Throughout the Victorian age, our political ideas were in the ascendant : it was to England that all political reformers looked, while from foreigners we had nothing to learn. But when we come to social and economic ideas, the influence is the other way. It is we who look abroad, to America, to Germany, to France. And as European Liberalism evolves towards Socialism, so does ours. But always with that difference, which we have noticed so often, when European ideas have to be fitted into the island framework.

But : will the framework hold them, or will the explosive elements in the new doctrines shatter it to pieces ? Are Socialism and Parliamentary methods really compatible ? Are you in your heart convinced that self-government *is* better than good government ? Can you make the welfare of the people your aim without sacrificing their liberty ? Can you bring progress under control and not take the heart out of the pioneer, thus damping initiative and responsibility together ? It is in questions like these that you hear late-Victorian Liberalism—the Liberalism of men who had grown up under the influence of Mill and Morley—taking its stand, measuring itself against the new ideas : questions which they have left us to answer.

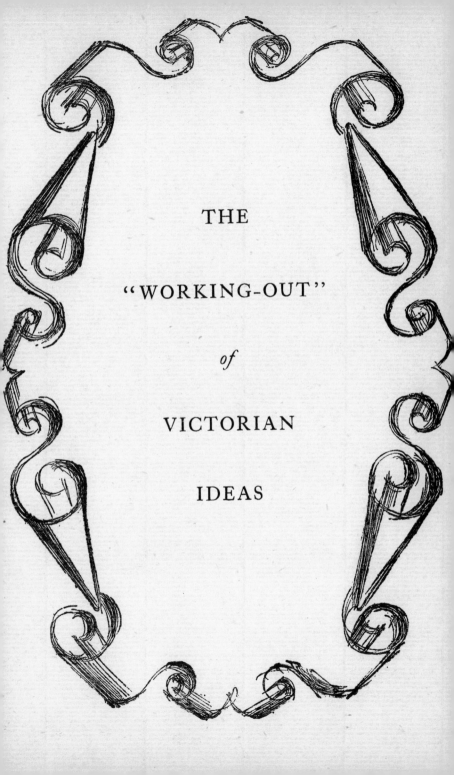

THE

"WORKING-OUT"

of

VICTORIAN

IDEAS

The Victorian Family

H. L. BEALES

THE WORD "family" like the word "society" means different things when spelt with a small initial letter and when spelt with a large. I am not going to talk about Family with a large capital F. Aristocracy, political or social, patrician or plutocratic, throws no special light on family spelt with a small "f"—on the family as a social institution. What I am concerned with is ordinary little bunches of parents and children, the small universal social groups in which most but not all adults live out their lives, and in which most but not all children are raised and grow to adulthood.

The Victorian family won a reputation for itself as a noble social institution, upon whose continuance depended all that was fine and stable in British civilisation. It was exemplified for many in the Royal Family itself. What could be better, morally and socially, more definitely Christian and tenderly benignant, than that high exemplar? What harder blow had any family, any wife, to bear than that which deprived it of its devoted, and so far as may be, selfless father in 1861? Yet even that family had its imperfections. Inherent in the apparently simple grouping of parents and children, a non-political though an economic unit in the Victorian period, were difficulties—for instance, that of harmonising sexual and parental relationships. There were problems of discipline, training, relations with the outside world of non-personal values, as well as problems of personal psychology. It is easy to see that all sorts of strains and stresses could not but arise. The external environment of this difficult social institution was changing too. The rigours no less than the opportunities of the new industrialism put a heavy strain on those to whom technical progress and its business problems were matters of day-to-day urgency. Those who had no cushioning from the onset of unemployment or other economic insecurities equally though in different ways found their family life hard to manage. To be successful a family requires, in general, a settled outlook about the present and the capacity to look ahead. So for the middle class internal strains were apt to develop, and for the workers external influences were apt to threaten collapse. And so, stable as it looks at a first glance, the Victorian family shows signs of wear and tear as the decades draw on.

The Victorian family was, as near as might be, a self-sufficient unit. Every Englishman's home was his castle. In its sanctities and privacy a man might escape from the trials of the outer world and be safe from its prying eyes. The family was indeed a kind of estate, like, say, the British Empire, and subject like it to the benevolent despotism of its lord and master. For it *had* a lord and master, and his ways were expected to be authoritarian. An incident when Lord Melbourne was Prime Minister just before Queen Victoria was called to the throne illustrates that aspect of the family. Melbourne was cited as a co-respondent. Both he and the respondent escaped with their reputations well nigh intact, but there followed a sharp struggle between Mrs. Norton and her husband. The husband claimed the custody of the children, and claimed also complete control of his wife's literary earnings. Caroline Norton, who reappeared for a later generation as Meredith's *Diana of the Crossways*, was not the person to lose battles without a fight. She fought with her pen and her personal influence for her children and the modification of the one-sided marriage contract then prevalent. And it was one-sided, so much so that a man could deprive his wife, though she were of proved virtue, of her children and give them over to the care of another woman. Mrs. Norton was no feminist. " I never pretended," she said, " to the wild and ridiculous doctrine of equality. . . . I believe in the natural superiority of the man as I do in the existence of a God. The natural position of woman is inferiority to a man, that is a thing of God's appointing, not of man's devising." All the same, her struggle aided in securing the Infant Custody Act of 1840. She struck a blow of some value in the re-definition of woman's place in the home and in society.

Another memory might be added. In 1873 the Rev. Frank Besant and his wife came to the parting of the ways, theological and personal. " I was told," writes Annie Besant in her *Auto-*

biography, " I was told that I must conform to the outward observances of the Church and attend Communion. I refused. Then came the distinct alternative : conformity or exclusion from home, in other words hypocrisy or expulsion. I chose the latter." And the two children ? She obtained a legal separation and the guardianship of one of them, the daughter. But she lost home, friends, social position . . . and as " a lady in reduced circumstances " she found herself earning four shillings and sixpence a week by fancy needlework, and then a little more as governess-cook-nurse in a family. When in 1877 she was in trouble, with Charles Bradlaugh, for publishing a birth-control pamphlet, an application was made to the High Court to deprive her of the custody of her child. Though the judge admitted that she had taken excellent care of her, her refusal to give religious instruction was decisive. She describes how her child was taken from her " shrieking and struggling, still weak from scarlet fever, nearly frantic with fear and passionate resistance ". An appeal failed. " In the days when the law took my child from me," she wrote later, " it virtually said to all women, ' Choose which of these two positions, as wife and mother, you will occupy. If you are legally your husband's wife, you can have no legal claim to your children, if legally you are your husband's mistress, your rights as mother are secure.' " It is easier for us now to sympathise with Mrs. Besant than to understand what the Court was trying to protect. It was the Victorian family as a social institution, as a complete social commonwealth in miniature, whose stability was imperilled by Mrs. Besant's high-souled independence.

Mrs. Besant, Josephine Butler and others won victories which led to a substantial modification of the internal relations of the marriage-partnership, and therefore of the institution of the family. In 1857 divorce became possible through the newly established Divorce Court. It required an Act of Parliament before that, though Ecclesiastical Courts could grant separations. But divorce was too expensive for the poor and grounds for it, acceptable to the court, were very one-sided. It played little part in the regulation of the Victorian family because it was little used. There were less than two hundred cases a year before 1870, and fewer than four hundred a year in the 'nineties.

There was a literature about the family, but it was a literature of acceptance and praise, not of discussion. The family was, in fact, a going concern. Its validity was not in doubt. It fitted in to the golden age of the self-made man. But it wasn't everybody's choice. Florence Nightingale, for example, refused to marry. " She was asked in marriage," says her biographer, Sir Edward Cook, " by one who continued for some years to press his suit. . . . The match would by all have been deemed suitable, and by many might have been called brilliant. And Florence herself was strongly drawn to her admirer . . . because she admired his talents, because the more she saw of him the greater pleasure did she find in his society." And yet she refused to marry him. Why ? She explained her refusal in these terms : " I have an intellectual nature which requires satisfaction, and that would find it in him. I have a passionate nature which requires satisfaction, and that would find it in him. I have a moral and active nature which requires satisfaction ; that would not find it in *his* life. . . . I would be satisfied to spend a life with him combining our different powers in some great object. I could not satisfy this nature by spending a life with him in making society and arranging domestic things. Voluntarily to put it out of my power ever to be able to seize the chance of forming for myself a true and rich life would seem to me like suicide."

Florence Nightingale was not a warped person. She understood the claims of family life. But in her life she stated a case for the individual alternative. And she was aware of the narrowness of prevailing ideas. " Daughters," she wrote, " can only have a choice among those people whom their parents like, and who like their parents well enough to come to their house." There were sides of the family relationship which caused doubt or resentment to arise ; and as in all ages the appearance of felicity and its actuality was not always identical. The family as it was in this Victorian Age before either biology or psychology had begun to throw a generally accessible light upon its realities leaves necessarily indirect rather than direct records of its true qualities. These records are available in the unconscious evidence of novels, newspapers, magazines, even in such popular sayings as " Children should be seen and not heard ". The heavy ceremonial entertaining portrayed in the brilliant pages of Thackeray's *Cornhill* magazine, the quieter fullness of the days of William Arthur's *Successful Merchant* (which ran through over forty editions in the 'seventies) reflect the middle-class habit and outlook before the epoch of economic grace was over. The clear impression that emerges is that of established routine, of a division of labour between man and woman that correlates with known social habits, known ambitions and prestige values, and approved positives and negatives of personal behaviour. For at any rate the ascending middle class this was a settled outlook. That class did not appear to be haggard with frustrations. They couldn't have produced or tolerated a D. H. Lawrence, though of course they had their escapes and escapisms, their safety valves and extra-marital adventure equipments. The typical Victorian novel was a happy-ending, wedding-bell stereotype ; there was a *cult* of the home then, and family prayers, family magazines, bowdlerised Shakespeares, the family photograph album, the annual family holiday were standard family equipment.

Perhaps it would be fair to say that the chief defect of the Victorian middle-class family was that it lived too much in the present. It was rooted in a tradition that did not allow much room for development, for the acquisition of new freedoms, and new enjoyments. The new public schools that were created for the middle class came to be dominated by Arnold's Rugby. The ideal behind that system was that of the English gentleman— people must be pressed to conformity on that matrix. It is beautifully delineated in Newman's *Idea of a University*, in which he draws an ironical picture of his kindly but amateurish inefficiencies. Muscular Christianity had its limitations.

No wonder Herbert Spencer complained that " though some care is taken to fit youth of both sexes for society and citizenship, no care whatsoever is taken to fit them for the position of parents. While many years are spent by a boy in gaining knowledge of which the chief value is that it constitutes ' the education of a gentleman ' and while many years are spent by a girl in those decorative acquirements which fit her for evening parties, not an hour is spent by either in preparation for that greatest of all responsibilities—the management of a family ".

But what of the family lower down in the social scale ? The determinants of personal and social welfare in the lower social strata were strictly conditioned by the crudities of the new urbanisation and the sad deficiencies of life in our villages. For a big proportion of the population food was scanty, housing disgraceful, and leisure inadequate. There were the clerks at a pound a week or less, the agricultural labourers of the south-west at, say, eight shillings, and the multitudes of dock and other general labourers, with intermittent employment relieved only by intemperance—however shocking that may sound. The way the problem presented itself may be gathered from a discussion of the employment of mothers in manufactures. The speaker, Cooke-Taylor, is an experienced authority on the factory system.

" We have hitherto prided ourselves in this country—and prided ourselves justly—on the liberty of the subject, on the sanctity of the domestic hearth, and on the decency and privacy of our family life. That unit, the Family, is the unit upon which a constitutional Government has been raised which is the admiration and envy of mankind. Hitherto, whatever else the laws have touched, they have not dared to invade this sacred precinct ; and the husband and wife, however poor, returning home from whatever occupations or harassing engagements, have there found *their* dominion, *their* repose, *their* compensation. . . . There has been a sanctity about this . . . home life which even the vilest law acknowledged and the rashest law respected. . . . But let the State step in between the mother and her child . . . domestic confidence is dissolved, family privacy invaded and maternal responsibility assailed. For the tender care of the mother is substituted the tender mercies of the State ; for the security of natural affection, the securities of an unnatural law ! Better by far that many another infant should perish in its innocence and unconsciousness than to be the victims of such a state of things."

In all such circles poverty was an omnipresent theme. Anyone who is willing to uncover the social history of the " submerged tenth", "the dangerous classes," will soon discover how many are the paths that lead to the work of Octavia Hill or Beatrice Webb or Mary Carpenter, to the writings of W. T. Stead or George Godwin or the anonymous author of the *Bitter Cry of Outcast London* (1884) or the statistics of Charles Booth, or the struggle to mend broken human earthenware of General William Booth. Let anyone who will look below the improving material surface of Victorian life ask what alternative there was to Charles Booth's conclusion that only the State could handle the problem of the hard core of insufficiency and squalor in which a third of London lived ? The long record of child-murder, of baby farming, of parents cashing in, through the pittances of minute insurance policies, on what was rather too tamely called " infanticide ", is still under discussion in the last years of the century. A Select Committee of 1890 faced the question of whether then there was any appreciable amount of child-murder and their evidence is affirmative. Said Mr. Justice Wills : " I have no doubt there is a very considerable number of children in this country who are starved to death by parents who could prevent it if they chose " and who added his belief that pecuniary gains played its part in their untimely end. But in any case the figures of high infant mortality tell their own grim story. So does the widespread influence of occupational diseases, sweated trades, and all the rest of the sordid degradation, neglect, waste of the supposedly self-regulating economic system. I could quote horrifying descriptions of the physical environment of a large proportion of the working-classes. Take the two volumes of letters contributed to the *Times* by the Dorset-born Sidney Godolphin Osborne, or the *Seven Curses of London* by James Greenwood, or Alexander Paterson's *Across the Bridges*. There is no Victorian decade in which housing is adequate. That is why it comes to be the State's concern. Education likewise. Under the same sort of social pressures, the State took over functions, earlier regarded as those of the family, in relation to food, health and welfare generally. The spheres of public concern and public enterprise had to be enlarged because of the threat and the reality of physical and moral deterioration. It is a simple truism that a family cannot be what too many people thought it was if it lives in a cesspool.

And the factory family ? There too was failure. How could it be otherwise. Fathers, mothers and children, all working in mills, brickfields, Black Country workshops and elsewhere *could not* live as their betters told them they must, yet not till 1847 was a Ten Hours' Act passed. The vital statisticians warned every year that things were not right ; doctors repeated their warnings. Preventable death, child labour and woman labour, squalor and disease caused the premature disintegration of families.

Increasingly, birth control and rising standards of living, collective bargaining and shorter working days, athletics, parks, education and libraries, made for better ways of living. But these external factors did not strengthen the Victorian family. On the contrary they tended to modify it in all sorts of ways. The family began to look outward more and more, as it became smaller, better environed, better equipped culturally and educationally. It was coming, too, under the influence of new biological and psychological knowledge. Its hold was weakening.

Change has become incandescent in the writing and discussion, and in the behaviour, of recent years. Listen to Samuel Butler, at the end of the century :

" I believe that more unhappiness comes from this source (the Family) than from any other—I mean from the attempt to prolong family connection unduly and to make people hang together artificially who would never naturally do so. The mischief among the lower classes is not as great, but among the middle classes it is killing a large number daily. And the old people do not really like it much better than the young ".

That passage comes from the *Note Books* ; it is written out in full in *The Way of All Flesh* (1903).

Scepticism was beginning to be articulate. Those things that took parents and children out of the family circle for their enjoyments and their freedoms were developing. Internally and externally the family had to face new influences. People had begun to wonder whether it could survive.

Victorian Ideas of Sex

H. L. BEALES

THOMAS MORTON, author of the play, *Speed the Plough*, died in 1838. A character in that play was Mrs. Grundy. The Victorians took that lady to their hearts and homes. Was it Mary Russell Mitford who got into trouble for calling a certain pudding a roly-poly ? But Mrs. Grundy was insistent on more than verbal respectability. She was dictator of manners. But she lived and ruled in most circles of Victorian society. Out came the drapings for the piano-legs—was it the high polish which was vulnerable, or were legs just things that should not be seen ? A conspiracy of silence was established on the subject of sex which has never been completely broken up. A system of conventional negatives or taboos was devised for it. In 1862, George Meredith's friend, Sir William Hardman, was saying that a public meeting with the purpose of abolishing the crinoline was futile. " Crinoline will never be extinguished by public meeting and female combination. The girls of our time like to show their legs. . . ." The history of fashion in dress and undress contains more mysteries than certainties ; some Victorian fashions were so surprising as to prove that Mrs. Grundy had blind spots ; but the Victorian period, especially its earlier decades, was adamant in its refusal to let the subject of sex come into the open, whatever the vagaries even of Fashion might be.

To get to know Victorian beliefs on this subject it is necessary to examine behaviour rather than books. It would be misleading to take Mrs. Grundy at her face value. She was the child of reaction—of reaction from the period of the Regency and Queen Victoria's Wicked Uncles. You remember in Thackeray's *Four Georges* the description of Queen Caroline's death-bed ; she advises the King, George II, to marry again. " No, no," said the King, " I'll have mistresses." Thackeray's disgust at this is a representative expression of Victorian unwillingness to understand. . . .

" What satire is so awful," Thackeray wrote in 1848 to G. H. Lewes (not yet living with George Eliot), while there was still a trace in him of his earlier radicalism, " What satire is so awful as ' Lead us not into Temptation ', what is the gospel of life of our Lord (excuse me for mentioning it) but a tremendous protest against pride and self-righteousness ? " Thackeray was explaining that if Becky Sharp (delivered to the world in that astonishing year 1848) had had £5,000 a year " she would have been respectable ; increased her fortune ; advanced her family; laid up treasures for herself in the shape of three per cents., social position, reputation, etc. I am quite aware of the dismal roguery which goes all through the *Vanity Fair* story—and God forbid that the world should be like it altogether ; though I fear that it is more like it than we like to own." This Victorian epoch was an age of aggressive money-making industrialism; still young when Victoria became Queen, it pushed sex into the background of its *prime* interests. Beatrice Webb a generation later turned her sharp eyes on " The London Season " of the 'eighties. The London Season, she wrote, " with its derivative country-house visiting, was regarded by wealthy parents as the equivalent, for their daughters, of the university education and professional training afforded for their sons ; the reason being that marriage to a man of their own or a higher social grade was the only recognised vocation for women not compelled to earn their own livelihood. It was this society life which absorbed nearly half the time and more than half the vital energy of the daughters of the upper and upper middle class ". That heterogeneous society, whose social and intellectual habit deeply disturbed the sensitive Matthew Arnold, was devoted to " riding, dancing, flirting, and dressing up (I'm quoting Beatrice Webb again). As one form of entertainment was piled on another, the pace became fast and furious ; a mania for restless talking, for the experimental display of one's own personality, ousted all from consciousness. . . . I discovered that personal vanity was an ' occupational disease ' of London Society ".

Mrs. Webb's brilliant description was to her, and is for many of us, an indictment. The Victorians exalted the economics, but debased the ethics of sex relationships. They set truth at a discount. They maintained a "degraded and coarsening scale of values", which bred a poisonous cynicism about human relations. There is a forgotten descriptive literature of this epoch which I may exemplify by recalling the books of E. C. Grenville Murray. Murray was an ex-diplomat who was dropped, or victimised, for indiscretions, not entirely of his own making, in the premature divulging of important foreign news. He turned to "society" journalism—was indeed a pioneer in founding this new branch of it. He wrote such books as *Under the Lens*, which was a series of, as he calls them, " Social Photographs ", descriptive of persons whose names were thinly disguised but who were classified as "Jilts, Adventurers and Adventuresses, Spendthrifts, Roughs of High and Low Degree, semi-detached Wives, Our Silvered Youth and so on ". In the light of this precious stuff Mrs. Webb's indictment is obviously true. "There may be," as she said, " saints who can live untainted in such an environment, exactly as we know that there are men and women who retain their moral refinement in a one-room tenement, inhabited by persons of both sexes and all ages. But the true-born saint, whether rich or poor, is an uncommon variety of the human species." The Victorians were mammon-addicts. Bankruptcy and sexual irregularity or conspicuousness were the great sins. Yet all through Victorian society sexual irregularity was prevalent—at the top, at the bottom and in the middle.

In an earlier talk in this series Bertrand Russell pointed out that the growth of religious toleration was accompanied by an intensification of intolerance in all matters connected with sex. He added that intolerance in general springs from two main sources—fear of a threat to the power of the privileged and fear of the loss of cherished convictions. But there was, I think, more than that in this intolerance. There was that sort of warped narrowness which is visible in the Parnell episode. Did anyone really bother whether Parnell was involved in any way in the outbursts of Irish violence, Phoenix Park murders and the rest, or was it only his adultery that could not be tolerated ? The word "immoral" in England was (and still is to a considerable extent) a technical term. An " immoral " book was a book which dealt with sex in a direct way. Hardy's *Tess*, Meredith's *Ordeal of Richard Feverel* were immoral books. . . .

How tyrannical the earlier and mid-Victorian attitude was can be illustrated abundantly. Readers of the *Amberley Papers* will recall the South Devon election of 1868, with its vilifications of Lord Amberley because he took part in the discussion of such problems as Malthus had raised from 1798 onwards—problems of over-population and birth-control particularly. Dr. Drysdale concealed his identity under the initials G. R. or George Rex when he published in 1854 the *Elements of Social Science; or Physical, Sexual and Natural Religion*—it was a necessary precaution because he had views which he did not hide on such social evils as prostitution and the enforced celibacy of a considerable section of the population. The Census of 1851 had shown twenty-six as the average age of marriage for males and twenty-four-and-a-half for females ; it had shown, too, that on existing birth-rates, if all adults of child-bearing age were married, the annual births would go up from seven hundred thousand to one million six hundred thousand annually. There were forty-two per cent. of the women between twenty and forty who were spinsters—there were, that is, what contemporaries like W. R. Greg called " redundant women ". There was a conflict between social facts and conventional attitudes—that, perhaps, is the simplest way of putting things. But the conventional attitudes were commonly too strong for reason effectively to play on them, and the more so because of the strength of Mrs. Grundy in that get-rich-quick age. As late as 1887 a doctor was struck off the register for issuing *The Wife's Handbook* at so low a price as sixpence. The taboos, that is, had their class character—it would be dangerous to equalise knowledge of family limitation procedures.

Behind the Victorian barricade of conventional rectitude is the vast reality of prostitution. A Swiss traveller in England long before the age of the great Victorian Compromise remarked of us that the great cruelty of the English lies in permitting evil rather than doing it. The Victorian Age permitted it, did it, and looked the other way. In saying that I don't mean to draw up an indictment of the whole Victorian epoch. I'm sure there were good and happy people in plenty. I doubt if epochs are as different from each other as they seem to be. But the Victorian social setting was one of a vaster and more rapid urbanisation than had ever taken place before. Wealth accumulation had new powers and new sanctions behind it. The rise of industrialism, and its expansion, were even cradled in destruction as well as invention—the destruction of crafts, known patterns of social simplicity and of personal deferences of behavoiur, conceptions of value and of happiness and of public and private function that seemed to have had their day. The result is written in stark terms in the public reports and the private denunciations of moralists, poets, doctors, publicists of all sorts. No one who has seen them can forget the writings of the brothers Mayhew, or George Godwin, or Gaskell, or, to take a still remembered example, Thomas Hood's poem

" One more unfortunate weary of breath !
    Rashly importunate gone to her death."

Look at the maps at the end of the supplementary volume of Mayhew's *London Labour and the London Poor*—maps of the prevalence, among other things, of sexual crime. Turn to Dr. Acton's *Prostitution, considered in its Moral, Social Aspects in London and other large Garrison Towns.* Acton peers into the houses and streets where the vast armies of metropolitan and provincial prostitutes live. He examines the economic foundations of this considerable occupational stratum—sweated trades and ill-paid jobs and the rest—but he finds too the vast influence of the prevalent taboos. What occupation but the streets is open to the mother of an illegitimate child ? Acton gives an unforgettable picture of—what ?—a working system, an underworld that is concealed but known, largely invisible but omnipresent. " Prostitution," he says " is a transitory state through which an untold number of British women are ever on their passage."

In this centenary year of the Communist Manifesto we can recall a passage in which Marx and Engels are replying to those who declared that Socialism meant moral collapse :

" Bourgeois marriage is in reality a system of wives in common, and thus, at the most, what the Communists might possibly be reproached with is their desire to introduce in substitution for a hypocritically concealed, an openly legalised community of women. For the rest, it is self-evident that the abolition of the present system of production must bring with it the abolition of the community of women springing from that system, i.e. of prostitution both official and unofficial."

Both in letters and in life the 'eighties and 'nineties are something of a watershed. In life the practice of family limitation was coming to be firmly, and so far as one can tell, permanently established. The large Victorian family was shrinking, and with it the place of women, and therefore of fallen women, as they were called, in society, economic and social, was changing. The setting of ideas and taboos was being undermined. With what result ? Liberation of mind, slow in developing, was on the way, but there were rearguard actions of sheer intellectual Whiggism that made a great stir. The Bradlaugh-Besant trial of 1881 was one of them. It made the wide and open diffusion of birth-control literature possible, but it also showed how divided opinion was. The Lord Chief Justice summed up for acquittal and the jury returned a contradictory verdict. " The book in question "—a forty-year-old medical booklet, which Mrs. Besant and Charles Bradlaugh had circulated as a challenge—" is calculated to deprave public morals," was their verdict, " but we exonerate the defendants from any corrupt motive in publishing it." That trial cleared the air.

Yet in 1889 a publisher was fined £300 and sent to prison for three months for publishing translations of Zola's novels—bowdlerised though some of them were. The same old taboos still had power as they had forty years earlier when the Vice-Chancellor at Cambridge put pictures by Titian in out-of-the-way corners of the Fitzwilliam Museum so that ordinary people would not get wicked ideas from them ! Shaw's *Widower's Houses* was produced in 1892 though begun seven years before. " The very qualities which had made it impossible for ordinary commercial purposes in 1885 now recommended it " he said. W. T. Stead's *Maiden Tribute of Modern Babylon* had thrown open the whole conspiracy of silence in the *Pall Mall Gazette* in 1885. This exposure of the traffic in young girls for home and foreign sale was flamboyant in manner but too obviously true to be disregarded. It made the same sort of stir as had been made half a century before by Oastler on child slavery in factories. It is an unquotable document, which " the prudish, the squeamish, and all who prefer to live in a fool's paradise of imaginary innocence " were advised not to read. Stead showed how the purchase of girls was carried out—he bought nine within ten days for less than £30 ; he showed the processes of juvenile prostitution, of imprisonment in brothels, employment agencies and servants' registries, and how the law aided the criminal.

One thinks of Mr. Gladstone's twenty-nine speeches against a single clause of the Divorce Bill of 1857. Or of Josephine Butler's experience with government-controlled prostitution in garrison towns. At Chatham, for instance, in 1882, she talked to a couple of hundred young soldiers—mostly of about eighteen or nineteen years of age—herded in a brothel. " I was struck by the want of anything like gaiety or mirth ; it was solemn as hell itself . . . a businesslike exhibition of superintended vice." And one of the recruits explained to her, " The military authorities expect us to be bad, and of course we are bad ". One thinks, too, of the impoverished political career of Mr. Stansfeld, who worked with Mrs. Butler to clean up this business of the Contagious Diseases Acts, and the quick victory when Stead's *Maiden Tribute* forced open the shut doors of minds that had refused to open.

There was the new realistic literature, too, of Arthur Morrison and others, as well as Beardsley, Oscar Wilde and the *Yellow Book* of the 'nineties. In this field of sex we have no data upon which the statistician can work to establish levels or trends of happiness and unhappiness, harmony and frustration. Even Bentham had failed to devise a felicific calculus. Broad contrasts between phases of industrialist experience can be postulated, though little more than that. But a new era was opening all the same. Women were moving towards " emancipation " in this Victorian period—they staked a claim for certain rights and equalities, personal and legal, social and political, which made wives less than chattels, and daughters less than domestic drudges or commodities in the marriage market. They won their way to new occupations, new professions, a new dignity and status. They gained immeasurably from the widening acceptance of birth-control, and when, ultimately, on this account and others, the State built up a system of social welfare provisions, it was the individual rather than the family group that was made the basis of the new social order. Thus was the earlier Victorian conception of sex morality rendered obsolete.

Some steps in that direction, steps that broaden out into a positive progress, can be mapped. In the 'eighties there were the writings of Edward Carpenter, whose *Love's Coming-of-Age* helped many to a clearer view. In his widely read *Civilisation, its Cause and Cure* he postulated the case for a new morality. There is Havelock Ellis, whose earlier writings seem so slight an indication of his later power in research and interpretation. There was G.B.S., with his astonishing power to break down the Jerichos of Convention and Taboo. Beatrice Webb in *Our Partnership*, recalls a week-end in 1903 at which the Shaws, the Webbs, the Graham Wallaces listened to *Man and Superman* with a growing sense of its power. She notes : " We cannot touch the subject of human breeding—it is not ripe for the mere industry of induction, and yet I realise that it is the most important of all questions, this breeding of the right sort of man. G.B.S.'s audacious genius can reach out to it ".

In Samuel Butler's *Note Books* the section on " Elementary Morality " opens thus :

" These (the Foundations of Morality) are like all other foundations ; if you dig too much about them the superstructure will come tumbling down ". The digging was necessary and had begun. Too much had the Victorian sex code, if it can be so described, been "honour rooted in dishonour"; there had been too much " faith unfaithful ", too much pressure to keep too many people " falsely true " to frustrating taboos.

EDWARD GLOVER

THE DISCUSSION of sexual problems might with some propriety be scheduled as a dangerous trade. Many well-established reputations for scientific integrity have been wrecked in the process. The fact, too, that we are discussing the sexual habits of our grandfathers or great-grandfathers only adds to the difficulty. The man who takes too close an interest in the reproductive habits of his forefathers has usually an emotional axe to grind. I suggest therefore that we fortify ourselves this evening with some psycho-biological reflections. Consider in the first place the immeasurable strength of the forces that serve the purposes of reproduction. A blind force that can compel simple unicellular organisms quite literally to tear themselves in two, for reproductive purposes, a force that can drive multicellular organisms, including man himself, to subordinate and sometimes to sacrifice their lives to the necessities of love is not likely to let itself be run on gossamer leading strings : nor, unless it encounters even more powerful forces, is it likely to undergo fundamental changes. Let us remember too that forces which can produce dramatic physico-chemical changes in the body are also capable of playing fantastic tricks on that fragile organ the intellect. They can in fact cause men to hide their sexual strivings and prejudices behind a mask of calm and scientific detachment.

As for the Victorians it would appear that the mere mention of the word provokes in us some of the feelings with which Dr. Blimber's pupils reacted to any allusion to the Romans. Those of us who do not worship our ancestors tend to disparage them. Confusing youth and modernity with progress, we seek to comfort ourselves for the unacknowledged sexual deficiencies of our own period by castigating the pruderies and lubricities of our forefathers. So much is certain : until the Edwardians die off we cannot expect to be objective about the Victorians, least of all about their sexual habits.

So much for emotional prejudice. Unfortunately, a still more crippling obstacle confronts us. We have no reliable statistics on the subject either of Victorian sexuality or of present-day sexual habits. Moreover, such non-statistical information as we possess is based on the most superficial observation of adults. The mere existence of infantile sexuality, the fact that the love life of the adult is determined by the sexual vicissitudes he has endured from infancy to the fifth year of life was totally unsuspected by the Victorians. And to this day statistics concerning sexual matters are for the most part produced by experts who have little more than formal knowledge either of the early childhood stages of sexual development or of the immense strength of unconscious sexual impulse.

Under these circumstances there is only one scientific course open to us. Before allowing ourselves to be emotionally influenced by the evidence we must consider the tendencies which govern the scientific study of sexuality.

Now on the question of modification of sexual habits (it is better by the way to talk of modification than to beg the question by using the term " evolutionary progress ") there are two schools of opinion, namely a " Central " school and a " Peripheral " or environmental school. Members of the central school believe that, constitutional factors apart, the decisive factors in sexual development originate within the mind, i.e. are internal factors. Psycho-analysts, for example, incline to the view that no important modification of the sexual instincts has taken place since those prehistoric times when an *internal taboo* on incest was first established. Consequently they are not disposed to believe that any very fundamental differences exist between one generation and another.

Members of the peripheral or environmental school, on the other hand, believe that even adult man is extremely malleable and that his behaviour is deeply and decisively influenced by *external* influences; in other words, by the cultural patterns to which he is subject. For example, they regard even war as a culturally determined trait. Such observers are more ready to believe that fundamental differences in sexual behaviour may exist between one generation and another, provided always some important changes have taken place in the cultural attitude to sexuality.

Such being the case, it is safe to assume that whatever historical period is examined the results will appear to be self-contradictory. In the end we may be forced to accept a compromise. We may have to admit that as far as internal regulation of sexuality is concerned, there is no important difference between the Victorians and ourselves but that in so far as external social and cultural influences are concerned definite changes in sexual habit can be established. How important these changes are and whether they are for the better or the worse, each listener must decide for himself.

Now the sketch of Victorian sexuality as drawn by Mr. Beales leaves us in no doubt as to his own position. Mr. Beales is quite frankly an environmentalist. That is to say, although ready to concede that epochs may not differ so much as they appear to do, he is nevertheless convinced that the sexual behaviour of the Victorians was determined by two main factors : first, the existence of a definite cultural pattern ; in other words, of an externally imposed sex taboo, including a conspiracy of silence on sexual matters ; and secondly—and here he follows Mrs. Webb, Marx and others—an economic factor promoting sexual licence. This economic factor also, it would appear, makes the rich less idealistic in sexual matters and lays the (presumably more innocent) poor open to sexual exploitation by the rich. Hence the contrast he draws between the excessive prudery of the Victorians and the organisation of Victorian prostitution.

At this point Mr. Beales reveals himself a true Victorian. One might almost imagine from his remarks that prostitution was something peculiar to the nineteenth century—almost a transitory phenomenon, a product of capitalist industrialism, urbanisation and the amassing of profits. Typically Victorian, and, indeed, one might say part of an unconscious conspiracy of silence is the attempt to explain sexual disorders exclusively in terms of non-sexual (economic) factors. As a matter of fact, this theory of the economic causes of prostitution had already reached its acme of absurdity in the naïve, almost adolescent formulations of Marx, Engels, and the Communist Manifesto. Curiously enough, the theory is based on a perverted romanticism—" she sold her virtue to the squire "—and despite the work of normal psychologists like Sir Cyril Burt, and of the psycho-analysts, the economic shibboleth persists to this day. Modern investigations have shown that a surprisingly large number of prostitutes are mentally backward to the point often of borderline deficiency. And psycho-analysts have clearly demonstrated the unconscious and conscious factors in infantile development that are responsible respectively for the larval prostitute, and for the comparative chastity of the normal person.

Prostitution apart, Mr. Beales dismisses the Victorian lower and middle classes with a caution, and concentrates on the habits and prejudices of the leisured well-to-do. His evidence is based largely on the sociological and general literature of the times, starting with the legend of Mrs. Grundy and ending with Beatrice Webb. But here his argument becomes two-edged. The " progressive " was also a Victorian product. Had Mr. Beales chosen to quote more extensively from Thackeray, from Charles Dickens, the idol of the middle class who, interestingly enough gave one of the first sympathetic pictures of the gang-ster's moll, from Carlyle, Ruskin, Morris, from Charlotte Brontë, from Kingsley, Tennyson, or Matthew Arnold, to say nothing of Havelock Ellis, Edward Carpenter, Archer the Ibsenite and the earlier Bernard Shaw, he would have been able to establish that the most weighty and the most popular Victorians were themselves violently anti-Victorian.

The truth is, we tend to use the term Victorian when we mean either human or specifically Georgian—eighteenth-century Georgian. The Victorian taboo which from one angle might be regarded as a rather laudable striving towards decorum is also regarded as being a reaction from Regency licence. Yet after all Regency England was the England of Jane Austen, whose work, by the way, the Regent greatly admired. The blameless Walter Scott, it will be remembered, catered for a pre-Victorian public. (He, too, was much cultivated by the same Fourth George.) Going further back for more than super-Victorian prudery we find Mr. Shandy disgusted at his wife's innocent interest in the courtship of Uncle Toby. In truth the history of Victorian puritanism is longer and more complicated than Mr. Beales is disposed to believe.

Indeed, if we pursue this matter of action and reaction more closely than literary investigations permit, it becomes clear that *each* period manifests unmistakable signs of *two antithetical movements*, a struggle against the restriction of sexuality and an exaggeration of the forces of sexual inhibition. All the naked figures in Michael Angelo's *Last Judgment* were provided with pinafores long before Victorian times. Riches combined with tolerable respectability were normally honoured in early ages. Prostitution, an ancient cult, is not unknown in latter-day urbanised England. Patriarchal attitudes to sex have existed since everlasting. In short, female unchastity, especially that of wives and daughters, has never been tolerated in this country. The Victorian tendency to mealiness of mouth merely accentuated an existing tradition.

But although we may question Mr. Beales's assumption that Victorian sexual taboos were part of an organised conspiracy of silence covering an economically determined Victorian depravity, we are still under obligation to establish some correlation between prudery and licence. To do this we must take into account three factors : first, the unconscious laws that regulate sexual life from infancy onwards ; second, the enormous range of sexuality ; and third, the fact that many social manifestations are profoundly influenced by hidden psycho-sexual interests. To give one example only, no survey of sexuality can be regarded as complete that does not take into account the manifestations, from infancy to adult life, of conscious and unconscious homosexuality. Psychologically man is a bisexual animal. And so, for example, when we compare Victorian crinolines with eighteenth-century hoops and with the capacious corduroy slacks by means of which modern woman indicates that she possesses buttocks as well as ankles, we must at least pause before we assume that Victorianism is obsolete or before we congratulate ourselves on progress, either psycho-sexual or aesthetic. For it is always possible that either the latent homosexuality of women or the unconscious sexual rivalry existing between the sexes has had a finger in the pie.

Nor can we estimate the position of adult heterosexuality unless we prepare what I should like to call a *functional balance sheet,* setting off the total expression and the total inhibition of sexuality during any given period, preferably not so long a period as the Victorian—unless we trace the total sexual thrust, not just its direct adult manifestations, but as it is found in family life, education, marriage and divorce laws and a hundred other and more indirect channels of expression and inhibition.

But to come back to prudery. Psycho-analysis of unconscious mental mechanisms has shown that whereas an unconscious impulse can be held in check by impulses of an antithetical nature, there is always a danger that the unconscious impulse can turn the tables. It can, as it were, infect the antithetical impulse. And so, as in the parallel case of the spinster's fear of a burglar under the bed, prudery is an indication that a normal inhibition, modesty, has become perverted, i.e. sexualised. The woman who draped the legs of her piano, so far from concealing her conscious and unconscious exhibitionism, ended by sexualising the piano ; no mean feat. (This particular manifestation was, by the way, American in origin, but no matter.) Prudery, like sexual licence, sexual perversion and neurosis, is a sign of conflict and frustration, and although its expressions may change from period to period, it is like neurosis and perversion, always with us.

Now although the functional view of sexuality with its elaborate systems of regulating and compensating " balances " warns us to be sceptical regarding the importance of differences existing between generations, we must not therefore deny the possibility that cultural factors may bring about real and concievably permanent changes within the total system. But if a change is permanent we must postulate a new and permanent cultural influence to account for it. We shall only end in confusion if we regard those changes as fixed that depend on variable influences. When, for example, divorce laws change we must not make capital out of the increased numbers of divorces.

Similarly if we establish that present-day prostitution has decreased, we must correlate that decrease with the increase in the habit of pre-nuptial intercouse that followed the 1914–18 war. For the matter of that we may recall that the professional prostitutes of 1920 complained bitterly of the unfair competition of " fine ladies ".

Leaving out of account a more negative factor, namely, the decay of religion, it is not hard to indicate a new and positive cultural factor which has led to a legitimate contrast between Victorian times and our own. This is surely the development of objective science, not only of physical science, as witness the influence of contraceptive methods on limitation of families and on pre-nuptial sexual gratification, but of psychological science. Psycho-analysis has laid the foundations of an objective science of sexuality, and because it is an objective science, its influence is more likely to be permanent. In other words, it is not based on fluctuating emotional reactions to some existing system either of licence or of prudery ; indeed it includes among its studies the influence of sexual prejudice.

But to exert effective influence on the community at large scientific discoveries must penetrate every nook and cranny of our social fabric from the nursery to the laws of inheritance. A beginning in this direction has been made, but it is only a beginning. We cannot say whether even a satisfactory spread of psychological knowledge, upbringing and treatment would bring about a decisive modification of ancient patterns of sexual habit and regulation. Perhaps in the twenty-first century some observers, holding a finger on the emotional pulse of the community, in other words, measuring differences in the incidence of neurotic and other mental disorders, may be in a position to say whether or not this new cultural pattern has brought about new and better adaptations. But by that time, no doubt, it will have been discovered that so-called Victorianism in sex was neither confined to these islands nor peculiar to any one epoch. By that time too it will be generally recognised that the spirit of those progressive Victorians who fought against the sexual obscurantism of their own times reached its finest expression in the work of Sigmund Freud, who although for many years vilified and boycotted by the obscurantists of Europe succeeded at last in letting light into dark places.

Fin de Siècle

LORD DAVID CECIL

"Aesthetic", according to the dictionary, means someone whose chief concern is the appreciation of the beautiful. This sounds a very admirable kind of person. All the same, the word, as it is commonly used, isn't altogether a word of praise. When we hear a man say that " Mr. So-and-so is an aesthete ", there is generally a note of scorn and disapproval in his voice. This is very strange—strange enough to start us wondering why. The reason is, that the word " aesthete " has become associated with a movement which began in the late Victorian era. Then and now this was not a movement generally well thought of. What was it ? The expression of a philosophy of living taken up at that period by people whose temperament led them to find their chief satisfaction in beauty. Beauty is such a loosely used, overworked term that I suppose I must say in what sense I am using it. It is the ordinary obvious sense we intend when we say "what a beautiful picture !" or "what a beautiful sunset !" We mean to convey by these exclamations that the object appeals to our senses, and through them to our imagination ; that looking at them both pleases our eyes and sets up all sorts of pleasant dreams and associations and trains of thought in our minds. Almost everybody responds in this way in some degree. But there are people to whom it is far the most important and precious satisfaction which life has to offer : their experience of the beautiful is their most significant experience. And naturally they need a philosophy of life which justifies the value they set on it. Up to the middle of the last century it was not difficult for them to find one ; for the generally accepted philosophy by which most men lived was based on a belief in some absolute idea, religious or otherwise. Beauty was the revelation of the Divine Mind in all things ; " Beauty was Truth, Truth Beauty ". Personally, I think this view is still the true one. However, in the nineteenth century people began to doubt it. Rationalism and scientific discovery between them seemed to many people to have undermined the foundations of religious faith : and with it all other ideal interpretations of the nature of existence. So far from the world being a manifestation of the divine mind, it was an expression of some automatic and mechanical material force arising from no one knew where and progressing towards no one knew what. The whole idea of a spiritual world lying behind the material one was a figment of man's imagination. If this was true, clearly it was not possible to justify the love of beauty on moral and religious grounds.

However, people were still born who did care for beauty more than anything . They had to find some view of reality which would allow them to. It was to meet this demand that what was called " aestheticism " grew up. Now this was first of all an intensely subjective point of view. Beauty is just something that we feel. Why try to relate it to anything absolute ? Nothing is absolute. Life is just a stream of impressions dissolving one into the other as they flow continuously through our minds. Some, however, are peculiarly pleasant. While they are with us we feel our spirits expanded, enriched, delighted. Our aim should be so to direct and arrange our lives that we have as many of these pleasant impressions as possible—and as few of any other kind. If we can succeed in doing this, we have done all we can. It is futile and fruitless to ask for more. The purest and most satisfying of those impressions comes from the works of art and nature. The wise man concentrates most on these. Aestheticism therefore rests on the perception of two facts : life's essential transience and unintelligibility on the one hand ; and, on the other, its capacity for bringing us impressions of beauty.

But why should I waste your time in translating into my own lame words what has already been said with supreme eloquence by the great prophet of the aesthetic movement, Walter Pater :

> " The service of philosophy, of speculative culture, towards the human spirit, is to rouse, to startle it to a life of constant and eager observation. Every moment some form grows perfect in hand or face; some tone on the hills or the sea is choicer than the rest ; some mood of passion or insight or intellectual excitement is irresistibly real and attractive

to us—for the moment only. Not the fruit of experience, but experience itself, is the end. A counted number of pulses only is given to us of a variegated, dramatic life. How may we see in them all that is to be seen in them by the finest senses ? How shall we pass most swiftly from point to point, and be present always at the focus where the greatest number of vital forces unite in their purest energy ?

To burn always with this hard, gemlike flame, to maintain this ecstasy, is success in life. In a sense it might even be said that our failure is to form habits : for, after all, habit is relative to a stereotyped world, and meantime it is only the roughness of the eye that makes any two persons, things, situations, seem alike. While all melts under our feet, we may well grasp at any exquisite passion, or any contribution to knowledge that seems by a lifted horizon to set the spirit free for a moment, or any stirring of the senses, strange dyes, strange colours, and curious odours, or work of the artist's hands, or the face of one's friend. Not to discriminate every moment some passionate attitude in those about us, and in the very brilliancy of their gifts some tragic dividing of forces on their ways, is, on this short day of frost and sun, to sleep before evening."

Such was the aesthete's general view of life. Certain consequences followed, when he came to put it into practice. First of all, it tended to make him contemplative rather than active. If we are always occupied in practical action, our minds are not open to receive impressions of beauty as they fleet by. The true aesthete is a cloistered out-of-the-world kind of man. He turned away, as much as the mediæval monk, from the activities of the world of affairs. They were snares and delusions that distracted the mind from following the true good. He was all the more disposed to do this because the active world of Victorian England had peculiarly little satisfaction to give to the aesthete. That industrial progressive middle class which gave the tone to the life of the time held a view which offered as little scope to lovers of the beautiful as any view well could. On one side it was usually utilitarian ; on another, Puritan. Utilitarianism made it contemptuous of the imagination, Puritanism made it hostile to the senses. The two together blinded men's eyes to the beautiful. In consequence they looked on art as at best a harmless pleasure and at worst a dangerous frivolity : never an activity for a serious self-respecting man. In Elizabethan times the lover of beauty and the man of action were often the same person ; in the Victorian era the lover of beauty felt himself an alien who must turn his back on the world of action if he were to fulfil his true nature.

The gulf between him and the average Victorian philistine was still further emphasised by another consequence of his point of view. The fact that he valued experience in proportion as it satisfied his sense of beauty, meant that he did not divide things according to their moral categories. Anything was good, in his sense of the word, if it gave him a rich and delightful feeling, if it was vivid and brilliant and stirring. A great many things did this which were not approved by Victorian standards of virtue. Chastity might create its own effect of beauty ; but so might sensuality. A work of art might be grave and noble : it could also be flippant and irresponsible. If it was good in its own kind, the aesthete approved of it. Charles Kingsley has said— and he speaks with the very voice of the Victorian Age—" Be good, sweet maid, and let who will be clever ". The aesthete might have replied, " Be beautiful, sweet maid, and let who will be good ".

People instinctively feel it when their fundamental values are threatened : and though Pater expressed his views in a very restrained and unprovocative way, he immediately stirred suspicions in the minds of the orthodox Victorian pundits. He was an Oxford don, at a time when Oxford was dominated by the public-spirited Dr. Jowett. "I should not wish," Jowett is rumoured to have said, " any young man in whom I took an interest to come under the influence of Mr. Pater ". To Jowett Pater's doctrines were morally irresponsible. And what was to be thought of a philosophy of life which stressed feeling and contemplation at the expense of thought and action ? Why, such ideas take us back to the benighted idleness of the mediæval monastery—and an immoral monastery at that !

It must be admitted that some of Pater's first followers—the bohemian poets and artists of the 'nineties—like Dowson and the lesser contributors to the *Yellow Book*—did give a certain colour to the suspicions of the respectable. They tended to exaggerate the most questionable aspects of aestheticism, without having the talent or the self-discipline to develop its stronger side. For it did need self-discipline, strict and strenuous, if it was to be carried out according to its precepts. Intelligence and sensibility must be kept continuously at work in detecting and discriminating what is most exquisite in experience. And then a rigid self-control must be exercised : the attention must be wholly concentrated on these things, rejecting any temptation of ease or ambition that might lead to living at a lower level. Like the monk again, the true aesthete must be prepared to sacrifice the whole world to save his own soul. This devotion to the beautiful is brilliantly expounded in Whistler's famous ten o'clock lecture. But the minor aesthetes of the 'nineties, hangers-on and camp followers of the movement, did not see it like this. More often than not, they took up aestheticism because they were sensual and sentimental or because they wanted to shock their prim and proper fathers and mothers. Contemplation, for them meant doing nothing in particular ; the love of beauty, hardly more than a taste for bric-a-brac and for wearing peacock blue trousers. Furthermore, they tended to emphasise the most doubtful aspect of aestheticism, its moral aspect ; and to develop it in directions that would have horrified Pater or any other serious exponent of the gospel. His writings had suggested that beauty could be found in ways of life thought immoral by orthodox Victorianism. Some of his followers appear to have argued from this that it was to be found only in such ways of life. And they conducted themselves in keeping with such a belief. Beauty to them became inextricably connected with moral corruption. Naturally enough, the ordinary citizen disapproved of them.

As a result, they disapproved of aestheticism too. But here they were wrong. For, as I've said, these aesthetes of the 'nineties did not really understand the doctrine they professed to follow. Their works showed it. These do not exhibit a particularly intense or varied sensibility of the beautiful. On the contrary, they were, for the most part, feeble tasteless productions —thin little stories and poems about pierrots and prostitutes— written in a derivative and a devitalised manner. The aesthetic philosophy should surely be capable of producing better works of art than these ? It did. It produced the essays of Max

Beerbohm, the wit of Wilde, the early dreamy poems of Yeats. And later works, too ; for the situation that had produced them remained; it has remained for many people to this day. Ever since the beginning of the century people have been born to whom aesthetic experiences are the most precious, but who can find no absolute philosophy to which to relate them. Their view, like Pater's, rests on an intense realisation on the one hand, that life is insubstantial and transient, and on the other that it is capable of great beauty. Some of the most distinguished writers of our time have held this view and expressed it in their works. Virginia Woolf, in particular, may be looked on as the final exquisite flower of Pater's doctrine. Her lovely delicate books are remarkable equally for their power to convey the shifting fleeting quality of life and for the radiant perception of beauty which shimmers over their every page.

Yet even Virginia Woolf cannot make pure aestheticism completely satisfying as a gospel for living. It is not practical, for one thing. Human life is inevitably full of ugly and insignificant stretches of experience ; it is no good trying to extract aesthetic pleasure from them. Further, even if by some miracle it were possible to contrive a form of existence from which the ugly was excluded, it would not be possible continuously to enjoy the beautiful. The human spirit has not the capacity to maintain itself all the time in the right receptive frame of mind : its power to respond gets dulled with overwork. The most musical person could not listen to a concert indefinitely. Moreover, aestheticism rests in an unresolved discord, a confusion of thought. It says on the one hand that life has no absolute significance, and on the other, that beauty gives one a feeling of absolute significance—that we enjoy Shakespeare or Beethoven, not just because they give up pleasant sensations like a chocolate, but because they make us understand life more deeply. Now both of these propositions cannot be true. The meaningless cannot give one a feeling of meaning. Virginia Woolf herself seems to have realised this as time went on. Her last books give hints that she had occasional intuitions of some eternal principle behind the fleeting shows of time. Such a view followed to its logical conclusion, must lead to the old idea that beauty is, in some sense or other, a revelation of divinity. The fact that the aesthetes did not perceive this at once is a measure of their limitations. But it must be said to their credit that, whether they intended to or not, they have helped in the end to make other people perceive it. Without the aesthetes, English ideas in the last thirty years might have become wholly material and utilitarian. People might have grown to judge things to be good, only in so far as they made the mass of mankind comfortable. Aestheticism did, in its way, uphold the standard of the spiritual ; it did assert that a play of Shakespeare is more precious than good sanitation. It also conferred a humbler benefit on mankind by showing it new means to day-to-day happiness. I know myself that during these last troubled years I have listened less to the voice of high-minded vociferous moral teachers than to Pater and Virginia Woolf.

"Don't worry so much," they said to me, "about future dangers ; look at the street outside, observe the delicate shadow cast by a passing aeroplane, note the delicious stroke of colour made by that shred of orange peel lying in the gutter. These things are just as real as all the horrors of war. Why let yourself be despondent, when so much of your daily experience is brimful of matter for delight ? "

Personal Responsibility

G. D. H. COLE

THE VICTORIAN Age, and more particularly the earlier part of it, was an age of "self-made men"—that is, of men who, from poverty and obscurity, had risen to positions of wealth and influence in society. To most of these men, and to most of their contemporaries, this rise seemed to have been due to certain personal qualities which they possessed above other people. Their admirers spoke of these qualities as "initiative, enterprise, personal driving force", and also as "abstinence, frugality, and a self-control which enabled them to brush aside pleasure and other distractions, and to concentrate their energies on doing with all their might the job they had marked out for themselves". Their detractors painted a different picture, in which initiative and enterprise were metamorphosed into greed and overreaching, personal driving force into lust for irresponsible power, abstinence and frugality into meanness, avarice and a will to impose privation upon others, and self-control into a soulless lack of cultural values which left the new capitalists with no other interest in life than the pursuit of wealth in this world and of salvation in a next world conceived in the image of their own spiritual poverty.

The truth, of course, lay betwixt and between these estimates. The age in which the early Victorians grew up was one in which, though many fortunes were made from lowly beginnings, the competitive struggle was always hard. Though many succeeded, many more failed, and were thrust down again into poverty ; and most of the successes were not achieved without the aid, not only of very hard work, but also of big risks, tough times in the early stages, and, not least, hardness, sometimes approaching savagery, in dealing with other men, and in particular with the men, women and children who ranked with the machines they tended as indispensable "factors of production". For many among the successful the causes making for harshness in social behaviour were aggravated by a kind of religion that stressed above all else the "other-worldly" values and looked on this world as a vale of tears and tribulations through which men must pass to a "hereafter" to which the final values of life were firmly relegated. Religion, indeed, among the early Victorians, faced two ways ; and this was true above all of the various forms of Methodism, both inside and outside of the Established Church. One kind, much the most prevalent, stressed the need for the saving of souls, and made little of the material tribulations of men's—or even of children's—bodies and minds under the impact of the new industrialism. The other kind, expressed in the work both of the Christian Socialists, such as Frederick Denison Maurice and Charles Kingsley, and in the efforts of the factory reformers, Richard Oastler and Joseph Rayner Stephens as well as Lord Shaftesbury, insisted that the Kingdom of God was of this world as well as of the next, and denounced as intolerable in the eyes of God and man the hideous exploitation of the factory children—and indeed of the grown-ups as well. The Methodists of the first kind were intolerant of these criticisms : they had a feeling that worldly success was a test of achievement and that they could set about making money to the glory of God, provided only that they were scrupulous in the spending of it. In this spirit, even while they fought bitterly against all wage increases, all reductions in the hours of labour, and all attempts to impose on them even the most elementary rules of sanitation, heating, lighting and ventilation of factories and employer-owned houses and tenements, they gave largely to build chapels, to support revivalist and temperance crusades, and to encourage societies for the suppression of vice and mendicancy. They felt no contrast in these attitudes, because they were so carried away by the immense achievements of the new industrial system in increasing productivity as to regard anyone who threatened to interfere with it as opposing himself to an order of natural development that was plainly ordained by God.

These conditions, prevalent over more and more of the economic and social field despite all the efforts of the reformers, bred an attitude of self-righteous assurance which was in most of the protagonists totally inaccessible to argument. The effect was to exalt self-reliance, which is undoubtedly a virtue, into a contemptuous sweeping-aside of " failure ", which emphatically is not. I am not at all suggesting that this attitude went to any stage unchallenged. It did not. Indeed, the revolt had begun long before the Great Queen ascended the throne. Thomas Carlyle was already fulminating against the " dismal science " ; Lord Shaftesbury was already heading the crusade for factory reform ; Robert Owen had long been proclaiming the superiority of co-operation over competition, when William IV died. The Chartist agitation, with its impassioned cry for social justice and against the horrors of the New Poor Law and the factory system, was already beginning. Trade Unionism, though heavily crushed in 1834, was again raising its head. Nevertheless, though always challenged, the attitude I have been describing was largely dominant among the " successes " ; and it spread downwards through the social structure, infecting every grade of minor manager, supervisor and foreman—indeed, everyone who, having got a foot on any step of the social ladder, saw, in imitation of those higher up the line, hope of rising both in status and in social prestige. The early Victorian Age was one in which the thoroughgoing believers in the benefits of *laissez-faire* had most things their own way. Employers refused to discuss anything with their operatives except on a basis of purely individual bargaining, on the plea that anything else violated freedom of contract and undermined the personal relation between man and man. The Poor Law, the only form of public relief open to the destitute or the unemployed, was administered in a spirit of ferocious deterrence which even humane men sought to justify as necessary if the springs of self-reliance were not to be weakened. Nor was it only against State charity that the shafts of the enthusiasts were directed : they attacked " indiscriminate " voluntary charity just as fiercely, and sought to limit it to the " deserving " and to those who could be helped by it to help themselves.

Let us remember that what was occurring in the early-Victorian era was a stage—in a sense the first stage—in the process that leads on to democracy. Under the impact partly of ideas let loose by the French Revolution and partly of the new conditions of mass-aggregation of workers in factories and in factory towns the " lower classes " were making, incoherently and often turbulently, their claim to be recognised as men entitled to equal claims and rights. This challenge was not so much resented as *feared* both by the older governing classes, who saw in it a threat to their conceptions of good and civilised standards of living, and also by the "new men" who had raised themselves out of the mass by making themselves the masters of the new techniques of production and of control. Fear, as always, prompted repression, and conduced to sheer inhumanity towards those of whom the superior classes were afraid. Even the more progressive and the more humanitarian among the educated classes were subject to this fear of the mass. Shaftesbury, ardent for factory reform, was intensely hostile to every sort of Radicalism ; and such men as John Bright, who were ardent political Radicals, bitterly opposed factory reform. Most middle-class Radicals, even if they wished to bring in a wider electorate in order to reinforce their power against the older aristocracy, stopped short at the will to enfranchise the "respectable" artisans—as was done in 1867 by the second Reform Act—and remained full of fear of the great illiterate mass below. They could never join hands with Chartism, because it derived its strength as a movement so largely from these very untutored masses of which they were afraid.

Hostility to demands for social legislation, and insistence on self-reliance as the sovereign virtue which nothing must be done by the State or by private charity to undermine, thus proceeded from a mixture of motives and attitudes—from a feeling of triumphant self-assurance resting on the new industrialism ; from fears that anything done to meet the claims of discontent would serve only to strengthen the dangerously uneducated and uncivilised mass of common people ; and from an other-worldliness which discounted the importance of suffering in this world, and even regarded it—at any rate for others—as wholesome purgation for the life to come.

The second half of the Victorian era saw a powerful reaction against these attitudes, and converted the protesters against them from voices crying in the wilderness into increasingly influential inspirers of many movements of social reform. Each battle was hard fought, and, of course, there was no complete victory of one attitude over another ; but, by and large, the change was great and unmistakable. Now why ?

Not, I think, mainly because the reformers made out a better case than they had been making earlier, when they were kicking vainly against the pricks. It was much more because the classes which had some share in social power—classes enlarged by the Reform Acts of 1867 and 1884—were very much less afraid than they had been of the classes below them. As the wealth generated by high productivity filtered down—and it had to filter down if there were to be outlets for the vastly increased output of goods and services—a larger proportion of the common people became more civilised, turned away from the violence of hunger-revolts, set to work to imitate in some degree the behaviour of its " betters "—and, in doing these things, became less a source of both rational and irrational fears. The cry " We must educate our masters " was heard : the prospect of democracy became, for the time, much less terrifying both to the cultured and to the rich. There was accordingly less opposition to anything that looked like concession to the claims of the poor, and also more readiness to regard the poor as men and women possessing elementary rights and claims. Nor can we afford to disregard the fact that the industrial system itself was becoming less a jungle of unregulated struggle to survive. Joint stock companies were spreading fast ; more power was in the hands of big businesses, and more of the big businesses were run by men of the second or third generation—men who had inherited fortunes, even if they went on greatly to enlarge them, and had not started with nothing and made their own way in the world. Such men were less ruthless, because any act of ruth exposed them much less to the threat of ruin. They were beginning to take for granted that they must treat certain minimum conditions in their factories as objective costs that had to be met, and would fall upon their competitors as well as on themselves. The more the scale of business increased, the more these new conditions applied, and the less resistance was offered to the growth of Trade Unions and to the recognition of at any rate some rights of collective bargaining. As business became more impersonal, there was less insistence on the purely individual character of the wage-contract, as between each master and each separate workman. Where the business was a collectivity, it was easier for the workers' collective, the Trade Union, to force its way. There was also under these conditions much less resentment of factory legislation as an infraction of the employer's personal rights—for a company could less easily plead to be the embodiment of the virtues of individual self-reliance.

How far did this change go—how far has this change gone in the much further development of it in the world of today—in undermining personal qualities which are indispensable for the health of society? The answer is not nearly so simple as many who have attempted to give one would have us believe. In the first place, of whom are we speaking? The Victorian Age—particularly in its earlier phase—was an age of sharp contrasts. If it encouraged in some people—the successful and the climbers who were seeking success—not merely a spirit of self-reliance but a perversion of that spirit into an exaggerated pushfulness and disregard of others, equally, at the other end of the scale, it discouraged these qualities in the great mass of the people. It did this by keeping them much too low to give such attitudes of mind any scope. The thriftless and the slavishly dependent were fully as much characteristic products of the early Victorian Age as the abstinent and the self-assertive; and it is quite beyond doubt that as social conditions in general improved later in the century a very large number of people were lifted up to a position which gave them the chance both of practising thrift and self-reliance and of becoming members of the community in a far more real sense. This aspect of the great change must be kept always in mind. The huge scope which the conditions of the early-Victorian era offered to personal initiative and enterprise—for both good and evil—for *some* of the people had as their correlative a sheer denial of such opportunities to a much greater number. True, the two groups were not marked off from each other by any sharp definition of status. Men could rise out of the one into the other; but for one man who possessed the qualities required for such self-elevation there were a hundred who did not, and were condemned to the fate of " devil-take-the-hindmost " by the arduous conditions of the struggle.

The other factor working against the current of *laissez-faire* doctrines in the 'forties I shall call, with picturesque licence, " Chadwick's nose ". Edwin Chadwick, the architect of the new Poor Law and the most hated man in England, was fanatically devoted to *laissez-faire* notions in many respects, and no man believed more strongly in the supreme virtue of self-reliance. But this same Chadwick was also the principal inspirer of the first *effective* Factory Act—that of 1833—and when, in the 'forties, he visited the factory districts again and smelt out the fetid odour of poverty for himself, no man cried out louder that it was the public's business to ensure the supply of pure water and of efficient drainage in the growing towns, to enforce reasonable sanitary precautions against infectious and contagious diseases, and to give the town populations an environment that would afford them at any rate some chance of living decent, happy and self-reliant lives.

Chadwick was a disciple of the great Jeremy Bentham, who preached at all seasons the paramountcy of the utilitarian principle—the greatest happiness of the greatest number. It is important to understand this principle aright, if you wish to understand the movement of ideas in Victorian England. I say this, because it is so often misunderstood by those who confuse Benthamism with *laissez-faire*. The two were in truth radically different. The *laissez-faire* advocates said—as Herbert Spencer said later—that everything would come reasonably right if only the State would let matters alone, to take their natural course. Bentham, on the other hand, maintained that, where men's interests were not naturally harmonious, it was the State's business, by legislation, to establish an artificial harmony of interests that would serve to promote the greatest happiness of the greatest number. Bentham did indeed argue that most of the existing forms of State regulation were harmful because they neither promoted nor were designed to promote this harmony of interests. He wanted to sweep most of the existing regulations away, and he believed that most things would be better unregulated than ill-regulated as they were. But the Benthamites, as far as they were true to their master, were never against State regulation as such. They were in favour of it, wherever it could be applied in such a way as to procure the greatest happiness of the greatest number.

That brings me back to " Chadwick's nose ". Chadwick smelt the towns, knew that they were not good, and set out to get them put to rights. He was not tactful about it, and he encountered ferocious opposition ; but, helped by the cholera scare, he did start modern sanitary legislation right in the middle of the heyday of capitalist *laissez-faire*.

In the case of the Factory Acts, it was possible to argue that, as the legislation applied only to children and later to women—

who were not regarded as able to look after themselves—the sacred principle of leaving he-men to sole reliance on themselves, under the system of free contract, was not being infringed. But pure water and drains could not be provided for women and children only : the Health legislation of 1848 embodied a recognition of the fact that individual men were not in a position to look after themselves and that public compulsion was needed to protect them—and therewith the whole community—against preventable disease and misery. It was the thin—I agree, the very thin—end of a wedge which has been hammered in harder and harder ever since. That was why a *laissez-faire* Parliament, as soon as it dared, swept Chadwick's General Board of Health away. But Parliament could not sweep away the Local Boards which had been set up under the same Act ; and from that time on the health activities of Local Government began steadily to grow, until in the 1870's two great Public Health Acts gave full recognition to the principle of State responsibility in that particular field.

The growth of social legislation, of education, of Trade Unions and Co-operative Societies, and of the standard of life, in the latter part of the nineteenth century created, I feel sure, a much greater sum-total of self-reliance and personal sense of responsibility than it did away with by mitigating the severity of the competitive struggle. If we are simply counting heads that is a sufficient answer. But, of course, it will be replied that this is a quite illegitimate way of stating the case. The qualities of a community, it will be said, depend, not on the characteristics diffused over the main body of the public, so much as on those which are found among its leaders in the various walks of life. Thus, even if a hundred households gained in self-reliance and personal responsibility for every one that lost, the gain may be regarded as more than outweighed if the one that lost was performing an indispensable function of social leadership. I am not stating this as my view—for it strikes at the very heart of the democratic conceptions in which I believe. I am stating it as a view, much more widely held than clearly expressed, which has to be taken into account.

My contention on this point is that the development of State intervention, of social legislation, and of collective bargaining based on the recognition of Trade Union rights was not the cause of any decline that occurred in the initiative, the enterprise and the self-reliance of the leaders of late-Victorian and of more recent society. The causes of the change in attitude among these leading groups arose, as did the social legislation and the rest of the new developments, out of the changes in the underlying social and economic situation. The era of scrambling competitive capitalism passed away as the scale of enterprise increased, as the leading types of business became less personal, as team-work of necessity superseded purely individual business adventure, and as ownership and management were more and more divorced. I do not say that the change was exclusively the result of this economic process ; but I do say that the economic changes brought into the big business partnerships based on wide shareholding an *élite* which was much less able, or even minded, to resist to the last the increasing pressure of an enlarged electorate, an enlarged body of educated opinion, and a growingly powerful movement demanding social security. Under these circumstances, the early-Victorian type of hard-faced man ceased to be admired as he had been, or to command the same prestige ; and the attractions of behaving as such a man grew less. I am entirely unable to regret this : indeed, it appears to me as an enormous advance in civilisation and decent living ; but what I have to admit is that the problems of eliciting the required responses of initiative and enterprise *under the changed conditions* were most inadequately faced.

This inadequacy has three distinct aspects. In the first place, whereas the preceding conditions had left the individual *entrepreneur* always on his toes, in the pursuit of fortune or for the avoidance of bankruptcy, the new conditions made it much harder to go bankrupt, and much easier to arrange " gentlemen's agreements " to lessen the competitive struggle *between firms*. Thus, the road was cleared for the development of various forms of monopoly—from trade agreements between competitors to vast mergers into trusts and combines which could dominate the market. Personal risks were greatly reduced in this way, and it became much easier for big businessmen to survive both without any great effort to improve their methods and without going nearly so far as they had done in screwing the last ounce of energy out of their workers for the lowest possible wage.

Secondly, management, divorced more and more from ownership, and no longer staking personal survival on the fortunes of the business it served, could afford to relax, and to accept a customary standard instead of trying continually to keep a step ahead.

Thirdly, pressure on the workers grew less, both because they had organisations behind them to fight their competitive battles, and because the State no longer took sides, at any rate not so openly, against them, and also because there were less urgent purely physical compulsions of threatened starvation and destitution to drive most of them on.

In face of these new factors—which, I would remind you, were necessary concomitants of the new phase of industrial development—there was a clear need to work out new incentives and new ways of eliciting initiative and enterprise, at all levels, within the limiting conditions set by the changed structure of the economic system. These problems of a changing society were, however, simply not faced—mainly because the new conditions came in gradually and piecemeal, and in such a way that their nature was seldom clearly recognised. The result, seen in our own day, has been a society in which, on the one hand, the qualities of self-reliance and personal responsibility are more widely *diffused* than ever before, in the sense that they reach further down the social scale, but at the same time the intensity of their application to production and to business generally has been in some degree lessened because, in these fields, they need now to be applied in a different, and a much more democratic, way.

And yet . . . quite a number of people will say . . . surely the present generation is a good deal less . . . strongly personal than the people portrayed by Charles Dickens or even than the types who appear in lesser Victorian novelists—by whose writings, in default of other evidence, most of us are apt to judge of the characteristics of the generation before us. I agree : of course the modern age is much more standardised in manners, and therewith less obviously idiosyncratic or, if you will, less eccentric, as well as less proud of being masterful . . . or even bullying. Popular education has combined with the growing standardisation of working conditions to produce this effect. The Sam Wellers and Mark Tapleys of today are less flamboyantly individual ; the Silas Marners too have been largely obliterated by the growth of large-scale production, and the Gradgrinds grind a good deal less hard, and with less pride in grinding, than used to be the case. But, even after we have discounted the novelist's licence in presenting such characters as these, we cannot reasonably identify personality with peculiarity, or responsibility with eccentricity, or enterprise with bullying. A man can be as self-reliant as Mark Tapley without expressing himself in so Dickensian a fashion. And he can be a much better businessman than Gradgrind and have better morals as well as better manners. The real question is whether men have become less enterprising, as well as less idiosyncratic.

On that point, I have said already what I believe the truth to be. I believe it to be nonsense to suggest that modern social legislation, in limiting the burdens falling on the individual, has lessened self-reliance or the feeling of personal responsibility. There are, I know, a good many people who maintain that personal responsibility has been undermined by the modern growth of social security. I agree, of course, that it has been *limited*, in the sense that the State now does a great deal more for the individual than it used to do. I deny, however, that this has involved a destruction of personal responsibility. On the contrary, it has enabled a great many more people to face up to their responsibilities, by making them less impossibly burdensome. The modern parent, by and large, does not feel less responsibility for the welfare of his children than his parents or grandparents did : he feels more. There are a great many fewer cases of neglect, of sheer abandonment, of what readers of Dickens will recognise if I call it " Tom-all-alone-ness " than there were in the Victorian Age ; and this is not only because parents are compelled to behave better, but at least as much because they are given a better chance and a more manageable task. Nor does the case of children stand alone : there is also much less insanitariness of personal and household behaviour, except among a quite small group, not only because higher standards are enforced and slums cleared, but also because there are fewer down and outs who have been left, in the cause of personal responsibility, to stew in their own juice under the conditions of free contract and no State interference. Doubtless the new conditions have made some men less *abstinent*—less willing to sacrifice present enjoyments for the sake of the future. But is this a bad thing ? I am sure it is not ; for I am sure that the Victorian exaggeration of the virtue of abstinence and thrift was the cause of a great deal of quite unnecessary suffering. This does not mean that I under-estimate the need to secure, in the community as a whole, a level of saving high enough to provide for increasing population and for a rising standard of life. Assuredly I do not ; but, in the first place, I hold that the requisite level of productive saving can be achieved by collective action as well as by personal abstinence, and in the second place I deny that thrift has decreased among the poorer classes—whatever may have happened among the rich. The decline in abstinence among some sections of the people has been much more than offset by the spread of saving to a much larger proportion of the whole—a spread made possible by the general improvement in living standards, which is itself partly a product of the very social legislation that is accused of undermining personal responsibility.

That is half the answer ; but the other half remains. The early Victorians relied on the drives inherent in a particular sort of temperament to impel both the possessors themselves and the rest of the people—the great majority. Such a solution was essentially undemocratic, and its inconsistency with political democracy has been sufficiently proved here, and is, I think, being proved even in the United States. We, as a democracy, at any rate in purpose and in the making, have to find ways of getting the drives and incentives that are requisite for high industrial production on different and on more democratic terms. How we should set about the task it is none of my business to attempt to say in this talk : all I can say, in conclusion, is that I feel sure the thing can be done, and that we ought to have set about doing it a very long while ago. Indeed, I have been saying just that—not, I fear to much purpose, for the best part of forty years.

The Onus of State Action

GUY CHAPMAN

DURING THE war of 1914-18, one of the commonest remarks one heard was : " Well, we always have muddled through; and we always shall ". It was said with a kind of gloomy pride, as if muddling were a virtue and peculiar to ourselves, the virtue of taking things as they come, instead of meeting them half-way with a set of cut and dried theories. We looked on our empiricism as a biological virtue, and never wondered how this legend of " muddling through " arose.

" Muddling through " was neither a virtue nor a vice, but an historical phenomenon, which came about through the expansion of England in the nineteenth century. If we go back to the last years of George III, we shall see a country which might be said to govern itself. In contrast to France with its centralised system, and' its State-appointed officials, *préfets, maires* and judges, England was decentralised. National government was bit by bit shedding the last remnants of mediæval restraint and Tudor paternalism, and confined itself to national finance and defence, the colonies and foreign affairs. The Post Office apart, the rest lay in the hands of landowners and the corporations who combined the duties of the judiciary, the administration and the executive. Whitehall was staffed by a handful of gentlemen, appointed through patronage, supported by a body of copying clerks and messengers. How one got into the Civil Service and how one spent one's days when one got there can be read in Trollope's *Autobiography*. The emphasis was on " freedom ", implying freedom from royal autocracy and no inference with local custom and privilege. And though the interpretation of the word " freedom " differed, it had penetrated even to the poorest classes.

To this almost Arcadian society was suddenly presented a problem. It derived from two sources. The first was the impact of technical invention. The second was the rapid and unexampled growth of the population. These, combining with the difficulties of financial readjustment after Waterloo, formed a single labyrinthine problem which the State was unequipped to handle. Conventionally, the Industrial Revolution has been cast for the part of villain ; and the pursuit of profits indicted as the cause of low wages, starvation, the condition of the towns and the high death rate. That many masters were brutal and predatory there is no doubt. But the ultimate cause of the misery of the 'thirties and 'forties is the sudden teeming of new life into an unprepared society. Between 1801 and 1851, the population of England and Wales doubled, and doubled again in the next sixty years. No other European nation went through a similar experience. The leaders of industry may have been rapacious, but they were wrestling to convert a country-minded people, accustomed to working in their own time at their own pace, into an effective, punctual, machine-handling labour force. If they had failed, the misery might well have been doubled. It was a period very like that through which Russia has been going since 1917, but with this difference. Under the English parliamentary system, no government was in a position to decree. Every step proposed, every measure recommended, must be debated. At all points, working compromises must be reached ; and on all sides there were critics. The major issue, obscured by controversy on every conceivable subject, was—what is the responsibility of the State ? Can it constitutionally intervene ? Will intervention not mean a revival of the tyranny defeated in 1688 ? Can the State interfere when it is a law of nature that the economic system is automatically self-righting ?

For the admitted evils, the prescribed remedies came from personal mythologies. Universal suffrage, free trade, currency reform, a return to the land and rural simplicities, primitive socialism of different brands all had their prophets. There were the Benthamite Radicals who combined a belief in *laissez-faire* with what amounted to a vast government information and preventive service. And there was Toulmin Smith who held that the most beneficent unit of government was the parish—Toulmin Smith, the prototype of Mr. Podsnap ; " I knew it, from the first. Centralisation. No. Never with my consent. Not English ".

Part of the government's shyness of responsibility lay in the firmly-held tenet that government must be carried on as cheaply as possible, a belief dating back more than two centuries. The National Debt was a menace ; down to 1914, it was the aim of every Chancellor to reduce it. Economy was the perpetual watchword. " No country," said Disraeli in 1859, " can go on raising £70,000,000 a year in time of peace with impunity ". In the same year, Gladstone claimed that " Economy is the first and great article of my financial creed ". Remember, Gladstone dominated public finance for another thirty years and three-quarters of the budgets of that period are his or his disciples' work.

Again, most of the leading ministers for the first sixty years of the century came from an earlier and more leisurely age. The " Why can't you let it alone ? " of Lord Melbourne is matched thirty years later by Lord Palmerston : " We can't go on adding to the Statute Book *ad infinitum* . . . we cannot go on legislating for ever ".

The art of government, let us remember, is not to make laws but to fit them to the ideas of the day and to apply them. The question for every Minister was : can this or that measure be applied without causing a revolt. Ministers lacked reliable information. Commissioners and inspectors were few, sometimes amateurs, occasionally corrupt. The execution of remedies, especially in the towns, had to be carried out by magistrates themselves involved in the abuses. Hence so much social legislation in the early years was tentative, limited in scope, directed to immediate objectives. Often it failed to fulfil the intentions of Parliament, and needed additions and amendments as the gaps and the unforeseen consequences became apparent.

Nor were the bit constructive measures encouraging. The Poor Law Amendment Act of 1834 was a measure of economy through uniformity. Its crude surgery stimulated Chartism, and the violent reaction reinforced timidity. The General Health Act of 1848 was due less to the Sanitary Commissioners than to the fear of cholera sweeping over the Continent. Even so it was only permissive, and the general hatred of Chadwick's emphatic crusading led to a very gingerly handling of the whole health question down to the 'seventies. Even when faced by so strictly national a problem as the railways, the main preoccupation apart from safety regulations, was to control monopoly. True, State purchase was envisaged to take place in twenty-one years; but when the time came, the Committees shied off. Most of the work was piecemeal, patching here, restraining there, saving life and where possible, salving bodies—a long line of Acts, dealing with factories, mines, hours, merchant ships, truck, the exploitation of children and young people. But there is no hint that the state can (or should) do anything positive to eliminate poverty, save by not hindering production, which must be left to the natural economic laws.

Certainly down to the middle 'sixties, the repugnance to State intervention was lively. Even economic thinkers were divided on the limits of government action, and not a few held that the State was not only incompetent but actively malignant. We cannot of course lay our finger on any date and say, " Here is the turning point ". But new ideas and new knowledge were at work. For one, the rising influence of the physical sciences with the conception of prediction and control. For another, the growth of *expertise*, the need to have on hand a body of efficient administrators in Whitehall, though it took from 1853 to 1870 to carry out the recommendations of the Northcote-Trevelyan Report on the recruitment of the civil service. Then again there is John Stuart Mill. In 1848 he had condemned bureaucracy as a " continental nuisance ". But even with all his reservations and doubts, with his insistence on the necessity for private property, he was to reach the stage where he could say that socialism, " with all its risks," " with all its restraints," was preferable to a society resting on the resignation of the poor. The next generation, Jevons and Cairnes, reinterpreted Mill and began the revolt against *laissez-faire*. At the same time, the philosophers, Green, Ritchie and Bosanquet, began the undermining of the prevalent conception of liberty, formulating the theory that the State action is not of necessity the antithesis of freedom. As Bosanquet put it : " In submitting even to forcible constraint when imposed by society in the true common interest, I am obeying only myself, and am actually obtaining my freedom."

Such paradoxes of course were not for the average man. Yet he could not avoid the material influences. In the 'twenties, 'thirties and 'forties, the emphasis had been on thrift to provide the capital to enable industry to make the machines to make the goods that the new mouths needed, goods which, let us not forget, handicraft was unable to provide. The country was growing rich. The national income at a guess trebled between 1820 and 1870 ; it doubled again in the next forty years. Increased efficiency produced dividends. By the middle 'seventies, Birmingham under the lead of the redoubtable Joseph Chamberlain was demonstrating that an efficient municipality, a local State within the State, could render profitable services to the community.

Within the next decade, it was beginning to be accepted that parsimony was not economy, that waste was inefficient, and that ignorance and squalor were wasteful of both money and energy. In 1886, the Chancellor of the Exchequer, Lord Randolph Churchill, resigned from a Conservative Cabinet which would not tolerate his economies. As Lord Rosebery said, Lord Randolph, Mr. Gladstone and the Treasury officials were the only ones who had not realised the changed attitude to government spendings. In the same year, Chamberlain's " Unauthorised Programme " boldly claimed " the intervention of the State on behalf of the weak against the strong, of the interests of labour against capital, of want and suffering against luxury and ease."

With the running-out of the 'eighties, the obscure battle which had been little more than a series of guerilla skirmishes was as good as over. The State was seen to be destined co-ordinator of conflicting organisations. Efficiency rather than liberty was the new note. People as distinct in their social philosophies as the Webbs and Kipling were at one ; the Webbs upbraiding what they called " our real rulers in point of administrative detail ", the Civil Servants, for their invincible ignorance of modern economics ; Kipling jeering :

> " All along o' dirtiness, all along o' mess
> All along o' doing things, rather more or less."

In that indeterminate period between, say, 1893 and 1914, which is neither Victorian nor yet twentieth century, the debates are less on principle than on ways and means. The interpenetration of the State and Democracy was being tacitly accepted— Democracy which Mr. Gladstone had said would prove a costly mistress. There were, of course, still the critics : Herbert Spencer, who in *The Man versus the State* warned the nation that it was centralised government which had produced the French Revolution ; Dicey spoke of irresponsible power ; even Trade Unionists dimly perceived that one day this many-armed giant would restrict their own power ; but they could not push back the tide.

As one looks back from 1901 over the past seventy years, only one clear fact emerges. Parliament had continued to legislate in piecemeal fashion, without any long view, paying little attention either to consequences of action or principles involved. Even in the noonday of *laissez-faire* belief, it was taking steps which would hamper economic freedom. In each case a problem had been met and partially solved. The economists examined the new situation and adjusted their formulas. The philosophers reconsidered their basic assumptions. The interests protested, surrendered and often found a way round. Almost unwittingly, the State, setting up board after board, creating ministry after ministry, reaching out to amend an abuse, taking up another shirked responsibility, was answering an unvoiced but urgent public need. The seventy years is the record of a society faced by wave on wave of complex, unforeseeable, menacing problems for which there were no guides, rules or tables. Many clumsy, partial and even wrong solutions had been produced. There had been injustice, cruelty and fierce hatred ; but at least society had held together. There had been no violent revolt, no civil war and the modern State had arrived. The English, they rightly flattered themselves, had " muddled through ".

Anthropology — the Victorian Synthesis and Modern Relativism

DARYLL FORDE

ANTHROPOLOGY WAS a creation of the Victorian Age. The conception of a comprehensive science of Man; a synthesis which should illuminate the history and variety of mankind as a whole; this was typical of the intellectual ambition and industry of the Victorians.

This conception of Anthropology resulted largely from the impact of the doctrine of biological evolution on eighteenth-century ideas of social progress. The achievements of geologists and naturalists had given a greatly lengthened perspective of the age of the earth, of life on the earth and of mankind himself, and so, also a new importance to speculations on the cultural and social development of Man. Some eighteenth-century thinkers like Hume and Ferguson had formulated general schemes of social development, and the social progress of Man was already being schematised in stages of savagery, barbarism and civilisation.

Another aspect of the Victorian Age led to remarkable changes in the vantage point from which human life was viewed. Alongside the more general conviction of the immense benefits which Western science and a mechanised Christendom were conferring on the world, there was a growing recognition of the unity of mankind, which helped to break down the dichotomy between God-fearing civilised man and the heathen savage. The variety of behaviour and belief among the many peoples of the world could no longer be disposed of so simply.

The theory of organic evolution first propounded by Lamarck had brought coherence into the bewildering diversity of living forms by assuming a gradual but prolonged process of small cumulative changes. A similar development from more elementary forms would account satisfactorily for the immensely varied details of form in the social life of man. This app owed an immense debt to Herbert Spencer. The ope chapters of his *Principles of Sociology* can hardly be bettered t as a comprehensive statement of the general connection between the physical, biological and cultural phenomena involved in the study of man.

But in its speculative enthusiasm, Evolutionary Anthropology developed weaknesses. Western views, skills and institutions were tacitly assumed to be the culminating point to which human evolution had been moving through millennia. Western Europe was the point of reference for the world.

Thus the anthropologists of the later nineteenth century cast their theories about social institutions and culture in a pseudo-historical form. Features of custom and belief among modern savages were sometimes projected backwards into the past as the origin of western institutions, while explanations of the customs of savages themselves were sought not in the constitution of their own society or in its actual history, but in some hypothetical pre-existing condition. For some writers, the widespread rule of exogamy of kin groups pointed to an earlier condition in which such groups had first captured wives from one another and later arranged a regular system of exchange. Even Tylor saw the origin of religion in a belief in spirits and the soul generated early in the development of mankind when primitive man was unable to distinguish between waking life and things seen in dreams. The religion of savages at least was accordingly to be regarded as an inherited body of erroneous beliefs leading to pointless activities.

The study of actual societies was neglected for the construction of their hypothetical precursors presented as plausible starting points for an evolution that culminated in our own Western institutions. This distracted attention from enquiry into the actual forms and working of living communities. The Victorians by and large accepted their world and society as satisfactory and stable. They were curious as to the past but less anxious as to the future. They were not preoccupied as we are today with what is to come next.

Anthropology today, while eschewing speculative origins, has attempted to go beyond mere description of observable behaviour, to discover its meaning in terms of adaptation. This study of the meaning of cultures has taken two broad directions which may be distinguished as sociological and psychological. By analysing the apportionment of different tasks and privileges among people, by examining the character and distribution of leadership and authority ; by determining which people join together and which are absent or excluded in a task or feast or ceremony—in brief, by analysing the customary behaviour of persons of different age, sex, status and kinship in all phases of activity, we pass beyond the concrete activities of individuals and groups to the pattern of social relations among them. We analyse the social structure of the community to determine its coherence as a system and the tensions within it, and its relation to basic drives for livelihood, continuity and prestige.

Analysis of a series of societies provides us with a means of comparative study of social processes, a means of discovering fundamental similarities and differences between social systems which can be examined in relation to differences of physical environment, technical equipment, external relations and so forth.

But the customary behaviour of any people can be analysed from another point of view. We can formulate underlying attitudes and ideas that are expressed in that behaviour. So far as they are self-conscious about them, the people themselves regard such attitudes and feelings as ultimate values. Social stability and social conflicts and change are closely linked with harmony and discord in these dominant ideas. Both patterns of value and the processes whereby they are established and decay can be seen more clearly in the simpler and comparatively isolated primitive cultures which involve only thousands of human beings than in our own complex civilisation.

The anthropologist approaches such cultures from outside and against the background of the cultural variety of mankind. The relativity of what is considered good and bad, dignified and degrading, social and anti-social, is seen in a new light. For between differing cultures there are startling contrasts in what is approved and disapproved, in what energises the group and calls for the united action, and what discourages and dismays. Customary behaviour far from being commonplace and uninteresting as compared with the peculiarities and originality of the individual, is seen to be a predominant factor in all human belief and experience. It is through the spectacles of custom that every human being is trained from childhood to do his seeing and thinking. Cultural anthropology takes up one half of the problem. What are the conditions and processes, over and above the uniformities of human psychology, that produce this diversity of values and attitudes ? And in posing this problem the anthropologist takes as his working hypothesis the relativity of such values and of the social systems they inform.

This recognition of the grip of custom on human behaviour and ideas affects the anthropologist's view of personal responsibility. For the Victorians in general, as earlier speakers in this series have shown, the notion of personal responsibilty was a very high value. People were held to be responsible for the rightness and also for the consequences of their beliefs and acts. In the religious context man was responsible to God and under obligation to act in accordance with fixed and absolute rules. For the Victorian, circumstances did not alter cases in ethical judgments. In everyday life it was felt that what happened to a man was mainly the result of his own decisions.

To the anthropologist nowadays this appears to ignore both the relativity of values and also the way in which those values enshrined in custom condition human behaviour and narrow down personal choice.

For the anthropologist, the notion of personal responsibility is relative to the culture or social order in which a person has been reared. It is arbitrary and meaningless to hold persons responsible in terms of beliefs sanctioned by a group or community in which they do not socially belong ; in other words, to moralise objections to the conduct of peoples of other cultures. But since men live by and through values as much as by techniques, they are inevitably attached to them and will reject and oppose the values of another group which appears to threaten their own. The missionary seeks to uproot savage beliefs that conflict with Christian values. The political leaders of nations and classes denounce and organise action against the ideas as well as the acts of those who threaten or thwart their values. Much emotional heat is generated in the process. But, anthropologically speaking, these are conflicts between systems of ideas which cannot be set in opposition as right or wrong nor are they ideas for which their supporters are to be held personally responsible by opponents. If the anthropologist makes any judgment it will be a practical one, an estimation of the likelihood of the survival or dominance of one or other according to its consistency with technology and social organisation, and to the energy in material resources and man-power that will be mobilised in support of one or other.

Both the approaches I have referred to—the analysis of social structure and of patterns of value—are very different from that dominant in Victorian Anthropology. Values and the duties of persons in a society are considered in relation to the stability and continuity of the society itself, in its particular physical and technical environment and external relations. A culture is not regarded as a step on a single upward path of progress. There is no judgment by an external standard and in the abstract of the rightness of a custom or the fitness of a social rule. The question is rather what combination of external factors and internal processes help to maintain them, and how does it contribute to the harmony and continuity of the life of the group.

The cult of ancestral spirits, for example, is not to be regarded as a fixed stage in the spiritual evolution of man, nor as a credulous dogma of weaker minds, but as one symbolic expression of sentiments of social continuity and cohesion. The anthropologist seeks to discover the relation of such a cult to other phases of group life. Ancestor cults in fact vary in form with the social structure. Among the Ashanti of West Africa, the ancestors of territorial chiefs were the symbolic guardians of order in the chiefdom. Through them the chief maintained the customary code of law and morals and was himself bound to rectitude and responsibility.

The distinctive feature of anthropology as a social science is that it includes as an essential basis of study other societies than our own and that it formulates its hypotheses in terms of cultures of all kinds. For scientific study must be comprehensive. It must test any hypothesis against all known types of relevant phenomena. Too often in the social sciences and even more in common-sense judgments about human nature, only one variety of culture and social tradition is studied or used as the standard of reference. So long as civilised Western belief is true and the savage, the barbarian and the pagan are merely superstitious, the significance of neither can be objectively analysed. The dominance and the expansion of Western civilisation since the Age of Discovery have led those reared in it to forget its own historic development and its manifold internal changes and varieties. Knowing other cultures only as dissolving entities in the onward march of Western Civilisation, Western beliefs have been equated with Truth and Western customs and attitudes with Human Nature. This outlook is neither exceptional nor surprising. Savages agree in regarding their own people as Mankind—in fact, tribal names are commonly the name for Man—outsiders are not human, nor within the moral law.

Relativism is characteristic of these approaches to the understanding of culture and society and of the position of the individual within it. A given culture or social system is considered as a more or less coherent adjustment to a particular set of conditions. As we learn more, we can try by comparative study of different systems to detect more general principles and to return with a surer grasp to the problems of the evolution of culture and society which our Victorian ancestors made the goal of Anthropology.

The Recession of Liberalism

R. C. K. ENSOR

THE PERIOD in the history of British Liberalism, with which I am here concerned, is one which people nowadays are apt to forget, unless like myself they have lived in it. They remember that back in the nineteenth century the Liberals were the dominant party ; and they remember that early in the twentieth century, in the epoch of Asquith and Lloyd George, the same situation recurred. What they do not remember is that between these two periods of triumph extended for nearly thirty years a period of frustration and defeat. How did Liberalism slide down into the trough of that great depression, and how was it able eventually to rise out of it to heights beyond those that it had reached before ?

The greatest Liberal Government of the nineteenth century was that of 1868-74, presided over by Mr. Gladstone. In the Civil Service it substituted entry by competitive examination for entry by jobbery ; in the Army it abolished the sale and purchase of officers' commissions, and carried the Cardwell reforms ; in elections it introduced the secret ballot ; in Ireland it disestablished the church and passed the first great Irish Land Act ; in England it opened the doors of Oxford and Cambridge to Dissenters, carried the first great Education Act laying the foundations of universal education, and straightened out the tangle of our historic law-courts into the pattern which has served us ever since. Add that it attempted several other major tasks—notably the reform of liquor licensing and that of local government ; in which, though it was less successful, it expended much energy— and incurred an unpopularity that in the case of liquor licensing dogged it for forty years.

Now that is a prodigious record of work for one Government, at any rate by nineteenth-century standards, which allowed of no short cuts in Parliamentary procedure. It is small wonder that, as their period of office neared its close, the Ministers became tired, spent, stale ; so that Disraeli could describe their front bench as a row of extinct volcanoes ; while Mr. Gladstone himself told the Queen ten months before he asked her to dissolve Parliament, that his work was done, his mandate exhausted, and he himself in need of a long rest. In these circumstances the General Election of 1874 returned a solid Conservative majority to Parliament— the first that there had been since the party was split in 1846 over the repeal of the Corn Laws. Though helped by a swing of the pendulum, it had deeper causes than that. It not only enabled Disraeli to rule the country as Conservative Prime Minister for six eventful years, 1874 to 1880, but it ushered in a period of thirty-one years, 1874 to 1905, during which the Conservatives held office for twenty-two and a half and the Liberals for eight and a half only, and in which no single Liberal administration ever stood really firm on its feet.

Mr. Gladstone himself in 1874 may have divined something of this ; for when he resigned office after the election he privately resigned the Liberal leadership as well. In January, 1875, Lord Hartington publicly succeeded him as the Liberal leader.

Nevertheless, when his seventy-first year was less than half through, there was Mr. Gladstone back in office as Prime Minister for the second time. On paper he had a good majority— one hundred and thirty-seven over the Conservatives and seventy-two over the Conservatives and Irish Nationalists combined. But his following had little coherence. He had won, not by the attractions of his own policy, but by the unpopularity of his opponents. We know now, as it was not known then, that by a sort of natural law whenever a Parliamentary nation makes a great war, the election that follows it brings defeat to the party under which the war was begun. The sequels to two world wars show, I think, no exception to that rule. Disraeli had not, it is true, made a great war. But he had brought the country within an inch of one, and he had followed that closely by starting two little wars—one in Afghanistan, the other in Zulu-land—each of which led to an episode—in the one case, the massacre at our Legation in Kabul, in the other the appalling butchery of Isandhlwana—which profoundly shocked popular feeling. In his Midlothian campaign and elsewhere Mr. Gladstone had with consummate skill and eloquence fused these three matters into one terrific accusation ; but even had he not done so, the showing of all parallel cases is that the Beaconsfield Government would have been defeated.

The resulting House of Commons, which sat from 1880 to 1885, expressed therefore a negation rather than an affirmation. And it was the most chaotic that this country has known in modern times. I do not mean merely that its proceedings were disorderly, though at times they were ; both the squabbles over Mr. Bradlaugh and the unseemly episodes of Irish obstruction tended to lower the prestige of Parliament and with it that of the party which formed its majority. The party, which had originally been an amalgam of Whigs, Radicals and Peelites, threatened to lose that intellectual unity it had acquired in the 'sixties and 'seventies, and to break up again into Whigs and Radicals. From 1880 to 1885 there was a series of Cabinet conflicts, mostly revolving round the Radical leader, Joseph Chamberlain ; while outside there was a growing trickle of secessions. I myself can remember (it is my earliest serious political recollection) how in 1884 my father, till then a Liberal with a special veneration for John Bright, was impelled to change over to Conservatism by the violence of Joseph Chamberlain's Radical speeches.

Putting personalities and minor issues on one side, what was the chief reason for the Liberal disintegration ? Was it the emergence of new conflicts between Labour and Capital, between the proletariat and the bourgeoisie ? You might perhaps guess so, but speaking as an historian I think your guess would be wrong. Historically the main cause was the agrarian revolution in Ireland. Let us take a glance at this.

In 1869 Mr. Gladstone passed his Act disestablishing the Irish church and in 1870 his first great Irish Land Act. These measures sought to heal Irish discontent by removing its causes, and down to past the middle 'seventies they had a remarkable degree of success. But in 1877 something happened which nobody had foreseen. Europe was suddenly invaded by imports of American prairie-grown corn at prices with which no European farmer could compete. By 1879 every country west of Russia faced the alternative—either to put on a corn tariff or to see its agriculture ruined. France and Germany both put on corn tariffs, and saved their farmers. Britain almost alone continued admitting the prairie-corn free, and her farmers were ruined.

Now three things may be noted about this. First, the British decision was probably inevitable, because the circumstances under which the Corn Laws had been repealed in 1846 had left in the people's minds a peculiarly rigid aversion to duties on food. Secondly, while it did irreparable damage to English agriculture— till then the finest and most efficient in the world—England had far more men employed in industry than on farms, and in that way could absorb the shock. But thirdly, Ireland outside Ulster had virtually no industries ; almost the whole nation depended on agriculture ; and almost the whole nation faced ruin. The tenants could not pay their rent ; the landlords and their agents had nothing else to live on ; and two centuries of agrarian strife, which the Act of 1870 had abated, flared up again into a sort of civil war. What with murders, moonlighting, cattle-maiming, boycotting and terrorism of every kind, there was in most of rural Ireland no security for life or property left.

Now this fire burned for some years. It began in the time of the Beaconsfield Government, which did nothing to arrest its spread. Irish land was not a subject within Disraeli's normal range of interest. With Mr. Gladstone it was otherwise ; few Englishmen knew so much about it. But in the first year of his Ministry he was prevented by the House of Lords from doing what was essential ; and although during the second year he succeeded in passing his second and greatest Irish Land Act, which eventually enabled the agrarian situation to settle down, the intervening period of inevitable coercion had raised the temperature of controversy to its highest point. English society was deeply stirred during those terrible years by the spectacle of refugees in England belonging to the Irish landlord class. Most of them were simple attractive people of a God-fearing Protestant type ; they had never been very rich, but now, through no fault of their own, they were penniless ; and the tales they had to tell of murders and cattle-maimings and all the other midnight barbarities of the moonlighters made their hearers' blood run cold. You have to remember that the Victorians had a much stricter moral sense than we ; for them the Ten Commandments were still a corner-stone of life ; and public reprobation of a crime like murder had not been blunted as it so extensively has been ever since the first World War. Remember, too, that the Victorian ideology, and especially the Liberal ideology, regarded law and order and the enforcement of contracts as the root conditions of progress and prosperity, the foundations on which rested the whole marvellous fabric of enterprise and invention, which had so vastly raised Western standards of life. Consider then the shock to Englishmen, and not least to English Liberals, when they looked across the few miles of the Irish Channel, and there saw all these basic principles of theirs cast down and trampled upon—and that, while a Liberal Government ruled at Westminster ! This was the current of feeling which destroyed the inner unity of the Liberal party. The actual split came in 1886 over Mr. Gladstone's first Home Rule Bill. But that is why it came then ; why that measure, in the main so just and timely never stood a dog's chance with English public opinion. Above all, that is why at the parting of the ways the anti-Gladstone and anti-Home Rule way was chosen, not merely by a Whig leader like the great Lord Hartington, afterwards the eighth Duke of Devonshire, but by the two chief leaders of the English Radicals, John Bright and Joseph Chamberlain.

Between 1886 and the end of the century the Home Rule split, as it was called, only gradually abated its depressing influence over the fortunes of Liberalism. In the late 'eighties Mr. Gladstone made a great effort to rally his forces, and in 1889 the exposure of the Pigott forgeries before the Parnell Commission was a real help to him. But only a year afterwards came the O'Shea divorce case, with Parnell as co-respondent—a case in which Parnell, for private reasons not known till this century, had to cut a much worse figure than the facts really warranted. The result was that not only the British Liberals but the Irish Nationalists were split. In 1891 Parnell died ; and in 1892 Mr. Gladstone became Prime Minister for the fourth time with a majority (including Irish) of only forty. With this he passed through the Commons in 1893 his second and best Home Rule Bill ; but the Lords threw it out, and the evidence of public approval, which greeted their action, showed that the feeling of revulsion against Irish crime still dominated the English electorate. On 4th March, 1894, Mr. Gladstone, now in his eighty-fifth year, resigned ; but his colleagues decided to carry on. The question who should be Prime Minister was answered by Queen Victoria, who sent for Lord Rosebery. The party, could it have voted, would have elected Sir William Harcourt ; and Mr. Gladstone, if consulted, would have advised Lord Spencer. Either choice might on some grounds have been preferable ; but the personal unpopularity of Harcourt within the Cabinet itself caused the choice of Rosebery to be acquiesced in. Nevertheless, in it lay the germs of yet another Liberal split—which, beginning as that between Rosebery and Harcourt, became eventually that between the Roseberyites and the majority of the party. The precarious Government fell in the summer of 1895 ; thereafter the party remained in the wilderness for a period of over ten years ; and during all that time the split that has just been described persisted. In the period 1899 to 1902 it was complicated by a yet further split—between those who supported and those who opposed the South African War.

How was a party so long torn by so many dissensions able between 1905 and the first World War to produce and maintain strong Governments and to win successive General Elections by large majorities ? In the similar case of the Conservative party's re-birth in 1874, credit must go to the educative brilliance of Disraeli's very long preceding leadership. Who was the Disraeli in the Liberal case ? The answer is that there was none. From December, 1898, the leader was Sir Henry Campbell-Bannerman. He was a Scot with a good measure of his countrymen's shrewdness, and his strength of character had been shown by his dealings as War Minister with Queen Victoria. But he could not be claimed as a great brain ; and on his legs, where I have myself heard him, he was probably the least eloquent speaker who ever in this country reached the highest office. It is true that he commonly said the right things, but his actual delivery of them was so halting as to be painful ; and most of the time, although with occasional memorable exceptions, he stuck to the merest party commonplaces. Possibly his greatest virtue as a leader was just this—that people always knew where he was going, as with men like Gladstone or Lloyd George they seldom could. He never wavered from a simple faith, that if his party went stolidly on repeating its familiar shibboleths, in the long run it would come into power, no matter what happened by the way. And eventually time rewarded him.

From that happy ending it is easy to draw, as many Liberals often have drawn, a quite incorrect conclusion. They infer that, no matter how much a party's members squabble and wrangle, it will be saved, if its leaders repeat the shibboleths. The Liberal party between 1895 and 1905 survived—and survived to triumph —not through its shibboleths, but because under the two-party system which is established and necessitated by our British mode of conducting elections, it was then one of the two great alternative parties in the State. Its opposite number, the Conservative party, could never, no matter how victorious, deprive it of that position. It could only be deprived by a third party coming in and ousting it from its claim to be the alternative ; as between the World Wars, three decades later, was in fact done by the Labour party. But in 1895-1905 no such potential substitute existed. Its germinal form, the Labour Representation Committee, only started in 1900. Hence in the years after 1902, when the nation had tired of the Conservatives, it had no alternative but the Liberals to turn to ; and in spite of all past Liberal mistakes turn it did.

Benjamin Jowett

GEOFFREY FABER

SOME YEARS ago an eminent Balliol man urged me to get a book written which would explain how the famous Master of Balliol, Benjamin Jowett, provided his young men with reserved seats in express trains to destinations of importance.

A younger Oxford friend, to whom I once confided that I should myself like to write a book about Jowett, replied incredulously : " What ? That dull, bogus old man ! "

Both views are typical. Both are false.

Let me begin by recalling the essential facts of his career. Jowett was born in 1817 and died in 1893. He spent his whole life from the age of nineteen to seventy-six as scholar, fellow, tutor, and finally Master of Balliol College, Oxford. Beginning from nothing, he ended up as a kind of mentor-in-chief to most of the great Victorians, men and women alike. His best period was his tutorship—1842 to 1870, age twenty-five to fifty-three ; and the best part of it was the first half. He was incomparably the greatest educator of able young men England has ever produced.

In the world of learning, Jowett led the way to a new understanding of St. Paul ; rediscovered the early Greek philosophers ; translated, analysed, and commented upon the works of Plato— an immense life-long task, superbly done ; he did the same for Thucydides, and began it for Aristotle ; he was the first Oxford man to decipher the philosophy of Hegel.

In the world of affairs he played many leading parts—especially in the reform of mediæval Oxford and the reconstruction of the Indian Civil Service. It is worth noting, by the way, that he fell out with Gladstone over the method of reforming Oxford. That was in 1854. He believed in making people and institutions reform themselves. Gladstone believed in having it done for them ; and this view prevailed.

He became a figure of legendary influence in his own lifetime ;
but is now often misrepresented as merely an ill-mannered old
autocrat, with a squeaky voice and an exceptional capacity for
frightening nervous young men :

> " I am the great Professor Jowett.
> What there is to know I know it,
> What I don't know isn't knowledge,
> And I am Master of this College."

The affectionately intended caricature has somehow acquired the
aspect of a malicious lampoon.

As Jowett's influence took possession of Balliol, an increasing
number of his young men—many of them brilliant, and all of
them hard workers—became State servants at home or abroad.
Some of them achieved proconsular fame. When Curzon went
to Balliol in 1878, as his biographer says, it was " the obvious
setting ". By the late 'seventies, Balliol—dominated by Jowett—
had become " a famous nursery of Public men ". Curzon himself, and a little earlier Milner, were perhaps the greatest of its
" proconsuls ".

But neither Milner nor Curzon, let alone the lesser men, who
went out from Balliol into Whitehall or India or Africa or elsewhere, had been specifically trained by Jowett for the tasks they
eventually performed—any more than Asquith or Grey were
trained by him to be statesmen, Bowen or Loreburn to be
lawyers, Gore or Lang to be ecclesiastics, Morier or Spring-Rice
to be diplomats, Tout to be an historian, Caird to be a philosopher,
Swinburne to be a poet, and so on *ad libitum*.

It is wrong to think of Jowett as a kind of super-crammer or
trainer of candidates for public service. If one analyses the
worth-while Balliol output from 1840 to 1893, the " Public
men "—administrators at home and abroad, plus statesmen and
diplomats—scarcely make up a quarter of it, if so much. A
remarkably high proportion, certainly, and one that tended to
increase. But not so high as to overshadow everything else. A
full half of the output were scholars, historians, philosophers,
teachers, men of letters. Churchmen, lawyers, land-owners, and
unclassifiables, make up at least another quarter.

It looks as if the quality, which made Jowett's young men
count, was a universal quality. Whatever they did, they did it well.

The question, then—if I may take a single instance—is not " How did Jowett train Alfred Milner to be High Commissioner of South Africa " but " What did Jowett *do* to Milner ? "

Milner's case is rather remarkable. Going up to Balliol in 1873, he was never one of Jowett's pupils. Jowett had ceased to be tutor and become Master, three years earlier. But Milner stood to him very much in the relationship of pupil to tutor. Here are a few fragments from a very long letter which he wrote to Jowett in 1882, breaking his decision to give up the Bar—a decision which he plainly felt himself obliged to justify before the Master.

" You will ask me what I mean to do. Frankly speaking, I have no idea. I am rising eight and twenty and cannot afford to waste time. . . There are two things I want to say for fear you should think me light headed. The first is, I am not dazzled by the prospect of a great political career. A man without money can scarcely hope to go into Parliament. But there are many useful careers outside Parliament, any one of which I personally should prefer even to great success at the Bar. Secondly you must not think that I want to escape hard work. My only idea is hard work, provided my heart is in it. . . If I live, I mean to do you some credit yet."

This letter—I wish I could quote more of it—shows the lasting force of Jowett's personal influence. It does not suggest that he was an architect of empire. Does it suggest too strong a pre-occupation with the ideal of worldly success ?

It is essential to understand Jowett's attitude towards success. The view is common that all he desired for his pupils was a distinguished career. It contains an element of truth. Jowett rightly desired his young men to make their mark. But the flow of Balliol successes bred envy and malice outside Balliol, and even inside Balliol maintenance of the flow tended to become an objective in itself. The present view of Jowett stems from this envy and reaction, beginning before you and I were born. Is it perhaps being kept alive by a modern error—our egalitarian dislike of individual merit ?

Whatever you may think of that question, in Jowett's own mind the desire to see his young men succeed sprang from hatred of failure. He had good reason for that hatred. His father had been a failure. From twelve to nineteen the future Master of

Balliol lived all by himself in lodgings, attending St. Paul's
School. It was a boyhood of extreme poverty and unimaginable
loneliness, far divided from his mother, brothers and sisters. No
doubt it forged self-reliance. But the iron entered into his soul
—he never spoke or wrote of those days, and even his young
Oxford contemporaries thought of him as Melchisedec, " without
father, without mother, and without descent ". " The greatest
of evils and the worst of crimes is poverty ". Jowett would have
seen nothing paradoxical in this paradox of Bernard Shaw's. For
him poverty—the poverty whose synonym is failure—was a sin,
perhaps, rather than a crime. It means undeserved suffering for
others. And it usually results from indolence of mind or spirit.
It was indolence, therefore, that he took as his chief enemy. Sir
Robert Morier, his best loved pupil, owed his ambassadorial
career to Jowett ; not because Jowett pulled strings or taught him
diplomacy, but because—as his friend Palgrave said—" he had
come up to Balliol a lax and imperfectly educated fellow, but
Jowett, seeing his great natural capacity, took him in the Long
Vacation of 1848 and practically ' converted him ' to the doctrine
of work ".

The same doctrine was effectively preached to men who had
no need to earn their living. So Walter Morrison, heir to a great
fortune, went to Balliol from Eton in 1853, with no idea of doing
anything but have a good time.

Forty years later, after Jowett's death, Morrison wrote : " One
day he said to me, ' Morrison, you are a fool. You must be sick of
idling. . . . You have fair ability, but it is too late for you to do
much. . . . But the class matters nothing, what does matter is the
sense of power which comes from steady working '. I thought
the suggestion good. I *was* tired of idling ".

Morrison, to his own and his friends' amazement, got a first
in Greats.

There are innumerable stories describing Jowett's way with
young men. Morrison's comes as near as is possible to explaining
how it was that he turned idlers into workers.

Power ? What did he mean ? Not power over others.
Power over self, power to direct life, instead of drifting on currents of circumstance and emotion. Power over self *means* power
over others. Its index-mark, in the western world, *is* success.
The lure was a cunning one. But it wasn't used by a man of mere

cunning. His biographer, Campbell, one of his earlier pupils, recalls " the singular personal charm" which made the thirty-year-old tutor " irresistible to a younger man", his " candour of judgment", his " penetrating sympathy", his way of coming to his pupil's aid " unasked in difficulties which his sagacity had divined".

Asquith, in his autobiography, recalls the unique " union of worldly sagacity with the most transparent simplicity of nature ; ambition, keen and unsleeping, but entirely detached from self, and absorbed in the fortunes of a great institution and its members."

Asquith gives us the old man, at his best ; Campbell the young one, at his better best. Both had in mind a personality which both remembered as unlike any other they had known. I will try to suggest a few further features. The humour that salted his seriousness. His silences. The stories of those dreadful silences are legion. It is not clear how far they were the result of shyness or abstraction, or were a deliberately used instrument. But it *is* clear that they enhanced his influence, instead of diminishing it— as one would have expected.

The reverse side of these silences was his exceptional power of throwing himself into somebody else's position. Let me give two examples : First, the published series of letters written, when he was an old sick man, to his former pupil, Lord Lansdowne, Viceroy of India from 1888 to 1893. I don't find any "philosophy of empire" in them. But their wise pragmatic counsel, their imaginative awareness of Lansdowne's day-to-day problems, are almost uncanny.

My other example comes from two unpublished letters to a schoolboy cousin, Sidney Irwin, written when Jowett was in his early 'forties. They warn the lad against schoolboy immorality ; and urge him to " make himself a good cricketer" and gain the respect of the other boys " in this way as well as in books". " As to your work," he wrote, " you should always do everything as well as you can. . . But don't try to do too much. . . . The real effort is to do well without spending a long time at your books".

Here is a hint of Jowett's secret. At the busiest, most creative, point in his life he has time to write to a young boy, of no peculiar talent, long, wise, tactful, cherished letters, which rebuked their own writer. *He* had never tried to make himself a cricketer ; *he* had always spent a long time at his books.

Jowett never played any game, never learned to dance, never acquired any vice. Campbell says that he once confessed to smoking a cigarette—" abroad " and " in the company of a lady " whom he refused to name. He never made love. There is some unpublished evidence that he once thought of a particular woman as a possible wife. Fortunately it came to nothing. Marriage would have impaired that complete devotion to his pupils which made him great and his pupils worth while. He had an immense capacity for friendship. He collected friends ; writing lists of their names in his notebooks. Loyalty to a single person would have stopped that kind of collective, passionate, attachment. It would have killed the tutor of genius.

The devotion, the charm, the formidability, the learning, the doctrine of work, the clear-sighted reasoning, the loathing of failure, the mixture of sagacity and innocence and ambition—if we add these qualities up and put them at Jowett's unique moment of opportunity, have we not sufficiently explained him ?

No. Something vital is missing. A philosophy of adminis-tration ? He had none, beyond the truism that the ruler is the servant. A philosophy of liberal imperialism ? He had none. He was a mere amateur, now inclining to a paternal government of backward peoples by combined European nations, now desiring the annexation of Egypt because the " greater India " of Africa must sooner or later be a British possession.

What is missing from our picture of the man is his religious faith. It used to be said that Jowett gnashed his teeth when he saw his undergraduates filing into Chapel. Asquith puts this legend where it belongs. But Asquith omits to say—and perhaps never knew—that Jowett all his life earnestly believed in a personal God and in the validity of Christ's teaching about God. He lived his own life, and made other men live their lives, according to the Parable of the talents. This fact makes the exact complexion of his temporal opinions relatively unimportant. " In the essentials of his personality and of his convictions "— wrote Asquith—" he had not undergone any fundamental change. He had never been an iconoclast, or a pioneer, or propagandist of revolutionary dogmas and ideals. Even his political Liberalism had always been of a temperate and semi-sceptical kind, and no man was by nature and habit of thought more repelled by what his friend Tennyson called the "falsehood of extremes'".

Jowett would have very much liked to hear that said of his attitude to worldly affairs. But inwardly he did obey an extreme call. Not very many men in human history have bettered him in that obedience, or in its practical consequences.

The Proconsuls

JACK SIMMONS

IN THE course of Queen Victoria's reign the British Empire expanded with an astonishing rapidity : in North America, in Africa, in India and the Far East and Australasia—everywhere it was the same. But what strikes one most about this Victorian expansion is not really its speed : it is the haphazard, almost casual way in which so much of it came about. In a familiar phrase, much misunderstood, Seeley said that England seemed "as it were, to have conquered and peopled half the world in a fit of absence of mind ". He meant, of course, that the great majority of Englishmen thought little about the Empire—as he went on to add, " we constantly betray by our modes of speech that we do not reckon our colonies as really belonging to us ". That was true when he wrote, in 1883 ; and for all the efforts of conscious imperialists like himself, it has remained true ever since. The interest of Englishmen in the Empire has always been vague and intermittent.

But that does not mean that there were no fixed principles on which British imperial policy was based, that Downing Street and the proconsuls merely devised solutions to the problems that confronted them as they turned up one by one. On the contrary, Victorian colonial policy bears a strongly-marked character of its own. It inherited great principles from the past, dropped some of them, modified others, contributed much that was new ; and handed on a powerful tradition that profoundly influences—it often dominates—our colonial policy today.

The first and greatest thing that the Victorians took over from the eighteenth century was the humanitarian tradition, which attained the highest point of its influence in the emancipation of the slaves, four years before Victoria came to the throne. It is interesting to see how that tradition fared as the century went on. In the West Indies the working of the Emancipation Act was far from an unqualified success. The officials on the spot pointed constantly to its defects, and especially to the inadequate provision it made for the difficult transition from slavery to freedom. Here is the Governor of Trinidad, writing in 1848 : " One of the many errors which have been committed since the granting of emancipation is the little attention paid to any legislation having for its end the formation of a society on true, sound and lasting principles . . . As the question at present stands, a race has been freed, but a society has not been formed."

For already in the 'forties a reaction against the older humanitarianism had set in. The movement had done a good deal to discredit itself. The Niger expedition of 1841 was a disastrous, a disgraceful failure ; and Dickens voiced, as usual, much of the feeling of his class when he attacked its promoters, the whole plan upon which it had been based, what he called " the ocean of ignorance at Exeter Hall ". The humanitarians had had their triumphs, but they had been with limited, fixed objectives. The prohibition of the slave trade, the freeing of the slaves—these were clear ends in themselves : when it came to more complex problems, demanding a close knowledge of West Indian or African or Maori society, a new approach was needed.

It came in the 'fifties, and most of all from Livingstone. He knew what he was talking about, as none of his predecessors had done ; for he had lived and worked in Africa for fifteen years before he first spoke out. To him that union of " Christianity and commerce " which had been advocated so incompetently by the promoters of the Niger expedition remained the right policy —the only policy to exterminate the Arab slave trade that was ravaging Central Africa when he saw it. But he understood that no quick triumph could be expected, that the old African order was breaking down, that it must be replaced with something else, which would be the work of many years of experiment. For that, the first thing necessary was a clearer understanding of the African, and it was to this that Livingstone addressed himself. He had an instinctive sympathy with Africans (a much closer sympathy than with his own countrymen), he had infinite patience with them, and something rarer, especially among missionaries : a real detachment, a disinterested mind. His passion was for the truth at any cost, even if it went against his own preconceptions, against Christianity itself. So you find him, quite early in his career, stating the case of the tribal rain-doctor, and later on inquiring pertinaciously of his brother-in-law—a missionary of a more orthodox kind—what was the real nature of initiation rites.

Livingstone went, in fact, some way towards the approach of the modern sociologist. He stands at the turning-point between the old humanitarianism and the new. In the second half of the century, as the Victorians were faced with a constantly-increasing responsibility for the government of primitive peoples, they developed a fresh technique : what has come in the twentieth century to be called "indirect rule". Its fundamental principle— that of ruling a dependent people as far as possible through their traditional institutions—was not novel. But the later Victorians turned something that had been merely a convenient device of administration into a system of government designed for the positive benefit of the people themselves : it was a new application of the principle of " trusteeship " that they had inherited from Burke. And that system has played a vital part in our colonial policy in the twentieth century—nor in ours alone, for it has influenced French and Belgian colonial practice too.

Now the principles of indirect rule were tried out and formulated in the colonies themselves, in Africa and Malaya and the Pacific. They were not in any sense the work of London, the Colonial Office, which wisely left such matters to the decision of the men on the spot. The makers of indirect rule were men like Sir Arthur Gordon in Fiji in the 'seventies and above all, at the end of the century, Frederick Lugard and Sir George Goldie in Africa : Lugard, the young Army officer who went out to tropical Africa almost by chance in the 'nineties, and stayed to make his life's work out there ; Goldie, the founder of the United Africa Company and its all-powerful director, who laid down with accuracy and imagination the lines on which the administration of Nigeria should develop. As Lugard wrote of Uganda in 1893 : " an arbitrary and despotic rule, which takes no account of native customs, traditions, and prejudices, is not suited to the successful development of an infant civilisation, nor, in my view, is it in accordance with the spirit of British colonial rule. The king has been proved incompetent and useless, but the Resident should rule through and by the chiefs." Here was a new conception of colonial government : it has proved very fruitful in our own time, and we owe it entirely to the Victorians.

It would be a mistake, however, to suppose that the Victorian Empire was run solely by men with such robust and positive ideas. The early Victorians had been very doubtful whether the Empire would, or should survive at all. In the 'forties and 'fifties responsible government was conceded to the colonies of white settlement in North America, Australia, and New Zealand ; and very few people believed firmly in the permanence of their imperial connection with England. Sir James Stephen, the great head of the Colonial Office, wrote in a gloomy mood in 1846 : " There are, at this moment, in Canada almost as many Europeans as there were in the United States when they declared their independence—a very pregnant fact in many ways."

There was similar doubt over the future of the dependent colonies. To many Englishmen they seemed valueless : the West Indies a group of islands whose prosperity had gone for ever, sinking into visible, rapid decay ; the West African settlements a series of posts in a pestilential and disappointing country. In the 'sixties the House of Commons showed itself anxious to undertake no further commitments there. A senior member of the Colonial Office summed up the problems of its government with remarkable honesty and clearness, minuting on a dispatch from Lagos in 1862 : " How long ought a man to take before he believes himself a good judge of the relative merits of obscure African tribes and villages ? . . . We want to use the different tribes as a means of extinguishing slave-dealing amongst themselves and those around them, while they want to use us as a means of oppressing their neighbours, and there seems to me to be a constant trial going on which shall be the tool of the other. . . . Wherever we go in Africa, our views are as enlightened and lofty, compared with those of the barbarous people amongst whom we find ourselves, as those of a superior race of beings : and if we choose to employ steamers and a few disciplined troops, our influence is paramount. The apparent good is so great that it is very fascinating. But still one cannot help occasionally asking oneself, where is it to end ? It is also uncomfortable to reflect on the disparity between our power and our knowledge. The first is so tremendous that we can at will exalt or destroy, but who is to ensure us a corresponding discrimination ? I feel afraid sometimes lest we should be like the kings in burlesques who with comical vigour dispatch one slave with a blow and cover the other with honours, long before they can know whether either deserves his fate." In plain matter-of-fact civil servant's prose, this is something very near to the mood of " Dover Beach ". How easy it is to overestimate the complacency of the Victorians!

It was not often, indeed, that doubts so grave were expressed with so much frankness. And gradually, in the 'eighties and 'nineties, a new spirit, tougher and more self-confident, appeared in British colonial administration. A new efficiency, too, for here, as in other branches of the Civil Service, the reforms of the 'fifties and 'sixties had their effect. The old system was based on a few simple rules, applied with an infinite talent for improvisation. Towards the end of the century the rules became rapidly more numerous, the scope of the individual less and less. In the Colonial Office, that is : for in the colonies themselves the officials retained a real measure of initiative and independence a good deal longer than their colleagues in London. We often speak of the closing years of the Queen's reign as a time of extravagant imperialism. But that jingoism, raucous and strident, was not as important as it is often made to appear. It was not characteristic of England, and its effects were transient. The 'nineties have much more positive and permanent achievements to show, in the development of the tropical African protectorates and the administrative reforms of Joseph Chamberlain.

Chamberlain's work as Secretary of State for the Colonies has hardly received the full recognition it deserves. So much of his eight years at the Colonial Office was passed in the glare of furious public controversy that a great deal of his quieter and more solid achievement has remained unnoticed. But his Secretaryship does mark an important new stage in the history of the dependent Empire. It was he who first proclaimed an imaginative programme for the planned economic development of the colonies— a policy modestly begun in his own time, but leading directly to the series of Colonial Development and Welfare Acts that have been passed since 1929. And his work for the colonial civil service was no less important. To take only one instance : he was the driving force behind the application of the new methods of preventive medicine in West Africa, the outward sign of which was the creation of the West African Medical Staff as a unified service in 1902. Mary Kingsley—who fought Chamberlain more than once, and fiercely, on other issues—paid him a ringing tribute. It was in her last lecture, delivered in London in February, 1900. (She sailed off next month to become a nurse in the Boer War, caught enteric, and died at Simonstown early in June.) "Mr. Chamberlain in this matter has done a grand good thing," she said, "and done it nobly, for no one urged it on him, it was done to catch no votes—white men in West Africa have none. It was not done to add to his own reputation or glorification as a statesman ; he has given time, thought and labour to it that he could, had he cared for that end, have spent in advertising himself. It was done from humane sympathy alone." Looking back over the career of that formidable Birmingham man, so masterful, in many things so uncongenial, the hard lines of his character soften for a moment, he becomes alive, something more than a mere efficient Cabinet Minister : one begins to understand why it was that so many of his subordinates held him in a respect that was tinged with affection.

Over against Chamberlain, his unwearied and venomous opponents, stand the anti-imperialists—an oddly-assorted group of Little Englanders, Liberals, and Labour men. They too have positive achievements to show : in Hobson's book, *Imperialism*, which influenced the mind of Lenin so deeply ; and in the pro-Boers' passionate, and bitterly unpopular, denunciation of the South African war. There was in that much exaggeration, wrong-headedness, and spite : yet when the war was over and the time for a settlement came, the Dutch South Africans remembered and trusted the Englishmen who had championed them as they would never have trusted Milner and the Conservatives.

The pro-Boers based themselves on a simple appeal to justice. Here they took strong ground ; for justice was the declared objective of Victorian colonial policy. Above all, justice between races, the most difficult sort to ensure : between British and French Canadians, between Africans and Europeans at the Cape, between settlers and Maoris in New Zealand. The problem arose, in many different forms, in India. Macaulay had been faced with it in 1836 over the Black Act, which established an exactly equal system of justice for Indians and Englishmen in Bengal : he maintained his position firmly and so earned the malignant hatred of some sections of British society in Calcutta. Elgin, as Viceroy of India at the end of his life, met the same problem in another form, when he was strongly pressed to reprieve an English soldier who had murdered an Indian. He was inflexible. " The verdict was clearly borne out by the evidence," so he told the Secretary of State. " The sentence was in accordance with the law, and the judge, to whom I referred, saw no reason to question it. The decision of the Governor-General in Council was that the law must take its course."

This steady, even justice was something that could be administered only by a paternal government, acting as arbiter between races, creeds and classes, where their interests were in conflict. And indeed Victorian imperialism remained paternal in its ideals to the end. Here was something on which all the great proconsuls were at one, whatever their other differences. Cromer's view is characteristic : " our primary duty," he said, " is not to introduce a system which, under the specious cloak of free institutions, will enable a small minority of natives to misgovern their countrymen, but to establish one which will enable the mass of the population to be governed according to the code of Christian morality ".

The Victorians lacked sympathy with the intellectuals, the educated minority, whether in Egypt or in India—though it is fair to remember that it was an Englishman, a retired civil servant, who did most towards founding the Indian National Congress ; and that though Lord Dufferin, the Viceroy, forbade the association of officials with it, he approved of the Congress in principle at its outset. For " the mass of the population ", on the other hand, the Victorians did a magnificent work, with affection and boundless energy : ending slave-raids in Nigeria and civil wars in Malaya, establishing security and peace and justice where those things had been forgotten or never known before. So much of it is summed up in that single story of Kipling's, *William the Conqueror* ; for, when all has been said about constitutions and laws, the Indian Famine Code may stand for the greatest work of the Victorian proconsuls.

The Leaders of Collectivist Thought

H. J. LASKI

AT THE height of the period we call the age of *laissez-faire*, we can see a change taking place in the minds of men. The philosophers began to be critical of a state-power which is merely a referee holding the ring. A good many people begin to realise that freedom of contract is a hollow mockery when the power to bargain on equal terms is absent. Charles Dickens saw that, and Mrs. Gaskell, and, above all, Disraeli in *Sybil* which is a manifesto rather than a novel. It is the principle underlying all Coleridge's thinking, and Mill himself has recorded the deep effect it had on him. Carlyle spoke out with passion against a society based on the " cash-nexus " only in his *Past and Present*. He, in his turn, converted Ruskin ; and among the major influences which made William Morris a socialist was Ruskin's famous chapter on the *Nature of Gothic* in the *Stones of Venice*. Nor must we forget the immense educative effect of the long debates on the Factory Acts. By 1870, they were a normal, even a necessary, part of the social landscape. And that landscape had been profoundly changed by Chartism, by the European Revolutions of 1848, by the growth of the working-class electorate after 1867, and by the organised power the trade unions were beginning to exercise. The Trevelyan-Northcote Report of 1853 on the Civil Service is a British contribution of major importance to the philosophy of representative government.

Overwhelmingly, before 1870, Victorian philosophies of the state are individualistic in character. It is an aggregate of separate persons, each of whom bears the main responsibility for looking after his own family and himself. It is assumed that, in general, the proper sphere of government activity is confined to internal and external defence. Otherwise, there ought to be freedom of contract. The more the government interferes, the more it destroys individual initiative and responsibility. These are the secrets of national well-being. With the decline of utilitarianism new winds of doctrine begin to blow. Mainly, they blow from Germany, and they sweep across the quadrangles of Oxford. Kant and Hegel begin to influence men like T. H. Green, like F. H. Bradley, like William Wallace, like Bernard Bosanquet. They begin to think of the state organically. The idea of freedom as negative begins to give way to the idea of freedom as positive. We begin to hear of corporate persons, as well as of individual persons. We are told, by T. H. Green, of the folly of talking about freedom of choice to a man whose only real choice is between " gin-shops on one side of the street and gin-shops on the other ". We learn from F. H. Bradley that all discussion of the " rights " of the citizen as something which are diminished by State action is nonsense ; for man is inside society, and not set over against it. Bradley makes morality a social product, and a man's duty is then not merely that of looking after his own pleasures. His duty arises from his place in society. He fulfils himself as he helps society to fulfil itself. With Bosanquet we go even further. The state, as in the *Social Contract* of Rousseau becomes the embodiment of the general will ; the citizen then ought to obey the general will because it represents what he would will if he were permanently at his best. The emphasis of social action shifts from the circumference to the centre of society. It becomes the function of the State power to organise the conditions of the good life for all its citizens. The state must remove the barriers in the way of his self-fulfilment. It must create for him, in T. H. Green's words, " the opportunity to do or enjoy something that is worth doing or enjoying ". The government ceases to be a mere policeman. It is a teacher, a medical officer of health, a factory inspector, a school attendance officer, a public librarian. By the end of the Victorian Age, the idea of the community as a body of persons organically related to one another, as itself a corporate person with a life of its own, is generally accepted. We have passed from the negative state to the positive state, from individualism to collectivism, within a generation of Queen Victoria's accesssion to the throne. Lord Melbourne would have been amazed at the extent of the changes. The Mr. Gladstone who, in 1837, was, in Macaulay's phrase, the " rising hope of the stern unbending Tories below the gangway " would hardly have recognised the Mr. Gladstone who was

Liberal Prime Minister in 1868. In the 'fifties, the Queen looked upon John Bright almost as a seditionmonger ; what she thought of the return of Keir Hardie to the House of Commons in 1895 it would be difficult to put into words. The age began by thinking that the cure for poverty is, when it is respectable, the charity of the rich ; it ended by preparing to believe that poverty must be provided against by State action. British freedom, a little hesitantly always, with doubt here and compromise there, has slowly broadened down from precedent to precedent. Even so faintly liberal a politician as John Morley had taken Sir Henry Maine and Lecky to task for their fear that political power for the masses would destroy prosperity and ruin civilisation. So, too, Kropotkin was showing that " mutual aid " was no less important a factor in social evolution than " natural selection ".

It should be clear that the trend to collectivism in the last third of the century did not mean an acceptance of socialism. No social philosopher of the period was more influential than T. H. Green. He was a liberal in politics, who thought of the state as concerned with the removal of the hindrances to the good life. Bosanquet was nearer to that veneration of the state which Fichte and Hegel introduced into German philosophy ; but he was very hostile to socialism, and an ardent supporter of the Charity Organisation Society. There was, of course, a socialist collectivism, but its influence was less profound than its advocates made it appear. The great difference, I think, between the first and second parts of the Victorian Age is that, in the first, government intervention is regarded with suspicious dislike, and, in the second, it has become a recognised instrument of social organisation.

The change from individualism to collectivism was not, of course, a change made by doctrinaire philosophers sitting in academic ivory towers, remote from reality. Their relation to the change was very like that of the French *philosophes* of the eighteenth century to the Revolution of 1789. Just as there would have been a revolution in France if Voltaire and Rousseau had never lived, so collectivism would have come in Great Britain without John Stuart Mill and Matthew Arnold, without Ruskin and Morris, without the neo-Hegelians at Oxford and the socialists of various schools. The changing relations of the complex production system, the new technologies which the discoveries of science made possible have the major part. These relations must be set in the perspective of the reforms in the franchise of 1867 and 1884. They must be seen in their connection with the growth in power, and the increase of status, in the trade unions. What the philosophers, like T. H. Green, or the men of letters like Ruskin, did was to provide the basis for understanding the necessity of the change. They prepared men to receive it. An illiterate Britain, to take an obvious example, could not have become the " workshop of the world ". Its craftsmen, in every skilled occupation, needed the knowledge of reading and writing if production was to utilise successfully the resources at its disposal. The " right to education " was the category of thought supplied by men like Matthew Arnold, by T. H. Green and T. H. Huxley, with remarkable power. The philosophers of collectivism made the needs of their time seem principles which were intellectually convincing and emotionally attractive. They established the canon of their age. They made what was in fact becoming socially outworn seem socially unsatisfactory. In their different ways they helped to effect the adjustment between the fact and the need.

I know no better illustration of the impact of their work than in its effect upon an eminent politician like the late Earl of Oxford, who, as Mr. Asquith, held office under Mr. Gladstone, and was himself Prime Minister. Mr. Asquith was a Whig by nature, with a good deal of the lawyer's instinctive conservatism, and the temperament which had a close affinity with Sir Robert Walpole's supreme political maxim that a statesman should let sleeping dogs lie. Yet, as Prime Minister, he presided over a government responsible for more collectivist legislation, and more profoundly collectivist, than any of his predecessors. I venture to doubt whether most of it was welcome to him ; yet he put very few obstacles in its way. It did not interest him very greatly ; but it never occurred to him to oppose it. So he allowed his colleagues, especially Mr. Lloyd George and Mr. Churchill, to embark on important collectivist experiments which, left to himself, I do not believe he would have been tempted to regard either with great interest or with eager approval.

Why did so natural a Whig take up this attitude ? Asquith was a Balliol man, in the era when Benjamin Jowett, its Master, had set out to make the College a nursery of statesmanship.

Jowett had already shown the direction of his interest in the important part he had played in helping to get civil service reform accepted. He was, too, engaged in his well-known translation of Plato, a task not, I think, unconnected with the return to the Greek ideal of the State, so essential a part of the new political philosophy. He gave the major " tone " to the college. And Asquith's tutor was T. H. Green, not only himself a man of noble heart and distinguished mind, but the thinker who—more than any other—symbolises the turning away from the old individualism. Green had a passion for social reform, especially for temperance legislation and for education. He served, too, on the Oxford City Council. The general atmosphere of Balliol and the special personal contacts he made there accustomed Asquith early in his life to the acceptance of doctrine to which, temperamentally, he would not have been naturally inclined. What the Oxford of his day did for him was to make possible a receptivity to collectivist schemes, mostly framed by others, which he would not early have embarked upon of his own initiative.

The same thing is true of many other men at much the same time. It is true of the remarkable civil servant, Sir Robert Morant. It is true of that Northumberland squire, Sir Edward Grey ; by nature he yearned to devote himself to fishing and bird-watching, but he entered Parliament very largely as a moral duty. He supported there, from the aloof eminence of Foreign Secretary in Mr. Asquith's cabinet, the collectivist measures of its radical wing. Mr. Lloyd George, of course, was an agrarian radical, to whom social reform came as naturally after 1906, as would Benthamite reform have come if he had been born in the epoch of Henry Brougham and Joseph Hume. Put " Young England " in the mental climate of 1906, and it is not difficult to see how Mr. Churchill's avidity for imaginative and dramatic action, at a time when social reform is in the air, brought him within the scope of Sidney Webb's Fabian tactics and led him, as President of the Board of Trade, to introduce a young Balliol man, eager for social service, to transfer his main theatre of effort from Toynbee Hall to the Board of Trade. The result was the foundation of our system of Labour Exchanges. That is the door which opens on the road to insurance against unemployment. Once our feet are upon that road, collectivism has become the foundation of our social life. An impersonal historical system sowed the seed ; the philosophers, Green and Bradley, Bosanquet and Webb, watered the tender plant as it grew ; and the statesman reaped the harvest. A generation afterwards, we begin to see the whole evolution as both a natural result of the early Victorian individualism, and an equally natural prelude to the swifter and more massive collectivism which, with its socialist emphasis, is the foundation of our own social effort.

The Testament of Change

R. H. S. CROSSMAN

ONE THING which has always impressed me about the Victorian epoch is the difference of atmosphere between the beginning and the end of it. It began in the turmoil and confusion of a social revolution, the rise to power of a new class with a new revolutionary philosophy : it ended with all the pomp and panoply of imperial fulfilment. It began in foreboding and it ended in complacency.

That is one reason why the later Victorians, like their Edwardian successors, seem so remote from our age. They had succeeded, vanquished their doubts and difficulties—achieved an equilibrium. They repel us by their success and their certainty. But the atmosphere of the first thirty years from 1836 to 1860 is entirely different. Here we can feel almost at home, the same sense of flux, the same prophecies of disaster, which W. B. Yeats expressed when he wrote :

" The best lack all conviction ; and the worst
Are full of passionate intensity."

I happen to be an inveterate optimist who believes that all the gloom and despondency of 1948 will seem unbelievably remote in twenty-five years time when our late-Georgian children will have become complacent and successful. And to prove that this optimism is not absurd, I want to look at the Victorian Age not backwards as in inevitable progress towards the Diamond Jubilee but forwards from the grim and anxious beginnings of British industrialism. Living in 1948 let's go back exactly one hundred years to 1848 and let's look forward from there towards the present.

All right. We are in the year of revolution. Paris, Berlin, Vienna, Budapest. Democratic revolutions everywhere. And even here in London there has been a monster Chartist demonstration at the Oval though it fizzled out in the rain. The

Chartists were demanding the most outrageous things, including " votes for all ".

Today in 1848 the trouble is that the French Revolution will not stay dead. We thought we'd done with it when we defeated Napoleon, but now twenty-three years after Waterloo the idea of democracy is still alive. Democracy in this year of grace, 1848, is the ideology which all loyal subjects of the Queen are united to defeat. Of course, there are, even here in Britain, some overt democratic agitators like the Chartists, and a few crypto-democrats, left-wing intellectuals who call themselves radicals and utilitarians. But educated public opinion and the Party leaders on both sides of the House of Commons are sound enough, thank God. They agree that there should be some reforms, some betterment in the condition of the working class. But democracy, no, Sir ! Not for us the rule of the mob. Kingdoms and thrones may totter and fall across the Channel. But here in Britain the ballot box shall never threaten the sacred rights of property.

You see, 1848 was not so remote from us after all. Then too we were fighting a long battle against a revolutionary ideology which was sweeping the Continent. We could argue quite reasonably that we had accomplished our own revolution in our own way. Since 1832 the Middle Class had achieved power and while sharing it with the landed aristocracy was imposing its own ideas on Britain. The old order had come to terms with these puritanical industrialists and shopkeepers and the terms had been capitulation. Middle-class Liberalism in 1848 was the British alternative to the revolutionary democracy of France. To get a taste of this classic British Liberalism, let us see how the London *Times* described the East End in the 1850's : " The East End is the most commercial, the most industrial, the most fluctuating region of our metropolis. It is always the first to suffer ; for it is the creature of prosperity. The whole of that region is covered with huge docks, shipyards and manufactories and wilderness of small houses. All full of life and happiness in brisk times, but in dull times withered and lifeless. Now their brief spring is over. There is no one to blame for this ; it is the result of nature's simplest laws ".

No wonder cultured people detested these rigid doctrinaire Liberals with their fanatical belief in money-making, their jargon about economic laws, their smug puritan religion and their contempt for culture and breeding. What they had done since 1832 was not very reassuring. They had turned large tracts of countryside into a smoky hell. They had created a proletariat living in filthy slums ; and the railways in which they were investing their money were beginning to upset the even flow of Britain's pastoral life. How could any decent civilised person fail to detest and to view with the gloomiest forebodings this new industrial Britain which the middle-class revolution was producing ? There was hardly a single Victorian writer who had a good word for them. Dickens who had suffered from it as a child detested their unconscious cruelty and immortalised one of them in Mr. Gradgrind of *Hard Times*. Thackeray laughed at their snobbery. Carlyle prophesied against them, and Matthew Arnold in lecture after lecture mocked at them as Philistines—to be distinguished from barbarians, the name he gave to the landed aristocracy. Listen to this : " We in Oxford, brought up amidst the beauty and sweetness of that beautiful place . . . our sentiment for beauty and sweetness, our sentiment against hideousness and rawness has been at the bottom of our attachment to so many beaten causes, our opposition to so many triumphant movements. We have not won our political battles, we have not carried our main points, we have not stopped our adversaries' advance, we have not marched victoriously with the modern world. But we have told silently on the mind of the country. We have prepared currents of feeling which sap our adversaries' position when it seems gained, we have kept up our own communications with the future ".

No, that isn't an Oxford Don writing sadly yet hopefully in 1948, the third year of the Labour Government. That is Matthew Arnold protesting against the Philistinism of the middle-class revolution and its Liberal theory. Indeed, until the coming of the Socialism of the 1940's there has never been a theory so widely condemned as the Liberalism of the 1840's. In 1848 the Liberals were supremely self-confident that they alone could save Britain from the democratic ideology of France ; and the men of culture were prophesying dire disaster if the Liberals had their way.

Of course the analogy with 1948 isn't exact. History never repeats itself. But it is close enough for us to feel ourselves at

home in the controversy. I guess that a hundred years ago I
would have been as ardent an advocate of Manchester Economics
as I am of Socialism today. Some of you probably would have
been on the side of Matthew Arnold, pensively yearning for the
golden age which passed away with the passing of the Reform
Bill, the stage coach and the glories of Holland House, and feeling
that the country is heading for disaster. In retrospect we can see
that both sides were partly right and that it was out of the
furious controversy that the synthesis of the 1890's was created.
But at the time ? At the time you can't be so objective. If you
care enough, you are bound to be a partisan.

But wasn't there one enormous difference between 1848 and
1948 ? Wasn't there for the Victorians the great comforting fact
of religion ? Politics may have divided them, but weren't they
united about God and progress. The outside world may have
been changing faster than they liked, but surely their beliefs
weren't falling to pieces like ours ? This may seem true in
retrospect, but I doubt if any of the great Victorians felt it at the
time. Read Dickens or George Eliot, not as respectable classics
but as what their novels really were, sensational exposures of
social and moral problems. You won't find much sense of intellectual stability. The Tennyson of the *Idylls of the King* had
certainly retired to an ivory tower, but the Tennyson of *In
Memoriam* and *Locksley Hall* was as much agonised by doubt as
any young poet of the 1930's. Of course millions of Victorians
even in 1848 were smug because they didn't know what was
going on around them. So are millions of people today. But
the important thing to notice is that the great Victorians, the
men and women who tried to understand the world around them
and contributed to the achievements of the Victorian Age, were
in a mental turmoil as violent as our own.

Two of the greatest Victorian self-portraits are John Stuart
Mill's *Autobiography* and Edmund Gosse's *Father and Son*. Read
again of Mill struggling to escape from bondage to his father's
narrow-minded *laissez-faire* Liberalism. Not much sense of
inner self-certainty or complacency there. Or have a look at
Father and Son. Edmund Gosse, the author, became a rather
precious literary critic and bibliophile. His father, Philip Gosse,
combined marine biology with membership of one of the
narrowest sects, the Plymouth Brothers, who believed in the

eternal damnation of everyone not baptised into their peculiar form of non-conformism. There is a wonderful passage in the book which describes the crisis in father Gosse's mind which was caused by the theory of natural selection and evolution. This is how Edmund Gosse describes it : " So through my father's brain in that year of scientific crisis of 1857, there rushed two kinds of thought, each absorbing, each convincing, yet totally irreconcilable. This was the great moment in the history of thought when the theory of the new mutability of species was preparing to throw a flood of light on all departments of human speculation and action. It was becoming necessary to stand emphatically in one army or the other. In this period of intellectual ferment, as when a great political revolution is being planned, many possible adherents were confidentially tested with hints and encouraged to reveal their bias in a whisper. It was the notion of Lyell that before the doctrine of Natural Selection was given to a world which would be sure to lift up a howl of execration, a certain bodyguard of sound and experienced naturalists should be privately made aware of its tenor. Among those who were thus initiated was my father. He was spoken to by Darwin after a meeting of the Royal Society in 1857. My father's attitude was critical in his career. Every instinct in his intelligence went out at first to greet the new light. It had hardly done so when a recollection of the opening chapter of Genesis checked it at the outset. Lyell had been threatening to publish a book on the geological history of man which was to be a bombshell. My father after long reflection prepared a theory of his own to take the wind out of Lyell's sails and justify theology to godly readers of Genesis. It was very briefly, that there had been no gradual modification of the surface of the earth or slow development of organic form, but that when the act of creation took place the world presented instantly the appearance of a planet on which life had long existed ".

Philip Gosse's theory that God hid the fossils in the rocks in order to tempt geologists into infidelity ruined his scientific reputation and was one of the causes why young Edmund Gosse ran away from home. It was not the act of a smug Victorian but of a man agonised by a mental conflict, as acute as any which faces us.

Or take another example. We think of the great Arnold of

Rugby as the typical Victorian headmaster. We forget that he had all the doubts as a young man which afflict our generation. The undergraduates I used to teach at Oxford in the 1930's argued about Marxism, Arnold's worry was on a different subject. Here is a letter about him written by a friend in 1819 : " I have not talked with Arnold lately on the distressing thoughts which he wrote to you about, but I am fearful from his manner at times that he has by no means got rid of them. The subject of them is that most awful one, on which all very inquisitive reasoning minds are, I believe, most liable to temptation. I mean the doctrine of the Blessed Trinity. Do not start, my dear Coleridge. I do not believe that Arnold has any serious scruples of the understanding, but it is a defect of his mind that he cannot get rid of a certain feeling of objections. He scruples doing what I advise him, which is to put down the objections by main force whenever they arise in his mind ".

There is a profound difference between an age of religion like the Victorian and an age of ideology like our own. But it is not the difference between certainty and doubt. At least in the first half of the Victorian epoch, the conflict of science and ethics seemed at least as irreconcilable as it does today. The minority who dared to think found that thought was tearing down the structure of theology and politics ; and Liberalism, like modern Socialism, was a conscious effort to replace a God-given set of commandments with a man-made humanist ethics. Liberalism in 1848 was not simply a political programme : it was a philosophy of life which tried to take account of science and to create a society based not on tradition but on reason. That is what made it so attractive to the new, thrusting, self-confident middle class, and so repellent to many cultured and educated people. Liberalism was certain that it had *all* the answers.

And what actually happened ? There is nothing more sobering to a practical politician than to look at the political controversies of a hundred years ago and to see how nothing happened according to plan. In 1848, the middle classes still believed that all State interference with the economic system was evil. They wanted to reduce both the power and the expenditure of government. Yet in the next two generations a State was created more powerful than ever before, with undreamt of expenditure on social services. And it began to interfere everywhere with the sacred right of profit-making. So much for Liberal theory. And the Tories fared no better. In 1848 they were still supporters of the Corn Laws and opponents of the Empire. They too could not foresee the future.

But actually none of what they planned happened. British capitalism was not permitted either to develop according to the iron economic laws of the Liberals or to be obstructed by the Tory landowners. Instead of this, Britain developed a state, a social service State designed to mitigate the severity of those laws. You can realise the extent of the achievement if you compare the spirit of the *Times* article on the East End which I have just quoted with the spirit of the minority report on the Poor Law, which Beatrice and Sydney Webb published at the turn of the century. Looking at the horrors of the East End in the 1850's the *Times* had viciously commented, " No one is to blame for this. It is the result of Nature's simplest laws ". The Webbs, defying both the main political parties, broke through this fatalism and compelled us to accept " the theory of an enforced minimum of civilised life ", which is today accepted by all political parties.

How did this miraculous change occur ? How did Britain refute the prophecies of Marx ? Why did the middle-class revolution with which the Victorian epoch began end by creating a State utterly different from the ideal which Liberal theory had outlined ?

The answer seems to be this. A class, in this case the middle class, achieves power by uniting *against* a social order which has become unworkable. The Liberals thought they had a con-structive solution of the world's ills in *laissez-faire*. But when they had destroyed the effete parts of the old order and enabled the industrial revolution to take place, when they had done this, they began to discover that *laissez-faire* didn't give the answer to any of the problems of the modern industrial State. If the Liberals had remained true to the classic theories of the Liberal economists ; if the middle class had really imposed its victorious ideology on Britain, the result would almost certainly have been democratic revolt of the working classes which Marx predicted exactly one hundred years ago in the Communist Manifesto. But what actually happened was that the Liberal theory was scrapped almost as soon as it had defeated its adversary and the

Victorian middle class set to work slowly and fumblingly to build, not the *laissez-faire* State of Mill and Ricardo but the welfare State of which the social security measures of the present Labour Government are only an instalment. This evolution from *laissez-faire* to welfare was the great achievement of the Victorian epoch and of the British middle class.

Seen in retrospect this transition seems smooth and almost inevitable, but it didn't feel smooth at the time. There was never a moment from the beginning to the end of the Victorian epoch when the controversy stopped and men of goodwill were all of one opinion. Britain was adapting herself to one of the most violent economic changes in the history of a nation and the adaptation was successful because political dogmas were modified in the light of changing circumstances.

And who modified them? Certainly not the politician. Here we come near to discovering the true secret of Victorian greatness. It was an age of intense political controversy. But the hard thinking, the soul-searching and the research and the experiment out of which the modern State evolved, took place below the level of party politics.

The transformation was carried out not by politicians or party machines—they merely reflected the change—but by non-party people, social reformers, educationalists, scientists, novelists, Civil Servants and men of letters. The Liberal ideology was turned inside out by a self-appointed army of middle-class people mostly belonging to no party and with little respect for politicians. They were the conscientious objectors against smugness and stupidity who shook the middle class out of its complacency and its *laissez-faire* ideology. They created the issues which the politicians were then compelled to attend to. Shaftesbury for factory reform, Howard for prison reform, Florence Nightingale, Charles Kingsley, Ruskin, William Morris and finally the Webbs, Wells and Shaw—it's a tremendous list. Add to them the host of scientists, the Darwins and Huxleys, battling against obscurantism, the great schoolmasters, who, without any Acts of Parliament, fashioned the Public School system, for training the middle class to a sense of responsibility. And then the men like Thomas Green who took hold of our decadent Universities and reformed them. Then there's another army, the men who without much public recognition, until their work was mostly over, developed the Empire and the Indian Civil Service and the Colonial Service.

We most of us realise the tremendous industrial advance which took place under the Victorians, the increase of British wealth and power. But all this would merely have intensified the class war which Marx predicted in 1848 if it hadn't been accompanied by the creation of an impartial machinery of state and of a completely new class—neither a land-owner nor a factory-owner but a public servant—to manage the State for the community. The vast wealth which the Victorians bequeathed to us has been dissipated in two wars, but the impartial State and the tradition of the men and women who man it survive. They are the most valuable possession which we as a nation possess.

But great administrators and civil servants by themselves would not have been able to create the modern welfare State. Something else was needed—a social conscience. If millions of people in Victorian Britain were complacent, there were armies of intellectual non-conformists breaking in on that complacency and compelling their countrymen to accept the facts of change and the discoveries of science, ready to court unpopularity by challenging the Victorian bishops and shattering the illusions of the Victorian politicians. It was this ferment of controversy which prevented the newly-created State machinery from becoming a sterile bureaucracy, a collection of Mandarins composing their minutes in a Ministerial vacuum. Victorian Britain was not a democracy—the working class was still excluded from any real share in government. But it was a free society in which the ideas bubbling out of the controversy of public opinion fashioned and re-fashioned the form of the State. And in the course of sixty years, a middle class, which had come to power politically uneducated and religiously narrow-minded, proved its ability to confound the prophets of gloom, like Matthew Arnold, and to adapt itself to the needs of the times.

Today in 1948, we are not so far away from the mood of 1848. Another class, the working class, has broken through and once again, as in 1848, there are prophets who foretell catastrophe. But I believe the prophets will once again be confounded. There is no reason why the working class should not make a contribution to the twentieth century just as remarkable and just as unsuspected as that which the middle class made in the Victorian epoch. But on one condition—the British Socialism shows itself as adaptable as British Liberalism a hundred years ago. The Victorians averted what looked like an inevitable revolution because the complacent majority was never left in peace for a moment, their ideas were constantly being knocked about to suit the needs of a changing age. The result was that between 1848 and 1900 the middle class matured with astonishing speed and they did it, not by some special innate virtue but because they were worried and bothered by independent-minded men and women who had no respect for political or social or religious orthodoxy, or, I must add, for most politicians.

Well, in 1948, Britain is theoretically a full democracy with full working-class participation in government. But we shan't become a real democracy unless we can recapture the Victorian spirit of rebellion against cant and unless we can maintain the ideals of voluntary social service and intellectual non-conformity in our socialist State. The majority in all classes hate change and oppose it to the bitter end. Have we got that minority of rebels and iconoclasts who will crusade for reforms long before they are necessary and won't be ashamed of being called cranks and interfering busybodies and of being abused by all the political parties ? If we have, then the British working class will be able to grow into its vast new responsibilities as miraculously as the middle class did in the Victorian Age.

Continuity and Contrast

A Discussion between D. M. Mackinnon, R. H. S. Crossman, K. B. Smellie and M. Polanyi.

SMELLIE : Our relation to the Victorian period is unlike our relation to any other, and probably the relation between ourselves and the Victorians is different from the relation of the Victorians to any previous period. The essential point is that the idea and the understanding of history grew up with the Victorians themselves. That is to say, in that period—and of course, it wasn't peculiar to Victorian England, it was common to the whole nineteenth century—the perspective of history was in fact transformed. We, looking back at them, have I think a very special perspective. We have, so to speak, a double perspective on them. We probably know more intimately than we know of any other period what the Victorians themselves were thinking, and at the same time we know more about what was actually happening at the time they were thinking than we know of any other period. We are far better documented. So much so, that the initiator of the analysis of the Victorian Age in modern times, Mr. Lytton Strachey, said that the history of the Victorian period would never be written because we knew too much about it. In his view, the technique of scrupulous direct narrative was inappropriate to the Victorians. As he put it, you would row out over that vast sea, let down a bucket and bring up certain curious objects for examination. Well, Mr. Lytton Strachey certainly, so to speak, looked over the side ; I don't know that he saw much of the Victorians (probably, I think, rather narcissus-like, he saw himself), but there is the fundamental point, that the Victorians are more understandable than any previous period. We have the analytical technique of the economist ; we have the detailed reports of a multiplicity of

28

official enquiries ; and, what I think is most important—the effort to understand what was happening was conducted without the distorting technique of propaganda. Lord Acton, I think it was, stressed this. Somewhere about the middle of the nineteenth century, he was indicating that while the Chancelleries of Europe were filled with lies, there was nevertheless a sign that the spirit of morality, the spirit of truth, the overcoming of despotism had been achieved, and that common decency and common order might spread. The Victorians were the only people to be in a position to understand what was happening in that period and to see their relation to previous periods.

MACKINNON : I'm glad that Smellie said that our relation to the Victorians was a unique relation. I think it is very dangerous to speak too glibly about one historical epoch and another historical epoch as if they were a lot of beads, strung out on a string. Some people who talk about the relevance of the Victorian Age to ourselves seem to write as if we could find, in the study of the Victorian Age, challenges met by responses in a way which would help us to meet the challenges which we encounter. Almost they suggest that we should go to the Victorian Age for a kind example to edify us. I'm not at all sure that there aren't some very questionable assumptions behind that. For one thing, and I think Smellie did bring this out, we wouldn't be where we are today if it weren't for the Victorians. We're in their debt in all kinds of ways. You know the catch-phrase : " The past is always incapsulated in the present ". We stand where we are today because the Victorians stood where they stood, and the challenges that we have to meet are challenges to some extent set us by their achievement and by their failure. I'm sure, therefore, that in thinking about the relevance of the Victorian experience to our own we oughtn't to get too much into the habit of thinking of the Victorian epoch as if it were something self-contained, like a bead.

POLANYI : I, too, am sure that in many ways we stand where we stand today because of the Victorian Age which preceded us, but also—and I want to emphasise that more than Smellie and Mac-Kinnon—we stand there because of a cataclysmic change which has occurred since, which first of all brought a breaking away from the Victorian ideas in this country, and, of course, very much more on the Continent of Europe. There was the first beginning of the literary movement of D. H. Lawrence about 1912, before the first World War ; then the incursion of psychoanalysis, which came, I think, in the early 'twenties, and most significant of all, the influence of Marxism which arose around 1930. That movement is very relevant ; it culminated, I should say, round the period of the Spanish Civil War.

The Victorian Age, seen from the Continent from where I saw it, continued solidly till 1912, '13 or '14, and actually did not relax its complete hold on this country, it would seem to me, until the middle of the 1930's. After about 1937 there came a reversion to Victorian ideas all over the world, and also in this country, which has continued ever since.

CROSSMAN : I don't know what you mean by " *the* Victorians ". Some Victorians seem relevant to me and some don't. Whether they seem relevant roughly depends on whether you're faced with a similar problem, and I think I'd maintain that whereas I find the Victorians of the 1890's as remote as the eighteenth century, I find the Victorians of the 1830's to the 1850's as close to me as Plato, who is also, of course, as close as anybody could be today. They, like Plato, were faced with catastrophe. They were certain there was going to be a revolution, and half of them were certain there was going to be collapse, and England was going to the devil. The 1830's, 'forties and 'fifties were a period of profound doubt and scepticism about the future. The drama of the Victorian Age is that it started with a crisis, and ended with a temporary settlement of that crisis, out of which has come the new crisis of which we are members.

POLANYI : I agree with Crossman. I think that the present situation is in many ways a repeat of the 'thirties and 'forties of the last centuries, with a great national cohesion in this country overcoming the problems which disrupted the Continent. But I would like also to answer Smellie by saying that I do think that the great feature of the Victorian era was precisely its isolation ; that it managed to keep itself aloof from the philosophic excesses —or philosophic adventures or philosophic achievements if you like to call them that—which eventually led, in my view, to the condition of Europe, which I think is a state of philosophic or sophisticated violence : the theory of violence transmitted into mass movements. And I think, if I may say so, this is a valid criticism of these admirable broadcasts; they were too much immersed in the Victorian Age and looked upon it without realising the contrast between the temper of the Victorians' speculation and that of European thought, how extremely timid it was compared with that of Europe at the same time.

For example: talking about the discussion in the Metaphysical Society about the Efficacy of Prayer or the Existence of God, I think how remote such a discussion would have seemed to any intellectual on the European Continent at that time. There there were two kinds of people :—those who didn't discuss questions like the Existence of God because they were good Catholics and those who didn't discuss it because they were confirmed atheists and had been so for three or four generations. Their grandfathers were educated by Voltaire. A profound division went right through politics in Europe, between those who were radically adherents of what was called Reaction and the Church, on the one hand, and the Progressive Atheists and, finally Nihilists on the other hand.

CROSSMAN : Yes. The Victorians paid for their political maturity, by their philosophical immaturity; that is why we look at their age as a haven of peace across two world wars. They resolved their crisis without thinking it out. When you mention the timidity of the Victorians, I think you've put your finger on an important point; that the civic habits of the Victorians, the sort of Gladstonian atmosphere, was based on some very superficial metaphysics and still more superficial theology.

POLANYI : One couldn't put it better. I'm sure that is exactly what I wanted to say, and I think some of the Victorians did realise it very well. Lecky writes about it and Morley writes about it; how the supreme political art which Britain had achieved, and in which it stood out high above everything on the Continent of Europe—certainly east of the Rhine—how that naturally limited the audacity of speculation, because it always had its concern with the necessities of political and social life.

CROSSMAN : Yes, but I still don't quite accept this word " timidity " and lack of audacity. No human being thinks unless he has to, and all you're saying is that the Victorians—fortunately for them—were in a position where they didn't have to think about certain things that people had to think about on the Continent. If you were a German and you hadn't got a nation and you hadn't got a State, you thought about the fundamental question, what is a State ? If you were in Britain, and you had a nation and you had a State, you didn't raise the problem because it wasn't relevant.

POLANYI : Well, I'm afraid that in this respect I am Victorian and I would accept that people think because of the natural urge to discover the truth, rather than because of certain historic necessities which point in a particular direction. And I would urge that, say, a movement like the Russian Nihilist Movement in the 'fifties of the last century, which was a direct outcome again of the Radical Materialist Movement in Germany, was of great significance to our age in its further consequences ; in fact, it was the precursor of the Russian revolution, and was due to the kind of philosophic audacity which, fortunately perhaps, was not at home during the Victorian Age in this country.

MACKINNON : And yet, you see, in one way it was at home. For after all, the tradition on the Continent, which you have mentioned, was fed by the work of the British Empericists. You can't understand eighteenth-century Continental thought (which is clearly, in your mind, the background of nineteenth century), unless you know something about the Empiricist School ; unless you know something about the methods of people like Locke and Hume.

CROSSMAN : Yes, but surely—here I reply to Polanyi—it is quite untrue that people just naturally think. I cannot accept that. I fear that we actually think when we have to and we always are idle when we possibly can be. Locke and Hume thought because the Britain in which they lived was faced with a desperately difficult situation. The Victorians didn't need to think —they were prosperous and wealthy and they developed without thinking. I don't blame them for it ; and it isn't timid, because they put all their courage and their energy into making money, developing the Empire, developing our parliamentary institutions.

SMELLIE : But some of the best people thought it was their duty to think. Throughout the whole Victorian period, there is a continuous and profound criticism—starting, shall we say, with Coleridge in the beginning, with Bradley in the middle. There is criticism and awareness by those persons. I don't agree that you just think because you are in a mess : some people think because they think it is their duty to think, and some Victorians did quite definitely criticise and, I think, anticipated the future troubles which have come, by pointing out the unanalysed presuppositions upon which the Victorian order was based. Mill does it to a certain extent.

POLANYI : Well, I'm going to agree now for the moment with Crossman that we are in a mess and we have to think now about what we are going to do about it. And I do think that this disaster which has divided Europe has brought us back to a reappreciation of the Victorian Age, and of the great period of progress by peaceful methods, of the great triumphs of civic responsibility, of the great triumphs of constitutional life. Our problem is—if I am at all right in what I said before—how to restore those virtues for the world, how to regain that spirit for the Western Union and for the West in general, while facing the fact that we cannot return to the innocence of Victorian authoritarianism or of the naïve rationalism of the Victorian Age.

CROSSMAN : Yes, I agree about the innocence. I think you've hit it off there. That is how, looked at from the Continental point of view, Victorian thinkers appear. They do appear naïve and innocent ; but I think you'd probably agree, Polanyi, we can't go back. Our problem today is that we have become Continentals. That's why we've got to think, just as the Continentals had to think in the last century always, because the very existence of the State and the nation is now in question. The fundamental issues are forced on us by our situation. As long as we sat safely on our island, the fundamental problems of power and politics never impinged on us. We were fortunately insulated. Now we're Continentals, and our greatest problem in Western Union will be that we are so idle in these fundamental questions of thought that it's an issue as to whether or not we ever catch up with the French and the Germans and the Dutch and the Belgians in the sort of thinking we shall have to do in common to get rid of our innocence. We're the idlest nation in the world intellectually—including the Americans. They're just a little better than we are. We never think unless we have to. And we never think until after the disaster has occurred. Take the major advance in thought of the last hundred years, which is the Dialectic. As I well know from teaching at Oxford, we are still today so Victorian that Oxford philosophers will say Hegel was complete nonsense and Marx an idiot and Kierkegaard they haven't even heard of ; that is the situation we live in today. In our University teaching we are completely out of touch with the biggest single intellectual concept of Europe ; wouldn't you agree, MacKinnon ?

MacKinnon : I would entirely, and, of course, the joke is that people like Green and Caird have so well cushioned us in our attitude towards Continental thought of that kind, that we don't realise that it's more radical than the positivism which is all the academic fashion. There's a kind of radicalism in parts of Hegel, in Marx, in Kierkegaard, that you just don't get in, let us say, Carnap.

Crossman : I agree. The logical positivist is, in fact, the most timid, the most Victorian type of philosopher you can possibly have.

Smellie : I disagree. I would argue that while this Victorian millennium was growing, while the Pax Britannica was spreading, while collectivism was growing ; while, if you like, modern Socialism was being born, the best thinkers in England, the Greens, the Bradleys, and I think perhaps, also, even the early Bertrand Russell, but at any rate the late Oxford School and the late Cambridge School, were criticising and were developing a sense of history. They were criticising the Utilitarians ; that was the domestic quarrel.

Polanyi : We seem to be coming to the question of what we are going to do about it, how we are going to link up again with the Liberal tradition of the nineteenth century, which is an enormous problem, and I think will be decided on a much larger stage than in academic discussions between philosophers.

MacKinnon : What I think we ought to realise is, that if you want to get back the sound coherence of the Victorian system you can't go back to what they did, which was to have a system and not understand it, but take it for granted ; you can't be naïve. We've got to be self-conscious about principles and not merely have them and take them for granted.

SMELLIE : May I ask one thing there ? If the Victorians had a sound system, how is it that it exploded ? How is it it exploded in two world wars ? What was the nature of this soundness which has produced our rottenness ?

MACKINNON : The answer is that life goes on ; the social development continues, and a system which was valid in one generation becomes completely invalid in the next. That is part of the historical dialectic : you are always having to adapt and even revolutionise your system, in terms with the changing order.

POLANYI : But those two world wars, the revolutions of our time, were not of the making of the Victorians. All the time during which the Victorian Age was making that wonderful progress politically, by isolation from the Continent, the tide was running in rapidly all over the Continent of the philosophic movement which finally culminated in the European disaster.

CROSSMAN : Well, now, what was the disaster which the Victorians didn't face before it came, and which came on us with a sudden shock after two world wars ? I think it's the central problem of power. But that is a problem which all European philosophers of politics were grappling with, struggling with— whether they were Marxists or clericals—for at least a hundred years. Now, the Victorians had such a tremendous lot of power, that they thought that power politics were wicked—it's a most comic situation. That's the essence of the Victorian attitude, to have so much power that you don't even need to think about it, or know about it, or study it, or study its dangers. Now isn't that the central problem ? Is it not almost the definition of a Victorian to say that you can grow out of these ugly underlying realities—Power, Evil ? These are the fundamental problems, but they just turned them aside by saying, " We're all going to get better and better."

POLANYI : But differently. They did believe (and I believe that they were right, and we must believe it again), that it is possible to exercise power with restraint—moral restraint. They did believe that it is possible to shape public affairs by the guidance of moral principles. They did believe that nations hold together by the coherence of their consciences, by the common holding of beliefs concerning the nature of their community—of the moral nature of their community. And that, I believe, is a thought which will become alive again through the action which it will call forth in the field of international minds, through the shaping of Western Union ; through the policies which Western Union will have to undertake in order to save itself, and through the consciousness of its own value which it will have to give in order to save itself.

CROSSMAN : Well, Polanyi, I think I follow you, but, may I put to you this specific problem which seems to me to be facing us, which the Victorians managed to get through without thinking it out. What do we mean by Democracy ? We really mean civilising the use of power ; seeing the people use it in a reasonable way and have discussion instead of hitting each other. Now, here we are, a civilised group in Western Europe—just as Victorian England was civilised—faced with another group which does not believe in the civilising of power—which believes that power is an eternal fact of politics and it's your duty to use it whenever you need it. The problem of how to live together is a fundamental political problem which I don't think the Victorians had to face, because there wasn't anybody else at that time who had enough power to challenge the British Navy. Now, we're in a situation where we have to think that problem out.

MACKINNON : We've got to face, haven't we, the question of what it is to have the fundamental assumption that power is the servant of law—not the source of law—challenged all along the line. It's challenged everywhere. The abandonment of this kind of assumption all along the line is to involve us, almost absent-mindedly in the spiritual predicament in which some of the Continentals, of whom Polanyi spoke, stood. People like Nietzsche did see that this view of the world, the beginnings of which were laid in the sixteenth and seventeenth centuries, drove a wedge right between what people really thought mattered, and what the world was like. And somehow or other, on the intellectual and on the spiritual plane, some of the great Victorians were cushioned against facing that issue. There was something that prevented the issue being raised for them in the nakedness with which it's raised for us. And the few who did raise it were really completely uninfluential in the practical life of the country.

SMELLIE : The idea that Palmerston and Salisbury were unaware of the problem of power seems to be rather startling ; *and* the idea that the people who were responsible for the North-west Frontier were unaware of the problem of power, and even, if I may say so, the idea that the early Chartists and the early Trade Unionists and all the people from whom the modern Socialist movement sprang, were unaware of the problem.

CROSSMAN : No, no ! The issue is not whether they were unaware, but whether they tried to behave as though the problem didn't exist.

POLANYI : I do think that it is fair to say that Gladstone was unaware of the problem of power, in the sense that he never thought of such a ruthless use of power as quite logically followed from the philosophic catastrophe on the Continent, embodied there in various dictatorships, and still with us today.

SMELLIE : Gladstone, of course, was a Christian, a rather naïve Christian.

CROSSMAN : I would take an even later example of innocence, Smellie. Take Neville Chamberlain. The fact about Chamberlain is—he wasn't a wicked man, but he could not conceive of the philosophy of power which in fact inspired the Continental Dictator. That is what appeasement meant—a man who had lived in such a civilised community that he couldn't recognise evil when he saw it. But Joseph Chamberlain was aware of the problem of power, and that is why Joseph Chamberlain, who was one of the very few Englishmen who understood this, was suspect by nearly all of his contemporaries ; because of his extraordinary understanding of power. It was men like Neville and Baldwin who won public confidence.

SMELLIE : That, of course, is the difficulty—that the person who is aware of the problem of power in a Christian community can only talk about it if he has a metaphysic to which he can appeal, and that was Bradley's whole point—that there was no metaphysic to which political realities could be related.

CROSSMAN : I believe we've got to some agreement here, because what we're really saying is, that you could get on without a metaphysic in the Victorian epoch, but we doubt whether if we're going to create a Western Union we can get on without a metaphysic.

MacKinnon : Yes—but we can't create a metaphysic to order or it will be a national religion or worse, just an ideology.

Polanyi : I think that cushioning of Victorian milieu which MacKinnon talked about was not altogether a philosophic affair, but very largely an emotional and civic strength. On the continent of Europe, that coherence, that love between fellow-countrymen which was common in Britain, was not an active political force. It was not capable of building up a peaceful Germany and of developing German affairs peacefully. When the Germans hung together, when the Germans formed a solid State, it was not in order to love each other and to get on with one another, but usually for aggressive purposes.

Smellie : Well, all the good metaphysicians—all the good Victorian thinkers—Bradley is the classical example—were concerned that English Liberal thought, that is to say, on the side of economic and on the side of representative Government, never considered the problem of power. What I was disturbed about in your earlier remarks was the implication that somewhere or other that problem was being discussed, and that I'd overlooked it, and presumably most listeners had overlooked it, and that it was to be found in the Dialectic. Now I agree that now there is no longer a Pax Britannica, there has to be some kind of metaphysical, philosophical, or other ground for any political order which may be created. Many people seem to think that we're to find it by a return to Aquinas. I would like to return your question to you : what is your alternative ground to, so to speak, St. Augustine and Aquinas ? If it isn't the Utilitarians, and if it isn't the Liberal economic system, is it Fabian Socialism ?

Crossman : I think that's a perfectly fair question, and I will reply to it perfectly openly. I do not think that Fabian Socialism is a philosophy at all. I think it's a series of *ad hoc* proposals for dealing with *ad hoc* problems, which has practically worked itself out. One of our problems in Britain now is that we've worked out all these *ad hoc* practical approaches. Today when we have to deal with the real problem of power there are two dangers we face : one is what I call " understanding power " and that means being corrupted by it and saying : " Well, there's nothing but power politics, so let's beat the dictators at their own game ". That's what happened to the Marxists of the 1930's.

The other is Pacificism. You understand power and are so shocked by it, that you retire into a monastery: you "do an Aldous Huxley".

POLANYI : I think that the centre of our problem lies in what Bertrand Russell once put as the philosophic position of our age ever since Hume. He said, if I remember rightly, that ever since that great critical philosopher, we have to choose either between profundity with a certain amount of madness, or sanity coupled with or based on superficiality. The Victorians, of course, had that supreme sanity, and the superficiality in the sense in which I am using now this word.

How are we to get out of this dilemma, since we cannot return to that state of innocence, and yet want to regain the great sanity and all the other great civic virtues which Victorianism brought and preserved to the world ? I would say first of all through action, through doing everything possible to preserve peace and unity and progress between the people of the West, so that that mutual love and understanding, which is the basis of all civic arts in my view, should be re-established in this group of people. And out of that, I believe, will grow a positive metaphysical belief in the foundations of the free society.

MACKINNON : I think that we've got to think through anew the relation of the philosopher to society. You get people like Huxley saying—in effect—all that matters is contemplation carried on in deliberate isolation from the problems of society. On the other side you get the cult of power and even those who speak pragmatically of the possibility of a new muddling through. Now frankly, I think myself that muddling through is ruled out as much as the other alternatives I've mentioned. I don't think myself we can muddle through now ; we can't escape facing the issues that were raised, as Polanyi said, at a much earlier date on the Continent. I don't think that the Thomist solution is any good, because ultimately there are depths of the problem on which Thomism and I think I must say Institutional Catholicism as we know it turn their backs. Our problem is fundamentally, I think, the problem of integrity.

CROSSMAN : I thoroughly agree with MacKinnon about this problem of muddling through. I think the relevance of the Victorians to us, as I said at the beginning, is that they were faced in the first half of the epoch with a revolutionary situation, with a catastrophic situation, and somehow they achieved a synthesis which got them through without the revolution. That's the relevance of it. But once we study the way they did it, we see we can't possibly repeat that way because they got through, frankly, by a providential dispensation without really thinking out the basis of their actions.

And so they left us—well, let's list it—they left us a Christian community without Christianity. They left us a free community without democracy. They left us an Imperial nation without Imperialism.

Now, none of that is possible today. Unless we can make our spiritual contact with the problems of Continental thought today, the politicians won't make anything of Western Union at all. There has got to be a common ground between those of us in Western Europe who are trying to " civilise power "—which, after all, is the definition of a free society. We've got to have a common philosophy dealing with that, and we—the British— have got to cease to be insular not only in our economics and politics, but also in our Universities, and in our whole way of thinking. Muddling through, as MacKinnon said, is the one thing we know from the start will lead to the disintegration of the Western Europe we're trying to build.

SMELLIE : I thoroughly agree that we, if you mean by we, the English-speaking peoples of Europe, cannot muddle through, because muddling at the moment is being done by very vast and powerful Continental powers. I cannot accept or I do not quite understand the dialectical solution ; to take a more general and common-sense view, I think that one's feelings for the Victorians are nostalgic. There was a period of order comparable to the order of the Greek City State ; there was, so to speak, a wedge of high pressure over the British Isles in which things were set fair, and now a series of complex depressions is approaching, and in that context I think one has to look to philosophy.

THE CONTRIBUTORS

ANNAN, N. G. O.B.E., M.A. Fellow of King's College, Cambridge.

AYER, A. J. M.A. (Oxon). Grote Professor of Mind and Logic, University College, London. Publs. include : *Language, Truth and Logic ; Foundations of Empirical Knowledge* ; etc.

BEALES, H. L. Reader in Economic History, London University ; Member of Council ; British Institute of Adult Education. Publs. include : *Industrial Revolution ; Early English Socialists* ; etc.

BOWLE, JOHN. Lecturer in Modern History, Wadham College, Oxford. Publs. include : *Western Political Thought ; The Unity of European History* ; etc.

BRAILSFORD, H. N. M.A., LL.D. Editor, Leader-writer. Publs. include : *Socialism for Today ; Property or Peace* ; etc.

BRONOWSKI, J. Scientist, mathematician, poet. Publs. include : *The Man Without a Mask.*

CECIL, Lord DAVID. C.H. Fellow of New College, Oxford ; Goldsmith Professor of English Literature ; Trustee, National Portrait Gallery. Publs. include : *Early Victorian Novelists ; The Young Melbourne ; Hardy the Novelist* ; etc.

CHAPMAN, GUY P. O.B.E., M.C., M.A. (Oxon), B.Sc. (London). Professor of Modern History, Leeds University.

COBBAN, ALFRED. M.A., Ph.D. Reader in Modern French History, University College, London. Publs. include : *Dictatorship, Its History and Theory ; The Crisis of Civilisation* ; etc.

COLE, G. D. H. Chichele Professor of Social and Political Theory, Oxford ; Fellow of All Souls. Publs. include : *Brit. Working Class Politics, 1832-1914 ; Intelligent Man's Guide to the Post War World* ; etc.

COPLESTON, F. C. M.A. (Oxon), D.Phil. (Rome). Priest of the Society of Jesus ; Professor of History of Philosophy, Heythrop College. Publs. include : *History of Philosophy ; Friedrich Nietzsche ; Arthur Schopenhauer* ; etc.

CROSSMAN, R. H. S. O.B.E., M.A., M.P. Lab. M.P. for Coventry East ; Asst. Editor *New Statesman.* Publs. include : *Plato Today ; Socrates ; How We Are Governed* ; etc.

DANIEL, GLYN E. M.A., Ph.D., F.S.A. Fellow and Steward of St. John's College, Cambridge : Lecturer in Archeology in the University.

DAVIDSON, J. W. Ph.D. Fellow of St. John's College, Cambridge ; Lecturer in Colonial Studies in the University.

DAVIES, E. SALTER. C.B.E., M.A. Chairman, Carnegie United Kingdom Trust. Publs. include : *The Aim of Education ; Education for Industry and for Life ; Technical Education* ; etc.

DAWSON, CHRISTOPHER. M.A., F.B.A. Gifford Lecturer, 1947. Publs. include : *Progress and Religion ; Religion and the Modern State* ; etc.

DEMANT, V. A. D.Litt. (Oxon), B.Sc. (Durham). Canon and Chancellor of St. Paul's. Publs. include : *God, Man and Society ; Christian Polity ; The Religious Aspect* ; etc.

DINGLE, HERBERT. D.Sc., A.R.C.S. Professor of History and Philosophy, University College, London. Publs. include : *Relativity for All ; Science and Human Experience ; Through Science to Philosophy ;* etc.

ENSOR, R. C. K. M.A. (Oxon). Member Exec. Comm., National Trust ; Member Royal Commissions on the Population and on the Press. Publs. include : *Modern Socialism ; England,* 1870-1914 ; etc.

FABER, GEOFFREY. Fellow Estates and Bursar, All Souls, Oxford. Publs. include : *A Character Study of The Oxford Movement ; A Publisher Speaking ;* etc.

FORDE, C. DARYLL. B.A., Ph.D. Professor of Anthropology, London University. Publs : Numerous books on Anthropology.

GLOVER, EDWARD. M.B., Ch.B., M.D. Director, Psychopathic Clinic, London. Publs. include : *The Psychology of Fear ;* etc.

GRISEWOOD, HARMAN. Joined BBC 1932 ; Asst. Director of Programme Planning ; 1939 ; Act. Cont. European Service 1945 ; Dir. of Talks 1946-48 ; Controller of Third Programme since March 1948.

GRYLLS, ROSALIE GLYNN. M.A. Publs. include : *Mary Shelley ; Queens College,* 1848-1948 ; etc.

HOUSE, HUMPHREY. Late Lecturer in Eng. Lit., Wadham College, Oxford ; William Noble Fellow, Liverpool 1940 (resumed 1945-46). Publs. include : *Notebooks and Papers of Gerard Manley Hopkins (Ed.) ; The Dickens World ;* etc.

HUTTON, GRAHAM. Economist and broadcaster on economic subjects.

HUXLEY, JULIAN. F.R.S., M.A., D.Sc. Dir.-General UNESCO. Publs. include : *On Living in a Revolution ; The Living Thoughts of Darwin ;* etc.

KLEIN, VIOLA. Ph.D. Publs. include : *The Feminine Character.*

KNOX, Rt. Rev. Monsignor RONALD. Domestic Prelate to His Holiness the Pope, 1936. Publs. include : *The Belief of Catholics ; The Holy Bible, a New Translation ; God and the Atom ;* etc.

LASKI, HAROLD. Professor of Political Science, London University ; Connected with London School of Economics since 1920 ; Member Exec., Labour Party. Publs. include : *Autobiography of J. S. Mill (Ed.) ; Rise of European Liberalism ; Studies of Law and Politics ;* etc.

LINDSAY of BIRKER, Baron. C.B.E., Hon. LL.D. (Glasgow and St. Andrews). Master of Balliol. Publs. include : *The Essentials of Democracy ; The Two Moralities ;* etc.

MacKINNON, D. M. Regius Professor of Moral Philosophy, Aberdeen University.

MOTT, N. F. M.A., F.R.S. Melville Wills Professor of Theoretical Physics, Bristol University. Publs. include : *The Theory of Atomic Collisions.*

NICHOLAS, H. G. Librarian and Lecturer in Politics and Modern History, Exeter College, Oxford.

PARKER, T. M. Asst. Chaplain, Exeter College, Oxford ; Librarian, Pusey House, Oxford. Contributor to *Union of Christendom.*

POLANYI, MICHAEL. F.R.S. Hon. D.Sc. (Princeton). Professor of Social Studies, Manchester ; late Professor of Physical Chemistry, Manchester. Publs. include : *Atomic Reactions ; USSR Economics ; Science, Faith and Society ;* etc.

RAVEN, Canon CHARLES E. D.D., Master of Christ's College, Cambridge ; Regius Professor of Divinity in the University ; Chaplain to H.M. The King. Publs. include : *The Gospel and the Church ; In Praise of Birds ;* etc.

RUPP, Rev. GORDON. Lecturer in Ecclesiastical History at the Methodist College, Richmond.

RUSSELL, BERTRAND, *Third Earl.* M.A., F.R.S. Fellow of Trinity College, Cambridge. Publs. include: *Principles of Mathematics; Freedom and Organisation; History of Western Philosophy;* etc.

SIMMONS, JACK. M.A., F.R.S.L. Professor of History, University College, Leicester. Publs. include: *African Discovery; Southey;* etc.

SMELLIE, K. B. B.A. Reader in Public Administration, London School of Economics. Publs. include: *A Hundred Years of English Government; Reason in Politics;* etc.

SMYTH, *Canon* CHARLES. M.A. Hist.S. Canon of Westminster and Rector of St. Margaret's; Fellow of Corpus Christi, Cambridge. Publs. include: *Religion and Politics; The Art of Preaching;* etc.

SUMMERSON, JOHN. B.A.(Arch), F.S.A., A.R.I.B.A. Curator, Sir John Soane's Museum; Dep. Dir. National Buildings Record. Publs. include: *Georgian London; The Bombed Buildings of Britain;* etc.

TAYLOR, F. SHERWOOD. Curator, Museum of the History of Science, Oxford. Publs. include: *The World of Science; The Fourfold Vision;* etc.

TREVELYAN, G. M. O.M., C.B.E., F.B.A. Regius Professor of Modern History, Cambridge, 1927-40. Publs. include: *British History in the Nineteenth Century; English Social History; History of England;* etc.

VIDLER, *Canon* ALEX. R. M.A., B.D., Hon. D.D. (Edin). Warden of St. Deiniol's Library, Hawarden. Publs. include: *The Modernist Movement in the Roman Church; A Plain Man's Guide to Christianity; The Orb and the Cross;* etc.

WHYTE, L. L. Scientist, author and broadcaster. Publs. include: *Everyman Looks Forward; Next Development in Man;* etc.

WILLEY, BASIL. M.A. (Cantab)., F.B.A. King Edward VII Professor of English Literature, Cambridge; Fellow of Pembroke College. Publs. include: *The Eighteenth Century Background.*

WOODRUFF, JOHN DOUGLAS. Ex-President, Oxford Union; Editor *The Tablet;* Broadcaster. Publs. include: *The British Empire; Plato's Britannia;* etc.

WOODWARD, E. L. M.A., Hon. Lit.D. (Princeton), F.B.A. Montagu Burton Professor of Modern History, Oxford; Fellow of Balliol College, Oxford. Publs. include: *The Age of Reform; War and Peace in Europe,* 1815-1870; etc.

YOUNG, G. M. C.B. Trustee, National Portrait Gallery; Member Standing Commission on Museums and Galleries; Trustee, British Museum. Publs. include: *Early Victorian England (Ed.) .Victorian England; Mr. Gladstone* (Romanes Lecture); etc.